# Values and Virtues for a Challenging World

ROYAL INSTITUTE OF PHILOSOPHY SUPPLEMENT: 92

EDITED BY

Anneli Jefferson,
Orestis Palermos, Panos Paris,
and Jonathan Webber

T0384649

CAMBRIDGE
UNIVERSITY PRESS

PUBLISHED BY THE PRESS SYNDICATE OF THE UNIVERSITY OF CAMBRIDGE
The Pitt Building, Trumpington Street, Cambridge, CB2 1RP,
United Kingdom

CAMBRIDGE UNIVERSITY PRESS
UPH, Shaftesbury Road, Cambridge CB2 8BS, United Kingdom
32 Avenue of the Americas, New York, NY 10013–2473, USA
477 Williamstown Road, Port Melbourne, VIC 3207, Australia
C/Orense, 4, planta 13, 28020 Madrid, Spain
Lower Ground Floor, Nautica Building, The Water Club, Beach Road,
Granger Bay, 8005 Cape Town, South Africa

Printed in Great Britain by Bell & Bain Ltd, Glasgow.
Typeset by Techset Composition Ltd, Salisbury, UK

*A catalogue record for this book is available from the British Library*

ISBN 9781009345262
ISSN 1358-2461

# Contents

# Notes on the Contributors

**Berys Gaut** (bng@st-andrews.ac.uk) is Professor of Philosophy at the University of St Andrews, Scotland. He has written numerous articles on creativity, aesthetics and the philosophy of film, and is the author of *Art, Emotion and Ethics* (OUP, 2007) and *A Philosophy of Cinematic Art* (CUP, 2010).

**Mandi Astola** (mandiastola@gmail.com) is PhD student at Eindhoven University of Technology. Her recent publications include 'Mandevillian Virtues' in *Ethical Theory and Moral Practice* (2021) and 'Can Creativity Be a Collective Virtue: Insights for the ethics of innovation' in *Journal of Business Ethics* (2021).

**Hugh Desmond** (www.hughdesmond.net) is a postdoctoral researcher at the Leibniz University of Hannover and Assistant Professor at the University of Antwerp. He received his PhD from the KU Leuven, and has held research and visiting positions at the Paris I-Sorbonne, KU Leuven, Princeton University, New York University, and the Hastings Center. His work centers on the philosophy and ethics of science, with particular emphasis on biology. His recent and forthcoming publications include *Human Success: Evolutionary Origins and Ethical Implications* (OUP, 2022) and 'The Logic of Status Distrust' (*Social Epistemology*, forthcoming).

**Taylor Matthews** (taylor.matthews@nottingham.ac.uk) is a PhD student at the University of Nottingham. His thesis investigates the relationship between intellectual character and epistemic vice. His research interests include epistemology, social and virtue epistemology, political philosophy, and the philosophy of technology.

**Alessandra Tanesini** (Tanesini@cardiff.ac.uk) is Professor of Philosophy at Cardiff University. Her latest book is *The Mismeasure of the Self: A Study in Vice Epistemology* (OUP, 2021).

**Kathleen Murphy-Hollies** (KLM276@student.bham.ac.uk) is a Philosophy PhD student at the University of Birmingham. Her research is on ethics, moral psychology and mental disorder.

**Lani Watson** (lani.watson@philosophy.ox.ac.uk) is a Research Fellow at the University of Oxford. Her research in epistemology

doi:10.1017/S1358246122000297     © The Royal Institute of Philosophy and the contributors 2022
*Royal Institute of Philosophy Supplement* **92** 2022

# Notes on the Contributors

focuses on questioning and curiosity and she has recently published *The Right To Know: Epistemic Rights and Why We Need Them* (Routledge 2021).

**Anneli Jefferson** (jeffersona1@cardiff.ac.uk) is lecturer in philosophy at Cardiff University. Her research focuses on issues surrounding moral agency and philosophy of psychology and psychiatry. She recently wrote a book entitled *Are Mental Disorders Brain Disorders?* (Routledge, 2022).

**Katrina Sifferd** (sifferdk@elmhurst.edu) is Professor and Chair of Philosophy at Elmhurst University, where she holds the Genevieve Staudt Endowed Chair. Her recent publications include *Responsible Brains: Neuroscience, Law, and Human Culpability* with Bill Hirstein and Tyler Fagan (MIT Press, 2018).

**Kristján Kristjánsson** (k.kristjansson@bham.ac.uk) is Professor of Character Education and Virtue Ethics, University of Birmingham. His publications include *Virtuous Emotions* (OUP, 2018) and *Friendship for Virtue* (OUP, 2022).

**Jonathan Webber** (webberj1@cardiff.ac.uk) is Professor of Philosophy at Cardiff University. His most recent books are *Rethinking Existentialism* (OUP, 2018) and *From Personality to Virtue: Essays on the Philosophy of Character* (coedited with Alberto Masala; OUP, 2016).

**Carissa Phillips-Garrett** (carissa.phillips-garrett@lmu.edu) is Assistant Professor of Philosophy at Loyola Marymount University. Her recent publications include *Why Aristotle's Virtuous Agent Won't Forgive* (Springer, 2022) and 'Completeness, Self-Sufficiency, and Intimacy in Seneca's Account of Friendship' (*Ancient Philosophy Today*, 2021).

**Panos Paris** (parisp@cardiff.ac.uk) is Lecturer in Philosophy at Cardiff University and a Trustee of the British Society of Aesthetics. Panos works mainly in aesthetics and ethics. He has published articles on a variety of topics, including functional beauty, moral beauty, immoralism, ugliness, and ethical reflection through television series.

**Nadine Elzein** (nadine.elzein@warwick.ac.uk) is an Associate Professor of Philosophy at the University of Warwick. She works primarily on problems relating to free will, moral responsibility, and moral obligations. She has several recent publications on this theme, including 'Undetermined Choices, Luck and the Enhancement Problem' (*Erkenntnis*, 2021), 'Deterrence & Self-Defence' (*The Monist*, 2021), and 'Determinism, 'Ought' Implies 'Can' & Moral Obligation' (*Dialectica,* 2021)

**Nicholas Shackel** (shackeln@cardiff.ac.uk) is Professor of Philosophy at Cardiff University. His recent publications include 'The Nothing from Infinity Paradox versus Plenitudinous Indeterminism' (*European Journal for the Philosophy of Science*, Forthcoming) and 'Constructing a Moorean 'Open Question' Argument: The Real Thought Move and the Real Objective' (*Grazer Philosophische Studien*, 2021).

**Cathy Mason** (cm865@cam.ac.uk) is a Leverhulme Early Career Fellow in Philosophy at the University of Cambridge. She has written, among others, on Iris Murdoch, love and friendship. Her recent publications include 'What's Bad About Friendship with Bad People' (*Canadian Journal of Philosophy*, 2021) and 'Hoping and Intending' (*Journal of the American Philosophical Association*, 2021).

# Introduction

ANNELI JEFFERSON, ORESTIS PALERMOS,
PANOS PARIS AND JONATHAN WEBBER

We all now know just how challenging an unexpected event can be. Every aspect of our lives was transformed by the appearance of Covid-19, as governments across the world struggled to limit the damage while vaccines were invented, produced, and administered. The ongoing implications of this pandemic remain unpredictable as the virus continues to mutate.

Our planet's climate is now changing at a rapid pace due to greenhouse gas emissions. Extreme temperatures and changes to traditional weather patterns are widespread, wildfires are more frequent, and the sea levels are rising. One effect of this will be the movement of people and their livestock away from lands that can no longer sustain them. These mass migrations may well cause wars over fertile land and water sources, displacing people as refugees and further reducing food supplies. They will also increase the likelihood of new viral pandemics.

Climate change and the Covid-19 pandemic have been fuelled by the rapid development of technology, which has brought an enormous increase in movement of people and goods around the world. At the same time, the emergence of almost ubiquitous digital technology has radically altered our interactions with one another and with our natural and built environments, with profound effects on our understanding of ourselves and one another, our emotional lives and wellbeing, our styles of inquiring and reasoning, our general political outlooks, and our aesthetic tastes.

All of this makes for an increasingly unpredictable physical and social environment. Even the most radical action to limit climate change will only stabilise the environment after a few decades. In the meantime, we are likely to be faced, both locally and globally, with a series of new challenges that will only be understood in detail some time after they have arisen.

How should we prepare for this unpredictability? What attitudes, skills, and values should we foster in ourselves and one another to enable us to respond well to the challenges of a rapidly changing world? The contributors to this volume present a range of suggestions, unified by a few recurring themes.

doi:10.1017/S1358246122000303      © The Royal Institute of Philosophy and the contributors 2022

One theme is that we need to counteract the growth of political polarisation, which seems to be an effect of technological change and the emergence of social media. Polarisation is movement towards a society's division into two sharply opposing ethical and political outlooks. It strongly mitigates against the development and deployment of effective responses to new situations by reducing the common ground from which consensus might emerge about which changes should be seen as problems, how these should be prioritised, and how best to solve them.

Contributors to this volume identify various sources of polarisation. The use of moral and political statements to identify oneself as a member of some social group and, conversely, the effect of peer pressure on opinions within an already constituted group are both amplified on social media, where a single message can easily reach hundreds of thousands of people at high speed and low cost.

These tendencies increase one's susceptibility to forming beliefs on partial information or outright misinformation without critical scrutiny, encourage the unthinking reproduction of other people's claims and conclusions in one's own social communications, both online and offline, and facilitate emphasising one ethical value at the expense of others in considering difficult problems.

All of this is compounded by the preference for certainty over uncertainty, even where the situation cannot justify any conclusion with a high degree of confidence, and by the propensity to give reasons for a belief or decision regardless of whether those reasons actually motivated it.

In response, the contributors to this volume argue that we should foster a more collective and collaborative outlook, where people act together to identify problems, analyse them, and work out how to solve them. The essays emphasise appropriate recognition of one's own limitations, the importance of understanding other people's perspectives on situations, and the need for serious commitment to open-minded reasoning. They recommend cultivating the concern to understand the world as it really is and the tendency to think honestly about what really matters.

That is not to say that the contributors to this volume each subscribe to a single multifaceted approach to preparing for unpredictability. Rather, each contributor addresses a different aspect of this overall problem and makes a specific recommendation. As a result, there are various tensions and contradictions between the essays. Yet in their collective emphasis on care, creativity, collaboration, curiosity, discernment, diversity, fallibility, forbearance, hope, integrity, responsibility, self-regulation, understanding, and wisdom, their recommendations together bring into view, if not entirely into sharp focus, an overall image of how we should prepare to deal with the challenges of an unpredictable world.

One major feature of this image is the recognition that our immediate responses, both in feelings and intuitive thoughts, can shape our behaviour in profound ways even when they do not represent the opinions we would form by reasoning about the situation. By learning how to reason better about how the world really is and how we should respond to it – reasoning that can be undertaken both individually and collectively – we can reduce the influence of our immediate responses and, at the same time, attune them to what really matters and bring them closer to the conclusions of our reasoning.

Another major feature is the role of our social environment in fostering the values and virtues we need in a challenging world. This includes thinking about how education can cultivate in students a better approach to facing new challenges, both online and offline, but also about how changes to the design of social media can reduce the kinds of behaviour that make it difficult to think clearly about new challenges as they arise.

We are very grateful to the Royal Institute of Philosophy for the opportunity to produce this collection of essays and to the authors for their excellent contributions. We hope this volume will inspire further work to bring its overall image of how to be prepared for unpredictability into sharper focus. This would involve enriching that image with details that have not been mentioned in this volume and resolving disagreements between these essays. We hope these ideas about our social environment will be refined and applied, but also extended to consider, for example, the regulation of mass media, the structures of companies and other organisations, and the designs of buildings and urban spaces.

There is certainly much more thinking to be done. We are well aware that we cannot predict the directions it will take. For that reason, we present this volume as an example of the open-minded, carefully considered, and public-spirited collaborative approach that its essays recommend, and we encourage its readers to continue the conversation in the same way.

*Cardiff University*

# Group Creativity

BERYS GAUT

**Abstract**

Group creativity is vital in overcoming the numerous challenges that the world faces. Yet group creativity is deeply puzzling. It seems plausible that only agents can be creative, so group creativity requires group agency. But how could groups possess the mental states required to be agents, let alone the rich range of them required to be creative? It appears more reasonable to hold that group creativity is not a real phenomenon, but is merely the summed creativity of the individuals forming the group. There is also much empirical evidence that groups are no more creative than their members. In this paper I examine the conceptual and empirical challenges to group creativity, defend its existence, and offer an explanation of how it is possible.

We live in a challenging world. Recently we have faced a global pandemic, accelerating climate warming, increased pressure on biodiversity, and since 1945 have acquired the ability to annihilate our species by nuclear warfare. Challenges require solutions, and the most promising solutions are collective ones. The vaccines against Covid-19 were all developed in group laboratories, involving many specialists: the Oxford Vaccine Group, for instance, has more than 100 members. More generally, scientific outputs have increasingly shifted from individual to group-authored papers. Collective action in meeting the challenges also needs to be creative to have much chance of success, given our mixed results in dealing with them so far. So group creativity is vital to solve our problems. But there are reasons for denying that group creativity is even possible, and if it is, that it can surpass individual creativity. I argue here that scepticism about group creativity can be countered, and so provide some reason to think that our global challenges can be met. And in so far as creativity is a virtue (Gaut, 2014), we can also conclude that it is a virtue of groups, not only of individuals.

## 1. Two challenges to group creativity

It is widely agreed that creativity requires the production of new things, at least in the sense that they are new to the person or entity that produces them. It is also generally agreed, though not so

doi:10.1017/S1358246122000145

widely, that the creative product must be valuable (Boden, 2004, pp. 1-10). Agency theories, which include virtue theories, of creativity also hold that it is only agents that are creative, in the core sense of 'creative' (Gaut, 2018; Kieran, 2014; Paul and Stokes, 2018). So on agency accounts of creativity, group creativity requires group agency. But some philosophers deny that groups can be agents, since they hold that groups cannot possess those mental states such as intentions, and related beliefs and desires, that are required to be an agent.[1] The problem is particularly acute in trying to show that groups can be creative, since creativity standardly involves a rich range of mental powers, such as imagination, that go beyond the minimal conditions, such as the possession of intentions, that are required for agency in general. How could groups possess the mental states required for agency, particularly the rich range of them required for creative agency? Call this the philosophical or *richness challenge* to group creativity.[2]

If the richness challenge cannot be met and agency theories are correct, then groups cannot be creative: it is the *individuals* who compose groups who are creative. If so, group creativity is merely the sum of the creativity of the individuals in the group. The creativity of the whole is merely the sum of its parts.

This individualist, summative alternative to group creativity admittedly does not sit well with our common talk: we speak of scientific research teams, jazz groups, filmmaking groups, companies or company divisions (such as Google DeepMind and Pixar) and even of political states as being creative. And these kinds of locution seem well-supported, even for the largest of entities: for instance, Mariana Mazzucato (2015) argues that the U.S. state has played a leading role in technological innovation, and that many innovations often credited to companies have emerged from US government agencies, such as DARPA (the Defense Advanced Research Projects Agency). But maybe we are mistaken in our attributions of creativity to groups.

---

[1]    The threat to group creativity applies if agency theories are correct. But not all theories of creativity are agency based. Notably, Darwinian theories (Simonton, 1999; 2014) hold that creativity requires a blind variation and selective retention (BVSR) process that occurs not only in agents, but also in other entities and processes, such as biological evolution. So these theories do not face the same challenge from group creativity.

[2]    Scepticism about the possibility of group creativity in the political realm, drawing on these kinds of considerations, is expressed by Matthew Noah Smith (2018).

The philosophical worry about groups also has empirical support, which forms the *empirical challenge* to group creativity. One of the most common techniques for enhancing creativity is brainstorming. The advertising executive Alex Osborn published the first book on the technique in 1948. He provided four rules for brainstorming: don't criticise the ideas generated (deferment of judgement: evaluation comes later); be freewheeling (the wilder the idea, the better); produce as many ideas as possible (quantity breeds quality); and build on ideas previously produced (Sawyer, 2012, p. 235). Osborn proposed brainstorming as a group technique.

From 1958 onwards (Taylor, Berry and Block, 1958), the method has been subject to intensive psychological study. Many of these studies compare group brainstorming with individual brainstorming: that is, with individuals using the same four rules on their own. A well-established finding is that group brainstorming, as standardly practised, produces only about half the number of good ideas as does individual brainstorming by the same number of individuals (see Sawyer, 2012, pp. 235–42 for a review). So asking people to be creative in groups, using the most influential creativity technique, is damaging to creative outcomes. Hypotheses to explain this include: free-riding on others' contributions (social loafing); evaluation apprehension (people are afraid of looking stupid in front of others); production matching (matching one's productivity to others', so there is convergence on the mean number of ideas produced); and production blocking (for instance, people cannot talk at the same time). These explanations suggest that creativity loss is deep-rooted in the nature of groups: tendencies to free ride, to be concerned with how others think of one, to converge on the average, and difficulties with people speaking at the same time are endemic to groups. Moreover, the larger the group, the worse the creativity loss is relative to the same number of individuals brainstorming. For instance, Thomas Bouchard and Melana Hare (1970) tested groups composed of five, seven and nine people: the larger the group, the fewer ideas were produced, relative to a nominal group of the same size (a nominal group is composed of a number of individuals who have no interaction with each other).

Adjusting the brainstorming technique can improve these results: for instance, 'electronic brainstorming' involves participants typing their ideas, which are then displayed on monitors to other participants without identifying who generated the ideas. But even electronic brainstorming, with a few exceptions, only produces at best the same number of ideas as does individual brainstorming. And since it works by paring down group interaction, preserving anonymity and removing face-to-face contact, these electronic groups are very unlike real-world groups. The less a test group is like a real group, it seems, the more likely it is to be creative.

This empirical evidence suggests that the summative account of group creativity is a best-case scenario. In practice, a group's creativity is likely to be *less* than the sum of the creativity of its members: the creative whole is likely to be less than the sum of its parts. So the evidence suggests that the creativity of a group is *no more than* the sum of the creativity of its members, were they operating independently. Call this the summative-minus hypothesis.

## 2. A method for meeting the challenges

What would be required to refute the summative-minus hypothesis?

One lesson from the brainstorming literature is that it is too simple to contrast the creativity of groups per se with individual creativity.[3] For the design of groups is crucial to determining their degree of creativity: electronic brainstorming groups can be up to twice as creative as traditional brainstorming ones. So the alternative hypothesis to summative-minus should hold only that some *kinds* of groups are more creative than are their members.

However, it may be that some kinds of groups are more creative than their members, but only because of contingent features of the groups. For instance, some groups may be better funded, in terms of the pay they offer and the research resources they provide, than their members would be, were they operating as solo researchers; and this extra funding explains groups' enhanced creativity. We need to rule out such possibilities. So the claim that needs to be demonstrated is this:

> (GC) The creativity of some kinds of groups is, because of the features that make them groups, greater than the summed creativity of their members, were those individuals acting separately.

So it is because of some of the features that make them groups – that *constitute* them as groups – that these groups are more creative than their members would be, were they working individually. If this can be shown, then the summative-minus hypothesis is false.

---

[3]    From now on I will sometimes use 'individual creativity' and 'the creativity of members' as shorthand for 'the summed creativity of the members of the group'.

Moreover, because the truth of this claim would show that the creativity of the group isn't the same as the summed creativity of its members, it would also follow that group creativity can't be reduced to individual creativity. Call this claim the group creativity (or non-summative) hypothesis.

## 3. Social groups

The group creativity hypothesis requires an account of what constitutes a group as a group. There is a plethora of competing philosophical proposals in social ontology and collective intentionality, and I do not propose to provide a definition of social groups and group agents, only an indication of some of the relevant factors.[4] A good start is Margaret Gilbert's (1990) famous example of walking together. What, she asks, is the difference between two people who are walking side by side, as it happens, and two people who are walking together, and so who constitute a (temporary) social group? The two people walking together are subject to some norms that those who walk side by side are not: for instance, if one of them walks too fast, the other walker is entitled to rebuke her and ask her to slow down; and the one walking too fast is obliged to slow down. In contrast, two people who are merely walking side by side are not thus entitled or obliged to alter their pace at the behest of the other. So when we do something together, when we form a social group, a framework of norms applies to our conduct that does not apply if we are acting individually. It is the norms about how its members ought to act towards each other that in part makes a collection of people a social group: that is, groups are partly constituted by interpersonal norms.

We can add that social groups are also partly individuated – are partly distinguished as different kinds of groups – by the norms to which they are subject. For instance, two members of the army marching together might be indistinguishable in their physical movements from our two walkers, if the walkers aim to match each other's stride. But the army group would be marching together, whereas our civilians are merely walking together. This is because the norms applying to the army marchers are different to those applying to the civilians: accelerating ahead by one marcher might be a violation

---

[4]    Leading accounts are by Michael Bratman (1999; 2014) Margaret Gilbert (1990; 2009), Christian List and Philip Pettit (2011), John Searle (2010) and Raimo Tuomela (2013).

of an order, and so subject to military sanctions, rather than merely grounding a rebuke. And the coordination of the walking movements of the army duo might be required, rather than being merely optional as with our walkers. The relevant norms may be elaborate, structuring the group internally by specifying a set of roles, each constituted by its rights and obligations, or 'deontic powers', as John Searle (2010) calls them, such as different ranks and positions in the army with different authority and responsibilities. So the army group forms a different kind of group to that of our sociable walkers, partly because of the different norms to which they are subject.

The norms that constitute groups extend beyond those governing the entitlements and obligations members have vis-à-vis each other. As Amie Thomasson has noted, the norms that partly constitute groups also include how members are to behave, what they should believe, how they are to dress, etc. (think of Orthodox Jews, for instance). And groups may even be defined by the norms applied to them by those who are not members, such as being an immigrant (Thomasson, 2019).

So collections of people become social groups in part because they are subject to norms that apply to members of the collection. And norms that distinguish between one collection of people and another partly constitute these collections as groups and individuate them from each other.

This normative approach to groups has considerable intuitive appeal and philosophical support. It also has its critics: Michael Bratman (1999, chapter 7) has objected that two people may act together, and so form a group, without giving rise to rights and obligations. This might either be because they are engaged in an immoral activity, and so neither has a right to demand that the other continue in the shared activity, or because one of the participants has coerced the other, and so has no right for the action to be performed, nor has the coerced person an obligation to perform it. So though groups typically generate rights and obligations, these deontic features are not necessary to groups and so do not constitute them. But, as Gilbert (2009) has noted, the obligations and correlative rights involved need not be moral ones and, as we can put it, they are only *prima facie*, since they can be outweighed or undermined by facts about the immorality or coerced nature of the joint action. What makes the action a group one depends on the *prima facie* status of the obligations, not on their all-things-considered status. This point also applies to the more general view of groups as partly constituted by norms: there are many norms besides moral ones (dress codes for instance are not usually moral codes), and norms may be only *prima facie*, so can be outweighed or undermined by other norms.

There is also empirical evidence in support of the normative view. The cultural evolutionary theorist Michael Tomasello and collaborators ran an elegant series of experiments in which three-year-olds were introduced to Max, a glove puppet (Henrich, 2016, pp. 185–87). Max sometimes made mistakes, as the children were shown when he used the wrong end of a pencil to draw. While Max took a nap, the children saw an adult with an odd assortment of objects engaging in a procedure which was one of several ways to use the objects. The children were then offered the chance to play with the objects. Max then awoke and used the same objects in a way that was sensible but different from that employed by the adult. Most children protested against Max's way of using these objects, even though nothing had indicated that there was a correct way to use them. The lesson is that young children are inveterate norm-inferrers: give them a regularity and they will conclude that it is the correct way to do something. In a variant of the experiment, the children encountered another puppet, Henri, who spoke French-accented German, unlike Max who was a native German speaker (the experiments were run in Leipzig). The children protested far less against Henri, when he played the game differently from the adult, than they did against Max. So they were associating norms of how to act with different groups, French or German (Henrich, 2016, p. 204). And this is what the normative conception of groups predicts.

Evidently, more needs to be done to develop this account into a complete theory of group constitution and individuation, and Gilbert (1990; 2009) and Searle (2010) in particular have done much work in this direction, but the foregoing suffices for our purposes. However, not all social groups are group agents, that is, can engage in group action: for instance, gender, ethnic and class social groups are usually not group agents. I will discuss later what more is required for group agency. But even as our account stands, since it gives a condition on what constitutes a group, it allows us to fill out and evaluate the group creativity hypothesis.

## 4. Evidence for the group creativity claim

That hypothesis, recall, holds that:

(GC) The creativity of some kinds of groups is, because of the features that make them groups, greater than the summed creativity of their members, were those individuals acting separately.

According to the normative account of groups, groups are partly constituted and individuated by the norms that distinguish them from other collections of people. So, if there are different norms, there are different kinds of groups, and if these norms play a role in explaining the greater creativity of the group, then that enhanced creativity is to be explained by group-constituting features, rather than by incidental features of groups, such as some groups' greater funding.

As the evidence from brainstorming groups shows, not all kinds of groups satisfy (GC). But are there some kinds of groups that do? The social psychologist, Charlan Nemeth, with collaborators examined the importance of dissent for group creativity. In one study they gave five-person groups of undergraduates the task of coming up with as many good ideas as they could in twenty minutes about how to reduce traffic congestion. The groups were given either no instructions about how to do so (the minimal condition), or brainstorming instructions with the standard 'don't criticise' requirement, or debate instructions: that 'you *should* debate and even criticize each other's ideas' (Nemeth et al, 2004, p. 369). The results were striking: including ideas generated immediately after the discussion was over, the no-instructions groups generated an average of 22.7 ideas, brainstorming groups 24.5 ideas, and debate groups 28.4 ideas. Thus the debate groups were substantially more creative than the brainstorming groups, and this was because of the difference in norms, either brainstorming or debate, that were specified in the instructions. Unfortunately, Nemeth and colleagues did not compare the performance of the groups with individuals, so the experiment provides no direct evidence for the group creativity hypothesis. They also framed their results in terms of Solomon Asch's paradigm of the surprising degree of conformity in groups and the role of dissent in breaking it down. However, the debate instructions specifically call for debate and criticism, i.e., for participants to come up with reasons for their own suggestions and against others' suggestions; and that suggests that the key to better creative performance lies in the role of reasoning in group activity.[5]

[5]  A distinct research programme about collective wisdom has shown that more diverse groups are more accurate predictors of events than are homogeneous groups (Hong and Page, 2012). However, in its main form this is a statistical model, depending on the fact that individuals' judgements are independent and so their biases tend to cancel each other out; it does not require individuals to be members of social groups.

Let us turn momentarily from the social psychological literature on creativity to research on reasoning. The Wason selection task, a canonical test of reasoning abilities, involves four cards, on the first of which a vowel is visible, on a second a consonant, on a third an even number, and on the fourth an odd number: for instance, E, K, 4 and 7. Participants are told that all the cards have a letter on one side and a number on the other. They are also given a rule: for instance, that if there is vowel on one side of the card, there is an even number on the other. What are the cards, and only the cards, that they need to turn over to test whether the rule applies to them? People are strikingly bad at this reasoning task: generally only about 10-15% produce the right answer, which is to turn over only the cards with E and 7 on their faces. David Moshman and Molly Geil (1998) tested participants individually on the Wason selection task, obtaining a score of 9.4% for individuals. But when they tested groups of 5 or 6 persons, an astonishing 70% of groups got the answer right. Groups are far better at reasoning than are individuals. Moreover, when they formed groups out of people who had previously taken the test individually, 80% of groups answered the problem correctly. Three of the groups who were successful were composed of individuals *none* of whom had answered correctly when tested individually. So these answers were not produced by one or more people in the group, who had discovered the answer individually, persuading the other members of its correctness. Rather, the groups discovered the answers collectively. As the transcripts show, group members did this by reasoning with each other; challenging each other's conclusions; adding new bits to an argument, part of which had been generated by their fellow members; extending each other's arguments; and so on. They were engaging in group reasoning.

Though Moshman and Geil don't remark on it, the participants who got the answer right were creative: they came up with something valuable (the correct solution to the Wason selection task), which was new to them (in Margaret Boden's, 2004, pp. 1-3 sense, they were psychologically creative, P-creative), and did so by intentional actions, involving discussion and debate. So in some cases people can be creative by employing reasoning. Since groups can, as these data show, reason much better than individuals, groups should be, other things equal, more creative than individuals when they employ norms of reasoning, rather than, for instance, brainstorming. And Moshman and Geil's findings directly compare groups to individuals, unlike Nemeth et al's (2004) experiment, which is the missing comparison we needed.

It might be objected that not all creative processes involve reasoning: there are sudden illuminations – the famous 'aha' experience – which have nothing to do with reasoning; so the data are of limited interest. However, the argument I have advanced relies on the claim that not all creative processes involve reasoning: the contrast between the effectiveness in group contexts of brainstorming and reasoning depends on brainstorming not being a type of reasoning. Moreover, reasoning can sometimes produce an experience of sudden insight: in his classic account of his own creative process Henri Poincaré (1985) gives examples of when conscious reasoning led to illumination during the course of the reasoning, and also examples of when illumination happened some time after he had stopped reasoning. He stresses in the latter cases that illumination would not have occurred without extensive preparation, including conscious reasoning. And Andrew Wiles' sudden moment of illumination about how to prove Fermat's last theorem occurred during the course of reasoning (Singh, 2005, p. 297).

There is also non-experimental evidence to show that groups can be more creative than individuals because of groups' superior deployment of reasoning abilities. Kevin Dunbar (1995; 1997) conducted a one-year study of how four world-renowned microbiology labs ran their research projects. All the labs held a weekly meeting which all members were required to attend, even those not working on the project under discussion, at which a presentation was given by one of the scientists working on the project. This was followed by extensive group discussion, and Dunbar notes that several insights were generated in the course of these discussions.

We can distinguish three reasons for why group members reasoning together enhance creativity. First, when they had experimental evidence confounding their hypotheses, individual scientists tended to explain this by assuming some fault in the experimental set-up. In contrast, other members of the group tended to explain the inconsistency by offering new hypotheses or getting the presenter to suggest new ones (Dunbar, 1995, p. 380). Mistakes in reasoning, such as confirmation bias, were countered because people can identify mistakes more easily in other people's thinking than in their own and are more motivated to find them.

Second, Dunbar shows that the labs used distributed reasoning, that is, reasoning where more than one member of the group contributed to providing the premises of an argument. Analysis of discussions in the HIV lab showed that 30% of the inductions or deductions generated involved premises supplied by more than one individual, and 12% of them premises supplied by more than two individuals (Dunbar, 1997, p. 483). And some of these premises involved knowledge that only one lab member had, so that the members operating separately could not have come up with the argument. This was important in the creation of new analogies, since the analogies that were most useful in hypothesis formation were to other organisms (Dunbar, 1997, p. 473), which might not be known to other members of the group. The importance of cognitive diversity was therefore also demonstrated (see also Jefferson and Sifferd, 2022, on the importance of diversity for making good judgements).

Third, group reasoning processes are sometimes enhanced by the organisational structures of labs, which may be elaborate: one of the labs had a total of 32 members, comprising a senior scientist, 22 postdoctoral fellows, 5 postgraduates and 4 technicians (Dunbar, 1995, p. 373). Each person in the lab could call on its other members to help her: that was part of the point of the weekly lab meeting. So specialists in labs were expected to share their subject-specific information with others. Participants in psychological experiments, in contrast, have a tendency not to share with other members of their group information that is unique to them (Stasser and Titus, 2003). The entitlements and obligations of group membership, to extend Gilbert's point, can be invoked in the service of creative reasoning.

It is worth noting that group creativity is not unique to science. Many art forms, such as cinema, are highly collaborative (Gaut, 2010, chapter 3) and similar group mechanisms are to be found there. For instance, Pixar is an enormously creative company, the maker of the first computer-animated feature film. Ed Catmull (2008), its co-founder and president, describes the group's creative process in the years to 2008. While acknowledging the importance of a few key people to the success of each film, Catmull also emphasises the role of group creativity. Daily meetings were held, in which draft film material was shown to all members of the animation crew, and everyone was encouraged to comment on it. There was also a 'creative brain trust', composed of John Lasseter and eight directors, who could be asked by a filmmaker to comment on her material. The constant feedback as described by Catmull was an intensified version of the back-and-forth of argument that is present in the microbiology labs: in Pixar's case the meetings were daily, not weekly. The similarity to an academic milieu is not entirely coincidental: as David Price (2009, pp. 24-25) has noted, Catmull recreated in an early incarnation of Pixar the atmosphere of the University of Utah Computer Science department, in which he had obtained his PhD. Even Pixar's Emeryville studio with its large atrium was designed, with considerable input from Steve Jobs, to get employees to mix with each other, and so to foster group discussions (Price, 2009, pp. 198–199).

So there is both experimental and real-life evidence that groups reason better than individuals thinking in isolation, and that reasoning can produce creative outputs. Hence there is evidence that groups, when operating according to norms of reasoning, as opposed to for instance norms of brainstorming, can be more creative than their members, and their creative superiority is to be explained in part by the norms which partly constitute their identity as groups. And that is what the group-creativity hypothesis holds.

There is also a plausible explanation of why group members when reasoning together are superior to individuals reasoning on their own. Hugo Mercier and Dan Sperber have argued that reasoning is a social competence: its function is to produce arguments to convince others and to justify one's own actions; and also to evaluate others' attempts to persuade oneself and to justify themselves (Mercier and Sperber, 2017, especially Introduction and Conclusion; Sperber and Mercier, 2012). This interactionist or argumentative theory of reasoning is distinct from the traditional 'intellectualist' theory that holds that the function of reason is to advance the individual reasoner's cognition. The theory explains the biased nature of reasoning and its laziness when people are defending their own views, whereas the intellectualist theory is left with the puzzle of why reason is so bad in these cases. The interactionist view also explains why people are so much better at evaluating other people's arguments and justifications than their own, since evaluating others' claims is a form of 'epistemic vigilance' (Sperber and Mercier, 2012) that pays off because so many of our beliefs are grounded in claims made by other people. Since others' arguments may be directed to showing that one's own views are badly grounded, individuals will more likely change their minds when reasoning with others than when engaged in solo reasoning, so group reasoning is, other things equal, superior to solo reasoning.

If this explanation of the superiority of group over individual reasoning is correct, and we add the premise that reasoning may lead to creative results, then we can explain why groups, when they follow reasoning norms, are more creative than their members would be when engaged in solo thinking.[6] Recall that the individual scientists

---

[6] Mercier and Sperber (2017, chapter 18) also make the link between reasoning and creativity in science, and adduce some of the evidence employed in the present paper (I was alerted to the existence of the

in Dunbar's studies were loathe to accept experimental disconfirmation of their pet hypotheses, yet the other scientists had no problems in coming up with alternative and undermining hypotheses, which usually persuaded the presenting scientists to modify their views.

## 5. Group agency and creativity

So far I have argued that the empirical evidence that groups are less creative than their members applies only to some types of group, including brainstorming ones, and that other types of group, using for instance reasoning norms, can be more creative than their members; moreover, this is because of what in part makes them groups, their constitutive norms, rather than their incidental features, such as their financing.

This argument, however, is not yet sufficient to establish the group creativity claim. For it is consistent with groups not being agents or creative at all: rather, groups might be part of the background, causal conditions that merely make *individuals* in the groups more creative. Consider an analogy. There is evidence that having the colour blue in one's environment promotes creative outputs relative to the colour red, which fosters greater attention to detail, or a neutral colour, such as white (Mehta and Zhu, 2009). So blue-coloured environments enhance creativity, but it makes no sense to say that the colour blue *is* creative: it only has creative *effects* on people; colours cannot be creative since colours aren't agents. In the same way, someone might hold that individuals are more creative when they are members of groups, but that it makes no more sense to speak of groups as being creative than it does to talk of colours as being creative. So we need to show that groups can be agents and that they can have a sufficiently rich mental life to sustain creativity.[7]

---

Moshman and Geil paper by their discussion). Their main aim, however, is to show that apparently solitary geniuses are really participants in social networks and thus are not counterexamples to their interactionist view. This is true in many cases, but it does not fit all of them: Andrew Wiles for instance, up to the point when he submitted his proof for publication, carried on his work on Fermat's theorem in complete secrecy (Singh, 2005). A better response to such cases is to acknowledge the existence of individual, as well as group, creativity.

[7]   Even without establishing this further result we have, however, shown something about group creativity. For there is a weak sense of group creativity, in which it is sufficient to establish it that the creativity

Hence we need to return to our unfinished business of discussing what makes a social group a group *agent*: as noted earlier, not all social groups are group agents. Again, given the complexity and disputed nature of the terrain, I will only provide a sketch of the relevant factors (see Astola, 2022, for further discussion of some group-level properties).

Group agents come in many kinds. Some are corporate groups, such as charities, political parties, and companies; these have formal organisational structures, specified by often elaborate rulebooks of procedures (see List and Pettit, 2011, for discussion). But there are also informal, smaller scale groups, that lack these elaborate procedures, such as a group of people walking together, to return to Gilbert's iconic example. It is these more informal groups on which I focus here. Ordinary language licenses talk of them as group agents: we may talk of a group going for a walk, or equivalently of the individuals who comprise the group going for a walk together. In general, we can say that a group F's if and only if the individuals comprising it F together. For instance, a jazz group plays a song if and only if the members of the group play that song together. Let us employ a common philosophical parlance and call the action of doing something together a joint action.

There are two conditions that plausibly suffice for this modest kind of group agency. First, the individuals who comprise the group must have a common aim or purpose: for instance, speaking from their perspective, that we go walking, or that we play a particular song. The content has to include reference to the collection of individuals: the 'we' in the 'we go walking'. The aim is not merely that a walk happens, or a song is played, which could be satisfied by other people doing these things: the aim is that *we* walk or play a song.

Second, the individuals should coordinate their individual actions with each other so as to achieve this common aim. Without action the common purpose remains a mere aspiration, and without *coordinated* action, there are merely several individuals who act individually to bring about the same goal, and perhaps know this, but who do not act as a group. As argued earlier, the appropriate coordination

---

of individuals is enhanced by their group membership. Showing this might be the main aim of a psychological study, which is not concerned with whether it is the group or individuals to whom the enhanced creativity is correctly attributable, but only whether creativity is increased; or it might be the chief interest of an advertising executive who wants to know whether he should have his staff work in groups or individually to be more creative.

involves norms, specifying entitlements and corresponding obligations of group members to each other. Two people walking together are entitled to call on the other to slow down if one draws ahead, and they are obliged to make their excuses should they decide to drop out of the group.

How exactly to specify these common purpose and coordination conditions is, of course, a contentious matter. But for our purposes we need not take a stand on these more fine-grained issues. What matters is that these two conditions, or something similar to them, suffice for a group to be a group agent, in the modest sense of the term.

The creative groups mentioned are, by this test, group agents. Moshman and Geil show that their participants are engaged in collaborative reasoning, which they define as 'cases in which two or more individuals deliberately coordinate their thinking for the shared purpose of achieving justifiable results' (Moshman and Geil, 1998, p. 231), a definition that closely mirrors our two conditions for group agency. These participants are reasoning together, just as Gilbert's walkers are walking together; and in the course of reasoning together and as a result of doing so, they are creative together. Likewise, the research scientists are reasoning together, with a common purpose (that they solve the problem set by the research project) and coordinate their individual actions by supporting, or challenging, or extending each other's arguments, and so are creative together. They also exhibit distributed reasoning, and follow more stringent norms for helping their fellow reasoners than the more ad hoc groups of the Wason case. The Pixar filmmakers are also reasoning and being creative together.

So the people reasoning together constitute group agents, that is, they act as groups. It might be objected that, even so, this does not show that they are creative as groups, for the features that make them group agents are not the features that make them creative. But the objection is untenable: in the examples presented the group's creative activity is inextricably bound up with its members' actions of thinking together: it is because they are reasoning together that they are group agents and also why they are creative as groups.

Fully meeting the richness challenge requires us to show not only that groups can meet the general conditions for agency but also that they can possess the mental powers, such as imagination, that are standardly exercised in creative acts.

As we saw, when individuals have a common purpose and coordinate their individual actions to achieve it, acknowledging entitlements and obligations relative to each other, this suffices for group agency.

# Berys Gaut

Complex intentional states can also be ascribed to groups on this account. For instance, several people might decide on a project of imagining in detail a particular state of affairs, perhaps a hypothesis or a story; they have a common aim, each may contribute something to the scenario, and they coordinate their imaginings so as to produce a coherent outcome, typically using external props, such as written texts and storyboards of film sequences. The participants have jointly imagined the story and we can thereby ascribe to the group the content of that imagining. The act of joint imagining (imagining together) may be richer than individuals could accomplish on their own, since each may contribute only a part of the whole, as we saw in the case of distributed reasoning.

Moreover, not all of the mental states required for creativity need be attributed to the group, even when the group has been creative. For instance, if an individual comes up with an analogy that leads to a creative idea and she tells the group about the idea but not the analogy, the analogy is not attributable to the group. Nevertheless, the group's creativity depends on the analogy, because it depends on the creative idea generated by it. Since group actions depend on the common goals and coordination of individuals' actions, individual agency is always present when there is group agency, so there is plenty of scope to attribute creative states to individuals that are not states of the group. So some of the mental richness required for group creativity is plausibly ascribable to the individual members, rather than to the group. Nevertheless, some of it is correctly ascribed to the group.

## 6. Implications and reflections

I have argued for the group creativity claim:

> (GC) The creativity of some kinds of groups is, because of the features that make them groups, greater than the summed creativity of their members, were those individuals acting separately.

Social groups, as we saw, are constituted as groups partly by virtue of the norms applying to them. The argument ran that the empirical data that seem to contradict the group creativity claim, chiefly the ineffectiveness of brainstorming norms as standardly practised, merely show that the claim is true of only some kinds of groups; and groups employing reasoning norms were shown to be ones where the hypothesis is well supported. The objection that this evidence is compatible with only individuals being creative, boosted by the background condition of group membership, was met by arguing that group agency is a genuine phenomenon, and that a group's being creative is one way in which group agency can be exercised. And an array of mental states can be attributed to groups by, for instance, individuals imagining together, which may be richer in content than those possessed by individuals. Groups can be creative and are often more creative than their individual members.

This defence of the group creativity claim removes a serious challenge to agency theories of creativity. If group creativity is real, but incompatible with agency theories, we should abandon those theories. But far from that being so, we have shown that the philosophical literature on group agency can provide a plausible account of how group creativity is possible. Agency theories have sometimes been associated with 'genius' accounts of creativity, according to which the sole locus of human creativity lies in a small number of people possessed of exceptional gifts. But nothing within the agency claim requires the genius view. Creative agency is not to be equated with individual creativity, let alone with the creativity of a few outstanding individuals. Nor is the agency claim confined to humans: non-human animals and extra-terrestrial beings may be agents too.

The group creativity claim also locates creativity in a wider social and cultural context. This is partly because the groups in question are social entities, and also because of the central role played by social norms in group agency. According to cultural evolutionary theory, cultures evolve and cultural entities include social norms. Michael Tomasello (2009; 2014) has argued that core human achievements, particularly the cumulative evolution of knowledge, tools and practices, depend on the development of larger scale groups, themselves dependent on joint and collective intentionality, which in turn depend on shared cultural norms, particularly norms of fairness. As norms become more elaborate and more explicit (aided by the development of writing more than 5,000 years ago), groups can become larger, cooperation increases, and more creative achievements are rendered possible.

It might be thought that the group creativity claim leaves no room for competition and conflict as spurs to creativity, particularly given views such as Tomasello's that emphasise the role of cooperation. Whilst it is true that groups require a minimal degree of cooperation to exist, since they require common purposes and coordination to achieve them, they also permit and sometimes even require competition and conflict. There can be competition between groups, and in the case of competitive team sports and commercial firms, competition is standardly a requirement; and competition may incentivise creativity, producing innovations in sports techniques and commercial products. There can also be a degree of competition and conflict within groups which may similarly promote creativity, as with creative differences within rock bands and filmmaking groups (Gaut, 2010, pp. 130-32). Moreover, it is no part of the group creativity claim that only groups are creative (though some sociocultural theorists, such as Keith Sawyer, 2007, have advanced that view); the creativity of individuals is important too, as earlier noted. Individual creativity leaves room for more extreme forms of conflict and competition, which may enhance creativity, than does group creativity, since individual action does not require the minimal cooperative framework required by group action.

The existence of group creativity also renders intelligible the fact that groups have become more prominent in many creative areas. This is particularly important in science, as we noted earlier. Wuchty, Jones and Uzzi (2007), using a database of 19.9 million papers and 2.1 million patents, showed that between 1955 and 2000 the average number of co-authors of a scientific paper increased from 1.9 to 3.5, and the citations of team-authored scientific papers relative to citations to solo papers increased from 1.7 to 2.1 times. This is in part because as the knowledge frontier – the amount of knowledge individuals require to have a chance of improving on existing forms – advances in science, individuals have to specialise more, so teams of authors have a greater chance of making creative discoveries than do individuals operating on their own (Henrich, 2016, p. 325). In other cultural domains group creativity is also becoming increasingly important. As Wuchty, Jones and Uzzi (2007) also report, even in the arts and humanities more papers were group-authored at the end of the period they studied than at the start, which is partly because the knowledge frontier has advanced in these areas too. And many arts are now heavily dependent on science-based technology, which requires increasingly specialised knowledge: for instance, the digital revolution in filmmaking has caused substantial increases in the size of filmmaking teams, and some films are now made by thousands of people. So not only is group creativity real, but it is also increasingly pervasive in modern societies.

This is just as well. As I remarked at the start of this paper, the challenges we face are ones that call for group, and not merely individual, creativity. Our central example was the four world-leading microbiology labs studied by Dunbar: three of them were working on pathogens, either bacteria or viruses, including the

HIV virus. Group creativity was essential to getting their results, and the problems of eradicating pathogens are still very much with us. We also require creativity in solving collective action problems, finding ways to reduce the temptations of free riding on proposed policies. Fortunately, we are uniquely good as a species at cooperating on a huge scale with unrelated conspecifics (Raihani, 2021), and so scope for group creativity opens up here as well. There are reasons, then, to be hopeful in looking forwards, and a major reason for optimism is the existence of group creativity.[8]

*University of St Andrews*
*bng@st-andrews.ac.uk*

# References

Mandi Astola, 'Collective Responsibility Should be Treated as a Virtue', *Royal Institute Philosophy Supplementary Volume*, 92 (2022) 27–44.

Margaret A. Boden, *The Creative Mind: Myths and Mechanisms*, second edition (London and New York: Routledge, 2004).

Thomas J. Bouchard, Jr. and Melana Hare, 'Size, Performance, and Potential in Brainstorming Groups', *Journal of Applied Psychology*, 54 (1970), 51-55.

Michael E. Bratman, *Faces of Intention: Selected Essays on Intention and Agency* (Cambridge: Cambridge University Press, 1999).

Michael E. Bratman, *Shared Agency: A Planning Theory of Acting Together* (New York: Oxford University Press, 2014).

Ed Catmull, 'How Pixar Fosters Collective Creativity', *Harvard Business Review* (September 2008), 64-72.

Kevin Dunbar, 'How Scientists Really Reason: Scientific Reasoning in Real-World Laboratories' in Robert J. Sternberg and Janet E. Davidson (eds.), *The Nature of Insight*. (Cambridge Mass.: MIT Press, 1995).

Kevin Dunbar, 'How Scientists Think: On-Line Creativity and Conceptual Change in Science' in Thomas B. Ward, Steven M. Smith and Jyotsna Vaid (eds.), *Creative Thought: An*

---

[8]   For helpful comments on this paper or its precursors I would like to thank the editors of this volume, participants in the Creativity in Art, Science and Mind Conference in Cambridge in 2018, and attendees at the Values and Virtues in a Changing World Workshop in Cardiff in 2021.

*Investigation of Conceptual Structures and Processes* (Washington, DC: American Psychological Association, 1997).

Berys Gaut, *A Philosophy of Cinematic Art* (Cambridge: Cambridge University Press, 2010).

Berys Gaut, 'Mixed Motivations: Creativity as a Virtue', *Philosophical Aesthetics and the Sciences of Art: Royal Institute of Philosophy Supplement* 75 (2014), 183–202.

Berys Gaut, 'The Value of Creativity' in Berys Gaut and Matthew Kieran (eds.), *Creativity and Philosophy* (Abingdon: Routledge, 2018).

Margaret Gilbert, 'Walking Together: A Paradigmatic Social Phenomenon', *Midwest Studies in Philosophy* XV (1990), 1–14.

Margaret Gilbert, 'Shared Intention and Personal Intentions', *Philosophical Studies* 144 (2009), 167-87.

Joseph Henrich, *The Secret of Our Success: How Culture is Driving Human Evolution, Domesticating Our Species, and Making Us Smarter* (Princeton, NJ: Princeton University Press, 2016).

Lu Hong and Scott E. Page, 'Some Microfoundations of Collective Wisdom' in Hélène Landemore and Jon Elster (eds.), *Collective Wisdom: Principles and Mechanisms* (Cambridge: Cambridge University Press, 2012).

Anneli Jefferson and Katrina Sifferd, 'Practical Wisdom and the Value of Cognitive Diversity', *Royal Institute Philosophy Supplementary Volume*, 92 (2022) 149–66.

Matthew Kieran, 'Creativity as a Virtue of Character' in Elliot Samuel Paul and Scott Barry Kaufman (eds.), *The Philosophy of Creativity: New Essays* (New York: Oxford University Press, 2014).

Christian List and Philip Pettit, *Group Agency: The Possibility, Design, and Status of Corporate Agents* (Oxford: Oxford University Press, 2011).

Mariana Mazzucato, *The Entrepreneurial State: Debunking Public vs. Private Sector Myths*, revised edition (London: Anthem Press, 2015).

Ravi Mehta and Rui (Juliet) Zhu, 'Blue or Red? Exploring the Effect of Color on Cognitive Task Performances', *Science* 323 (2009), 1226–1229.

Hugo Mercier and Dan Sperber, *The Enigma of Reason: A New Theory of Human Understanding* (London: Allen Lane, 2017).

David Moshman and Molly Geil, 'Collaborative Reasoning: Evidence for Collective Rationality', *Thinking and Reasoning* 4 (1998), 231–248.

Charlan J. Nemeth, Bernard Personnaz, Marie Personnaz and Jack A. Goncalo, 'The Liberating Role of Conflict in Group Creativity: A Study in two Countries', *European Journal of Social Psychology* 34 (2004), 365–74.

Elliot Samuel Paul and Dustin Stokes, 'Attributing Creativity' in Berys Gaut and Matthew Kieran (eds.), *Creativity and Philosophy* (Abingdon: Routledge, 2018).

Philip Pettit, 'Corporate Agency: The Lesson of the Discursive Dilemma' in Marija Jankovic and Kirk Ludwig (eds.), *The Routledge Handbook of Collective Intentionality* (Abingdon: Routledge, 2018).

Henri Poincaré, 'Mathematical Creation' in Brewster Ghiselin (ed.), *The Creative Process: A Symposium* (Berkeley, Calif.: University of California Press, 1985).

David A. Price, *The Pixar Touch: The Making of a Company* (New York: Vintage Books, 2009).

Nichola Raihani, *The Social Instinct: How Cooperation Shaped the World* (London: Jonathan Cape, 2021).

R. Keith Sawyer, *Group Genius: The Creative Power of Collaboration* (New York: Basic Books, 2007).

R. Keith Sawyer, *Explaining Creativity: The Science of Human Innovation*, second edition (New York: Oxford University Press, 2012).

John R. Searle, *Making the Social World: The Structure of Human Civilization* (New York: Oxford University Press, 2010).

Dean Keith Simonton, 'Creativity as a Darwinian Phenomenon: The Blind-Variation and Selective-Retention Model' in Michael Krausz, Denis Dutton and Karen Bardsley (eds.), *The Idea of Creativity* (Leiden: Brill, 1999)

Dean Keith Simonton, 'Hierarchies of Creative Domains: Disciplinary Constraints on Blind Variation and Selective Retention' in Elliot Samuel Paul and Scott Barry Kaufman (eds.), *The Philosophy of Creativity: New Essays* (New York: Oxford University Press, 2014).

Simon Singh, *Fermat's Last Theorem* (London: Harper Perennial, 2005).

Matthew Noah Smith, 'Political Creativity: A Skeptical View' in Berys Gaut and Matthew Kieran (eds.), *Creativity and Philosophy* (Abingdon: Routledge, 2018).

Dan Sperber and Hugo Mercier, 'Reasoning as a Social Competence' in Hélène Landemore and Jon Elster (eds.), *Collective Wisdom: Principles and Mechanisms* (Cambridge: Cambridge University Press, 2012)

Garold Stasser and William Titus, 'Hidden Profiles: A Brief History', *Psychological Inquiry* 14 (2003), 304–13.

Donald W. Taylor, Paul C. Berry and Clifford H. Block, 'Does Group Participation When Using Brainstorming Facilitate or Inhibit Creative Thinking?', *Administrative Science Quarterly* 3 (1958), 23–47.

Amie Thomasson, 'The Ontology of Social Groups', *Synthese* 196 (2019), 4829-4845.

Michael Tomasello, *Why We Cooperate* (Cambridge, Mass.: MIT Press, 2009).

Michael Tomasello, *A Natural History of Human Thinking* (Cambridge, Mass.: Harvard University Press, 2014).

Raimo Tuomela, *Social Ontology: Collective Intentionality and Group Agents* (Oxford: Oxford University Press, 2013).

Stefan Wuchty, Benjamin F. Jones, Brian Uzzi, 'The Increasing Dominance of Teams in the Production of Knowledge', *Science* 316 (2007), 1036–1039.

# Collective Responsibility Should be Treated as a Virtue

MANDI ASTOLA

**Abstract**

We often praise and blame groups of people like companies or governments, just like we praise and blame individual persons. This makes sense. Because some of the most important problems in our society, like climate change or mass surveillance, are not caused by individual people, but by groups. Philosophers have argued that there exists such a thing as *group responsibility*, which does not boil down to individual responsibility. This type of responsibility can only exist in groups that are organized with joint knowledge, actions and intentions. However, often disorganized groups without joint knowledge, actions and intentions are precisely the kinds of groups that cause problems. Therefore, in such cases, it becomes difficult, according to traditional accounts of collective responsibility to attribute responsibility to such groups. This has problematic implications. Therefore, I propose a new way of seeing collective responsibility, which is able to attribute the vice of irresponsibility to such disorganized groups. This involves seeing responsibility not as a relationship between the group and some action, but rather, as a virtue. In cases where it is difficult to establish whether a group is responsible for something, we should ask 'is this group *responsible*, or *irresponsible*?' This line of questioning is likely to be a more productive and philosophically legitimate way of holding groups morally responsible in such cases.

## 1. Introduction

We often praise and blame groups of people, just like we praise and blame individual persons. Blaming Shell for climate change or a government for war is often as natural as blaming a friend for betrayal (Tollefsen, 2003). It makes sense that we blame groups. After all, wars, environmental degradation and pandemics are never one person's fault. Attributing responsibility to collectives is also often effective in driving change. Because being held responsible is often what drives us to fix the problems we have caused and to demand that others do so. For instance, the oil industry is responsible for much environmental degradation. This is why we may easily feel comfortable demanding that the oil industry take the largest steps to protect the environment. Group responsibility justifies globally

doi:10.1017/S1358246122000133

important group action. But what does it really mean to blame a group?

Philosophers have long discussed what it means for a group to be morally responsible for something. Does it boil down to individuals being responsible for their individual contributions? Or is there something like blaming a group, *as a group*, which is different from blaming individuals? Many theorists agree that group responsibility does not always boil down to individual responsibilities (Gilbert, 2002; Smiley, 2008; List and Pettit, 2011; Björnsson, 2020; Giubilini and Levy, 2018). Groups can be held responsible but only under certain conditions. Generally, what these conditions are depends on which aspects of the group are seen as supervening, or in some way 'over and above' the individual members (Giubilini and Levy, 2018). Supervening characteristics are those which cannot be explained with reference to the behavior of individual members only. Just like the elaborate shapes created in the sky by a flock of birds, many collective human behaviors emerge from many individual actions. These emergent phenomena however have their own characteristics, which are best described at the level of the collective. Some philosophers have argued that a group's actions supervene on the actions of members (Bratman, 2014). Others argue that a group's intentions or beliefs do so (Searle, 1990; Gilbert, 1987). The supervening qualities are what give the group a kind of unity. If this unified part of the group fulfills the conditions of moral responsibility, knowledge, control and moral competence, then it seems intuitive that the group can be held responsible as a group. This means that when one is praising or blaming a group for collective and emergent behavior, then one is praising or blaming the collective as a whole, not the individuals. Philosophers disagree on whether this praise or blame is always shared by individual members too.

Collective responsibility is an important concept to have. Many times, when for example a big corporate scandal is revealed, it is not clear which individuals were responsible for the transgressions. Often, each member may have played a small part, partaking only in a minor transgression or no transgression at all. In such cases, we must blame the collective rather than individuals for the crime. However, exactly these kinds of groups tend to be internally fragmented in the kind of way that renders them incapable of responsibility. Such cases, often referred to as a 'problem of many hands', is a situation where a collective has done something wrong, but no individuals can be blamed. Usually, this is seen as a problem because it

# Collective Responsibility Should be Treated as a Virtue

means we cannot hold individuals responsible. I argue that in such cases, it also becomes difficult to hold the collective responsible.

Should we do away with the idea of collective responsibility completely in such cases? I think that would be premature. I propose instead that we adopt another way to see collective responsibility, which does not run into this problem. I suggest we abandon the idea of collective responsibility as a relationship between the collective agent and the action in question. Instead, we should see collective responsibility as a virtue. A virtue is a long-term and stable positive character trait of an agent, in this case, a group. If we see responsibility as a virtue possessed by a collective then it becomes easier to attribute moral praise and blame to groups. Instead of thinking 'is this collective responsible for x' let us think 'is this a responsible collective? Or is it irresponsible?' Changing our conception of what responsibility means makes it possible to praise and blame groups, even if the group is fragmented, like in the case of an example I treat in section 3, the Deepwater Horizon disaster.

How can a group be responsible or irresponsible? To answer this, I use philosophical literature to show that groups can have a character, much like individuals. A group can be said to be, just like any of us, benevolent, foolhardy, responsible or irresponsible. This means that we can distinguish virtues and vices in the character of groups. According to virtue ethics, vices (bad character traits like foolhardiness or irresponsibility) are inherently blameworthy and virtues (good character traits like benevolence and responsibility) praiseworthy. Virtue ethics can, therefore, give guidance in praising and blaming groups. The guidance of virtue ethics, I will argue, is better than the guidance given by the more traditional philosophical concept of collective responsibility.

What then does a virtuously responsible collective look like? My answer to that is derived from the negative opposite of collective responsibility, which is the vice of collective irresponsibility, of which the problem of many hands is expressive. I outline some causes of the problem of many hands and show how these traits can be categorized as collective irresponsibility as a vice. Collective responsibility is the long-term and stable acquired trait of collectives to avoid these pitfalls.

Section 2 outlines what is needed for a collective to be held collectively responsible for something. Section 3 explains the problem of many hands. In section 4 I show how the notion of collective responsibility runs into problems in cases of problems of many hands, and why an additional way of holding groups responsible is needed. In section 5, I propose an alternative way of holding collectives responsible, based on the idea of groups having a character, which can be virtuous or vicious. The concluding remark reflects on the significance of collective responsibility as a virtue.

## 2. Collective moral responsibility

Let us begin with the question: what is collective moral responsibility? Two questions are important for understanding collective responsibility: 'what is *collective* about collective responsibility?' and 'How is collective responsibility *moral responsibility?*' Let us briefly consider each.

As for the first question, Giubilini and Levy (2018) have provided a coherent answer that summarizes the views of most collective responsibility scholars. Imagine a group of schoolchildren who are directed by their teacher to each draw themselves on one large shared piece of paper. Each enthusiastically picks out colored pencils and soon becomes absorbed in drawing, mumbling to themselves and blissfully ignoring everyone else. Of course, the children are creating something together, namely a collectively drawn class picture. However, if we follow Giubilini and Levy, the pupils are not collectively responsible for the drawing. Rather, the responsibility for the drawing is better explained by saying that the teacher is responsible for the idea and each pupil for their individual drawing. However, if the teacher asked a group of pupils to write a report together, then this would force the pupils to make agreements, form shared intentions and devise their contributions based on what others are contributing. Such an assignment would probably qualify as something the pupils are collectively responsible for.

As for the second question, 'How is collective responsibility *moral responsibility?*' let us take a closer look at what is required for moral responsibility in general. One comprehensive view, which serves our purposes here, and captures well the most dominant intuitions about moral responsibility, is Fischer and Ravizza's account.

Fischer and Ravizza's theory of moral responsibility focuses on the internal mechanism that brings about a certain action. For example: If a person knocks over a glass because of a seizure, then the mechanism that brings about the action is not reasons-responsive. A seizure cannot be reasoned with, it just happens. However, if a person knocks over the glass because they are angry, then this mechanism can be reasons-responsive. Because they may refrain from knocking the glass over if they are told that their behavior is scaring their friends. In the case of a seizure, the person is not morally responsible for knocking the glass over, in the latter case they are. The authors also specify an epistemic condition for responsibility, meaning that to be responsible one must have knowledge of what one is doing. For instance, if the person knocking the glass could not have known that it was glass, not plastic, and would break when knocked, then they would not be morally responsible for the glass breaking, although they would be responsible for knocking it over (Fischer and Ravizza, 1998 (The example is my own)). The mechanism by which the person acts must also be 'the agent's own' meaning that the agent: '(a) sees herself as the source of her behavior (which follows from the operation of K [the mechanism]); and (b) believes that she is an apt candidate for the reactive attitudes as a result of how she exercises her agency in certain contexts; and (c) views herself as an agent with respect to (a) - (b) based on her evidence for these beliefs' (Fischer and Ravizza, 1998).

We can distill three important components of moral responsibility from Fischer and Ravizza's account, which also align with other accounts of moral responsibility. Therefore, for a collective to be morally responsible for an action or event, it must be the case that:

- The collective agent has knowledge of what it is doing.[1]
- The collective agent's mechanism of control over the action is reasons responsive.
- The mechanism of control over the action is the collective agent's own in the sense that the agent believes to be in control of it.[2]

Armed with this definition of collective responsibility, let us move to what the problem is with applying this definition.

## 3. The problem of many hands

The problem of many hands, henceforth PMH, is a morally problematic situation which arises when a collective is morally responsible for something but no individual in that collective can reasonably be held responsible (Poel et al., 2015). For instance, take the Deepwater Horizon disaster, the oil spill that happened in 2010 in the Gulf of Mexico. This is a case that has been described as a PMH (Poel

---

[1]    For a discussion on how a group can know things, see Smith (1982). For a discussion of mutual know-how, see Miller (2020).
[2]    For a discussion on how a group can hold joint beliefs, see Gilbert (1987).

et al. 2015, pp. 1–11). The part of the oil rig that extended into the earth under the sea was not sealed off properly. No one intervened early enough because of various epistemic failures. For instance, British Petroleum's internal tests had shown the cement to be unstable. However, this was not communicated to the contractors implementing the cement seal. The site leaders at the oil rig even dismissed obvious signs of leakage. This was because they accepted a theory held by other oil rig staff, about the signs of leakage being caused by something harmless. The oil rig staff had not been trained properly. The necessary information did not reach the right people, because of a lack of necessary information, protocol and training at other places (Poel et al., 2015).

The PMH is problematic because it seems to cause a responsibility gap (Poel et al., 2015). A responsibility gap emerges when there is an event for which someone should be responsible, like an oil rig disaster, but no one can be held responsible. One could argue that each member of the collective that caused the disaster can be attributed a small amount of the responsibility, which all adds up. However, distributing responsibility in a piecemeal fashion still causes a responsibility gap, because a small piece of responsibility for 'not noticing that one's boss was not properly trained' or 'not taking great efforts to find out what was wrong' is something very different than the heavy responsibility of a disaster involving deaths and pollution (Poel et al., 2015). The heavy responsibility, for which we feel someone should be blamed, disappears, unless we attribute it meaningfully to the collective as a whole.

Groups with PMH can however also not be attributed collective responsibility. To illustrate why, let us consider the definition of collective responsibility from the previous section. To be collectively responsible, a group must fulfill all three conditions of moral responsibility: epistemic condition, control condition and moral competence condition.

The epistemic condition is: 'The *collective* has *collective* knowledge of what it is doing'. Think again of the Deepwater Horizon disaster. Information which could have been knowledge about the impending disaster was distributed in such a way that it was merely distributed information. No common knowledge of the danger was present until after the disaster. Therefore, although the necessary information may be distributed among members, the possibility to form the knowledge is not there in that state. The fact that crucial information is not distributed properly is generally a sign that the group suffers from an underlying collective behavior problem, like a lack of transparency, secretive culture, or insufficient collective attention to signaling problems. In such a state, it is group-psychologically impossible for the information distributed among group members to be used in a functional way to improve the actions of the group. Therefore, there is no collective knowledge, meaning that the collective agent does not meet the collective knowledge condition for moral responsibility. We also cannot resort to merely holding the individual members responsible for their lack of knowledge. In such cases, the individuals *do not know that they should know* something. Therefore, they do not fulfill the knowledge condition for individual responsibility either. In this case, the group not fulfilling the epistemic condition is what led to the PMH and the tragedy.

## 4. Collective responsibility as a concept must be revised

Problems of many hands, make it impossible to attribute a responsibility properly to individuals. They also make it impossible to attribute collective responsibility. We may be tempted to bite the bullet and admit that the concept of collective responsibility is not applicable to cases like climate change or engineering disasters, which involve PMHs. The alternative is to call these cases a combination of some individual fault, and bad luck. Engineering disasters and climate change would then be in the category of unfortunate events, like natural disasters.[3] Then we must argue that only epistemically and structurally well-organized groups can be held responsible for their mistakes.

However, there are good reasons not to bite the bullet. Climate change, corporate scandals and engineering disasters often happen precisely because a group is not a well-functioning collective agent. If we accept that all such cases are nobody's responsibility then we may lose the motivating force of responsibility attributions which is practically very important for remedying such situations. If a theory of collective responsibility fails to attribute collective responsibility in a case like the Deepwater Horizon disaster, then it seems intuitive that we should use another theory to justify the practice of attributing collective responsibility.

---

[3] This would be different from what van de Poel et al argue in their work on PMH. They argue that in a case of PMH, the collective is morally responsible, but individual responsibility attributions are impossible to make (Poel et al., 2015). This is where I disagree with the authors, because I argue that a group with a PMH cannot be collectively responsible either.

This does not mean that we must eschew the notion of collective responsibility completely. It works in many collective responsibility cases, after all. However, in cases of PMH, collective responsibility should be attributed differently. Because the traditional way of attributing it is not metaphysically sound for that particular situation.

One way to avoid biting the bullet might be to try to find ways of attributing individual responsibilities to members of the group. Fahlquist has suggested such an account (Fahlquist, 2015). She re-conceptualizes responsibility by viewing it as a virtue, meaning an acquired, stable, long-term disposition of actively taking responsibility. A person with this virtue is a *responsible person*. If each individual in an organization takes the responsibility upon themselves, even when they are not assigned it, then this can fill responsibility gaps that may have been left unaddressed by job descriptions and responsibility divisions. What is important here is that taking responsibility means that one makes it so that one can reasonably be held responsible for something (Fahlquist, 2015; Poel et al., 2015). A responsible person involves themselves with issues in such a way that others can hold them responsible for it, thereby eliminating responsibility gaps (Fahlquist, 2015; Poel et al., 2015).

This approach, however, cannot escape the limitation that it needs to break apart a large responsibility into small pieces, which means that the large responsibility, being of a different nature, disappears. If a group causes deaths, but each member has only contributed to it in a minimal way for which they are hardly blameworthy, then the piecemeal way of distributing responsibility fails in a significant sense. For this reason, I choose to further the concept of collective responsibility, rather than individual responsibility.

My proposal is a collective version of Fahlquist's. I propose seeing responsibility as a virtue, which is *the disposition to make oneself fulfill the conditions for moral responsibility* for important matters. Collective responsibility, therefore, refers to a desirable characteristic of groups. Instead of asking whether a group is responsible *for* something, we can ask whether a group is *responsible*. This provides an alternative possibility for philosophically justifying the praising and blaming of groups.

## 5. Collective responsibility as a virtue

Groups that regularly meet and undertake joint actions, can be said to have a character. And group characters can contain positive and negative traits. Just like individual character, group character can be developed to become virtuous or vicious. Instead of asking the

# Collective Responsibility Should be Treated as a Virtue

question 'Is Coca-Cola responsible for sugar consumption related health problems?' we should ask a different question 'Is Coca-Cola an irresponsible company?' This kind of thinking is not new in philosophy. Many philosophers have written about collective virtues, or what it means for a group to be, for example, clever, open-minded or benevolent (Fricker, 2010; Palermos and Pritchard, 2013; Pritchard and Palermos, 2016; Lahroodi, 2007; Byerly and Byerly, 2016; Palermos, 2020; Astola, 2021).

My proposal is to create a collectivist version of Fahlquist's argument. We should attribute collective responsibility as a virtue to collectives that act responsibly. Responsibility as a virtue has so far only been characterized as a trait of individual people (Williams, 2008). However, as various authors have argued, virtues and vices can also be possessed by collective agents (Fricker, 2010; Beggs, 2003; Lahroodi, 2007; Sandin, 2007; Astola, 2021). I will argue for a view of collective responsibility which includes the following claims, which I will treat in subsequent subsections:

- A responsible group has a responsible identity, constituted by the practical identities of members
- The problem of many hands is generally expressive of the collective vice of irresponsibility, which is the inverse of responsibility as a collective virtue
- Collective responsibility as a virtue is the long-term and stable, acquired trait of a group to make itself meet the three conditions for collective moral responsibility

## 5.1 A responsible group has a responsible identity, constituted by the practical identities of members

Collective responsibility must attach to a mechanism of action that is truly collective and does not boil down to actions of individuals (Giubilini and Levy, 2018). What then is this mechanism? I believe Fricker's work on institutional virtue provides an answer. Fricker argues that group membership often entails the development of a *practical identity*. If one becomes a member of a company or an association, then this means that one must sometimes speak and act *as a member of that group*. These practical identities are mutually dependent, because their existence in members depends on the commitment of other members to similar practical identities. When one acts in their capacity as a member, they sometimes act in ways that are different from how they would act if they were not in that capacity.

According to Fricker, this explains why people sometimes act against their own views in professional, or other membership-related, contexts (Fricker, 2010).

When the streets surrounding a fast-food restaurant are littered with straws and burger-wraps, we tend to hold the customers individually, not collectively, responsible. They are not, after all, organizing and coordinating their littering activities. We might however hold the fast food restaurant (perhaps even the franchise) as collectively responsible in their part in the littering. The restaurant and the chain coordinate their activities so that littering may be reduced, for example by handing out less packaging, providing more bins and reminding customers not to litter. They are, therefore, collectively responsible, because they are more organized and have a unifying group identity consisting of the practical identities of members.

What operationalizes this possibility for coordination, are the mutually dependent practical identities. If the fast-food staff decide that they must take action on this problem, this stance will become a part of every employee's practical identity as an employee of that restaurant. And the mutually dependent practical identities are the object of the responsibility attribution. When groups have practical identities, they also become candidates for blameworthiness if they are not responsible collectively. Because adopting practical identities means making a certain promise, to act in a certain way to internal or external parties.

It should be noted that if we see groups as entities that develop character, we must not judge the character of groups that have had no time to develop their character. If a violent mob bands together randomly in the span of an hour, we should attribute responsibility for the actions of the mob to individual members rather than the mob as a collective. The group is nobody yet. However, groups that exist over a long period of time and establish their own forms of operating, like organizations, can be held responsible as groups.

## 5.2 The problem of many hands as indicative of the collective vice of irresponsibility

The negative opposite of a virtue is a vice. It will be useful therefore to add some detail to our conceptualization of responsibility as a collective virtue by describing what its opposite is. If we think about collective responsibility as a virtue, we may think of its negative opposite as being collective irresponsibility. The problem of many hands is expressive of exactly that.[4]

PMHs should not be seen as mere events of instances where no responsible persons can be found. It is not merely by the unlucky circumstance that the Deepwater Horizon disaster occurs without a clear responsible person. The lack of responsibility was already there for a long time before the disaster. The procedures, attitudes and working practices within the collective were conducive to a lack of transparency, internal communication and perhaps also a lack of care for safety. The PMH was a symptom of this collective irresponsibility. The PMH developed and worsened over a long period of time, and the disaster in turn was a tragic symptom of it. PMHs are then indicative of collective irresponsibility. I propose to treat collective irresponsibility as a collective vice, which often leads to PMHs.

PMHs may not always be a symptom of underlying collective irresponsibility. It is conceivable that a virtuously responsible group fails to take responsibility appropriately for some given object in a specific situation, without doing so structurally. However, in such cases, as soon as the failure is signaled, the group will be equipped and capable of carrying out the correct response. It is in cases where a PMH is signaled but the group fails to take appropriate actions that one sees proof of an underlying collective vice of irresponsibility. An irresponsible group has a character that does not allow them to take responsibility, in the same way that an irresponsible person fails to take responsibility. In both cases, the appropriate response is to blame the agent for having developed an irresponsible character.

A vice is by definition blameworthy. But a collective irresponsibility is not always blameworthy. For group irresponsibility to be blameworthy, it is necessary that the group occupy a role where collectivization is required of them. Not every group needs to be a collective agent. Some groups, however, like companies, governments or other organizations whose members adopt practical identities related to their group membership should be considered collective agents that can have praiseworthy or blameworthy traits. Adherence to law or protocol and prevention of harm to society are generally tasks that require organizations to perform joint actions. These are the kinds of collectives for whom collective irresponsibility is a vice.

The collective vice of irresponsibility, which expresses itself in the PMH, is realizable in multiple ways. There are three distinctive ways

---

[4]    For a discussion on collective vices, see Fricker (2010) and Baird and Calvard (2019).

in which a PMH can occur, the epistemic, structural and motivational. Each of these categories shows a particular trait, all of which can be categorized as collective irresponsibility, because they culminate in a situation where the collective agent does not meet the three criteria for collective moral responsibility. This generally means that the collective agent generally does not have the disposition to make itself meet the conditions for moral responsibility or even the active disposition to avoid making itself meet the criteria for responsibility. When this tendency is negligent enough, we can speak about a collective vice of irresponsibility. Let us discuss each type of irresponsibility in turn.

### 5.2.1 Epistemic irresponsibility

Many stories exist of organizations compromising their ability to fulfill the epistemic condition. A group may fall into an epistemic problem of many hands if it begins to exercise collective habits that lead it away from transparency and information sharing, which prevents the collective agent from forming collective knowledge about its responsibilities. Just as an individual can adopt bad habits that compromise their epistemic agency and make them forgetful or ill-informed, a group can adopt habits that similarly compromise their epistemic agency. As in the Deepwater Horizon disaster, where knowledge was not spread efficiently enough for necessary conclusions to be drawn. Such a group fails to be virtuously responsible, because it operates in a state in which it cannot meet the epistemic condition for collective responsibility.

### 5.2.2 Structural irresponsibility

A PMH can also arise as a result of structural issues. Dysfunctional bureaucracies are an example of this. Inefficient policies or a lack of policies can however also constitute structural collective irresponsibility. Many PMH that have been investigated thoroughly show this kind of trajectory. For instance, the Volkswagen Diesel scandal involved probably a few hundred employees from Volkswagen. This group of people had concealed a portion of the emissions from Volkswagen vehicles. This was done by creating a test-rig setting for the automobiles that would give much lower than accurate emission readings when tested for emissions (Davis 2020, pp. 219–20).

We might say that everyone involved in the creation and implementation of the cheat code was individually responsible for their misconduct. To what extent this holds for the hundreds of people involved is unknown. However, the problem of many hands here rests on the rest of the organization not inquiring, signaling and intervening in this illegal practice. It is, after all, quite unusual that hundreds of employees in an organization take part in an illegal and fraudulent activity without anyone intervening. One analysis of why this happened is because of the lack of preparedness for misconduct. There were no internal processes that would allow for whistleblowing. And because of the lack of organizational structure and attention to whistleblowing, no whistles were blown by employees, perhaps out of fear of social sanction (Davis, 2020). VW had a long-standing collective habit of trusting upper management too much and not considering the possibility of misconduct. This eventually created structures which did not support responsible behavior within the organization. This makes it difficult for the company to meet the control condition for moral responsibility.

### 5.2.3 Motivational irresponsibility

A problem of many hands can occur due to motivational traits. As experience often shows, demotivation is contagious, and it is hard to stay motivated to do a task in groups where this contagion has already spread. One example of a motivational PMH is 'innovation trauma' in organizations. Companies that experience backlash following an innovation, or an attempt to innovate, sometimes develop a pessimistic company culture that is wary of trying anything new. Innovation trauma has been defined in management literature as 'the inability to commit to a new innovation due to severe disappointment from previous innovation failures' (Välikangas et al., 2009). The demotivation caused by a previous failure easily spreads even to those employees who did not experience the traumatic failure. And the pessimism persists even if there is a good reason to innovate (Välikangas et al., 2009). A company may stick to old and inefficient ways for much too long, because of such collective pessimism. This can happen even if the company possesses all the shared knowledge and capabilities to innovate. Such a state of inaction can lead to a problem of many hands, and a purely a motivational one. For example, innovation trauma can discourage members from proposing much needed improvements to the rest of the group, or make it shameful for anyone to get excited about them once they are proposed.

In some cases, motivational irresponsibility can go so far that it becomes irresponsive to reason. In a case of heavy collective trauma, it can become impossible for the collective to change its motivational patterns. In such cases, we can speak of the collective not meeting the collective moral competence condition. Because in a case of severe innovation trauma, the mechanism of control over the *joint* action, which is the fear of innovation in this case, does not respond to reason. This means that the collective does not fulfill one of the conditions of moral responsibility, indicating irresponsibility, or at least a lack of collective responsibility as a virtue. One sometimes hears about organizations that are 'beyond saving' because the collective culture is such that no new manager or no voice of reason can inspire change. In other cases, a collective lack of motivation for something can prevent the group from revising epistemic norms, information flows or structures that need revision. This can in turn lead to epistemic or structural problems which prevent the group from fulfilling the epistemic and control condition for moral responsibility, meaning that the group is irresponsible.

### 5.3 Collective responsibility as a virtue is the long-term and stable, acquired trait of a group to make itself meet the three conditions for collective moral responsibility

Having described the vice of irresponsibility, and how it can emerge in a collective through epistemic, structural and motivational issues, let us again turn to its positive opposite, collective responsibility as a virtue. The virtue of collective responsibility must be a trait to actively avoid the epistemic, structural and motivational pitfalls described in the previous section.

Possessing the collective virtue of responsibility means that the collective avoids vices of irresponsibility. However, it is also useful to characterize the virtue of responsibility in a positive sense, by what it is, rather than only what it avoids. Fahlquist's characterization of responsibility as virtue provides such a positive description, which aligns with avoiding the pitfalls which lead to PMH. Namely, a responsible agent actively takes responsibility (Fahlquist, 2015). A responsible agent acts in such a way that it fulfills the knowledge, control and moral competence conditions.

The collective virtue of responsibility can be defined as:

*The collective long-term and stable trait of a group to actively make sure that it fulfills the three conditions of moral responsibility. A responsible group makes sure it has collective knowledge of what it is doing, ensures that there is a feeling of collective control over what it is doing, and the process whereby the group acts is reasons-responsive.*

# Collective Responsibility Should be Treated as a Virtue

Virtues are traditionally acquired traits. Some philosophers also specify that a virtue must be acquired through significant effort (Zagzebski, 1996). The same goes for collective responsibility as a virtue. Similar to the way that a PMH is acquired, or created, over a long period of time, it takes time to fix it. It also takes significant effort.

Acquiring the collective virtue of responsibility is not easy and requires time and effort. This can be seen in how complex it is for companies to take on this kind of 'self-improvement' projects. For a company, particularly a big one, to change its personality usually requires many different effortful long-term interventions. Take for example the banana company Chiquita's corporate responsibility plan, which was executed in response to the negative attention on the company, which involved the following actions:

- hiring a corporate responsibility officer;
- selecting an external measurement standard (in Chiquita's case SA8000) to assess performance;
- creating a code of conduct, training employees in corporate social responsibility;
- 'mentoring and coaching managers to build decision-making skills that integrate CR-criteria in evaluating options' (Werre, 2003).

As this plan shows, the required changes are not merely effort-requiring for the top management, but for all levels in the company. Managers need to develop their skills and all employees need to be trained. New structures are created and new collective knowledge and joint action are introduced. The process of becoming a more responsible company can be characterized as effortful joint action based on collective knowledge about the company's goals.

Epistemic, structural and motivational elements can also be found in Chiquita's corporate responsibility program. For instance, epistemic functioning of the collective is improved by providing training for all levels of employees ensures that everyone is aware of corporate responsibility goals and responsibilities. This creates collective knowledge and a collective intention, making it easier for the group to fulfill the knowledge condition. Making corporate responsibility criteria a part of the evaluation of managers is a structural change, which makes it easier for managers to prioritize corporate social responsibility tasks. Motivation towards becoming a more socially responsible organization was also enhanced by training, setting incentives and mentoring programs. A collective that develops itself in this way is more likely to collectively fulfill the conditions for moral responsibility.

Mandi Astola

## 6. Concluding remarks

Whether we can attribute moral responsibility to groups matters. Many of the greatest challenges humankind is facing are in some way caused by groups. Being able to assign responsibility in a manner that is philosophically justified is important for legitimizing action to fix the problem. If it is true that such fragmented groups cannot be held responsible, then this means that we cannot blame groups like British Petroleum and the other partners for a mistake like the Deepwater Horizon disaster at all. Since it is also hard to hold individuals responsible for this disaster, the result would be that we cannot ascribe the responsibility to anyone. This is very counterintuitive and likely to lead to practical impasses where no individual or institution feels compelled to take responsibility for the problem. Our ascriptions of responsibility seem to fail us in such cases, indicating that they may need replacement. Using a virtue-based one allows us to judge that the conglomerate of parties involved at Deepwater Horizon was collectively irresponsible and hence have the duty to develop their collective character to a more responsible one.

Furthermore, groups often commit wrongful acts precisely because of internal fragmentation, disorganization or bad information flows. This means that the problem that applies to the Deepwater Horizon case, is likely to apply to other such problems too. Asking whether a group is responsible, rather than whether it is responsible for x, may also be a more productive way of approaching collective responsibility. Because it focuses on the long term operation of the group and prescribes realistic advice for the underlying cause for problems. Changing the way we think about responsibility as a system and a group character trait is more holistic than seeing responsibility as only *responsibility for x*. It is likely to be the kind of thinking that we need to solve humanity's greatest problems.[5]

*Eindhoven University of Technology*
*m.a.astola@tue.nl*

[5]   This project has received funding from the European Union's Horizon 2020 research and innovation programme under Grant Agreement No. 788359.

# Collective Responsibility Should be Treated as a Virtue

## References

Mandi Astola, 'Mandevillian Virtues', *Ethical Theory and Moral Practice*, (2021), 1–14 doi: 10.1007/s10677-020-10141-9.

Christopher Baird, Thomas S. Calvard 'Epistemic Vices in Organizations: Knowledge, Truth, and Unethical Conduct', *Journal of Business Ethics*, 160 (2019), 263–276, doi: 10.1007/s10551-018-3897-z.

Donald Beggs, 'The Idea of Group Moral Virtue', *Journal of Social Philosophy*, 34 (2003), 457–474. doi: 10.1111/1467-9833.00194.

Gunnar Björnsson, 'Collective Responsibility and Collective Obligations Without Collective Moral Agents', *The Routledge Handbook of Collective Responsibility* (Routledge, 2020).

Michael E. Bratman, *Shared Agency: A Planning Theory of Acting Together* (Oxford University Press, 2014).

T. Ryan Byerly, Meghan Byerly, 'Collective Virtue', *Journal of Value Inquiry*, 50 (2016), 33–50, doi: 10.1007/s10790-015-9484-y.

Michael Davis, 'A Whistle Not Blown: VW, Diesels, and Engineers', *Next Generation Ethics*, (Cambridge University Press, 2020).

John Martin Fischer, Mark Ravizza, *Responsibility and Control: A Theory of Moral Responsibility*, (Cambridge University Press, 1998).

Miranda Fricker, 'Can There Be Institutional Virtues?' *Oxford Studies in Epistemology*, (Oxford University Press, Oxford, 2010).

Margaret Gilbert, 'Modelling collective belief', *Synthese*, 73 (1987), 185–204, doi: 10.1007/BF00485446.

Margaret Gilbert, 'Collective Wrongdoing: Moral and Legal Responses' *Social Theory and Practice*, 28 (2002), 167–187.

Alberto Giubilini, Neil Levy 'What in the World Is Collective Responsibility?', *Dialectica* 72 (2018), 191–217, doi: 10.1111/1746-8361.12228.

Reza Lahroodi 'Collective Epistemic Virtues', *Social Epistemology*, 21 (2007), 281–297, doi: 10.1080/02691720701674122.

Christian List, Philip Pettit, *Group Agency: The Possibility, Design, and Status of Corporate Agents*, (Oxford University Press, 2011).

Seumas Miller, 'Joint Abilities, Joint Know-How and Collective Knowledge', *Social Epistemology*, 34 (2020), 197–212, doi: 10.1080/02691728.2019.1677799.

Jessica Nihlen Fahlquist, 'Responsibility as a Virtue and the Problem of Many Hands', *Moral Responsibility and the Problem of Many Hands*, (Routledge, 2015).

Orestis Palermos, Duncan Pritchard, 'Extended Knowledge and Social Epistemology', *Social Epistemology Review and Reply Collective*, 2 (2013), 105–120.

Orestis Palermos, 'Epistemic Collaborations: Distributed Cognition and Virtue Reliabilism', *Erkenntnis*, (2020), 1–20, doi: 10.1007/s10670-020-00258-9.

Ibo van de Poel, Lambèr Royakkers, Sjoerd Zwart, *Moral Responsibility and the Problem of Many Hands*, (Routledge 2015).

Duncan Pritchard, Orestis Palermos, 'The Distribution of Epistemic Agency', *Social Epistemology and Epistemic Agency: Decentralizing Epistemic Agency*, (Rowman & Littlefield, 2016).

Pär Sandin, 'Collective Military Virtues', *Journal of Military Ethics*, 6 (2007), 303–314, doi: 10.1080/15027570701755505.

John Searle, 'Collective Intentions and Actions', *Intentions in Communication*, (MIT Press, 1990).

Marion Smiley, 'Collective responsibility' *Stanford Encyclopedia of Philosophy*, Summer 2017 Edition, (2008), https://plato.stanford.edu/cgi-bin/encyclopedia/archinfo.cgi?entry=collective-responsibility.

Neilson Voyne Smith, *Mutual Knowledge*, (Academic Press, 1982).

Deborah Tollefsen, 'Participant Reactive Attitudes and Collective Responsibility', *Philosophical Explorations*, 6 (2003), 218–234, doi: 10.1080/10002003098538751.

Liisa Välikangas, Martin Hoegl, Michael Gibbert, 'Why Learning from Failure Isn't Easy (and What to Do About It): Innovation trauma at Sun Microsystems', *European Management Journal*, 27 (2009), 225–233, doi: 10.1016/j.emj.2008.12.001.

Marco Werre, 'Implementing Corporate Responsibility - The Chiquita Case', *Journal of Business Ethics*, 44 (2003), 247–260.

Garrath Williams, 'Responsibility as a Virtue' *Ethical Theory and Moral Practice*, 11 (2008), 455–470, doi: 10.1007/s10677-008-9109-7.

Linda Zagzebski, *Virtues of the Mind: An Inquiry Into the Nature of Virtue and the Ethical Foundations of Knowledge*, (Cambridge University Press, 1996).

# Reclaiming Care and Privacy in the Age of Social Media

HUGH DESMOND

**Abstract**

Social media has invaded our private, professional, and public lives. While corporations continue to portray social media as a celebration of self-expression and freedom, public opinion, by contrast, seems to have decidedly turned against social media. Yet we continue to use it just the same. What is social media, and how should we live with it? Is it the promise of a happier and more interconnected humanity, or a vehicle for toxic self-promotion? In this essay I examine the very structure of social media communications in order to sketch how we should engage with social media. Social media communications are, I argue, a public communication of private content. This allows connections to be made with others in ways that would not otherwise be possible; however, it also submits the private to a status competition, which in turn is linked to mental health challenges. A 'virtuous' engagement with social media means being aware of these dynamics, and choosing to subordinate social media to other, more important goods.

Nobody today seems to be genuinely indifferent to social media. Some of us are enthusiastic users, posting daily about our personal and professional lives. Others stay away entirely. Yet others are reluctant or ambivalent users. Nonetheless, as varied as attitudes may be, it is clear that social media provokes emotional reactions in ways that many other technologies – washing machines, for instance – do not.

Long gone are the days when the virtual spaces of the internet were populated by the proverbial nerds and misfits. Today, social media is where success is sought by politicians, corporations, and professionals of all stripes. Likes and followers have become a currency that can be converted into power, revenue, or prestige. Even in academia – that traditionally ivory-tower community – likes and followers are increasingly chased, as evidence mounts that they lead to citations, and hence funding and job opportunities (Luc et al., 2020).

There is something disturbing about the way social media is transforming our private, professional, and public lives. A recent Pew survey showed that 64% of U.S. adults believe that social media have a mostly negative impact on society, *six times* more than the 10% who were optimistic (Auxier, 2020). The cited reasons mainly concern misinformation, harassment, hate, polarization, and echo

doi:10.1017/S135824612200025X

© The Royal Institute of Philosophy and the contributors 2022

*Royal Institute of Philosophy Supplement* **92** 2022

chambers. Such opinions are now shaping public discourse. For instance, some politicians have taken to openly blaming social media platforms for promoting misinformation and vaccine hesitancy (*BBC News*, 2021).

One of the most worrying consequences concerns mental health. Teenagers are vulnerable, and especially teenage girls. Between 2000 and 2015, the suicide rate for teenage girls doubled, with two thirds of that rise occurring between 2010 and 2015 alone. Jean Twenge and colleagues (2018) point to the introduction of the smartphone as the turning point: with that invention, social media could be accessed anytime and anywhere, just as long as one hand was free.

Such challenges underline just how novel the social media environment is for a social species such as ours. For the overwhelming part of our history, we gossiped or joked with a relatively small number of people. In fact, according to anthropologists, our cognition cannot handle much more than about 150 social relationships (Dunbar, 1992). By contrast, on social media our banter and bragging reaches thousands or even millions. Social media has taken root in our evolved desire for community, then twisted it in new ways. For instance, psychologists notice how social media intensifies comparisons between one's own social status and that of others (J.-L. Wang et al., 2017) and promotes expressions of outrage (Brady et al., 2021).

How should we respond to these novel challenges? One approach is to seek reform of the social media environment, in order to reduce the challenges that users structurally face. Calls for privacy protection can be situated in this approach, as can proposals to make platforms less addictive, or to design other types of reactions to posts in order to reduce the anger and rage that can otherwise so easily flourish on social media platforms (Tanesini, 2022). The other approach adopted in in this essay (but also by e.g. Vallor, 2016) will focus on how users can adopt more appropriate responses to the social media environment. Given the structural challenges on social media, how can users better direct their agency? In effect, as expanded on later, this involves a virtue ethics of social media.

This essay's main message will be to bring attention to what I argue is the most fundamental structural challenge on social media: the intertwining of the private and the public in new and often deceptive ways. I will link this to some of the problems concerning social media's impact on mental health, but will aim to sketch how structural and unavoidable the public vs. private ambiguity is on social media.

This is the rationale to consciously reclaim space for the private aspects of our lives, as well as have practical wisdom to guide communication on social media. This task requires a certain detachment from the attitudes of 'hype and disappointment' that new technologies often provoke. It can be helpful therefore to digress briefly into how another technology also once transformed our daily lives, our communities, and even our sense of self: the automobile.

## 1. Technology and the Flux of Public Opinion

In one of the opening scenes from *The Wind in the Willows*, a children's novel from 1908, an encounter with a 'motor-car' is described in almost transcendent terms:

> … the magnificent motor-car, immense, breath-snatching, passionate, with its pilot tense and hugging his wheel, possessed all earth and air for the fraction of a second, flung an enveloping cloud of dust that blinded and enwrapped them utterly, and then dwindled to a speck in the far distance… (Grahame, 2010, p. 22)

This encounter has an immediate polarizing effect. It provokes a complete transformation in Toad, one of the central characters (an anthropomorphized upper-class English gentleman), who becomes entirely obsessed with motor-cars. By contrast, Rat is scandalized by the occurrence.[1]

Toad's adulation of cars was not merely a comic invention, but a parody of a general attitude in the early 20th century. Historians report how the car initially was imbued with all sorts of symbolic value: individual freedom, or the promise to make cities cleaner and quieter (Flink, 1972). The rival technologies of the railways and horses were associated with corruption and harmful monopolies, or with major burdens on quality of life. Horse-drawn carriages made a lot of noise (from the iron wheels and iron horse shoes hitting cobble stones), parking them required a lot of space, and removing horse excreta from the streets was a daily chore and expensive. Dried remains of such excreta turned into what was called 'street dust', which caused various respiratory diseases. Such was the draw of removing horses from public streets that one of the leading automobile periodicals of the era was termed *The Horseless Age* (Flink, 1972,

---

[1] "'You villains!' he shouted, shaking both fists, "You scoundrels, you highwaymen, you – you – road-hogs! – I'll have the law on you! I'll report you! I'll take you through all the Courts!'" (Grahame, 2010, p. 23).

p. 453). Due to this perceived potential, there was collective enthusiasm about cars: 'press coverage was overwhelmingly favourable; laws regulating the motorcar were overly lenient' (Flink, 1972, p. 454).

However, not all were like Toad – a sizable minority sided with Rat. There were those who blamed the technology for a range of social ills: 'increased sexual promiscuity, a decline in church attendance and the breakdown of the family and neighborhood solidarity' (Flink, 1972, p. 460). It seems that few could be genuinely indifferent towards the automobile, as is the case with social media today.

By the late 1950s public consciousness of the automobile had reached what could be called a 'mature' stage. Public spaces were no longer maximally sacrificed to cars. Issues regarding safety and pollution were also no longer disregarded. Thus, in the U.S. context for instance, laws on both air pollution and vehicle safety were passed in 1965 and 1966 respectively (Flink, 1972, pp. 469–470).

Today, cars remain status symbols for many and an obsession for a minority. However, collectively we are more acutely aware of the downsides of cars compared to a century ago. They are loud and a danger to vulnerable pedestrians. They pollute and take up large tracts of public space. The gentrification of inner cities starting in the 1960s and accelerating in the decades afterwards (cf. Lees, Slater, and Wyly, 2013) reflects how many prefer not having long daily commutes by car. The high real estate prices in leafy, quiet neighbourhoods reflect the undesirability of busy roads. In cities, pedestrianized zones have been promoted as a way to reclaim public space from cars (Gallo and Marinelli, 2020).

## 2. Between hype and disappointment

Like the automobile before it, social media seems to be going through a 'hype-disappointment cycle' (Borup et al., 2006). Today disappointment seems to dominate. However, not too long ago social media was hyped: it was supposed to transform democracies, turning citizens from passive consumers into active participants, and allowing the oppressed to connect and organize (Loader and Mercea, 2011). The Arab Spring and Euromaidan Revolution were seen as early confirmations of this view. And not just politics, but also science was supposedly going to be revolutionized by social media's facilitation of free-flowing information (Bartling and Friesike, 2014).

One overinflated expectation is the promise of how social media was going to transform our *social life*. Consider one of Facebook's earliest mission statements (from 2008):

# Reclaiming Care and Privacy in the Age of Social Media

Facebook helps you connect and share with the people in your life. (Reagan, 2009)

The use of the definite article – '*the* people in your life' – gives the mission statement an unmistakeably intimate ring. You are not connecting and sharing with 'people' in the generic, but with your family and friends, whom you need and who need you. Social media was going to be a tool for maintaining intimate friendships and caring communities, even while at a physical distance.

This taps into a deep-seated human desire for community. It may have been what led to the vast adoption of social media, going from 5% of adults in 2005 to 72% in 2020 in its initial U.S. market (Pew, 2021). However, it clearly has also led to deep disappointment.

First of all, since social media thrives on the desire for social approval, many users tend to communicate 'idealized selves' (Harris and Bardey, 2019) – also termed an *avatar* (e.g. Brunskill, 2013) or a *curated self* (Hogan, 2010). We seem to distort basic features of our personality on social media. For instance, introverts often attempt to appear to be (much) more extraverted online than they are in offline life (Harris and Bardey, 2019, p. 11). This strongly contrasts with the way social media is promoted by corporations as a vehicle for empowerment and self-expression.

Dating platforms are where idealized self-presentation is at its most intense (though unsurprisingly so). Users not only touch up their profile photograph, but also mispresent height, weight, or age (Toma and Hancock, 2010; Ellison, Heino, and Gibbs, 2006). The vast increase in partner choice, far from representing an increase in freedom or autonomy, seems to promote the 'fear of missing out' in users. It can even trigger a 'rejection mind-set', where even good potential partners are rejected in the hope of finding someone 'better' (Pronk and Denissen, 2020). Instead of promoting free choice, dating platforms stimulate us to *rank* potential partners more than we otherwise would. This commodification of romantic partners seems to be a draining process, and researchers speak of 'Tinder fatigue' or 'dating burnout' (see Pronk and Denissen, 2020).

Rankings did not originate with social media. Status hierarchies exist across many animal species (L. Ellis, 1995). However, social media does seem to have added a new twist, where we identify with the success of *online* personas. For instance, our social media following is rapidly becoming part of who we are in society (Harris and Bardey, 2019, p. 9). The result is that we, in the words of the psychiatrist David Brunskill, identify with a 'socially-derived and socially-driven composite online image' (Brunskill, 2013), to the detriment of genuine self-awareness.

A specific mechanism by which social media can lead to harm is that it promotes *competitive* communication. We compete in order to capture attention, likes, and affirmation; the winners are rewarded with status. This leads to social media users engaging in what researchers call 'upward social comparison', where users compare themselves to people they perceive as 'superior' (Wheeler, 1966; Vries et al., 2018; Schmuck et al., 2019). This upward social comparison has clear negative impact on the subject's self-esteem and well-being (J.-L. Wang et al., 2017).

So should we just conclude that social media is harmful for our mental health? Such a blanket generalization seems to be difficult to make. Not everybody engages in upward social comparison. Some users report *more* positive feelings after viewing a positive post. This is a form of what is called 'emotional contagion': instead of feeling inferior due to other's successes, some feel genuinely happy (Vries et al., 2018).

Nonetheless, even if only a fraction of users develop serious mental health consequences from social media, this is still significant. Compare this to an epidemic of viral infections. A virus may only provoke very mild symptoms in the vast majority of a population, but even if it 'only' kills 1% of all infected, this can still lead to a dramatic population-level effect. Similarly, even if only a small minority is driven to depression and even suicide (Twenge et al., 2020), this is still sufficient to warrant a rethink in how we approach social media.

Ultimately, it is darkly ironic that a technology designed to 'connect and share with the people in your life' should have such pernicious effects on *anyone*. According to the interpersonal theory of suicide (Van Orden et al., 2010; Joiner, 2005), suicidal desire is caused by two beliefs. The first is that one no longer 'belongs' which is taken to refer to feelings of loneliness and the absence of reciprocally-caring relationships. The second is the belief that one is a 'burden' on others: the belief that one's self is a liability to others, and self-hatred. Hence, apparently, when some use a technology in an attempt to be 'more connected' and to 'share more', they experience the feeling that they do not 'belong' and that they are a 'burden' on others.

## 3. The role of ethics

The type of approach offered by ethics can be contrasted with the predominant response among policymakers or corporations: to draw up measures to *protect* users. Sometimes it is the government that is called upon to take action (e.g. Udorie, 2015). At other times it is the corporate owner of social media platform (e.g. Miller, 2018). For instance, one of the very first protective policies is the ability to set privacy controls (Keys, 2018). These increase the control of users *over whom* a social media post is shared with – whether a post is 'more' or 'less' public.

Privacy controls have been around on a platform such as Facebook since 2008, that is, before the observed uptick in mental health problems related to social media. One might therefore be sceptical about whether they go to the heart of the problem. Another far more controversial – but also more thought-provoking – proposal is to remove the feature of 'likes' from social media platforms. This, it is argued, minimizes upward social comparison and addictiveness (Miller, 2018). Or in the words of one executive: removing likes will 'remove the pressure of how many likes a post will receive, so you can focus on sharing the things you love' (Deguara, 2019).

Would users even *want* the likes on their posts to not be visible? Would removing likes resolve the problems associated with upward social comparison and competitive communication? Nobody currently knows for sure, but in the following sections I sketch some reasons to be sceptical: social media communication *is* public and *is* inevitably competitive; introducing privacy controls or even removing likes will not change this.

This is not an argument *against* the need to protect users, even from themselves. Just look at the history of the automobile: at some point, the government needed to step in and *mandate* the use of seat-belts – in the UK, an initial law was passed in 1981 (for drivers and front-seat drivers only: UK Parliament, 1981). Similarly, it sounds eminently sensible that social media applications should be redesigned so as to be less addictive (Miller, 2018). My argument is that policy measures should occur in tandem with a general change in user attitudes.

Such a change may happen without any conscious collective effort, through letting the hype-disappointment cycle play out. However, this may take years or even decades. In the meantime, an ethics of social media can help us navigate social media environments.

When I use the word 'ethics' here, I do not have in mind a system of rules and judgments which guide our moral approbation, but the more Aristotelian sense of the art of living: to act *appropriately*. This sense of ethics has only an indirect link with utilitarian principles such as avoiding causing harm to others, or with principles of duty such as respecting others. The classic example of an

Aristotelian virtue is courage. Attempting a summit of Mount Everest may be considered courageous for a professional alpinist, but would most likely be a form of recklessness for an armchair philosopher, resulting from a lack of self-knowledge and perhaps arrogance.

One particularly instructive dimension of this Aristotelian sense of ethics is the requirement to attach the 'right amount' of importance to social realities. Here Aristotle speaks not of status or popularity as we might do today, but of 'honour'. Aristotle deemed honour to be of more value than wealth or power, but even then, he claimed that the virtuous person 'does not care much even about honour' (*Nicomachean Ethics, 1124* a1).

Similarly, a virtuous engagement with social media could be thought of as not caring too much (or too little) about social media success, but subordinating it to other, more important goods. It is in this sense that 'indifference' should be understood. Just as the automobile lost its romance at some point in the 1950s, paving the way for subordinating the technology to safety and clean air, it would be desirable if most of us could, one day, achieve a similar 'virtuous boredom' with social media.

## 4. Relational trust on social media

To achieve a little more clarity on the nature of social media interactions, consider the following recognizable type of social media communication. Imagine some acquaintance posting about a holiday on an exotic island, replete with pictures of him or her laughing with friends, having a good time, and doing adventurous activities. Call this person, for the sake of convenience, 'Rich Acquaintance B'. The user who sees the post is 'Poor Person A'.

Do you 'trust' B? In one sense, you probably do trust B: you trust that they have told the truth. After all, your first assumption would probably not be that B has entirely fabricated the photos. However, in another, deeper sense, you don't trust B. Some philosophers distinguish a type of 'trust' where you trust a person if you believe that person has a benevolent attitude or 'good will' towards you (following Baier 1986). For instance, you may trust your mother in this fundamental sense. Even though you may doubt her competence in some domain or even her truthfulness in some situations (e.g., she may tell you a white lie), you would still agree that you trust her because you know she *cares* about you, in some general, unqualified sense. This lack of qualification is related to the 'unquestioning' aspect of some of the most basic forms of trust (Nguyen, forthcoming): the care is directed to a person as a whole, and is not dependent on either competence or the nature of the task at hand (contrast with Hawley, 2014). The expectation of care is closely related to what we sometimes call the 'unconditional trust' we place in our family members, or close friends.

For future reference, let us call this deeper sense of trust, 'relational trust'. My concern is what social media does to relational trust. Interestingly, and not coincidentally, Facebook's early mission statement can be read as an indirect promise of relational trust to its users, to 'connect and share with the people in your life'. However, does this promise make sense, given the nature of the social media environment?

Let us return to the example with this concept of relational trust: does the post of Rich Acquaintance B help promote the relational trust that Poor Person A may place in B? In other words, does the communication help bring across that B cares about A? The answer seems to be: not particularly. To see this, imagine the same communication in a private setting. Imagine that B met with A privately. Would B then still communicate with the same transparency about their exotic holiday? If B cared about the well-being of A, then, knowing that A could not afford the holiday, B would likely downplay the news. Instead of mentioning the spearfishing expedition, B might complain about the hotel instead, or emphasize how nice it was to be back home. The communication would have been shaped by the value of relational trust: B cares about A, and thus wants to preserve the relational trust that A has in B, even if B is only an acquaintance.

This illustrates how private communications are governed by norms that (at least currently) seem to be absent on social media. B may post about an exotic holiday without being considered particularly inconsiderate, self-centred, or mean-spirited. Is this because social media is public, rather than private communication?

## 5. Private versus public

To say that a communication is 'private' does not mean it is 'secret'. My conversations with a romantic partner may be private, but I may not put any particular effort into keeping them secret. Governments keep secrets: they expend considerable effort in preventing certain information from becoming public. By contrast, most of my private communications are hardly a secret. If someone would wish to know the mundane details of my daily life, my response would closer to indifferent bemusement rather than to one of betrayal or indignation.[2] What is private about such communications lies not in the content of the communication, but in the *manner* in which that content is communicated. I might be slightly embarrassed if my terms of endearment were to become public knowledge. If I knew other people were listening in, I would likely craft my message in a different way.

As another example of a distinctively private communication, consider telling a bad joke to a good friend. If you were to broadcast the same bad joke on national television, you might feel a mixture of shame and embarrassment – perhaps because the joke was in poor taste, or perhaps because it was just not very funny. Yet, in the context of a 1-to-1 conversation, the bad joke may have been entirely appropriate. You know that the good friend will appreciate the joke, and you know that only the good friend will hear it.

To generalize, a *private communication* can be understood as a message that is conveyed by one person with the intention that a *specific* person is the receiver. By contrast, a *public communication* is a non-private one: a message conveyed *without* any specific receiver in mind. Political communications, meant for all citizens of a country, are one of the most indiscriminate public communications. However, public communications can also target a *type* of receiver. For instance, scientific publications are written for an audience of scientific peers. They are not crafted with the general public mind, but at the same time neither are they private communications. Once there is any degree of uncertainty (in one's intention) as to who precisely will receive a communication, then the communication can be said to be public.

Private and public communications are (often unconsciously) structured by different social norms. Private communications typically take place in trusting relationships, and aim to enhance relational trust rather than merely to convey information about a state of affairs. The bad joke is not told for its information content, but is told knowing that the good friend will appreciate that bad joke, and hence that the bad joke can give pleasure. Similarly, by saying 'rainy day, isn't it?' to your neighbour, your intention is not to convey information about the meteorological state of affairs, but to create a (weak) bond by acknowledging a common challenge or common experience. The absurdity of a government issuing a

---

[2]    Note that it is precisely this attitude which underlies the 'nothing to hide argument' in support of surveillance programmes (cf. e.g Cofone, 2020). We may not deem our private information worthy of being kept secret, but third parties can nonetheless find ways to abuse it.

communiqué 'rainy day, isn't it?' – let alone a social media user posting the same message as a status update – underlines just how different the norms governing private communications are from those governing public communications.

Communication, in general, is not always simply about the transmission of information content about causal states of affairs, like why snow is white. Communication can serve to transmit information about the sender's view of his or her relationship with the receiver, including what value or status is ascribed to the receiver. This is partially why we make small talk, or communicate tautological propositions or make observations that are clear for everybody: to convey that we *care* about the other person because we deem them worthy of being spoken to.

Given this analysis, it is quite clear that online communication on social media (Facebook, Twitter, Instagram, and so on) has a *public* character. However, this public character is often not obvious, and not only because of the mission statements of social corporations couched in terms such as 'caring' and 'sharing'. The public character of social media communication is often hidden because a lot of the content is private. If I post something about my dog, then that is 'private content' in the sense that it is not particularly of 'public interest'. Before the advent of social media, gatekeepers such as journalists or editors would have screened away content about my dog (unless it bit me). With social media, we can broadcast information that does not make any obvious contribution to a common good, such as the state of scientific knowledge or the advancement of a political debate. As an academic, I can post my latest articles to Twitter, but I can also share what I happened to see on my afternoon run.

Not all social media platforms stimulate the sharing of private content to the same degree. Facebook seems more geared to sharing private content than Twitter is. This seems to be reflected in how, for instance, politicians gravitate towards Twitter as a forum for their public communications (Silva and Proksch, 2021). One could also ask whether the confusion of private and public is inevitable. As used by some politicians, Twitter can come to resemble a kind of newsletter or bulletin-board, where the posted content is carefully curated in light of political goals. Where the confusion of private and public is more obvious is, for instance, in the communications by celebrities of the minutiae of their daily activities. If I see what Cristiano Ronaldo had for breakfast, or the loving attention he shows his children, I may be tempted to feel a misplaced connection with him as if he were a friend of mine. All this information draws me into the orbit of his life. However, he is not my friend, so how does the information really contribute to the good of *my* life? If service to a common good were a criterion for posting to Instagram, it would not be known beyond a closed circle of friends what some celebrity had for dinner or wore to a party. It is in this way that the private and public are confused on social media: private content is communicated publicly but in such a way that gives users the impression that the communication is private, feeding into the misplaced expectation that they can find friendship-like trust and intimacy on social media.

Are we entirely unaware of the public character of social media? Probably not. It would seem strange to post 'rainy day, isn't it' to social media, or to share a terrible joke. The fact that we are disinclined to post about today's weather illustrates how, at some level, we at least sometimes make the distinction between public and private communication. However, we often confuse the distinction, both when we post ourselves and when we read others' posts. We share private content without tailoring it to a particular intended receiver.

The concept of 'context collapse' can be useful in clarifying just how public and private relate here (Frost-Arnold, 2021; boyd, 2011).[3] Context collapse refers to how a particular message can be appropriate for one social group (within certain shared background assumptions), but inappropriate for another. It is seen as a misuse or ill-advised use of social media that is to be avoided. And the public vs. private distinction involves at least two contexts. A private communication is highly contextual insofar as its content is tailored to a *known* receiver, and governed by norms of relational trust. When this content is broadcast publicly, there is a kind of context collapse.

However, the context collapse is of a special kind. On the one hand, users usually are spontaneously led by different norms than in private communications. Hence, if private content is broadcast publicly, it is *re*contextualized to the extent that it is rephrased to adopt the contours of a public communication. On the other hand, the recontextualization is not complete, insofar as the content of the communication stubbornly evokes expectations more appropriate to private contexts (for instance, by being irrelevant for the common interest). Thus, the sender may have the misguided expectation that the receivers were motivated by relational trust. Or, the receiver may likewise have the misguided expectation that the sender was motivated by

---

[3]    My thanks to the editors and an anonymous reviewer for enquiring about this connection.

relational trust, and when this expectation is disappointed, reactions of anger or diminished self-worth can ensue.

Hence, if one were to rephrase the argument in terms of context collapse, social media communication involves a *partial* decontextualization and a *partial* recontextualization of private communication. Another distinctive feature of this kind of context collapse is that it is not an unfortunate misuse of social media, but rather a fundamental property of social media communication. In this respect, the ambiguous context collapse involved with the blurring of private and public is not like the context collapse present in the inadvertent quote or the ill-advised attempt at humour. Without the ambiguity between private and public contexts, social media loses its distinctive character and becomes like an electronic bulletin board, only containing announcements of public interest. The challenge for the user is to engage with ambiguous context collapse in a virtuous way (see later).

## 6. The dangers of suppressing the private

As a result, aspects of one's private life become grist to the mill of *status competition*. Status is the rank that persons ascribe to each other, such that persons can be, at least to a certain extent, slotted into 'status hierarchies'. Wealth, fame, or ability are some of the most central indicators. In the online environment status is, more or less, indicated by number of followers or likes.

It is entirely unsurprising that we use social media as a tool for status competition. The human concern for social status is sometimes listed as one of the possible 'human universals': we seem to care about status regardless of our gender, culture, age, or personality (Anderson, Hildreth, and Howland, 2015). Put a group of strangers into a room together, give them a task, and within minutes they will sort themselves into some kind of status hierarchy. Our caring about status is also not capricious. Status has very real impacts on our lives, and is ultimately correlated with health outcomes and even mortality rates (Wilkinson, 2001; Marmot, 2005).

Here it is crucial to distinguish between benevolent and perverse forms of status competition. Anthropologists sometimes distinguish between 'prestige' and 'dominance' (Henrich and Gil-White, 2001). The former comes from competence, ability, or a valuable service that benefits the community as a whole. The latter refers to the threat of violence: physical violence, but also alliance-formation, bullying, intimidation, or manipulation.[4] Most human societies try to keep perverse forms of status-seeking at bay (Price and Van Vugt, 2014; Desmond, 2020b; 2021).

What type of status competition does social media seem to promote? Status in the social media environment, measured by likes or follower counts, seems to interact with status in the broader society in several ways. On the one hand, offline status is often converted to online status. Humans upvote appearances of competence and service. They also upvote appearances of power: a U.S. president will typically command a large following by virtue of their position of power. In other words, both prestige and dominance can be converted into likes and followers. However, online status follows its own dynamic, and can be in turn be converted into prestige and dominance. A large following (think of social media influencers) can translate into wealth and influence.

However, status competition on social media seems closest to the dynamic of a popularity contest, which has been been mainly studied in groups of children. Popular children impact what types of behaviour become social norms in classrooms, and they are typically in demand as a friend (W. E. Ellis and Zarbatany, 2007). However, bullying also apparently increases a child's popularity (Redhead, Cheng, and O'Gorman, 2018, p. 3). Popularity is thus an ambiguous status measure – with similarities to both prestige and dominance.

Is social media enticing adults to enter popularity competitions – or other forms of perverse status competition? While more could be said about this than space permits, this competitive aspect of social media can help make sense of just how social media's confusion between private and public ultimately has corrosive effects on mental health. Private content has its 'natural place' in intimate contexts – friendships, romantic relationships – that are far away from the public eye, but with social media it is made public and submitted to competitive dynamics.

---

[4]   This dichotomy, while sufficient for purposes here, is oversimplified. Often prestige and dominance are intertwined in the offline world. For instance, those higher up on the corporate ladder may be more competent and thus may have high 'prestige'; however, their position may also give them the power to hire and fire, promote and demote others. For a discussion, see (Henrich and Gil-White, 2001; Chapais, 2015).

## 7. Social Media Virtues

In the past decade, we have gone from adulation to demonization of social media, but collectively we have not yet done much conscious searching for a golden mean. Perhaps the hype-disappointment cycle will play out of its own accord. However, there is also reason to believe social media to be more insidious than previous technologies. Social media attaches to our desire for community and thus plays with our sense of identity. It takes events and emotions from the intimate sphere and feeds them into the arena of public status competition, often without us realizing.

Some of this balance may simply involve not spending too much time on social media. In an experiment where groups of students disactivated Facebook for four weeks, not only did disconnecting increase well-being remarkably, but it also affected the users' priorities, as is well illustrated by one student's comment:

> I was way less stressed. I wasn't attached to my phone as much as I was before. And I found *I didn't really care so much about things that were happening [online] because I was more focused on my own life* ... I felt more content. I think I was in a better mood generally. I thought I would miss seeing everyone's day- to-day activities ... I really didn't miss it at all. (Allcott et al., 2020, p. 655, my emphasis)

What this participant is suggesting is that what was so beneficial was not the *limiting* of time on social media, but rather the *proper prioritization* of values or activities in his life. In particular, taking time away from social media allowed it to be *subordinated* to other activities that were clearly experienced as more central to the students' own lives and better for their well-being.

However, the public and competitive nature of social media communication is inevitable, regardless of how many privacy controls are instated, or whether likes are suppressed. The challenge therefore lies in finding ways to engage with this public, competitive character of social media in a virtuous way. Part of the response here surely lies in reforming the social media environment, in order to safeguard privacy and redirect competition. Thus, social media corporations have established forms of social status that are not brute popularity (e.g., 'blue checks' in Twitter), and proposals to introduce less anger-promoting interfaces (e.g., Tanesini, 2022) can help as well. Both help redirect the popularity competition towards more desirable values.

However, virtuous action presupposes user discretion in choosing the response, and thus a freedom to act inappropriately – precisely something that a policy response seeks to avoid. So how should we choose appropriately? Here the type of care shown by professionals is a useful model for ethical interactions on social media. A good physician, architect, engineer, or psychologist will care about their patient or client – but not in the exact same way a parent cares about their child. There is no prior intimate dyadic relationship that grounds the care. Professional care thus does not involve relational trust and cannot be called 'personal' in the way, for instance, filial care can. Instead, professional care reflects how the professional believes some standard of competent service to be valuable for the community (for more on professionalism, see Desmond, 2020a). Professional care shows how care can be relatively impersonal (indeed, a professional and their client may largely remain strangers to each other) and not necessarily involve the feelings of love that are often associated with care.[5]

Professional ethics is a useful analogy for thinking about social media because it points to a type of *care* that is appropriate outside of a merely private context. Interacting 'with care' on social media, at first approximation, means communicating something valuable for others, despite being uncertain about who the receiver will be and what their needs are. Especially given the dangers of misguided expectations of relational trust, both senders and receivers of messages on social media could evaluate their own and others' communications according to the standard of what is valuable for others. A sender may ask, does this message contribute to others' lives? A receiver may ask, does this message contribute to my life? If the answer is no, the message may be merely grist to the mill of online popularity competition, and therefore should be disregarded.

However, the analogy with professional care breaks down in considering social media's unique integration of private content within public communication. For instance, a psychiatrist may share their

---

[5]   For instance, Vallor defines 'technomoral care' as 'a skillful, attentive, responsible, and emotionally responsive disposition to personally meet the needs of those with whom we share our technosocial environment' (Vallor, 2016, pp. 138-39). This definition of technomoral care is appropriate for the examples of technologically-aided nursing she seems to have in mind. However, the concept of care is too personal to be applicable for social media interactions. Social media interactions are emotionally thin interactions (limited to a short text supplemented perhaps with emoticons), are not necessarily skillful, nor are they typically directed to the needs of specific persons.

opinions about the latest DSM on social media in a way they would never do during consultation. Indeed, to opine in this way to a patient could be a breach of professional ethics; yet, the very same content could constitute a virtuous use of social media. It can be of genuine interest to others to hear about these opinions. So, unless social media is to be reduced to an electronic bulletin board consisting of formal communication only, it should be possible for individuals to share their private thoughts, emotions, or actions in a way that is of genuine interest and value to others. In sum, sharing private content on social media can be a genuine form of care.

How precisely can we know if we are behaving in a proper 'caring' way? That is a different question.[6] My point here is to bring attention to care as a basic way of orienting one's online agency towards what is *valuable to others*. This is not a form of self-sacrificing altruism, but rather a prerequisite for online *flourishing*. If one's primary concern is for others, one is liberated from the need to receive instantaneous affirmation from others. Care for others helps avoid the dangers of increased anxiety or commodification of one's own identity.

At the level of policy, virtue ethics emphasises the primary importance of *education*. This is education for virtuous living – *paideia* (Aristotle, *Politics*, book VIII) – rather than education that merely aims at marketable skills or at intellectual knowledge for its own sake. What would this education look like? Based on the considerations of this essay, it would seek to raise awareness (especially among adolescents) about the public nature of social media, how social media communications are often competitive, and how this can impact a person's self-esteem. It would reveal what we know about our evolved psychology, and its sensitivity to status. It would warn of popularity competitions, and explain the importance of more benevolent types of status. It would emphasise that, as public communication, social media is best used not for seeking relational trust and signals that others care, but rather for broadcasting messages of value to one's wider social network.

By contrast, if one wishes to receive consolation or affirmation, then one should seek out friends or family. In this way, habits of care with regard to social media interaction seem also to depend on realizing what social media *cannot* give us: the joys we experience

---

[6] For instance, sharing private information can become an expression of narcissism rather than of care. How can we know that we are sharing virtuously, and not viciously? If the virtue ethics of social media is like other forms of virtue ethics, there is no general answer to this question. How to act with care can only be judged in particular situations, through *phronesis*.

with private, intimate, offline communication. If the collective realization of the joy of walking without having to worry about large, heavy metallic objects moving at high speeds gave rise to the growth of pedestrianized zones, similarly the joy of privacy and intimacy may give rise to social media-free zones in life. By helping users to adopt a wider perspective both on the nature of social media and even their own 'nature', social media education may help instil healthy habits, and thus a durable and effective response to some of the mental health challenges facing social media users today.

*Institute for the History and Philosophy of Science and Technology,*
*CNRS/Paris-I Sorbonne*
*hugh.desmond@gmail.com*

## References

Hunt Allcott, Luca Braghieri, Sarah Eichmeyer, and Matthew Gentzkow, 'The Welfare Effects of Social Media', *American Economic Review* 110 (2020) 629–76.

Cameron Anderson, John Angus D. Hildreth, and Laura Howland, 'Is the Desire for Status a Fundamental Human Motive? A Review of the Empirical Literature.' *Psychological Bulletin* 141 (2015) 574–601.

Brooke Auxier, '64% of Americans Say Social Media Have a Mostly Negative Effect on the Way Things Are Going in the U.S. Today'. *Pew Research Center* (blog). (2020). https://www.pewresearch. org/fact-tank/2020/10/15/64-of-americans-say-social-media-have-a-mostly-negative-effect-on-the-way-things-are-going-in-the-u-s-today/.

Annette Baier, 'Trust and Antitrust', *Ethics* 96 (1986) 231–60.

Sönke Bartling and Sascha Friesike, 'Towards Another Scientific Revolution'. In *Opening Science,* edited by Sönke Bartling and Sascha Friesike, (Cham: Springer International Publishing, 2014) 3–15.

*BBC News,* 'Covid Misinformation on Facebook Is Killing People - Biden', 17 July 2021, sec. US & Canada. https://www.bbc.com/ news/world-us-canada-57870778.

Mads Borup, Nik Brown, Kornelia Konrad, and Harro Van Lente, 'The Sociology of Expectations in Science and Technology'. *Technology Analysis & Strategic Management* 18 (2006) 285–98. https://doi.org/10.1080/09537320600777002.

danah boyd, 'Social Network Sites as Networked Publics: Affordances, Dynamics, and Implications'. In *Networked Self: Identity, Community, and Culture on Social Network Sites*, edited by Zizi Papacharissi, (New York: Routledge, 2011) 39–59.

William J. Brady, Killian McLoughlin, Tuan N. Doan, and Molly J. Crockett, 'How Social Learning Amplifies Moral Outrage Expression in Online Social Networks', *Science Advances* 7 (2021) eabe5641.

David Brunskill, 'Social Media, Social Avatars and the Psyche: Is Facebook Good for Us?', *Australasian Psychiatry*, 21 (2013) 527–532.

Bernard Chapais, 'Competence and the Evolutionary Origins of Status and Power in Humans', *Human Nature* 26 (2015) 161–83.

Ignacio N. Cofone, 'Nothing to Hide, but Something to Lose', *University of Toronto Law Journal* 70 (2020) 64–90.

Brittney Deguara, 'Instagram Removes the like Count for Your Own Good', *Stuff*, (2019).

Hugh Desmond, 'Professionalism in Science: Competence, Autonomy, and Service', *Science and Engineering Ethics* 26 (2020a) 1287–1313. https://doi.org/10.1007/s11948-019-00143-x.

Hugh Desmond. 'Service and Status Competition May Help Explain Perceived Ethical Acceptability', *AJOB Neuroscience* 11 (2020b) 258–60. https://doi.org/10.1080/21507740.2020.1830874.

Hugh Desmond. 'Precision Medicine, Data, and the Anthropology of Social Status', *The American Journal of Bioethics* 21 (2021) 80–83. https://doi.org/10.1080/15265161.2021.1891345.

Robin Ian MacDonald Dunbar, 'Neocortex Size as a Constraint on Group Size in Primates'. *Journal of Human Evolution* 22 (1992) 469–93. https://doi.org/10.1016/0047-2484(92)90081-J.

Lee Ellis, 'Dominance and Reproductive Success among Nonhuman Animals: A Cross-Species Comparison', *Ethology and Sociobiology* 16 (1995): 257–333.

Wendy E. Ellis and Lynne Zarbatany, 'Peer Group Status as a Moderator of Group Influence on Children; Deviant, Aggressive, and Prosocial Behavior', *Child Development* 78 (2007), 1240–54.

Nicole Ellison, Rebecca Heino, and Jennifer Gibbs, 'Managing Impressions Online: Self-Presentation Processes in the Online Dating Environment', *Journal of Computer-Mediated Communication* 11 (2006), 415–41.

James J. Flink, 'Three Stages of American Automobile Consciousness', *American Quarterly* 24 (1972), 451.

Karen Frost-Arnold, 'The Epistemic Dangers of Context Collapse Online' In *Applied Epistemology*, by Karen Frost-Arnold, (Oxford University Press, 2021) 437–56.

Mariano Gallo and Mario Marinelli, 'Sustainable Mobility: A Review of Possible Actions and Policies', *Sustainability* 12 (2020), 7499.

Kenneth Grahame, *The Wind in the Willows*, (Oxford: Oxford University Press, 2010).

Elspbeth Harris and Aurore C. Bardey, 'Do Instagram Profiles Accurately Portray Personality? An Investigation Into Idealized Online Self-Presentation', *Frontiers in Psychology* 10 (2019), 871.

Joseph Henrich and Francisco J Gil-White, 'The Evolution of Prestige: Freely Conferred Deference as a Mechanism for Enhancing the Benefits of Cultural Transmission', *Evolution and Human Behavior* 22 (2001), 165–96.

Bernie Hogan, 'The Presentation of Self in the Age of Social Media: Distinguishing Performances and Exhibitions Online' *Bulletin of Science, Technology & Society* 30 (2010) 377–86.

Thomas Joiner, *Why People Die By Suicide*, (Cambridge, MA: Harvard University Press, 2005).

Matthew Keys, 'A Brief History of Facebook's Ever-Changing Privacy Settings'. *Medium*, 4 May 2018. https://medium.com/@matthewkeys/a-brief-history-of-facebooks-ever-changing-privacy-settings-8167dadd3bd0.

Loretta Lees, Tom Slater, and Elvin Wyly, *Gentrification*, (Routledge, 2013).

Brian D. Loader and Dan Mercea, 'Networking Democracy?' *Information, Communication & Society* 14 (2011), 757–69.

Jessica G. Y. Luc, Michael A. Archer, Rakesh C. Arora, Edward M. Bender, Arie Blitz, David T. Cooke, Tamara Ni Hlci, et al., 'Does Tweeting Improve Citations? One-Year Results from the TSSMN Prospective Randomized Trial', *The Annals of Thoracic Surgery* (2020).

Michael Marmot, *Status Syndrome: How Your Social Standing Directly Affects Your Health*, (London: A&C Black, 2005).

Faye Miller, 'Ethical Design Is the Answer to Some of Social Media's Problems'. *The Conversation*, (2018). http://theconversation.com/ethical-design-is-the-answer-to-some-of-social-medias-problems-89531.

C. Thi. Nguyen, C. Thi, 'Trust as an Unquestioning Attitude'. *Oxford Studies in Epistemology* (forthcoming).

Pew, 'Demographics of Social Media Users and Adoption in the United States', (2021). https://www.pewresearch.org/internet/fact-sheet/social-media/.

Michael E. Price and Mark Van Vugt, 'The Evolution of Leader–Follower Reciprocity: The Theory of Service-for-Prestige', *Frontiers in Human Neuroscience* 8 (2014).

Tila M. Pronk and Jaap J. A. Denissen, 'A Rejection Mind-Set: Choice Overload in Online Dating', *Social Psychological and Personality Science* 11 (2020), 388–96.

Gillian Reagan, 'The Evolution of Facebook's Mission Statement', *Observer* (blog), (13 July 2009). https://observer.com/2009/07/the-evolution-of-facebooks-mission-statement/.

Daniel Redhead, Daniel, Joey Cheng, and Rick O'Gorman, 'Status Competition and Peer Relationships in Childhood'. In *Encyclopedia of Evolutionary Psychological Science*, edited by Todd K. Shackelford and Viviana A. Weekes-Shackelford (Cham: Springer International Publishing, 2018) 1–9.

Desirée Schmuck, Kathrin Karsay, Jörg Matthes, and Anja Stevic, 'Looking Up and Feeling Down: The Influence of Mobile Social Networking Site Use on Upward Social Comparison, Self-Esteem, and Well-Being of Adult Smartphone Users', *Telematics and Informatics* 42 (2019), 101240.

Bruno Castanho Silva and Sven-Oliver Proksch, 'Politicians Unleashed? Political Communication on Twitter and in Parliament in Western Europe', *Political Science Research and Methods* (2021) 1–17.

Alessandra Tanesini, 'Social media as affective technologies: anger and polarisation', *Royal Institute Philosophy Supplementary Volume*, 92 (2022) 87–109.

Catalina L. Toma and Jeffrey T. Hancock, 'Looks and Lies: The Role of Physical Attractiveness in Online Dating Self-Presentation and Deception', *Communication Research* 37 (2010) 335–51. https://doi.org/10.1177/0093650209356437.

Jean M. Twenge, Jonathan Haidt, Thomas E. Joiner, and W. Keith Campbell, 'Underestimating Digital Media Harm', *Nature Human Behaviour* 4 (2020) 346–48.

Jean M. Twenge, Thomas E. Joiner, Megan L. Rogers, and Gabrielle N. Martin, 'Increases in Depressive Symptoms, Suicide-Related Outcomes, and Suicide Rates Among U.S. Adolescents After 2010 and Links to Increased New Media Screen Time', *Clinical Psychological Science* 6 (2018) 3–17.

June Eric Udorie, 'Social Media Is Harming the Mental Health of Teenagers. The State Has to Act.' *The Guardian*, (16 September

2015). https://www.theguardian.com/commentisfree/2015/sep/16/social-media-mental-health-teenagers-government-pshe-lessons.

UK Parliament, 'Transport Act 1981'. Text. Statute Law Database. (1981). https://www.legislation.gov.uk/ukpga/1981/56.

Shannon Vallor, *Technology and the Virtues* (Oxford University Press, 2016).

Kimberly A. Van Orden, Tracy K. Witte, Kelly C. Cukrowicz, Scott Braithwaite, Edward A. Selby, and Thomas E. Joiner, 'The Interpersonal Theory of Suicide'. *Psychological Review* 117 (2010), 575–600.

Dian A. de Vries, Marthe Möller, Marieke S. Wieringa, Anniek W. Eigenraam, and Kirsten Hamelink, 'Social Comparison as the Thief of Joy: Emotional Consequences of Viewing Strangers' Instagram Posts', *Media Psychology* 21 (2018) 222–45.

Jin-Liang Wang, Hai-Zhen Wang, James Gaskin, and Skyler Hawk, 'The Mediating Roles of Upward Social Comparison and Self-Esteem and the Moderating Role of Social Comparison Orientation in the Association between Social Networking Site Usage and Subjective Well-Being', *Frontiers in Psychology* 8 (2017).

Ladd Wheeler, 'Motivation as a Determinant of Upward Comparison', *Journal of Experimental Social Psychology* 1 (1966), 27–31.

Richard G. Wilkinson, *Mind the Gap: Hierarchies, Health and Human Evolution* (Yale University Press, 2001).

# Deepfakes, Intellectual Cynics, and the Cultivation of Digital Sensibility

TAYLOR MATTHEWS

**Abstract**

In recent years, a number of philosophers have turned their attention to developments in Artificial Intelligence, and in particular to deepfakes. A deepfake is a portmanteau of 'deep learning' and 'fake', and for the most part they are videos which depict people doing and saying things they never did. As a result, much of the emerging literature on deepfakes has turned on questions of trust, harms, and information-sharing. In this paper, I add to the emerging concerns around deepfakes by drawing on resources from vice epistemology. As deepfakes become more sophisticated, I claim, they will develop to be a source of online epistemic corruption. More specifically, they will encourage consumers of digital online media to cultivate and manifest various epistemic vices. My immediate focus in this paper is on their propensity to encourage the development of what I call 'intellectual cynicism'. After sketching a rough account of this epistemic vice, I go on to suggest that we can partially offset such cynicism – and fears around deceptive online media more generally – by encouraging the development what I term a trained 'digital sensibility'. This, I contend, involves a calibrated sensitivity to the epistemic merits (and demerits) of online content.

On the 25<sup>th</sup> December 2020, the British television company, Channel 4, broadcasted an 'alternative Christmas Address', in which Queen Elizabeth II spoke of the challenges of the outgoing year (2020). Given the trajectory of 2020, it was unsurprising to hear her urge caution about the Covid-19 pandemic. Perhaps more surprising, though, was the Queen's admission that she wished to participate in the hit BBC television programme *Strictly Come Dancing*. Indeed, anyone who has listened to the Queen speak, let alone watched a Christmas Address on television, would have realised that this admission was out of character. In fact, the Queen's admission was not just out of character – it was entirely fake. Channel 4's 'alternative Christmas Address' took the form of a so-called *deepfake*.[1]

A deepfake is a video that depicts events, people, or states of affairs that never happened. Occasionally, the term is used to refer to any video that has been manipulated to create a false pretense, but what

---

[1]    To watch this video, go to https://www.youtube.com/watch?v=IvY-Abd2FfM.

doi:10.1017/S1358246122000224    © The Royal Institute of Philosophy and the contributors 2022
*Royal Institute of Philosophy Supplement* **92** 2022

people are usually gesturing at is a so-called *shallowfake*. These are videos that are slowed down, sped up, or whose audio is tampered with, all to depict people doing or saying things they never did. This occurred, for example, when the Speaker of US House of Representatives, Nancy Pelosi, was caught 'slurring' her words (Reuters, 2020). In reality, somebody had slowed down her speech on a recording, but it nonetheless convinced many that she was drunk. *Deepfakes*, by contrast, are far more sophisticated than this. The name itself hints at just how. Deepfake is a portmanteau of '*deep* learning' and '*fake*': the 'deep learning' aspect corresponds to a specific kind of 'artificial intelligence' (AI), and the fake element speaks for itself.

Despite their relative infancy, an increasing number of philosophers have begun expressing concerns about deepfakes. For example, Don Fallis (2020) claims that deepfakes will potentially reduce the amount of information videos impart to their viewers, Regina Rini (2020) worries that deepfakes will 'erode the credentials of all videos', leading us to increasingly distrust what we watch from videos, while the writer and political advisor Nina Schick (2020, p. 9) warns that deepfakes could usher in an 'information apocalypse' – where our digital environments are characterised by mis- and disinformation. These concerns are cleverly woven into Channel 4's deepfake. In the tradition of setting out a clear message to the Commonwealth, the Queen cautions about a world increasingly characterised by 'fake news', echo chambers, and disinformation, only for her actions and facial movements to manifest the very thing she warns against. In a rapidly changing world, whom we decide to trust and what sources of information we deem credible has never mattered more – and, as I will argue, the advent of deepfakes has made these tasks even more difficult.

My aims in this paper are twofold: to shed light on a currently unexplored problem with deepfakes, and then to offer a novel way of offsetting this problem. As the title of this paper suggests, the nature of this problem concerns the relationship between deepfakes and what I call *intellectual cynicism*, while the corresponding remedy lies in cultivating what I call a trained *digital sensibility*. The paper thus proceeds as follows. Section 2 sets out the technology behind deepfakes and demonstrates how these videos mark a watershed moment in media manipulation. Section 3 draws on resources in contemporary virtue and vice epistemology to illuminate how our social and digital environments can put us in a position to develop epistemic vices. Section 4 argues that deepfakes do just this; specifically, they encourage us to be intellectually cynical, to habitually distrust and disengage from viewing videos as a source of epistemic goods. In section 5, I develop the concept of a trained digital sensibility, a virtuously calibrated sensitivity to the merits (and demerits) of online content, that aims to ward off the vice of intellectual cynicism. Finally, section 6 concludes by briefly considering the relationship between a trained digital sensibility and the role of ethical and intellectual virtues in navigating an increasingly technological future.

## 1. Deepfakes and Deep-learning

Image manipulation has a rich history, pre-dating the advent of the internet and digital media. Under Stalinist rule, for example, political opponents and adversaries were not just executed but routinely removed from official photographs, deleting any trace of their existence from the public eye. The classic example is that of Nikola Yezhov – at one point, Stalin's right-hand-man and secret police official – who was notoriously removed from a photograph of Stalin and himself walking along the Moscow canal after he was assassinated. More recently, the advent of computing technology has ushered in programmes like Adobe Photoshop and CGI, which allows users to creatively edit images and video footage, inserting people and objects into places they never originally were. This has led to the creation of slightly more sophisticated versions of shallow-fakes called *cheap-fakes*, which rely on 'cheap, accessible software' to manipulate media (Paris and Donovan, 2019, p. 2). Given the extensive use (and misuse) of Photoshop and CGI, one might question whether deepfakes do pose a distinctive threat. That is, haven't people been able to subvert the truth with deepfakes and cheap-fakes alike (Paris and Donovan, 2019: 6)? Keith Raymond Harris (2021) has recently questioned whether the pessimism surrounding deepfakes is 'overblown'. To an extent, Harris is right. Currently, many deepfakes are blurry, costly to produce, and easily identifiable. However, this should not fool us into thinking that this will continue to be the norm. As I mentioned in the introduction, part of the name 'deepfake' derives from *deep learning*, and it is this technology that arguably sets deepfakes apart from their predecessors.

At its most basic, deep learning works by computing a process and then attempting to carry it out. If the process fails, the technology revises it and tries again until it is successful. In this way, deep learning operates using a similar 'trial and error' method by which the human brain learns. It is for this reason that the deep learning techniques behind many of the emerging deepfakes today – including that of Queen Elizabeth II – are called deep *neural networks*. Roughly, these can be understood as algorithmic models that predicts and generate an output – in our case a video – based on an input of images or video content. As the cyber-security researchers Yisroel Mirsky and Wenke Lee (2020) explain, the neural networks often used to make deepfakes are so-called Generative Adversarial Networks (GANs). GANs consist of two algorithms – one called the 'generator' and the other called the 'discriminator' – which *compete* against each other to manufacture highly authentic videos. After being fed the same input of images or recordings, the generator creates new samples based on the input that are good enough to trick the discriminator, while the discriminator works to identify which samples are fake. Eventually, through trial and error, the GAN produces a highly sophisticated video that is capable of manipulating the speech inflections and facial movements of a target person doing and saying things they never did.

In this process, GANs are able to manipulate the attributes on a target's face – adding or removing features, lightening or darkening the skin colour, or swapping certain expressions on one person and superimposing them onto another. By doing this, deepfake purveyors can quite literally swap the identity of one person with another, and in some cases, even generate entirely new, non-existent faces from scratch (Tolosana et al., 2020).[2] This sort of deep learning manipulation is popular in the video game and film industries, but it has also been exploited to create faces to match fake online profiles on social media platforms from Facebook to Twitter. In the early days of GAN technology, the photographic and video content required to create a compelling deepfake was often in the hundreds or thousands, but recently Samsung has developed a technology that allows purveyors to do this with only a handful of photos of videos (Zakharov et al., 2019). As the authors of the study report, a reasonably sophisticated deepfake could be created using only a single image. Alongside this, researchers at Princeton University have collaborated with Adobe to develop 'VoCo' technology, which allows video creators to modify the audio of a recording by typing the desired words into a transcript. The authors of the research observed how the algorithm was able to quickly analyse voice samples from a target, then synthesise what that person's voice would sound like, were they to say the words typed into the transcript (Jin et al., 2017). As the lead author, Zeyu Jin, (2017) reports, when the synthesised words were inserted in the context of a spoken sentence, the modified sentence was 'often perceived as indistinguishable from other sentences spoken in the same voice'.

[2]  Visit thispersondoesnotexist.com to see this in action.

Together, the use of VoCo technology and GANs marks a watershed moment not only in deepfake technology, but in media manipulation more broadly. For one, use of GANs has meant that purveyors can efficiently produce deepfakes that are increasingly indiscernible from authentic video footage. As the technology learns to improve, and the amount of video input required to produce a sophisticated fake decreases, deepfakes will inevitably become more widespread. This is observable, for example, in the rapidly growing number of deepfake apps and programmes available including Zao, Reface, Wombo, and DeepFace Lab, to name just a few.[3] As a result, deepfake production no longer lies necessarily in the hands of specialists as with CGI or Photoshop, but in the hands of a broader, non-specialist audience. Moreover, when VoCo technology is factored into this assessment, deepfakes become more credible than older forms of media manipulation because purveyors can design deepfakes with an accompanying, indistinguishable voice. In turn, we are more likely to accept the videos' testimony unless there are significant reasons not to. Considering these developments, its unsurprising that the pioneer and computer scientist Professor Hao Li (Stankiewicz, 2019) warns that we're going to get to a point where there is 'no way that we can actually detect them [deepfakes] anymore'.

## 2. Vice Epistemology and Epistemic Corruption

If there is any truth to the above statement, then it's understandable why philosophers would worry that these videos could jeopardise our trust in videos (Rini, 2020) or the information we gain from such a ubiquitous source (Fallis, 2020). My aim is not to press these issues any further but to address a currently unexplored problem that deepfakes risk generating. This problem is exposed by offering a *corruptionist* critique of deepfakes. Ordinarily, the verbal meaning of 'corrupt' refers to way in which the character of something or someone is made worse or degraded – like when we say that somebody has been 'corrupted by power'. When we talk of people becoming corrupted, we often invoke the language of virtue and vice, specifically that a person has lost certain virtues or gained particular vices in their place. This is the function of a corruptionist criticism: to demonstrate how an environment causes one to acquire vices. To

---

[3] Other honourable mentions include FaceApp, Deepfakes Web and My Heritage. See https://www.analyticsinsight.net/try-these-10-amazingly-real-deepfake-apps-and-websites/

get a better sense of the kind of vices that I'm interested in here, we need to say something about *vice epistemology*.

Epistemology is the branch of philosophy concerned with knowledge, beliefs, and thinking, while vices are often considered to be defects, faults, or failures. Together, it is the job of the *vice epistemologist* to study what makes one's beliefs and thinking bad or faulty. Generally, when vice epistemologists approach this task, they tend to focus on failures of *intellectual character* – that is, the traits, attitudes, and habits of attention that hinder good thinking or knowledge, and which reflect badly on us. Some classic examples include close-mindedness, arrogance, and snobbery. Intellectual character failings such as these are what Quassim Cassam (2016; 2019) calls the 'vices of the mind', or simply *intellectual vices*. These are contrasted with what Linda Zagzebski (1996) calls the 'virtues of the mind', such as open-mindedness, intellectual humility, and creativity. Intellectual vices are bad for several reasons. First, they often reflect poor or deficient motivations towards engaging in knowledge-related practices. Call this the *motivational account* (Tanesini, 2018; 2021). Second, they systematically obstruct responsible inquiry and the transmission of knowledge. Call this the *obstructivist account* (Cassam, 2016; 2019), Third, they reflect entrenched patterns of bad judgement. Call this the *judgement account* (Baehr, 2020; Crerar, 2018).

Regardless of how one's vices play out in the actual world, they're usually the product of what we might call our *intellectual environments*. Think of these as physical or virtual spaces where *epistemic practices* take place. Amongst other things, these include practices such as inquiry, deliberation, educating, and evidence-sharing. They are 'epistemic' in the sense that they usually aim at discovering the truth of some matter. While some of us are lucky enough to engage with relatively healthy intellectual environments – where these practices are encouraged and facilitated – it's more likely that many of us will inhabit less than healthy intellectual environments; one's where inquiry is facilitated up to an extent then shut down after a certain point, where questioning authority in deliberations is a risky business, and where the evidence available to us can come from dubious or untrustworthy sources. In a world of disinformation campaigns, 'fake news' and 'alternative facts', it's hard not to find oneself in steadily deteriorating intellectual environments.

Ian James Kidd (2019b; 2020) introduces the concept of *epistemic corruption* to draw attention to the way in which our intellectual environments can encourage the development and exercise of intellectual vices, or lead to the loss of intellectual virtues. Those environments which fail to nurture intellectual virtues are what Kidd calls 'passively corrupting', while environments that encourage the exercise of intellectual vices are 'actively corrupting'. Importantly, this distinction is not clear-cut and the two will typically reinforce each other in a mutual fashion. For example, suppose you attend an elite debating club that encourages and rewards 'kill or be killed' argumentative styles. Within that environment, arrogant or dismissive tendencies are likely to become entrenched in one's intellectual character. Simultaneously, the longer one is exposed to such conditions and styles, the harder it will become to cultivate humble or attentive behaviour and traits towards others. Of course, not all environments are equally corrupting.[4] Some might contain structures that are conducive to the development of many vices or lead to the loss of numerous virtues. At other times, the environment might only feed a handful of vices in a small number of domains. My participation in a football fan club might cause me to develop a close-mindedness towards other football clubs but leave my political or music tastes wholly unscathed.

How might these environments contribute to the corruption of intellectual character? Kidd says that epistemic corruption can occur in multiple ways. A particular environment might contain conditions that cause one to *acquire* certain traits or habits that one didn't previously possess. Only after joining and engaging in the activities of the football fan club, for example, might I realise that I have acquired an intellectual vice – assuming I'm even in a position to recognise it in the first place! (Cassam, 2019). Other environments might draw out and *ignite* one's previously managed intellectual vice(s). Suppose that you recognise your arrogant tendencies but nonetheless keep them contained. By participating in the debating club, the norms, rules, and structures present could unlock your arrogance and allow it to flourish. Furthermore, the same environments could well *amplify, stabilise, or intensify* particular intellectual vices, thereby corrupting one's intellectual character from many different angles (Kidd, 2020, p. 72). In short, epistemic corruption is a complex phenomenon with real implications for our character and conduct.

## 3. Intellectual Cynics

Using the concept of epistemic corruption, I now want to argue that deepfakes encourage us to develop the epistemic vice of *intellectual*

---

[4]    Indeed, it's plausible that some intellectual environments are not corrupting at all.

*cynicism*. To see just how deepfakes might put us in this position, it will be useful to consider Rini and Fallis' concerns in more detail. According to Fallis (2020), deepfakes are epistemically harmful because they risk undermining the information videos carry to viewers. On Fallis' view, a video carries information if there is a low probability of watching a false positive, i.e., a video that looks and sounds just like a genuine video but turns out to be fake. If this probability is low, a video will accordingly carry *more* information. However, Fallis worries that if deepfakes become sufficiently sophisticated and wide-spread, they will increase the incidence rate of false positives. As such, the information depicted in a genuine video will be undercut by the deepfake, increasing the likelihood of us suspending judgement about a video or simply accumulating false beliefs.

For Rini, meanwhile, the worry with deepfakes is that they will cause us to 'reflexively *distrust* all recordings' (2020, p. 8, my emphasis). This starts with the concept of an 'epistemic backstop', the idea that videos acutely *correct* other people's testimony and passively *regulate* what people say in public. After all, the possibility of being recorded tends to encourage people to be sincere and competent testifiers. However, Rini worries that as deepfakes become more sophisticated and widespread, they will lead to a sense of 'displaced epistemic reality' (2020, p. 8), where the *very possibility* of an authentic video being a deepfake lingers in people's minds. In turn, deepfakes could undercut the corrective function of videos by eroding their perceived evidential status. If deepfakes make it more difficult to ascertain the veracity of a recording, Rini believes that people will have less incentive to testify sincerely and competently if they can quite easily 'cry deepfake' on a video.[5] As a result, people will plausibly invest less trust in what they hear or see from videos, and thus videos will lose the ability to *passively regulate* what people say in public. For these reasons, Rini believes that deepfakes will usher in 'backstop crises' and erode the epistemic credentials of *all* recordings (2020, p. 8).

While we needn't endorse the full extent of Fallis and Rini's arguments here, I do want to press the idea that deepfakes could plausibly lead us to increasingly distrust videos or cause us to suspend judgement about what a given video depicts. In particular, I want to draw parallels with this behaviour and the distrust and

---

[5]    Of course, this is only the case *insofar* as first-hand, direct testimony is unavailable. However, since videos increasingly provide 'second-hand', indirect testimony, this is where Rini's worries would seem applicable.

disengagement that is central to what Samantha Vice (2011) calls *moral cynicism*. What makes cynicism specifically 'moral' is that it primarily concerns our attitudes and beliefs towards other human beings and ourselves. For Vice (2011, p. 173), moral cynicism can be thought of as a habitual and cultivated attitude of 'scepticism or distrust regarding people's professed values and motivations' or their 'strength and nobility of character'. Underpinning this distrust is the cynic's core belief that humans are ultimately self-interested or of little worth. In this way, cynicism 'structures our perception, interpretation, evaluation, and expectations of others', while also affecting our own actions. At its darkest and broadest, Vice claims, cynicism can even lead one to disengage from humanity and its institutions altogether, due to a habitual wariness of what drives people (2011, p. 172). Those who adopt this stance are what Vice calls 'pure cynics', someone whose 'pervading and fundamental character is cynical' (2011, p. 174).

If deepfakes are able to spark distrust towards online videos, thereby prompting us to suspend judgement more readily about their depictions, then we can begin to see a kind of cynicism on the horizon. This kind of cynicism, I contend, exists presently but will be exacerbated by deepfakes. In particular, it concerns our behaviour towards intellectual or epistemic matters as opposed to people and human relations. Call this *intellectual cynicism*. Much like its moral counterpart, we can think intellectual cynicism as a negative stance or cluster of attitudes towards a particular epistemic object. Here, the object in question needn't necessarily be epistemic goods such as truth, knowledge, or understanding, but rather the *source* of these goods themselves. In the past, this source has typically been directed at testimony. Think of those, for example, who adopt negative attitudes towards Facebook's recent claims and pledges to improve online safety. What makes these cynical attitudes 'intellectual' as opposed to 'moral', I suggest, is that they are grounded in a belief about the epistemic status of Facebook's pledges and claims *qua* propositions, that it whether their statements are true or false, rather than a belief about Facebook as a corporation or agent itself.[6] Adopting this kind of moderate cynicism might therefore be warranted, so long as one is receptive to evidence to the contrary.

Given this, how does intellectual cynicism factor into the spread of deepfakes? As the world has 'moved' online during and after the

---

[6] It goes without saying that the beliefs underpinning intellectually cynical attitudes will often emerge and reinforce those which ground the moral cynic's attitudes (Vice, 2011, p. 180).

Covid-19 pandemic, the source of many of our epistemic goods has increasingly shifted to *videos*. We watch, listen, and rely on videos for work, education, and information. However, suppose at some point you find out that they've recently spoken to a deepfake or been tricked into believing a deepfake's content, or worse. As deepfakes grow more sophisticated, a natural reaction might be to adopt a cynical attitude towards online, unregulated videos. At first blush, this move would bear similarity to the cynical attitudes adopted towards Facebook's safety pledge. Yet in both cases, I want to suggest that there is a problematic element to this. Just as Vice carves off 'pure cynicism' as a particularly acute kind of moral cynicism, so too can we draw attention to a similarly damaging kind of intellectual cynicism. This involves distinguishing intellectually cynical attitudes from the *trait* of intellectual cynicism. As deepfakes become more sophisticated, it's plausible to think that people will come to adopt cynical attitudes towards unregulated, online videos more and more, and through doing so have these attitudes congeal in their intellectual *character*. Why is this a bad thing? Well, take one familiar feature of character traits: they necessarily involve being *disposed* to think, feel, and act in particular ways. Those who cultivate the trait of intellectual cynicism, I contend, will come to habitually view videos in a negative light, which will in turn generate corresponding habits of thought and action towards them. In particular, the trait will dispose its possessors to make inferential leaps that all unregulated, digital, audio-visual information online is potentially deepfaked.[7]

How can we make sense of this inferential leap? In habituating certain traits, people also develop corresponding *sensibilities*. One way to think about sensibilities is in terms of one's characteristic patterns of seeing the world. For instance, a distinct feature of those who cultivate the trait of attentiveness is that they are more likely to notice certain behaviours, actions, or people than those without this trait. A similar story holds for the trait of intellectual cynicism. In fact, Vice alludes to this when she observes that moral cynicism 'structures our perception, interpretation, evaluation, and expectation of others' (2011, p. 172). By the same token, the trait of intellectual cynicism

---

[7] By 'unregulated', I mean the videos and digital content that does not come from established TV channels, news sites or newspaper. This will typically mean sites or domains on which deepfakes have had a presence, most notably social media websites. In an extreme form, this cynicism might even cause one to make inferential leaps about the intellectual merits of established content, but I do not commit myself to that view here.

will manifest cynical sensibilities that infect one's intellectual character at large, leaving one with a "corrupt sense of value' (Vice, 2011, p. 175). Specifically, those who habituate this trait will be driven by a belief in the sub-optimality of online, unregulated videos as a source of epistemic goods *as a whole*, much in the same that the moral cynic views humanity. Consequently, the intellectual cynic is unable to attend to the possibility that such content possibly aims at the truth or other epistemic goods. Instead, their sensibilities are too highly attuned to the foregone conclusion that these videos never serve intrinsically good purposes or are instrumental to the success of a dubious agenda. To put this point another way, we can think of the intellectual cynic as somebody who habitually fails to consider the intellectual *merits* of online, unregulated videos. In this way, the trait of intellectual cynicism is self-sufficient: the more one habituates it, the more pronounced the accompanying sensibilities are at structuring what the intellectual cynic sees and evaluates – or perhaps more apt, what they fail to see and misevaluate. It is for this reason that the intellectual cynic makes such large inferential leaps.

If this is the case, then we can say that deepfakes are actively corrupting: they risk encouraging consumers of digital media to develop the *epistemic vice* of intellectual cynicism. We can make good on this claim by reference to the three accounts of epistemic vice canvassed above. First, those who habituate the trait intellectual cynicism might be said to possess *bad motivations* towards wanting knowledge if they are disposed to distrust and associate videos with suspicion. Second, in cultivating this trait, the intellectual cynic *obstructs* the transmission of knowledge and information. Third, by developing the cynical sensibilities associated with this trait, the intellectual cynic makes poorly judged decisions about the merit of videos as a source of epistemic goods because they perceive them in such a skewed light. These three manifestations will, of course, overlap and be borne out more strongly in some than others. Regardless, though, by habitually distrusting and disengaging from epistemic practices, the intellectual cynic never engages with the very sources and practices that could potentially shake their cynicism. If this is the case, deepfakes have the potential to encourage an ultimately damaging intellectual character trait that deprives us of the knowledge and information needed for a flourishing intellectual life. It's beyond the scope of this paper to give a full account of the nature of intellectual cynicism, but I hope it's at least clear what both the attitude and trait consists of, and how deepfakes might encourage this intellectual vice.

## 4. Cultivating Digital Sensibility

In the previous section, I argued that deepfakes are epistemically corrupting because they risk encouraging consumers of digital media to develop the vice of intellectual cynicism. However, as Kidd rightly emphasises, identifying corrupting environments – or in our case technologies – enables us to work out what sorts of corrective measures to put in place (2019, p. 227). The corrective approach I want to advance is somewhat analogous to our everyday treatment of the testimony we hear from informants. The motivation for this comes from Rini's worry above. Part of the reason why videos play such an important role in her idea of an 'epistemic backstop' is because of their justificatory or evidential status. It is widely acknowledged that videos and photographs provide us with *perceptual* evidence of states of affairs (Cavedon-Taylor, 2013; Hopkins, 2012), which is more authoritative than, say, testimonial evidence. Rini worries that by eroding our trust in videos, deepfakes will relegate the justificatory status we assign to recordings from perceptual evidence to that of testimonial evidence. In other words, we will take videos to be less authoritative of the states of affairs they depict.

If Rini's concerns are correct, then why don't we treat videos like testimony? So, just as we deal with liars and bullshitters (Frankfurt, 2005) by exercising particular caution, hesitance, and critical evaluation in our credibility assessments of what they say, I suggest that we deal with the threat of deepfakes and intellectual cynicism by cultivating a countervailing sensibility, what I will call a *digital sensibility*. The basis of this sensibility is rooted in Miranda Fricker's (2007) idea of a *testimonial sensibility*. This a carefully cultivated way of experiencing and evaluating other people's testimonies, informed by an awareness that our ability to properly listen to others is corrupted by all sorts of biases and prejudices. It involves training oneself and gaining more understanding of social prejudices, which is no mean feat. By cultivating this sensibility, one comes to gradually acknowledge and, to an extent, nullify the prejudices that interfere with one's credibility assessments of others (2007, pp. 72–81). For Fricker, there are two components of this sensibility that stand out for our discussion: its *perceptual* nature and its *affective* dimension.[8] I will look briefly at each as a way of modelling the digital sensibility

[8]     Fricker adds that a trained testimonial sensibility will also be grounded by 1) good judgement that is uncodifiable i.e. it will not be rule-based, 2) be intrinsically motivating, and 3) be reason-giving i.e. generate reasons to act in certain ways (2007, pp. 72–80).

required for mitigating the intellectual cynicism promoted by deepfakes.

Fricker's starting point is an idea dating back to Aristotle, for whom the good or *virtuous* person is one whose 'moral perception' is drawn towards ethically salient aspects of a situation. This perception is carefully cultivated and trained to be reflexive and spontaneous, so that upon being confronted with a morally charged scenario, the good person comes to 'just see' the situation in a certain light and is able to pick out the best course of action to help. Fricker suggests that we do something similar with what she calls an 'epistemic perception'. Similarly, this is a calibrated sensitivity to salient aspects of a speaker's situation and is informed by a number of background assumptions about the speaker's trustworthiness, including cues relating to their sincerity and competence on the matter at hand (2007, p. 72). Importantly, the work of calibration should also be an interpersonal project, rather than an individual one, though obvious care should be taken in deciding whom to trust – something that gradually improves with practice. With the help of a conducive intellectual environment – one that encourages and emphasises the virtues of the mind – people can develop an ability to see the world in a certain light, enabling them to assess their interlocutors in a fair, open-minded, and non-inferential manner.

This perceptual sensibility is also supported by an affective dimension. In order to properly judge the competency and sincerity of a speaker, one needs to be able to sufficiently empathise with them. Only by invoking a degree of emotional engagement with a speaker can one fully appreciate the socially situated factors that might be in play when it comes to 'reading' another's body language or the competence one displays in their testimony (2007, pp. 79–80). In order to better determine the level of trust one ought to place in another's word, Fricker observes that good advice is 'to listen to one's emotions' insofar as the virtuous person's emotional response to different speakers across different contexts is only improved by training and experience (2007, p. 80). By exposing ourselves to different speakers in different contexts, we can build up a sophisticated emotional radar for detecting trustworthiness in speakers. In doing so, we not only cultivate a trained testimonial sensibility, but we also manifest the virtue of 'testimonial justice' – a disposition to reliably neutralise prejudice and bias from our credibility assessment of speakers (2007, p. 92).

Taking these points into consideration, we can develop a model for digital sensibility. For starters, this will be a reflective and spontaneous sensitivity towards online content, so that when we're confronted with certain videos, images, or website we learn to 'just see' them as trustworthy. Again, this will turn on features like the content's sincerity and competence. For instance, it is common nowadays to stumble across an online video or see adverts on websites and immediately withhold judgement about the claims made, or outright flag them as deceptive. One reason for this hesitance is that the content seems insincere: it makes claims that do not accord with the background assumptions against which we ordinarily evaluate videos or other media. Another reason is that the content appears incompetent: its presentation and configuration fail to conform to established norms of publishing and communication. A further factor in our assessments of trustworthiness might also include our worries about clicking on videos and developing computer viruses, being scammed, or losing personal information.

This last factor draws out the affective dimension of a digital sensibility. While Fricker takes empathy to be an important emotion in judging the sincerity of an interlocutor, I think that past, present, and future experience with our digital environments will require the kind of 'healthy scepticism' that, as Pierre Le Morvan (2011, p. 98; 2019) puts it, 'guards' against both gullibility and close-mindedness'. Fine-tuning this, he claims, bolsters our 'doxastic immune system' from the threat of false beliefs (2011, p. 91). Successfully exercising this healthy scepticism will partly rely on us listening to our 'gut feelings' when they flag a video as unscrupulous or dubious, the effectiveness of which will come from prior experience and exposure to a range of claims, depictions, and sources of digital content. An important part of this fine-tuning, then, will be the perseverance to fact-check such content, and a degree of humility in recognising that our credibility assessments will not always be watertight. Over time, this healthy scepticism will inform our emotional radar and help us to judge certain content as more trustworthy – established news media and websites that adhere to communicative norms – than other content which fail to adhere to such standards or are at odds with the catalogue of past experiences we have built up. In this way, we continually fine-tune the 'radar' that comes with cultivating a digital sensibility. Eventually, a trained digital sensibility, like its testimonial counterpart, will develop to be an active, automatic, and critical alertness towards online content.

Crucially, though, the development of a digital sensibility is as much about individual caution and critical awareness as it is about developing a *collective* safeguard against deceptive online media. As Fricker makes clear, the formation of our testimonial sensibilities is partly individual and partly collective (2007, p. 82). Accordingly, the cultivation, exercise, and regulation of a trained digital sensibility relies on cooperating with our peers across digital environments.

Those who are more technologically savvy will have duties to flag potentially untrustworthy content, allowing those less well-versed in digital matters to observe how to decide how much trust to place in websites and online media. Gradually, those with less experience can learn from the 'digital exemplars' in their community and slowly fine-tune their perceptual and emotional radar towards trustworthy online content. This collective dimension not only illustrates the educational role that training one's digital sensibility entails, but it also emphasises the socially-scaffolded nature on which the effectiveness of this sensitivity is premised. This is particularly salient when it comes to regulating the affective dimension of one's digital sensibility. It's not hard to imagine somebody who exercises a deficiency or excess of scepticism towards digital content, perhaps sympathising with the claims made by a video or website or being overly sceptical of authentic content. To ensure that one's healthy scepticism is kept in check, one's peers will need to hold them to account, warning them when their emotional radar fails to track the merits or demerits of digital content.

However, even a collective effort to cultivate a trained digital sensibility might not be sufficient to fend off the cynicism that deepfakes and emerging technologies might encourage. In addition to individual and collective practice and cultivation, a well-trained digital sensibility requires *institutional* and *structural* scaffolding (Anderson, 2012; Medina, 2013). This will require social media companies and news corporations to cultivate the virtue of *collective responsibility* (Astola, 2022). In our case, this responsibility will manifest in the companies flagging deepfakes, correcting mis- and disinformation, and raising awareness of other untrustworthy sources of information. For a long time, Facebook allowed users to post 'parody' deepfakes on its website, which could be exploited by malicious actors to indirectly spread misinformation and sow distrust (Shead, 2020). If efforts to cultivate a trained digital sensibility are to succeed in the long-term, institutions with regulatory powers like Facebook, Google, Microsoft, and Twitter will need to work in tandem with their user-base. Only then, will a trained digital sensibility be sufficiently socially scaffolded and effective.

## 5. From Digital Sensibility to Techno-Intellectual Virtue

In a world increasingly characterised by deepfakes, fake-news, and emerging technologies, how can we best flourish? I want to briefly conclude by reflecting on this question. According to the philosopher, Shannon Vallor (2016), the cultivation of what she calls *techno-moral virtues* will help us achieve this end. Techno-moral virtues are an extension of our existing moral capacities or traits, adapted to a rapidly changing techno-socially opaque world, which require a collective moral wisdom on a global scale (2016, p. 10). Some notable examples include techno-moral courage – 'a reliable disposition toward intelligent fear and hope with respect to moral and material dangers and opportunities presented by emerging technologies' (2016, p. 131), and humility – 'a renunciation of the blind faith that new technologies inevitably lead to human mastery and control of our environment' (ibid, pp. 126–27). In the face of emerging technologies, Vallor rightly stresses the need to cultivate these virtues as a means of offsetting any potential harm to our ethical character.

While Vallor is certainly right to draw attention to this prospect, my aim in this paper has been to demonstrate just how deepfakes can degrade our *intellectual* character by encouraging us to develop the vice of intellectual cynicism. In light of this, I proposed a way to fortify our intellectual character against the potentially corrupting nature of deepfakes. I believe that developing a well-trained digital sensibility will be a major step towards doing this. This will not simply lead those wishing to navigate online spaces to acquire a number of 'virtues of inquiry' towards digital content, but to specifically cultivate the techno-*intellectual* virtue of digital attentiveness, a corrective disposition to carefully attend to the merits and demerits of digital media. Just as cultivating a trained testimonial sensibility helps one nullify prejudices and biases against speakers, a trained digital sensibility enables one to offset the vice of intellectual cynicism and fortify one's intellectual character described above. For those wishing to flourish in a rapidly changing world, a trained digital sensibility and the correlative techno-intellectual virtue of attentiveness will help to make this a reality.[9]

*University of Nottingham*
*apxtm1@exmail.nottingham.ac.uk*

[9]    Sections of this paper were presented at the University of Nottingham's Postgraduate Research Seminar, and I am grateful for the feedback I received from friends and colleagues. I would also like to thank Ian James Kidd, Jennifer Chubb, the participants at the Values and Virtues Workshop, and the editors of this volume for helpful feedback and discussion that improved this paper. This paper was written whilst in receipt of a Midlands4Cities Doctoral Award.

## References

M. Astola, 'Collective Responsibility should be treated as a Virtue', *Royal Institute Philosophy Supplementary Volume*, 92 (2022) 27–44.

E. Anderson, 'Epistemic Justice as a Virtue of Institutions', *Social Epistemology*, 26 (2012) 163–173.

Q. Cassam, 'Vice Epistemology', *The Monist*, 99 (2016) 159–180.

Q. Cassam, *Vices of the Mind*, (Oxford, Oxford University Press, 2019).

Dan Cavedon-Taylor, 'Photographically Based Knowledge', *Episteme*, 10 (2013), 283–297.

C. Crerar, *Bad Judgement: An Essay in Vice Epistemology*, Doctoral Thesis, University of Sheffield (2018). https://etheses.whiterose.ac.uk/21243/1/Thesis%20%28library%29.pdf

CBS News, 'Artificial Intelligence Project Lets Holocaust Survivors Share Their Stories Forever', *CBS News 60 Minutes Overtime*, April 3rd, 2020, accessible at: https://www.cbsnews.com/news/artificial-intelligence-holocaust-remembrance-60-minutes-2020-04-03/.

Channel 4, 'Deepfake Queen: 2020 Alternative Christmas Message', *YouTube*, 25th December 2020, accessible at: https://www.youtube.com/watch?v=IvY-Abd2FfM

R. Chesney and D. Citron, 'Deepfakes and the New Information War: the coming age of post-truth geopolitics', *Foreign Affairs*, 98 (2019) accessible at: https://www.foreignaffairs.com/articles/world/2018-12-11/deepfakes-and-new-disinformation-war.

Meenu Eg, 'Try These 10 Amazingly Real Deepfake Apps and Website', *Analytics Insight* (2021) accessible at: https://www.analyticsinsight.net/try-these-10-amazingly-real-deepfake-apps-and-websites/.

D. Lee, 'Deepfake Salvador Dalí takes selfies with museum visitors', *The Verge*, May 10th, 2019, accessible at: https://www.theverge.com/2019/5/10/18540953/salvador-dali-lives-deepfake-museum.

D. Fallis, 'The Epistemic Threat of Deepfakes', *Philosophy and Technology* (2020).

H. G. Frankfurt, *On Bullshit* (Oxford: Oxford University Press, 2005).

M. Fricker, *Epistemic Injustice: power and the ethics of knowing*, (Oxford: Oxford University Press, 2007).

K. R. Harris, 'Video on demand: what deepfakes do and how they harm', *Synthese* (2021) https://doi.org/10.1007/s11229-021-03379-y

R. Hopkins, 'Factive Pictorial Experience: What's Special About Photographs?', *Noûs*, 46 (2012) 709–731.

Z. Jin, G. J. Mysore, S. Diverdi, J. Lu, A. Finkelstein, 'VoCo: Text-Based Insertion and Replacement in Audio Narration', ACM *Transactions on Graphics*, 36 (2017).

I. J. Kidd, 'Epistemic Corruption and Education', *Episteme*, 16(2019) 220-235.

I. J. Kidd, 'Epistemic Corruption and Social Oppression', in I. J. Kidd, H. Battaly, and Q. Cassam (eds.) *Vice Epistemology*, (Abingdon: UK, Taylor and Francis, 2020) 69–85.

F. Lang, 'Adobe Trains AI to Detect Deepfakes and Photoshopped Images', *Interesting Engineering* (2019) available at: https://interestingengineering.com/adobe-trains-ai-to-detect-deepfakes-and-photoshopped-images.

P. Le Morvan, 'Healthy Scepticism and Practical Wisdom', *Logos and Episteme*, 2 (2011) 87–102.

P. Le Morvan, 'Scepticism as Virtue and Vice', *International Journal for the Study of Scepticism*, 9 (2019), 238–260.

J. Medina, *The Epistemology of Resistance: gender and racial oppression, epistemic injustice, and resistance imaginations*, (New York: Oxford University Press, 2013).

Y. Mirksy and W. Lee 'The Creation and Detection of Deepfakes: A Survey', *ACM Computing Surveys*, 54 (2020) 1–41.

B. Paris and J. Donovan, 'Deepfakes and Cheapfakes', *Data and Society* (2019) accessible at: https://datasociety.net/wp-content/uploads/2019/09/DS_Deepfakes_Cheap_FakesFinal-1-1.pdf

Reuters, 'Fact-Check: "Drunk" Nancy Pelosi" video is manipulated', *Reuters*, August 3rd, 2020, accessible at: https://www.reuters.com/article/uk-factcheck-nancypelosi-manipulated-idUSKCN24Z2BI.

R. Rini, 'Deepfakes and the Epistemic Backstop', *Philosopher's Imprint*, 20 (2020) 1–16.

N. Schick, *Deepfakes and the Infopocalypse*, (London: Monoray, 2020).

S. Shead, 'Facebook to ban 'deepfakes'', *BBC News*, January 7th 2020, https://www.bbc.co.uk/news/technology-51018758.

K. Stankiewicz, '"Perfectly real" deepfakes will arrive in 6 months to a year, technology pioneer Hao Li', *CNBC*, September 20th 2019, accessible at: https://www.cnbc.com/2019/09/20/hao-li-perfectly-real-deepfakes-will-arrive-in-6-months-to-a-year.html.

A. Tanesini, 'Epistemic Vice and Motivation', *Metaphilosophy*, 49 (2018) 350–367.

A. Tanesini, *The Mismeasure of the Self: A Study in Vice Epistemology,* (Oxford: Oxford University Press, 2021).

R. Tolosana, R. Vera-Rodriguez, J. Fierrez, M. Aythami and J. Ortega-Garcia 'DeepFakes and Beyond: A Survey of Face Manipulation and Fake Detection', *Information Fusion*, 64 (2020) 131–148. https://arxiv.org/pdf/2001.00179.pdf

S. Vallor, *Technology and the virtues: A philosophical guide to a future worth wanting,* (New York: Oxford University Press, 2016).

S. Vice, 'Cynicism and Morality', *Ethical Theory and Moral Practice*, 14 (2011) 169-184.

L. T. Zagzebski, *Virtues of the Mind: an inquiry into the nature of virtue and the ethical foundations of knowledge,* (Cambridge: Cambridge University Press, 1996).

E. Zakharov, A. Shysheya, E. Burkov, V. Lempitsky, 'Few-Shot Adversarial Learning of Realistic Neural Talking Head Models', (2019) accessible at: https://arxiv.org/pdf/1905.08233v1.pdf. For a demonstration of the research, see https://www.youtube.com/watch?v=p1b5aiTrGzY.

# Affective Polarisation and Emotional Distortions on Social Media

ALESSANDRA TANESINI

**Abstract**

In this paper I argue that social networking sites (SNSs) are emotion technologies that promote a highly charged emotional environment where intrinsic emotion regulation is significantly weakened, and people's emotions are more strongly modulated by other people and by the technology itself. I show that these features of social media promote a simplistic emotional outlook which is an obstacle to the development and maintenance of virtue. In addition, I focus on the mechanisms that promote group-based anger and thus give rise to affective polarisation. In the final section, after a discussion of the positive value of some forms of anger, I argue that SNSs should not be designed to prohibit or suppress anger, but that its encouragement should also be avoided. I conclude with a suggestion about how this might be achieved.

Social media are, seemingly, a fertile ground for hate speech, misogyny, racism, and abuse. They might also be partially responsible for the emergence of 'culture wars' in the UK but especially in the USA.[1] These 'wars' would be characterised by hostile, and often hate-filled, disputes over numerous topics including police brutality, critical race theory and Black Lives Matter, feminism, and the rights of transgender women. These disputes are conducted on new and old media by members of sharply polarised groups. It is not the first time, however, that European and North American societies have been riven by deep, seemingly unbreachable, divisions. In the Early Modern period, for instance, Europe was devastated by a series of religious wars. Then like

---

[1]    For example, a recent report by the Policy Institute at King's College London recommends several measures to guard against further polarisation on 'culture wars' issues in the UK. These include 'holding media and social media to better account for the role they play in this [polarisation] process' and enjoining 'political leaders on all sides to cool things down rather than raise the temperature further' (Duffy et al., 2021). The report, however, also suggests that the media's contribution primarily consists in amplifying, and giving unwarranted prominence to, the polarised views of a tiny fraction of the population. That said, this amplification process might turn 'culture wars' in the UK into a reality.

doi:10.1017/S1358246122000261

now, disagreements were hostile, full of anger and aggression. People thought of members of the other camp as beyond the pale, and were not afraid to make the contempt in which they held their opponents manifest (cf., Bejan, 2017).

Even though polarisation, hostility, and 'culture wars' are not unique to contemporary circumstances, there are aspects of the current situation that make it different from historical episodes of deep social divisions in ways that require novel ameliorative strategies. More specifically, I argue in this paper that social networking sites (hereafter, SNSs), like Facebook, Twitter or Instagram, are technologies whose design features facilitate the triggering and mass contagion of group-based anger; that is, anger experienced by individuals because of perceived slights to their social identity. I argue that some strategies aimed to address the negative consequences of such expressions of anger should be targeted at the design features of these platforms rather than at encouraging users to cultivate virtues such as discreetness (Frost-Arnold, 2021) or care (Desmond, 2022; Vallor, 2016).

This paper consists of five sections. In the first I offer a brief survey of empirical results that strongly suggest that SNSs are essentially emotional environments where strong negative emotions can spread quickly and to many users. In section two, I offer an account of SNSs as emotion technologies that promote a highly charged emotional environment where intrinsic emotion regulation is significantly weakened, and people's emotions are more strongly modulated by other people and by the technology itself. I show that these features of social media promote a simplistic emotional outlook which is an obstacle to the development and maintenance of virtue. In section three I explain how SNSs cause deindividuation and promote group-based emotions, including group-based anger. Section four focuses explicitly on the mechanisms that facilitate this affective polarisation. In the final section, after a discussion of the positive value of some forms of anger, I argue that SNSs should not be designed to prohibit or suppress anger, but that its encouragement should also be avoided. I conclude with a suggestion about how this might be achieved.

## 1. SNSs as Emotional environments

SNSs are online platforms, like Facebook, LinkedIn, WhatsApp, Twitter and Instagram, that are designed to facilitate and promote social relationships. Users construct personalised profiles and establish connections of 'friendship' or 'followership' with others.[2] They are then able to communicate directly with individuals, via direct messaging, and to broadcast information publicly or to selected groups. Users are also able to view and navigate the contributions made by their connections and sometimes also by others within the network (boyd, 2011). There is now an established body of empirical research in information science, psychology, media studies and social science that strongly indicates that users' engagement with these sites is primarily affect- driven (Löwe & Parkinson, 2014; Papachrissi, 2015). SNSs provide an environment within which messages that communicate emotions spread faster and further than those that do not. Further, the amount of discussion generated by a message is directly proportional to the strength of the emotions it conveys (Chmiel et al., 2011).

In addition to evidence of generalised emotional engagement, several studies have also highlighted phenomena that are akin to emotional contagion (Kramer et al., 2014; Zollo et al., 2015). That is, users tend to experience the emotions conveyed by the messages with which they engage, and to spread these common emotional responses further by expressing them in their comments, shares or retweets. Emotional contagion occurs when a person, influenced by their observation of the emotion expressed by other people, experiences the same emotion as they have witnessed in others.[3] Emotional contagion is therefore a process that gives rise to emotional convergence. That is, to say it leads to the synchronisation of emotions among different people. At times, it also involves emotion regulation. The latter refers to any goal-directed conscious process, technique or strategy that influences which emotion a person has, how, when and for how long they experience it, as well as how (and whether) they give expression to their emotional experience (Gross, 2015, p. 5). Emotional contagion can be an interpersonal or extrinsic form of emotion regulation when one person regulates another's emotion by purposefully sharing with them their emotions with a view to encourage them to feel the same (Gross, 2015, p. 5). For

[2] Some, perhaps most, of these relationships are transient and superficial. This is true, for instance, of many Facebook 'friends'. Nevertheless, all social connections on SNSs are relationships of some sort.

[3] There are various accounts of the mechanisms involved in this phenomenon including social appraisal theory according to which others' appraisal of an event as conveyed by their emotions is factored into one's evaluation of the same event playing a role akin to testimony. Hence, the resulting evaluation as expressed in one's emotion is likely to agree with the appraisals that have informed it. This is a process that would lead to the convergence of emotions (Bruder et al., 2014).

example, a user can post a joyful message on a SNSs with the express
purpose of cheering oneself and others up. Such activity is a strategy
of emotion regulation that is both intrinsic (directed at oneself) and
extrinsic.

Contrary to what one would expect from many dire warnings about
the angry and hateful tenor of online communications the overall
emotional tone of conversations online is, as a matter of fact, positive.
For example, Kramer et al. (2014) found that among the Facebook
posts they examined there were twice as many positive emotional
messages as negative ones. This finding is what one would expect
of platforms designed to multiply social connections. People do not
like to engage with those they do not like or to discuss depressing
topics. In addition, there are unspoken social norms against posting
negative content (Waterloo et al., 2018). When negative content is
shared online, it is more frequently communicated as a request for
help or an offer of support to close connections by way of direct messaging (Bazarova et al., 2015; Ziegele & Reinecke, 2017). Therefore,
positive messages are prevalent in the public channels of SNSs.

It does not follow, however, that anger cannot also be on the increase. The evidence shows that online communication is emotionally
charged. It is thus entirely possible that emotions online are more
commonly positive than negative, and yet anger and hostility is also
on the rise. There is evidence that angry messages on SNSs are especially successful in spreading far and wide (Martin & Vieaux, 2015;
Wollebæk et al., 2019). In addition, anger online has been shown to
facilitate homophily effects (Song & Xu, 2019). That is, angry
people online have a propensity to communicate mostly with those
who share their anger, and to avoid those who do not. Importantly,
even people who do not interact with each other often or at all in
real life are susceptible online to emotional contagion when they
view angry content. Joy, instead, is less often shared among strangers
online (Fan et al., 2020).

## 2. SNSs as Emotion Technologies

The previous section has highlighted that SNSs are spaces within
which connections are emotionally charged, where emotional messages spread fast and wide by processes of emotional contagion
leading to emotional convergence. Although the tenor of SNSs communication is prevalently positive, the social media are also a fertile
ground for anger-fuelled emotional contagion. In this section I
argue that we can make some progress toward understanding these

phenomena by thinking of SNSs as emotion technologies. These are artifacts with features designed for the purpose of modulating and regulating emotions (Krueger, 2014; Krueger & Osler, 2019).

Emotion regulation is not a goal of the designers of SNSs. Their goal is to foster social connections.[4] However, even transient and superficial human relationships depend on emotions since the expression of emotions is one of the principal ways of communicating relationship-relevant information and of guiding behaviour. In short, emotions are an essential tool for the management and negotiation of human relations (Löwe & Parkinson, 2014; Parkinson et al., 2005).[5] For example, people show anger to indicate to another agent that their relationship is at risk (Löwe & Parkinson, 2014, p. 130). This emotional expression demands an emotional response such as an acknowledgment of fault that is conveyed in a demonstration of guilt. If this attribution of a communicative function to emotions is correct, then we can explain why humans are strongly motivated to express their emotions, rather than hide them (Goldenberg et al., 2020; Jakobs et al., 2001). We can also understand why we are predisposed to share some emotions when we see others express them (Rimé, 2009).

These considerations suggest that if promoting human connections is an important goal of those who design SNSs, they are successful only if they construct platforms whose features facilitate the communication of emotions. For this reason, the modulation and regulation of emotions is a proximate goal of SNSs design. It is therefore legitimate to think of them as emotion technologies. In the remainder of this section, I flesh out the notion of an emotion technology and focus on some of the design features of SNSs that explain why communication on these platforms is emotionally charged, biased in favour of positive emotions, and why emotional convergence is widespread. I also show that the same features also weaken the effectiveness of traditional strategies of intrinsic emotion regulation and promote the adoption of a simplistic and Manichean emotional outlook. These last two effects of the features of SNSs make them an especially fertile ground for anger. They also make these platforms environments where it is much harder for ordinary human beings, possessing an ordinary amount of virtue, to behave virtuously.

---

[4]    Their ultimate goals, however, might be commercial. Thanks to Orestis Palermos for reminding me of this fact.
[5]    These considerations offer some support for Macnamara's (2015) view that emotions serve a communicative function.

# Alessandra Tanesini

Human beings have always modified their environments to facilitate the performance of various tasks. Some of these tasks are primarily cognitive such as finding the way to a destination or the arithmetical sum of two numbers. To make problems easier to solve, humans have invented strategies (e.g., carrying when doing sums) and artifacts (e.g., maps, the abacus and calculators). These cultural and material resources function as a kind of cognitive niche designed to scaffold human cognition (Sterelny, 2010). But humans have also modified their surroundings to facilitate the task of emotion regulation. We create affective niches, where it is easier to achieve and maintain a desired affective tone (Colombetti & Krueger, 2015; Krueger, 2014). These niches include artifacts such as music or ambient lights designed to modulate our moods and emotions (Krueger, 2019). Thanks to these devices the task of successfully regulating one's emotions is made easier because it is scaffolded by cultural and material technologies.

Given that the goal of SNSs is to foster the increase of social connections, and the fact that in humans social relationships are created and sustained partly by way of expressing emotions, we would expect successful social media to have design features that call for emotional engagement. We would also expect these features to favour emotional contagion so that emotions are disseminated far and wide, and to promote positive emotions since people do not like to interact with disagreeable people. Whilst there are differences between SNSs, many have features that are particularly suited to promote positive emotional engagement and emotional contagion. Three prominent such features are: reaction buttons that encourage selection from a limited range of emotional responses; the availability of alternative channels for direct messaging and public broadcasting; the speed and ease of communication to a large public.

Facebook, for instance, explicitly encourages emotional responses to status updates by providing users with a fixed menu of reaction buttons (like, love, care, amusement, surprise, sadness, and anger).[6] These buttons call for emotional, rather than reflective, reactions and thus contribute to making Facebook an environment where communication is shaped by affect. The same buttons also give prominence to those aspects of a post that make it more likely to be shared because of its novelty or newsworthiness (surprise), its ability to generate positive feelings (like, amusement, love and care) or its capacity to harness support (like, sadness and anger). Hence, this design feature favours emotional contagion. In addition, the

---

[6]   Response buttons also feature in Twitter, Instagram and Tik Tok.

buttons are primarily designed to foster positive, rather than negative, emotions as four out of the seven existing options signal pro-social attitudes.

Furthermore, Facebook response buttons are an example of what Alfano et al. (2018) have labelled 'top-down technological seduction'. The platform design invites the readers to unthinkingly accept that the appropriate reaction to a post is one, and only one, among those pre-selected by Facebook. Users are thus taken down a path where there is no place for emotional complexity or ambiguity, and where the range of available emotional responses is rather limited. Users' adoption of Facebook's choice architecture for them has at least four consequences. First, all the available options consist in the expression of an emotion. Second, the available options are limited in number and thus promote emotional convergence. Third, the options are presented as exhaustive and mutually exclusive. Hence, users are led into the adoption of a Manichean emotional outlook where it is impossible for love to be tinged by anger, or vice-versa. It is an outlook that promotes simplicity, clarity, a 'with us or against us' mentality; it has no space for ambiguity or complexity.[7] Fourth, the platform gives prominence to anger as one among the standing available responses.

When users are seduced into the adoption of a simplified emotional outlook, they risk losing the ability to appreciate the complexities of human relationships and to respond emotionally to others in the right way. Thus SNSs, because of some of their features, obstruct the development and maintenance of virtues since these involve the capacity to appreciate emotionally the moral features of often complex situations.

Several SNSs also have different channels that separate public broadcasting from direct messaging (Bazarova et al., 2015). This design feature facilitates emotional engagements by creating private channels where one is able to share bad news with intimate friends, whilst maintaining an upbeat persona in the public broadcasting channel.[8] This characteristic of the platforms facilitates both emotional engagement and an overall positive tone in its more public facing channels. The opportunity to broadcast one's message far and wide in the more public channels is a great enabler of emotional

---

[7]    This is an aspect of what Nguyen (2021) has labelled the 'gamification' of communication.

[8]    There is evidence for instance that negative emotions are more prominent on WhatsApp than in other more public platforms (e.g., Facebook) (Waterloo et al., 2018).

convergence on a massive scale as Kramer et al. (2014) detected on Facebook.

Finally, SNSs make communication easy and near instantaneous (Baym & boyd, 2012). Because posting requires little effort, and sharing is even easier, contributing content on SNSs can be done on the impulse of the moment without giving it much thought. The speed of communication ensures that these contributions can reach other people almost instantaneously. In this way exchanges that would take some time face-to-face are accelerated so that they can be conducted over shorter time frames. The compression of the timeframe of conversation facilitates emotional engagement since one feels compelled to respond immediately to an immediate response. The speed of communication also partially disables some common strategies of intrinsic emotion regulation. For instance, we try to slow down and 'count to ten' to avoid giving expression to a negative emotion, we adopt similar delay strategies to dampen down the intensity of emotions. The speed of on-line communication makes it harder to deploy these strategies successfully. Given the role of intrinsic emotional regulation in promoting continence as the ability to resist urges that one does not endorse, this feature of SNSs constitutes another obstruction to the development of virtue.

The speed of online communication can potentially facilitate the escalation of angry exchanges, where anger is met with anger, that elicits more anger in response (Martin & Vieaux, 2015). It further contributes to the creation of emotional cascades (Alvarez et al., 2015). Whilst anger is generally a short-lived emotion, online communication could prolong its duration as instantaneous responses from others continually re-kindle the initial anger.

The speed and ease of communication on-line in addition to facilitating emotional engagements also encourages massive emotional convergence because it promotes emotional contagion at scale. Previously, mass emotional contagion was only possible when large crowds gathered. Whilst this phenomenon could already take place at concerts held in large stadia, sporting events, religious ceremonies and mass protests, it is potentially turned into an everyday and global occurrence by the speed of online communication. It is now possible for people located in different continents to experience simultaneously the same emotion triggered in part by one's knowledge that others feel in the same way as oneself. These events of mass emotional contagion have the potential to foster collective action across national boundaries and irrespective of location.

To summarise, SNSs are emotion technologies that call for emotional engagements, facilitate pro-social emotions, and promote emotional contagion at scale. Design features responsible for these properties of the platforms include reactions buttons that seduce users to respond emotionally and to adopt a limited emotional palette, the availability of both private and public channels of communication, and the speed and ease of on-line communication. Whilst these features are designed to promote positive emotions, they can also encourage anger by presenting it as a standing possible response, by partially disabling intrinsic emotion regulation, and by compressing the time frame of communicative exchanges.

## 3. Social identities, Group-based emotions and SNSs

Communication on-line also proceeds under conditions of relative anonymity. Users can, for instance, construct pseudonymous profiles. However, even when people's profiles feature information that identifies them, communication on some SNSs (but not others) mostly proceeds by text, emoticons, and pictures that do not often represent the users themselves. Hence, it is extremely rare to see a person's selfie on Twitter, Reddit, or Telegram. It is, however, more frequent on Facebook and positively ubiquitous on Instagram. When communication proceeds in contexts where the individuality of users is not prominent due, for example, to the absence of visual cues reminding one of the faces of each person with whom one is in dialogue, there is a tendency for users' social identities to become more salient, than their individuality. This phenomenon is known as the deindividuation effect (Spears & Postmes, 2015). It results in increased conformity with behaviours that are socially acceptable for members of one's social group. That is, it facilitates acting in accordance with stereotypes.

Deindividuation effects are partially responsible for the prevalence of pro-social emotions online. Since disruptive and negative behaviour is usually frowned upon, conformist users refrain from acting and expressing emotions that are generally disapproved. That said, the relative anonymity of users that makes them less individually identifiable by members of other social groups, also promotes behaviour that, whilst it is judged acceptable by members of one's own social group, is disapproved of by outsiders (Spears & Postmes, 2015). For example, if swearing is accepted by members of one's own social group but disapproved by others, the relative anonymity of the internet promotes an increase in sweary contributions by those whose group approves of swearing. Thus, although anonymity in computer-mediated communication increases conformity to social norms adopted by one's own social group, when norms might vary among groups, it also enables engaging in group-stereotypical behaviour that is disapproved by those outside of one's own group. Hence, anonymity should not be understood as primarily a cause of disinhibition and loss of accountability. To sum up, conformism promoted by anonymity is one of the reasons why the tone of communication on SNSs is usually positive. It can, however, be ugly and antagonistic if such behaviour is, on occasion, stereotypically acceptable for members of a given social group.

Either way, when computer-mediated communication occurs in the absence of prominent visual cues of a person's individuality it promotes self-categorisation as a member of some social group.[9] The increased salience of social group membership has important consequences on the nature of the emotional expressions which, as I have argued above, are ubiquitous online. More specifically, it promotes the experience of so-called group-based emotions. In turn, the prevalence of group-based emotions strengthens the tendency to self-categorise as group member but also to identify more strongly with the values, interests, and commitments of the group (Livingstone et al., 2011).[10]

Group-based emotions are emotions experienced by individuals as members of social groups. For example, the anger experienced by a woman because she is not taken seriously is an instance of group-based anger if it involves an evaluation of someone's actions as a slight that is inflicted upon her because of her gender identity. Hence, as in this example, group-based emotions can be experienced by individuals who are alone. What is distinctive of group-based anger is the evaluation that the perceived slight is inflicted upon one because of one's membership in a group, rather than because of individual characteristics of the person or of her situation (Goldenberg et al., 2020). Group-based emotions are capable of converging by means of emotional contagion. We would expect this phenomenon to be especially prevalent on those SNSs that facilitate emotional engagement whilst depriving users of cues of their individuality.

---

[9]   Or at least this is true of social identities that are not visible. It is at least possible that the absence of visual cues dampens, rather than enhances, the salience of identities such as gender or race that are tied to observable characteristics.

[10]   See Spears (2011) for the distinction between categorising oneself as member of a group and identifying with the group by investing one's membership with significance.

There is a two-way relationship between self-categorisation and self-identification as group member, and group-based emotions. Prior self-categorisation as member of a social group contributes to how we emotionally appraise situations. Conversely, the experience of a group-based emotion facilitates classifying oneself as members of a group, and investing that categorisation with importance, and thereby identifying oneself with the social group to which one belongs.

Anger, in particular, is triggered when one experiences the actions of some members of a different social group to have slighted the social group to which one belongs (Mackie et al., 2016; Mackie et al., 2004).[11] But the converse is also true. One might come to categorise oneself as a member of a subgroup upon realising that others who belong to the same social group as oneself and share some additional sub-group defining feature experience the same group-based anger as oneself (Livingstone et al., 2011).[12] For example, a person who categorises as a woman and is angry because of some disrespectful behaviour directed at women, upon discovering that other older women are also angry, if older might also be readier to categorise herself as an older woman than she was prior to knowingly share a group-based emotion with other older women.

In addition, group-based anger intensifies identification with salient social groups. That is, individuals who experience group-based anger because of the actions of members of outgroups, invest their own group membership with more significance so that it becomes a more important part of who they are (Kessler & Hollbach, 2005). But group-based emotions do not just promote self-categorisation and identification but also preparedness for collective activity (Livingstone et al., 2011; van Zomeren et al., 2004). In short, experiencing group-based emotions leads people to invest

---

[11]    Emotional responses are modulated by the social context. However, Mackie et al. (2016, p. 151) are mistaken in their claim that anger is experienced when the offending out-group is not powerful, and to suggest that fear is the response to a slight by a powerful outgroup. It is perfectly possible to experience both anger and fear at the same time. Being slighted by a powerful outgroup plausibly triggers both anger and fear.

[12]    The study was conducted with so called 'minimal groups'. These are made up groups that are created in the experiment. Livingstone et al. (2011) told participants who were all students that they were inductive reasoners. They then told these participants that other inductive reasoners were angry. As a result, angry participants were readier to classify themselves as inductive reasoners.

their group membership with more meaning, and thus to become more committed to act in defence of the interests of their group.

## 4. Hostile Identities, SNSs, and Anger

The two-way relationship between social identification and group-based emotions might be partially responsible for some forms of affective polarisation, where members of different social groups strongly dislike or even hate each other, irrespective of whether their disagreement are genuinely substantive (Hannon, 2021).[13] Group-based emotions such as anger are facilitated by the emotional tenor of SNSs and by deindividuation effects. These emotions in turn intensify the significance with which one invests one's social identity. The enhanced salience of social identity further promotes the experience of even more intense group-based emotions (Mackie et al., 2004). In addition, witnessing the group-based emotions of those with whom one identifies, especially when these emotions are intense, informs one's emotional appraisal of the situation leading to emotional contagion among those who self-categorise, and identify, as members of the same social groups. We should thus expect online environments to be places where some forms of emotional contagion spread among members of a social group but not across different social groups.

In the previous section I have argued that SNSs promote the adoption in users of a simplistic and Manichean emotional outlook where it is not possible for anger to be tinged by love or by sadness. This combines with those features that amplify social identification online and the intense group-based emotions that are often associated with it. We should expect that individuals caught in this dynamic to develop strong emotions, but we should also expect these emotions to be global emotions like hate or contempt.

Anger is not a global emotion. One may be angry at someone for something that they have done, and at the same time care for them because of something bad that has happened to them. Thus, anger has both a target (the person or persons with whom one is angry), and a focus (their action or feature that one appraises as deserving

---

[13]    Hence, affective polarisation is rather different from polarisation about belief which, in one of its many senses, occurs when people faced with the same evidence come to hold opposing views. The different mechanisms involved in these cases are discussed by Talisse (2019) and Shackel (2022).

to be met with anger). One can experience at the same time another emotion directed at the same target but with a different focus. Contempt is instead a global emotion because its focus is the whole person who is the target of the emotion (Bell, 2013). This emotion signals that the relationship is beyond repair. Because of its global character, it is not possible to experience both contempt and some positive emotion toward the same target at the same time.

The simplistic emotional outlook promoted by SNSs is one in which one cannot easily experience more than one emotion at same time about the same person. The consequent atrophy of emotional nuance, especially in the context of communication with virtual strangers, would seem to promote the experience of emotions that are global, such as contempt, or at least both extreme and without qualification. In short, the simplification of users' emotional palette, when combined with emotional contagion and strong social identification, is, I suspect, one important cause of affective polarisation on SNSs.

The argument so far has indicated that SNSs have features that promote emotional engagement, emotional contagion and increased social identification. I have noted that the overall emotional tenor of social media is positive but that there are several reasons why negative emotions, and especially anger, also thrive. First, anger is at least on Facebook one of the pre-selected standing reactions. Second, SNSs speed up communication making it hard to deploy successfully some forms of intrinsic emotion regulation standardly adopted to inhibit the expression of anger. Third, SNSs facilitate emotional contagion on a massive scale and thus the transmission and prolongation of anger once it emerges. Fourth, the relative anonymity of communication on some SNSs promotes social identification that facilitates group-based emotions. In turn, the experience of these emotions increases social identification which promotes the experience of even more intense group-based experiences. This phenomenon contributes to the segmentation of users into social groupings each of which is subject to emotional contagion. When this feature of SNSs communication is combined with its promotion of a Manichean emotional outlook, the separation of users into strongly emotive social groups provides fertile ground for affective polarisation where member of differing social groups develop a strong dislike for each other. Finally, the relative anonymity of online communication also facilitates stereotypical behaviour including behaviour that is frowned upon by society at large but is tacitly approved by members of one's given social group. In contemporary Western societies angry and hostile behaviour toward women is a

## Alessandra Tanesini

stereotypically acceptable expression of some forms of masculinity.[14] It is thus not a surprise that misogynistic angry messages proliferate online.[15]

There are two further design features of SNSs that play a significant role in making these platforms fertile grounds for the expression of anger: algorithm-driven personalisation and public broadcasting that is responsible for context collapse. The first of these two features has been the topic of intense study since it is usually singled out as among the most significant causes of filter bubbles online (Pariser, 2011). SNSs, such as Facebook, have proprietary algorithms which, based on a user's track record of responses such as likes, clicks and other engagements, select which posts appear in that user's news feed. Personalisation is described by Alfano et al. (2018) as a 'bottom-up' technological seduction. The technology learns from the user's past behaviour to serve them more of what they have previously engaged with. In this manner users are segmented into niches of like-minded individuals that primarily interact only with each other. This aspect of personalisation exacerbates homophily as the propensity to interact only with those with whom we agree that is a common human tendency but one that is made worse by anger (Song & Xu, 2019). Personalisation would thus make it more likely that users come across the angry posts of others with whose emotional appraisal they are likely to agree. That is, SNSs give access to content that these users would not otherwise have sight of, and which is likely to be anger-triggering for them, because it has been anger-triggering for others who are like them.

The second design feature of SNSs is their inclusion of channels for public broadcasting. I have mentioned this feature above when I contrasted it with direct messaging that allowed for more private expressions of negative emotions. There I highlighted the role of public broadcasting in enabling emotional contagion. Here I focus on another aspect of this design feature: context collapse (boyd, 2011). When users broadcast content using one of the SNSs public channels, their content potentially reaches multiple audiences and

[14] Such behaviour is a primary manifestation of misogyny understood as hostility directed at women.
[15] Overall, in the US at least, men are more likely to experience online threats and name-calling, but the harassment to which women are subjected tends to be more severe and have deeper effects (Pew Research Center, 2017). A study commissioned by Amnesty International revealed that online harassment has lasting impact on women in numerous countries (Amnesty International, 2017).

100

makes it impossible for one to tailor one's message to a specific audience. In face-to-face contexts, we would not convey the same information to close friends, mere acquaintances, parents and work colleagues.[16] Communications on SNSs facilitate the mashing up, or collapse, of these social contexts which we might wish to keep separate. One of the effects of this loss of the ability to tune one's message to one's audience is the increased likelihood of misunderstandings since messages reach people who do not know the messenger well (Frost-Arnold, 2021). Some of these misunderstandings might easily trigger angry responses.

Further, context collapse increases the risk of conscious or inadvertent violation of others' privacy. Partly because of its still relative novelty, users have not developed clear and firm conventions about sharing content and tagging pictures. Promiscuous sharing and tagging can make it easier for people to be targeted by malicious users, or have their content communicated to people whom they might have legitimately wished to keep in the dark (Frost-Arnold, 2021). In short, context collapse creates conditions that favour behaviour that might do speakers an injustice by violating their privacy and making them more vulnerable to harm. Since anger is the common response to these actions, context collapse creates conditions where anger triggering events are more likely.

It should now be clear that the character and distribution of anger on SNSs has many causes. It is inadvertently facilitated by many of those features of these platforms that are intended to facilitate social connections.[17] It is also parasitic on social norms that predate the SNSs and make some stereotypical aggressive behaviours acceptable for members of some social groups. Anger online therefore is partly continuous with the kinds of hostility, hate and social divisions that have often characterised Western societies, but it also exhibits novel features such as its ability to spread fast and at a massive scale, its disablement of intrinsic emotion regulation, and its formation because of top-down technological pre-selection. For these reasons, I

[16] Desmond (2022) might be thinking of the same phenomenon when he argues that messages broadcast on SNSs retain the feel of communications that are attuned to an audience despite being publicly communicated. He points out that different norms of trust govern private and public conversations, and that users online are especially vulnerable to having their trust betrayed.

[17] That said, a whistle-blower has recently alleged that Facebook has been aware of the divisive effects of some of these features and chosen to do nothing because anger keeps users engaged, and engagement brings advertising revenue (Whitwam, 2021).

**Alessandra Tanesini**

suspect, people who are reasonably thoughtful in their face-to-face encounters are more easily seduced into becoming on-line angry bullies.

## 5. Amelioration

My discussion has so far consciously avoided questions about the value of anger. In this final section, I address this issue before making a brief ameliorative suggestion to address some of the more problematic expressions of anger on-line.

It might be thought that anger and affective polarisation are always bad for democratic communities since angry and polarised individuals are unlikely to try to compromise with those they oppose. This conclusion is unwarranted. Perhaps, one should welcome the fact that SNSs have facilitated the expression of anger, at least in some cases. To see this, one first needs to realise that not all anger is the same. Sometimes anger is a fitting and proportionate response to slights and wrongs. On other occasions anger is not apt or fitting because it is a reaction that falsely appraises as a wrong or slight some action when it is not. In addition, showing fitting anger might at times be justified.[18] It might for instance be required by self-respect (Srinivasan, 2018). It might also be necessary to create an effective political community in the fight against grave social injustices (Cherry, 2021; Lepoutre, 2018). Hence, although anger can sometimes be misplaced, there are situations in which it is righteous and virtuous.

Perhaps, then, anger on social media should be welcome. The SNSs have offered an opportunity to the less powerful to voice their anger, and to resist oppression. SNSs' promotion of group-based anger and outrage might also have played some role in helping opponents of tyrannical regimes to create communities capable of collective action. These formations have not typically been very effective in achieving their goals (Tufekci, 2017). Nevertheless, the group-based emotions of members of these communities of resistance were often virtuous. Hence, one might wish to endorse the roles of SNSs in facilitating the expression and diffusion of anger as a way of giving a voice to the powerless and enabling the fight against injustice.

[18] See D'Arms and Jacobsen (2000) for the distinction between fittingness as accurate evaluation conveyed by the emotion and justification as moral propriety of experiencing the emotion.

That said, there are expressions of anger online that are clearly not fitting and are morally unjustifiable. Some of these, such as those involving misogynistic anger and hate directed at women online, are continuous with behaviour that can occur in face-to-face situations. These expressions are however exacerbated by the relative anonymity of some social media that promotes increased conformism to stereotypical behaviour. It is also true that SNSs facilitate misplaced anger because of its promotion of a Manichean emotional outlook. Hence, there is little doubt that this increase of anger on SNSs needs addressing. Whatever remedies one proposes, however, one should avoid having a silencing effect on the virtuous anger of those who struggle against inequality. One should also not lose sight of the fact that SNSs weaken intrinsic emotion regulation and thus obstruct a strategy frequently used to achieve continence. These platforms are somewhat addictive (Vaidhyanathan, 2018, chs. 1-2). They also have features that seduce us into adopting simplistic and distorted emotional outlooks. These considerations suggest that interventions aimed at individuals' characters requiring them to become more responsible, while valuable, might be of limited efficacy, and must be supplemented with measures that target the design features of the platforms themselves. These measures are likely to make SNSs less successful at establishing and maintaining social connections, and thus ultimately at generating advertising revenue. They are thus unlikely to be implemented without external intervention in the shape of regulation.

Nevertheless, some small interventions could, for instance, have a positive impact on Facebook's tendency to promote a simplistic emotional outlook without making it less successful as a platform that promotes social connections. I have already argued above that Facebook's reaction buttons are a form of top-down technological seduction that erodes users' ability to experience emotional complexity and ambiguity. Their introduction in 2016 is in my view a retrograde step. To understand why, one needs to be clear about the functions served by the original 'like' button and the reasons why users asked for more options.

In face-to-face encounters there is some conversational pressure not to ignore speakers when they address us.[19] In ordinary circumstances it is simply rude not to nod or respond when someone attempts to engage us in conversation. Some of that pressure survives, even though in a reduced form, on SNSs where users seek

---

[19] On this underexplored aspect of the norms of conversation see part one of Goldberg's (2020).

others' acknowledgement of their posts, whilst their friends feel a sense of obligation to respond especially if the content of the post is important. However, given the vast number of posts users shift through, they need a way to signal quickly that they have paid attention. Facebook's 'like' button served this function (Sumner et al., 2017). It would have served it better, if the term 'like' had not also potentially conveyed an endorsement of the content of the post. It is this implication that made its use awkward when the original post conveyed bad news or described an injustice. For this reason, users asked for a broader range of pre-selected emotional responses. But, as I argued above, this modification promotes emotional outlooks that should be resisted because it makes users less able to experience complex and ambiguous emotions even when they are the responses that fit the situation. This problem can be avoided if the reaction buttons are eliminated in favour of a single differently named button whose exclusive function is to convey that one has paid attention. It would be the Facebook equivalent of a head nod.[20]

Admittedly, my practical proposal concerns only one platform. However, I submit that other similar suggestions can be developed each tailored to the different features of SNSs. These engineering solutions would not on their own solve the problems of affective polarisation, inappropriate anger, and hostility online. They would, however, succeed in transforming social media platforms into environments that are less hostile to virtuous communication, including virtuously angry messages.[21]

*Cardiff University*
*tanesini@cardiff.ac.uk*

[20] This approach is to be preferred to the proliferation of response buttons that are not considered as mutually exclusive. Since reactions to posts need to be quick, the number of options for users must be limited to avoid trawling through endless possibilities. Hence, even if a broader range of emotions are enabled by additional buttons, users are still forced into the adoption of a limited palette of emotional responses.

[21] Thanks to Jon Webber and Orestis Palermos for their helpful comments.

## References

M. Alfano, J. A. Carter, & M. Cheong, 'Technological Seduction and Self-Radicalization', *Journal of the American Philosophical Association*, 4 (2018), 298–322.

R. Alvarez, D. Garcia, Y. Moreno, & F. Schweitzer, 'Sentiment cascades in the 15M movement', *EPJ Data Science*, 4 (2015).

Amnesty International, 'Amnesty reveals alarming impact of online abuse against women' (2017, 20 November). Retrieved from https://www.amnesty.org/en/latest/news/2017/11/amnesty-reveals-alarming-impact-of-online-abuse-against-women/

N. K. Baym & d boyd, 'Socially Mediated Publicness: An Introduction', *Journal of Broadcasting & Electronic Media*, 56 (2012), 320–329.

N. N. Bazarova, Y. H. Choi, V. Schwanda Sosik, D. Cosley & J. Whitlock, 'Social Sharing of Emotions on Facebook', Paper presented at the *Proceedings of the 18th ACM Conference on Computer Supported Cooperative Work & Social Computing - CSCW '15*, (Vancouver, BC, 2015).

T. M. Bejan, *Mere civility: disagreement and the limits of toleration*, (Cambridge, Massachusetts: Harvard University Press, 2017).

M. Bell, *Hard Feelings: The Moral Psychology of Contempt*, (New York: Oxford University Press, 2013).

d. boyd, 'Social Network Sites as Networked Publics: Affordances, Dynamics, and Implication', In Z. Papacharissi (Ed.), *A networked self: identity, community and culture on social network sites* (New York: Routledge, 2011) 39–58.

M. Bruder, A. Fischer & A. S. R. Manstead, 'Social appraisal as a cause of collective emotions'. In C. v. Scheve & M. Salmella (Eds.), *Collective emotions: perspectives from psychology, philosophy, and sociology* (OUP, 2014) 142–155.

M. Cherry, *The Case for Rage: Why Anger Is Essential to Anti-Racist Struggle*, (New York: Oxford University Press, 2021).

A. Chmiel, J. Sienkiewicz, M. Thelwall, G. Paltoglou, K. Buckley, A. Kappas & J. A. Holyst, 'Collective emotions online and their influence on community life', *PLoS ONE*, 6 (2011), e22207.

G. Colombetti & J. Krueger, 'Scaffoldings of the affective mind' *Philosophical Psychology*, 28 (2015), 1157–1176.

J. D'Arms & D. Jacobsen, 'The Moralistic Fallacy: On the 'Appropriateness' of Emotions', *Philosophy and Phenomenological Research*, 61 (2000), 65–90.

H. Desmond, 'Reclaiming Privacy and Care in the Age of Social Media', *Royal Institute Philosophy Supplementary Volume*, 92 (2022) 45–66.

B. Duffy, K. Hewlett, G. Murkin, R. Benson, R. Hesketh, B. Page, G. Gottfried,. *'Culture wars' in the UK* (2021). Retrieved from https://www.kcl.ac.uk/policy-institute/assets/culture-wars-in-the-uk.pdf

R. Fan, K. Xu, & J. Zhao, 'Weak ties strengthen anger contagion in social media' (2020) *arXiv:2005.01924 [cs.SI]*. Retrieved from https://arxiv.org/abs/2005.01924

K. Frost-Arnold, 'The Epistemic Dangers of Context Collapse Online'. In J. Lackey (Ed.), *Applied epistemology* (New York: Oxford University Press, 2021) 437–456.

S.C. Goldberg, *Conversational Pressure*, (Oxford: Oxford University Press, 2020).

A. Goldenberg, D. Garcia, E. Halperin, & J. J. Gross, 'Collective Emotions', *Current Directions in Psychological Science*, 29 (2020), 154–160.

J. J. Gross, 'Emotion Regulation: Current Status and Future Prospects', *Psychological Inquiry*, 26 (2015), 1–26.

M. Hannon, 'Political Disagreement or Partisan Badmouthing? The Role of Expressive Discourse in Politics'. In E. Edenberg & M. Hannon (Eds.), *Political Epistemology* (Oxford: Oxford University Press, 2021) 306–329.

E. Jakobs, A. S. R. Manstead & A. H. Fischer, 'Social context effects on facial activity in a negative emotional setting', *Emotion*, 1 (2001), 51–69.

T. Kessler & S. Hollbach, 'Group-based emotions as determinants of ingroup identification', *Journal of Experimental Social Psychology*, 41 (2005), 677–685.

A. D. I. Kramer, J. E. Guillory & J. T. Hancock, 'Experimental evidence of massive-scale emotional contagion through social networks', *Proceedings of the National Academy of Sciences of the United States of America*, 111 (2014), 10779.

J. Krueger, 'Emotions and the Social Niche'. In C. v. Scheve & M. Salmella (Eds.), *Collective emotions: perspectives from psychology, philosophy, and sociology* (Oxford: Oxford University Press, 2014) 156–171.

J. Krueger, 'Music as affective scaffolding'. In R. Herbert, D. Clarke, & E. Clarke (Eds.), *Music and Consciousness 2: Worlds, Practices, Modalities* (Oxford: Oxford University Press, 2019) 55–70.

J. Krueger & L. Osler, 'Engineering affect: emotion regulation, the internet, and the techno-social niche', *Philosophical Topics*, 47 (2019), 205–232.

M. Lepoutre, 'Rage inside the machine', *Politics, Philosophy & Economics*, 17 (2018), 398–426.

A. G. Livingstone, R. Spears, A. S. R. Manstead, M. Bruder & L. Shepherd 'We feel, therefore we are: emotion as a basis for self-categorization and social action'. *Emotion*, 11 (2011), 754–767.

I. v. d. Löwe & B. Parkinson, 'Relational emotions and social networks'. In C. v. Scheve & M. Salmella (Eds.), *Collective emotions: perspectives from psychology, philosophy, and sociology* (Oxford: Oxford University Press, 2014) 125–140.

D. M. Mackie, A. T. Maitner & E. R. Smith, 'Intergroup emotions theory'. In T. D. Nelson (Ed.), *Handbook of prejudice, stereotyping, and discrimination, 2nd ed.* (New York: Psychology Press, 2016) 149–174.

D. M. Mackie, L. A. Silver & E. R. Smith, 'Intergroup Emotions: Emotion as an Intergroup Phenomenon'. In L. Z. Tiedens & C. W. Leach (Eds.), *The social life of emotions* (New York: Cambridge University Press, 2004) 227–245.

C. Macnamara, 'Reactive Attitudes as Communicative Entities', *Philosophy and Phenomenological Research*, 90 (2015), 546–569.

R. C. Martin & L. E. Vieaux, 'The Digital Rage: How Anger is Expressed Online'. In G. Riva, B. K. Wiederhold, & P. Cipresso (Eds.), *The psychology of social networking* (Berlin and Boston: De Gruyter, 2015) 117–127.

C. T. Nguyen, 'How Twitter gamifies communication'. In J. Lackey (Ed.), *Applied Epistemology*. (New York: Oxford University Press, 2021) 410–436.

Z. Papachrissi, *Affective Publics: Sentiment, Technology and Politics* (Oxford: Oxford University Press, 2015).

E. Pariser, *The filter bubble: what the Internet is hiding from you* (New York: Penguin Press, 2011).

B. Parkinson, A. H. Fischer & A. S. R. Manstead, *Emotion in Social Relations: Cultural, Group, and Interpersonal Processes*, (New York and Hove: Psychology Press, 2005).

Pew Research Center. (2017). *Online Harassment*. Retrieved from Washington, D.C.: https://www.pewresearch.org/internet/2017/07/11/online-harassment-2017/

B. Rimé, 'Emotion Elicits the Social Sharing of Emotion: Theory and Empirical Review', *Emotion Review*, 1 (2009), 60–85.

N. Shackel, 'Uncertainty Phobia and Epistemic Forbearance in a Pandemic', *Royal Institute Philosophy Supplementary Volume*, 92 (2022) 271–91.

Y. Song & R. Xu 'Affective Ties That Bind: Investigating the Affordances of Social Networking Sites for Commemoration of Traumatic Events', *Social Science Computer Review*, 37 (2019), 333–354.

R. Spears, 'Group Identities: The Social Identity Perspective'. In S. J. Schwartz, K. Luyckx, & V. L. Vignoles (Eds.), *Handbook of identity theory and research*, (New York: Springer Science+Business Media, 2011) 201–224.

R. Spears & T. Postmes, 'Group Identity, Social Influence, and Collective Action Online: Extensions and Applications of the SIDE Model'. In S. S. Sundar (Ed.), *The Handbook of the Psychology of Communication Technology* (Malden and Oxford: Wiley Blackwell, 2015) 23–46.

A. Srinivasan, 'The Aptness of Anger', *Journal of Political Philosophy*, 26 (2018), 123–144.

K. Sterelny, 'Minds: extended or scaffolded?' *Phenomenology and the Cognitive Sciences*, 9 (2010), 465–481.

E. M. Sumner, L. Ruge-Jones & D. Alcorn, 'A functional approach to the Facebook Like button: An exploration of meaning, interpersonal functionality, and potential alternative response buttons', *New Media & Society*, 20 (2017), 1451–1469.

R. B. Talisse, 'The Problem of Polarization'. In *Overdoing Democracy* (New York: Oxford University Press, 2019) 95–128.

Z. Tufekci, *Twitter and tear gas: the power and fragility of networked protest,* (New Haven; London: Yale University Press, 2017).

S. Vaidhyanathan, *Antisocial media: how facebook disconnects US and undermines democracy*, (New York: Oxford University Press, 2018).

S. Vallor, *Technologies and the Virtues: A Philosophical Guide to a Future Worth Wanting,* (New York: Oxford University Press, 2016).

M. van Zomeren, R. Spears, A. H. Fischer & C. W. Leach, 'Put your money where your mouth is! Explaining collective action tendencies through group-based anger and group efficacy' *Journal of Personality and Social Psychology*, 87 (2004), 649–664.

S. F. Waterloo, S. E. Baumgartner, J. Peter & P. M. Valkenburg, 'Norms of online expressions of emotion: Comparing Facebook, Twitter, Instagram, and WhatsApp'. *New Media & Society*, 20 (2018), 1813–1831.

R. Whitwam, 'Whistleblower: Facebook Is Designed to Make You Angry' (2021). Retrieved from https://www.extremetech.com/

internet/327855-whistleblower-facebook-is-designed-to-make-you-angry

D. Wollebæk, R. Karlsen, K. Steen-Johnsen & B. Enjolras, 'Anger, Fear, and Echo Chambers: The Emotional Basis for Online Behavior', *Social Media + Society*, 5 (2019), 1–14.

M. Ziegele & L. Reinecke, 'No place for negative emotions? The effects of message valence, communication channel, and social distance on users' willingness to respond to SNS status updates'. *Computers in Human Behavior*, 75 (2017) 704–713.

F. Zollo, P. K. Novak, M. Del Vicario, A. Bessi, I. Mozetic, A. Scala, W. Quattrociocchi, 'Emotional Dynamics in the Age of Misinformation', *PLoS ONE*, 10 (2015), e0138740.

# Self-Regulation and Political Confabulation

KATHLEEN MURPHY-HOLLIES

**Abstract**

In this paper, I discuss the nature and consequences of confabulation about political opinions and behaviours. When people confabulate, they give reasons for their choices or behaviour which are ill-grounded and do not capture what really brought the behaviour about, but they do this with no intention to deceive and endorse their own accounts. I suggest that this can happen when people are asked why they voted a certain way, or support certain campaigns, and so on. Confabulating in these political contexts seems bad because we do not get a fully truthful account of why some political choice was made, and so the reasoning behind the choice is under-scrutinised. However, I argue that if people have a virtue of self-regulation, confabulation in political contexts can actually be part of the process of coming to better understand our political choices and embody more consistently the political values which we ascribe to.

When individuals make political decisions, such as voting for certain parties or supporting certain campaigns, they often give and receive explanations for why they are inclined to choose or behave in that way. Others who hear those explanations can find them implausible, unsatisfying and even frustrating. Imagine a woman who decides to vote for the UK to leave the European Union. When her peers ask her why she decided to vote in that way, she says that she doesn't like the power and influence from Europe in the UK and that it costs the UK too much money to be in the European Union. However, her peers are surprised to hear this because she did not seem to have paid any attention at all to these things before casting her vote. They suspect that other things, such as a sense of national pride, might have had a more powerful sway on her coming to vote for Brexit.

Explanations which are unsatisfying in this way may be frustrating because they are confabulations. When individuals confabulate, they don't track what has really brought about their decisions and actions, and they get something wrong about the world. Sometimes this means that harmful and irrational political decisions do not receive the scrutiny they deserve, from the individual giving the explanation or from others who receive it.

doi:10.1017/S1358246122000170

# Kathleen Murphy-Hollies

Individuals confabulate in many different contexts, whether it be consumer choice, moral convictions, or aesthetic preferences (Nisbett & Wilson, 1977; Hall et al, 2010; Haidt, 2001; Wilson et al, 1993). After elaborating on what confabulation is, in this essay I will explore confabulation in the context of politically charged decisions and behaviours, which have the potential to significantly affect the lives of many other people. Confabulations also often reflect self-concepts (i.e., traits and values which individuals ascribe to themselves) and identities (the type of person they see themselves overall as being).

It seems that confabulation is something we should try to avoid in political decision-making, but despite the problems it can cause, I will argue that confabulation can be an integral part of individuals coming to scrutinize their political actions further and make relevant changes to either their outlook or their political decision-making. Specifically, I suggest people will need the virtue of 'self-regulation' to do so. Exercising this virtue results in good management of the self, such that there is a good alignment between the descriptions someone gives of themselves and the reality of their behaviour. The virtue of self-regulation will consist in various attitudes such as being open-minded, curious, and receptive to the ideas of others about oneself.[1] With these attitudes in place, even confabulatory justifications of harmful behaviour can be conducive to the formation of behaviour which better aligns with values, in the long run. Both confabulation, recognised as a form of epistemic engagement and curiosity, and the virtue of self-regulation, as something which enables individuals to embody their professed values, can therefore be valuable.

I will focus on explanations which people gave for voting for significant political change, such as in voting for Brexit, or for Donald Trump, or in campaigning against lockdown restrictions during the Coronavirus pandemic.[2] I am interested in how confabulatory explanations made references to highly valued political ideals in order to justify

---

[1]  The attitudes which I outline as contributing to the virtue of self-regulation draw on ideas by DeBruin and Strijbos (2019) about attitudes which make up what they term 'self-know-how'; a skillset which enables individuals to preserve first person authority of their self-ascriptions despite confabulation.

[2]  Elsewhere, Lisa Bortolotti and I (2022) argue that justifications of certain behaviours during the global Covid-19 pandemic – particularly of behaviours which flouted the rules – were confabulatory and referred to distinctly political themes.

choices and behaviour. However, in these cases of confabulation, the explanations mask that the actions do not actually reflect and embody the values they refer to. This is not good for the agent, and if the value is a positive one, any harm incurred by not actually embodying the positive value can harm others and this harm is hidden. For example, in being mistaken about an action of theirs truly embodying compassion, that individual may inadvertently harm others.

## 1. What is confabulation?

Given how widely prevalent confabulation is, it is important to consider what influence it could be having in political contexts which are so often pressed with moral concern and expressions of one's identity. Confabulation has raised questions about the possibility and reliability of self-knowledge, and whether agents really are in any better a position to know their own mental states precisely because they are their own (Scaife, 2014). However, I think that the occurrence of confabulation highlights underlying features and motivations of how and why individuals give reasons for their behaviour, which are not necessarily bad. This will become clearer throughout my paper.

Confabulation was originally studied in the context of psychiatric disorders, where it is often seen as a component of a number of conditions such as Alzheimer's, Anosognosia, or Korsakoff's syndrome (Hirstein, 2005). However, I am focusing on less severe instances of confabulation which occur in everyday situations with healthy individuals. When people are asked why they have some belief or why they have behaved a certain way, they may confabulate if they do not actually have an accurate answer (Sullivan-Bissett, 2015, p. 552). This is the crux and mystery of confabulation; instead of their attention being drawn to their lack of explanation, individuals produce an explanation which they do sincerely believe. However, these explanations are 'ill-grounded' (Bortolotti, 2018, p. 237). This means that their answers are not based on the relevant evidence and fail to capture what actually brought that behaviour about. Their answers often include false statements about the world.

Crucially, confabulators do not realise that their confabulations are ill-grounded in this way, and that they can't be giving an accurate account of why they came to behave in the way that they did. There's no intention to deceive, as they fully endorse the account they put forward, thinking that it is the truth. This is partly because they do not have access to, or don't know of, more accurate explanations of their behaviour (Bortolotti, 2020, p. 15). This might be because some cognitive processes operate at the sub-conscious level and then individuals cannot know through introspection about the source of, for example, their intuitions or gut feelings, or of subtle external influences on their thinking and behaviour. This is the kind of 'gap' which can be filled with confabulation.

For example, in one study, participants read a vignette about a brother and sister who decide to sleep together, and are then asked to give reasons why the act was morally right or wrong (Haidt, 2001). Participants often gave reasons that cited factors which the vignette made clear did not apply; the siblings used contraception and their relationship was not affected, and so concerns about pregnancy and damage to the relationship were not applicable and could not have driven the moral judgement. When participants are reminded that these concerns do not apply, they continue to believe that the act was wrong nevertheless and are uncomfortably 'dumbfounded' as to why. Haidt suggests that these reasons were produced post-hoc, after a strong initial gut feeling of moral disgust. This disgust is what actually drove their decision, rather than the moral reasoning offered (ibid, p. 815).

Why do people do this? There are various possible motivations. Individuals do not want to be without an answer, unable to explain themselves and embarrassingly dumbfounded (Sullivan-Bissett, 2015, p. 552). But more generally, individuals want to provide an explanation which, although it may not be strictly accurate, meets other needs for them. They are motivated by the need to have a causal understanding of themselves and the circumstances they are in (Coltheart, 2017). They want to signal to other people that they are rational, competent, and trustworthy, (Ganapini, 2020) and so they are motivated to provide explanations which present themselves positively and protect positive self-concepts (Sullivan-Bissett, 2015, p. 552). Other, perhaps more accurate explanations such as 'I just felt like it' or 'I did it at random' put them at risk of looking foolish or unkind. So, individuals want to provide explanations which paint good pictures of themselves.

Confabulations can serve as explanations and justifications, and they often take a narrative form. These things have powerful benefits for people; weaving experiences and behaviour into a sense-making story or narrative helps people understand them and give them meaning (Örulv and Hydén, 2006). And then, these narratives facilitate social communication and the sharing of themes and values which are important to them (Stammers, 2018). Individuals might be particularly keen to fulfil these needs when it comes to moral issues, as is seen in Haidt's study. Individuals feel strongly about these topics and want other people to know that they are good, trustworthy, and share the same values.

Overall, I suggest that we can characterise something as confabulation if the explanation has the following features:

(1) It is produced post-hoc and the reasons given are not the ones which truly led the individual to act in that way.

(2) It is a false or ill-grounded explanation, in that it says something false about the outside world or, in some circumstances, is technically correct but only by chance.

(3) It is motivated in the ways discussed above; to paint a certain picture of the agent, and/or to create and communicate what is meaningful to them.

## 2. Politically charged confabulation.

I suggest that individuals will have a tendency to confabulate in explaining and justifying politically charged decisions and behaviours. Our political views can be close to our hearts, forming significant parts of our identities and relating closely to our moral views. Political choices affect not only ourselves and the people around us, but how we are represented on a global stage and work alongside other global bodies and powers. This motivates giving explanations, particularly ones that make us look rational and good, even if they do not accurately reflect the facts of the matter.

A number of tumultuous events recently have brought this out. Britain unexpectedly voted to leave the European Union in 2016, Donald Trump was controversially elected president of the USA in the same year, and in 2020 world governments had to navigate a global pandemic owing to the Covid-19 virus. Each of these events brought our moral convictions to the surface, as the consequences were highly significant for huge numbers of people. Individuals were keen to be able to justify their own decisions and to demand explanations from others for their choices. All these events were also plagued with issues of 'fake news' and 'alternative facts' being circulated, causing confusion, and making it difficult to know the facts of the matter. Sometimes this could provide more convenient versions of the 'truth'.

Return to the example of the woman explaining her decision to vote for Brexit, whose statements are found unconvincing. Perhaps the woman in question is generally quite patriotic, feeling particularly proud and protective of her country and its values. She is therefore drawn to the idea of Brexit through gut feeling, but she is not fully aware of the source of this inclination. After she votes for Brexit, she is asked by her friends why she did so. She doesn't want to seem politically ignorant or to have made such an important political decision flippantly, so she thinks about all the campaigning she saw for Vote Leave even though she didn't actually pay much attention to it before now. She recites that voting leave secures freedom from European lawmakers, means that the UK will keep more money, and will curb rates of immigration. She is confident that these are the reasons why she voted for Brexit.

I suggest that this kind of response is confabulatory; the reasons she gives for voting for Brexit never particularly crossed her mind in the run up to voting to leave, so the explanation is post-hoc. Her answer doesn't capture that her patriotic gut feelings and negative intuitions about European influence were factors in her coming to vote for Brexit, and so has feature (1) from the previous section.

We can see this kind of mechanism at play in considering the controversial case of extensive targeted advertising being used to show pro-Brexit advertisements to millions of people on facebook (BBC 2018). This could have had a significant impact on people's choices and the outcome of the referendum, yet this influence likely stemmed from merely an increased sense of familiarity with basic pro-Brexit sentiments and values. This could have contributed to, for example, our imagined voter's unexamined nationalistic gut feelings. But importantly, this is not a carefully considered change in decision-making. It is unlikely that the individuals would have endorsed this intervention on their decision-making, and agents are more likely to produce confabulatory explanations such as the one our voter gives, than acknowledge the role of persistent advertising on their decision. In overlooking the influence of these more basic feelings of familiarity and intuition in explanations, and instead citing more complex political and economic reasons for their decisions, confabulators are wrong about the psychological processes which led to their decisions.

The explanation also has feature (2); the explanation makes demonstrably false statements about the world. Specifically, her answer draws on false statements about the reality and scale of immigration. Rates of immigration are widely misconceived in the UK, with people guessing that the proportion of immigrants in the population is twice as high as it actually is (Ipsos Mori, 2014). Her answer also draws on false statements about how much money the UK sends to the EU, how it is spent, and how it may in fact be received back, facts that were difficult to ascertain even for experts. Yet, our

Brexit voter doesn't convey this in her simple assertion that the UK 'pays too much money' to the EU. It is also false to say that she paid considerable attention to these political and economic factors, deliberating about them *before* coming to make her choice. It is important to note that these are not incorrect beliefs which she acts on; she acts on her nationalistic intuition and draws on these mistaken beliefs in her confabulation because they make her decision seem more rational and acceptable.

I have used an example of voting for Brexit because it is an example of a politically charged explanation which is likely to have particularly high pressures to preserve positive self-concepts, as described in feature (3). This is because, akin to going against government-mandated lockdown regulations and voting for Trump, these were political behaviours which aroused particularly strong reactions and were votes for substantial change rather than for keeping more established political arrangements. Therefore, our voter is subject to particularly stark pressures to provide an explanation which justifies (in her eyes) her actions, meeting feature (3). She produced this explanation for her choice because she wanted to be able to share and communicate her values relating to Britain and Brexit with her friends when they asked, and not to seem uneducated on the issue or that she didn't actually have a particularly firm reason for voting as she did. One way that she makes her decision particularly acceptable and appealing to others is by drawing on a valued cultural ideal. Specifically, the value of freedom, particularly from European influence and law-making, was one such valued cultural ideal which she drew on and ascribed to herself. Anti-lockdown movements and marking the end of lockdown as 'freedom day' similarly drew on the same value, and so confabulatory explanations for rejecting measures to contain Covid-19 could work in the same way, emphasising a cultural and personal value for the individual at the expense of acknowledging scientific data and expert opinion on the spread of coronavirus.

This is not to say that explanations for voting in other directions (for Remain, for the Democrats etc.) could not also draw on rousing personal and political values which might not be strictly relevant, as nearly all political decision-making will bring pressures to confabulate. But the cases of Brexit and rejecting lockdown also provide a clear example of drawing on similar political values. For instance, the day the UK left the European Union (31 January 2020) and the final day of UK lockdown (19 July 2021) were both heralded as 'Freedom Day' (Duffield, 2021; Honeycombe-Foster, 2019). The political ideal of freedom is highly valued in the UK, and so it is powerful in glossing these political choices with some good-looking purpose.

## 3. Harms and costs of confabulation.

We are now in the position where an imperfect, confabulatory explanation has been offered, and the individual seems worse off for it. She is unaware of not having had a particularly well-formed reason for her decision and does not seem to be prompted to check whether her conceptions about, for example, immigration, are accurate.

The first type of concern relates to feature (1) of confabulations, when agents are wrong about the reasons they acted in some way and sometimes falsely posit certain psychological processes as being behind a decision. One reason we might care about agents 'filling in this gap' with an inaccurate explanation is that highly valued ideals get mis-applied, with consequences for others. For example, the decision to call the final day of the UK lockdown 'freedom day' was criticised for being directly at odds with the reality of the situation for many. For example, vulnerable individuals and young people who were not able to be vaccinated had to give up many freedoms in order to shield, and precipitating a fourth lockdown would reduce freedoms, and finally overloading the NHS to the point of barely functioning reduces freedoms (Ahuja, 2021).

It can sometimes seem that an individual's political choices bring about states of affairs which do not necessarily reflect that value very much. But, in their confabulations individuals draw on these highly valued political ideals and nevertheless ascribe them to themselves because it justifies the behaviour for them and satisfies other motivations in play described in feature (3); to have an explanation and understanding of one's decisions. We would want requests to explain and justify these decisions to be met with earnest thought and scrutiny, but this seems to be lost when a confabulation is offered instead. This fits the behaviour into a story that justifies it, protecting the reputation and self-concepts of the individual, and even imbuing it with a noble personal and political value.

A second type of concern arising from confabulation relates to feature (2) of confabulations; making ill-grounded claims. In drawing on false statements about the world, by fitting these false statements into narratives which make the decision more acceptable and rational, confabulation discourages the agent from thinking further about the possible falsity of those claims. Inaccurate claims about the nature of coronavirus put other people's health and lives at risk, as well as the wider project of containing the virus. Yet these false claims will be reinforced for a person if they are propping up a confabulatory explanation which holds meaning for them.

## 4. The role of confabulation in self-regulation.

So far, I have described what confabulation in political contexts looks like and why we might not welcome it. In the rest of this essay I will argue that political confabulation can be beneficial alongside a virtue of self-regulation.

I have already touched upon some of the motivations which underlie confabulation; people want to have an understanding, to display certain concepts of themselves, to construct meaningful narratives of their experiences, and to communicate them with others. These are very worthwhile endeavours which bring great benefits to people. Not only is it psychologically valuable to be able to organise our experiences into a coherent story which makes sense, but individuals can use these crafted personal identities and senses of themselves to actually guide their future behaviours, making them a reality (Velleman, 2006). Bortolotti suggests that confabulation can even mean that in the long-run, agents end up with *more* accurate beliefs about themselves and the world. This is because in giving reasons, even though they may not be accurate, their sense of agency is emboldened, their self-concepts are enhanced, and they engage with peers (2018, pp. 239–40). This 'active engagement with the world is also an epistemic goal' (2018, p. 241). Agents can receive feedback from others on their explanations and begin to think more explicitly about their behaviour and what is driving it. So, there is not anything distinctly bad about the motivations which individuals have for confabulating. They are primarily for understanding, for meaningfulness, and for connectedness with others.

However, there seem to be frustrating cases of confabulation in which someone re-casts themselves and the situation again and again in a way which preserves their good self-image, even when it's not deserved. In these kinds of cases, a good picture of the person continues, whilst the harmful and misguided reality of their behaviour continues too. There's an uncomfortable gap between what they *do* and what they *say*. Ideally, we want people to be able to bridge this gap; to give more accurate explanations of what is driving their behaviour, or for their behaviour to more reliably and consistently reflect an appreciation and adherence to these values. If every time someone is confronted for not wearing a mask they passionately espouse the value of personal freedom, they might only become more entrenched into that narrative despite the fact that they actually just couldn't be bothered to wear a mask and are indirectly curbing the personal freedoms of others.

So, while this is far from guaranteed, confabulation has the potential to impress valued self-concepts more explicitly into one's own mind and guide future behaviour to reflect those concepts and values.

## 5. The virtue of self-regulation.

The virtue of self-regulation will function like Cathy Mason's virtue of hope as described in this collection; as a structural virtue (2022). That is, rather than being directly related to a motivation for perceiving and responding correctly to certain values in the world, self-regulation is a valuable form of self-government which is called for in certain kinds of situations.

The situations which will call for the virtue of self-regulation are ones in which someone faces a possible inconsistency between their self-ascriptions and their behaviour, which is likely to happen when someone confabulates. Self-regulation is the matter of being able to effectively re-align these inconsistencies.[3] I suggest that someone with the virtue of self-regulation will be: open-minded about what may in fact be influencing their behaviour which is not being captured in confabulatory justifications; will be curious and attentive towards their own feelings, motivations and what may be causing them; will be receptive to the feedback received from others on the accuracy of their self-ascriptions, and will have the right amount of confidence in self-ascriptions such that they are not defended even in the face of compelling evidence to the contrary but neither do they crumble under the slightest pressure.

These attitudes are complex in that they equip the individual with the disposition to behave in the relevant ways when required (for

---

[3] Leon DeBruin and Derek Strijbos (2019) suggest that in order to close this gap, it helps if people have certain self-directed attitudes that make up a sort of skilful 'know-how' (as opposed to propositional knowledge of self-related facts). I also draw on their idea that how one goes about closing the gap is more important (and what we value more in others) than the gap itself, whether this be a large gap, as in cases of people with poor self-regulation, or a very small gap. They even describe *perfect* alignment as possibly indicating psychological, neurocognitive or personality vulnerabilities and an obsession with rigidity (p. 159).

example, actually changing one's mind when one encounters new evidence) and could be described as virtuous given that they reflect the virtue of self-regulation. They give the agent a mastery in managing their own behaviour given that it is in fact *their own* behaviour. Individuals do not simply 'read off' what their traits are from observing their own behaviour. Instead, in this process, they play an active role in shaping and negotiating their own behaviour and self-ascriptions.[4] Ideally, we want to be able to describe ourselves accurately but also live up to our own descriptions. This will involve dealing well with discrepancies between the two when they arise by adjusting either the ascriptions or the behaviour.

As with many virtues, the virtue of self-regulation will be subject to ideally operating within a 'golden mean'. Someone with a deficiency in courage might avoid dangers, or minimize and misrepresent dangers, and an excess of courage might lead someone to be reckless or to seek out confrontations. Similarly, a number of different attitudes and behaviours may come out of an excess or deficiency of self-regulation. In excess, individuals will be too preoccupied with the alignment of their self-ascriptions and behaviour to ever try anything slightly new, spontaneous, or 'out of character' for them. They would stringently avoid any self-ascriptions which could possibly be a little wishful or incorporate aspects of their idealised selves, which means that they lose the opportunity to regulate themselves 'up' to this desired self-image (as is suggested and described in Jefferson 2020). In deficiency, individuals live in a state of fantasy that they are already whatever person they perceive themselves to be, just in virtue of perceiving or desiring that they are that way. This could be completely at odds with reality. They will have no open-mindedness, no curiosity, and be utterly dismissive of the views and ideas of others with regards to their self-ascriptions and behaviour. Moreover, even in the right quantity, self-regulation could allow its possessor to be, for example, consistently unkind, impatient, or, in the political realm, fascistic. So, the virtue of self-regulation will also be subject to proper exercise in accordance with a more general ethical wisdom, or phronesis.

Finally, self-regulation also works as a corrective in Philippa Foot's sense (2002). That is, it prevents individuals from falling into the temptation of simply believing that they in fact are the type of person they admire and wish to be, simply because of their appreciation for that type of person. Generally, the appeal of being a good,

---

[4] For more on this 'regulative' dimension of self-knowledge, see McGreer (2015).

competent person is not difficult to find in people. The harder work of ensuring that they live up to such an image, avoiding the lures of self-deception and looking the other way when they do not live up to their ideals, is what takes some correcting.

In instances of political confabulation, individuals espouse certain political values and ascribe them to themselves. Then, if someone has the virtue of self-regulation, they are able to make the most of those self-ascriptions by more effectively and consistently embodying those values in their future decision-making and behaviour.

So, although we may have individual instances of confabulation, looking at a longer time-span, these inaccurate explanations can still have a role to play in bringing individuals to live up to the ascribed self-ascriptions. Without self-regulation and the attitudes described therein, individuals just continue to confabulate in all instances in which their behaviour does not reflect what they want it to. This is because they are unable to manage the misalignment; they can't consider other possible explanations for their behaviour, or integrate feedback from others about the plausibility of their offered explanations, or pay more attention to their thoughts and feelings. In the next section, I describe in more detail how this virtue and its associated attitudes could bring our Brexit voter to better embody the values she is espousing in her confabulatory explanation of why she voted for Brexit.

## 6. Confabulation and self-regulation at work.

Returning to our imagined Brexit voter, recall that she has provided a confabulatory explanation of her behaviour and the concern is that this has stopped her considering more earnestly what her reasons for voting for Brexit really were, and that sometimes harmful behaviour ends up being justified in this way.

I argue that this non-ideal, confabulatory explanation is better than being dumbfounded in that it affords the individual certain opportunities. Importantly, being dumbfounded is the only other option available to the would-be confabulator, because agents do not have access to more accurate explanations (Sullivan-Bissett, 2015, p. 552). Our Brexit voter does not have introspective awareness of the influence of her patriotic gut feelings on her decision to vote in that way. But her confabulation does make more explicit to herself and others the factors – and their associated values – which she wants and expects to be the causes of her behaviour. She signals that she values British independence and self-governance. Once she expresses these self-concepts of being protective of Britain, she can then be more mindful going forward of whether her decisions reflect those values. Thus her self-ascriptions of value and her behaviour can become better aligned.

How well individuals do this will depend on whether they have the virtue of self-regulation. It is hard to imagine someone without any of the attitudes involved in this virtue (curiosity, openness to others' interpretations, attentiveness to feelings) not confabulating (and instead being dumbfounded) because they both reflect an epistemic curiosity to understand oneself and the circumstances. One of the first things an individual with a curiosity and open-mindedness for explanations of themselves is going to do, is to come up with a possible – if unideal – explanation. They are likely only to be more comfortable with being dumbfounded when it comes to very neutral topics, which they don't regard as being particularly reflective of their values and personalities more widely. I think this is unlikely to be the case with political decisions and actions.

Without the virtue of self-regulation, confabulation carries important costs. For example, in these cases, it could drive entrenchment of the attitudes that actually motivated the action and prevent further reflection. At worst, confabulation is not only a missed opportunity for individuals to present themselves with self-ascriptions which they can work with over time, but could lead to them being perceived by others as unreliable describers of themselves. DeBruin and Strijbos describe this as the most significant possible cost for agents with regards to confabulation (2019, p. 154). If this happens, agents are not considered reliable, trustworthy and intelligible members of the community. However, the person who is serially dumbfounded has no epistemic curiosity with regards to their behaviour at all, and so is also unlikely to reflect on their explanations and to experience some lack of intelligibility and isolation from others. (Imagine our Brexit voter looking bored and saying that she has 'no idea' why she voted for Brexit, when she is asked.)

In summary, we should not immediately judge an occurrence of confabulation as a wholly negative thing. It stems from good and epistemically valuable motivations. By this I mean that these motivations can improve the state of an individual's knowledge about themselves and the world. What is even better is if, further than this, agents have the virtue of self-regulation and can navigate the resulting feedback well and negotiate competently between their ascriptions and their behaviour. In the next section, I illustrate this point by showing how this could happen in the context of navigating 'undermining propaganda'.

## 7. Navigating Undermining Propaganda.

There are some political phenomena in which there are particularly stark 'gaps' or 'mismatches' between the values being espoused and the reality of that political goal being realised. This is exactly what we see in cases of 'undermining propaganda', so here I consider how the virtue of self-regulation and its associated attitudes can help individuals navigate such propaganda.

Jason Stanley's (2015) influential account of propaganda includes the following sub-type of propaganda:

> *Undermining Propaganda*: A contribution to public discourse that is presented as an embodiment of certain ideals, yet is of a kind that tends to erode those very ideals. Undermining propaganda involves a kind of contradiction between ideal and goal. It's an argument that appeals to an ideal to draw support, in the service of a goal that tends to erode the realization of that ideal. (2015, p. 53).

The ideals in questions can be any sort of ideal, but Stanley's focus is, usefully, on political ideals. He cites a number of examples of undermining propaganda, one of which being the 'war on drugs' in America in the 1980s-90s. The 'war on drugs' invoked the ideals of justice, law and order, and fair sentencing in a campaign which in reality exacerbated sentencing disparities for white and black people using cocaine and crack cocaine (ibid, pp. 59-60).

When we consider for ourselves which political messages we want to adhere to and which values we wish to embody, the attitudes involved in self-regulation can be beneficial in helping combat the effects of undermining propaganda by improving alignment between our espoused political values and the realities of our behaviour. We may be better able to *spot* undermining propaganda, and not personally participate in furthering its goals by following its message and thereby eroding the value we initially espoused. The contradiction between the ideal expressed in a political message and the realisation of that message is masked by individuals having flawed ideological beliefs (ibid, p. 57). If these ideologies are accepted because there is something personally appealing about them, or in other words because the individual feels that accepting them exemplifies some trait that they (gladly) perceive themselves as having, then having the virtue of self-regulation would put pressure on the link between one's acceptance of this ideology and the reality of their behaviour responding to the propaganda.

# Self-Regulation and Political Confabulation

Here is an example. Imagine that Jack and Jill are both fed up with the state of American politics. They believe that politicians are out of touch and haven't made any changes which actually improve their lives in any way, because politicians are too caught up in various scandals and alliance-forging which make up political life. So they both have a general, unexamined sense of disenfranchisement, and this is what brings them to decide to vote for Donald Trump. Then, they are both drawn to Trump's presidential campaign messaging which invokes the values of anti-corruption ('drain the swamp'), law and order, and politics re-centering around the average American. In confabulatory explanations of why they voted for Trump, they cite an adherence to and having been moved by these values. However, this isn't a completely accurate explanation because adherence to these values isn't what drove their sense of disenfranchisement; in fact it is the other way around. Their basic sense of disenfranchisement drove their decision and then these values of law and order are drawn on post hoc in order to justify this political choice in a way which is more satisfactory to them. It has meaning for them and allows them to communicate with others that they appreciate these political values.

Over time it becomes clear that Trump appoints his friends and family members to key positions in the White House, engages in unlawful tax-dodging and lives a life very unlike the 'average American'. This points to Trump's election campaign being an instance of undermining propaganda because electing him did not further those values. It also raises issues about the possible falsity of claims about Trump's actions and practices, such as whether he engages in tax-dodging. Yet, these claims are unexamined when they become a part of Jack and Jill's confabulations about why they voted for Trump.

Jack not only subscribes to these political values, but in his eyes they support his conception of himself as being independent, self-sufficient, and able to take care of himself. Also, that he is savvy to the constant deceit and deal-making amongst politicians, and this explains for him why his general situation and quality of life never improves. He is too confident in his own appraisal of what is wrong with politics and receives psychological comfort from it because it satisfies his need for an understanding of the world. He has too little interest and respect for the opposing thoughts and experiences of those around him. He isn't curious enough and is too inflexible in his thinking to consider whether Trump being president really furthers the de-corruption of politics, and whether his illegal tax-dodging is actually an endorsement of breaking the law when it benefits you. Jack does not have the virtue of self-regulation and his confabulations about voting for Trump will include ill-grounded statements which prop up a narrative of having made a political choice which embodies his values, and these statements are unlikely to be scrutinised further.

Jill, on the other hand, despite self-ascribing the same values of being against political corruption and wanting average Americans to be more central to political decisions, is more open to the perspectives of others in considering what a Trump presidency would look like and mean for them. In talking through with peers her explanation as to why she voted for Trump, she comes to see how angry and disenfranchised she feels about American politics and she has an interest and inquisitiveness as to how and where that anger is best directed. Her self-confidence is not so low that she quickly assumes she is wrong about something if she hears an opposing view, but when some friends ask her whether avoiding paying your taxes really reflects her value of being law-abiding and understanding the lives of 'average Americans', she reflects on this. There is a possibility that she comes to stop seeing Trump and his presidential campaign as something that will truly further the values of anti-corruption, law and order, and a focus on the 'average American'.

Jill therefore demonstrates how having the virtue of self-regulation can mean that her confabulating actually played an integral part in her coming to consider whether a political action of hers – voting for Trump – actually aligned with her political values. In this turbulent political world, the drawing together of one's political outlook and political decision-making, unhampered by misleading political propaganda, is particularly valuable.[5]

*University of Birmingham*
*klm276@student.bham.ac.uk*

[5]   I would like to thank Lisa Bortolotti, Iain Law and Quassim Cassam for extensive and thoughtful comments on earlier drafts of this paper. Also, to the Women in Philosophy group at the University of Birmingham for listening to these ideas and providing invaluable feedback. Finally, to the editors Anneli Jefferson and Jonathan Webber, whose responses and suggestions I am incredibly grateful for and made this paper substantially better. Many of the other contributors to this volume also helped me better formulate these ideas.

## References

A. Ahuja, 'Monday is surrender day, not freedom day', Financial Times, https://www.ft.com/content/c9a6c0f0-985c-4563-91bb-aee51f0ab926. (2021) Accessed July 2021.

BBC News, 'Vote Leave's targeted Facebook ads released by Facebook', BBC News, https://www.bbc.co.uk/news/uk-politics-44966969. (2018) Accessed September 2021.

L. Bortolotti, 'Stranger than fiction: costs and benefits of everyday confabulation', in *Review of philosophy and psychology*, 9 (2018) 227-249.

L. Bortolotti, *The epistemic innocence of irrational beliefs*, (Oxford University Press, 2020).

L. Bortolotti and K. Murphy-Hollies, 'Exceptionalism at the time of COVID-19: where nationalism meets irrationality' in *Danish Yearbook of Philosophy* (2022), 1–22.

M. Coltheart, 'Confabulation and conversation', *Cortex* 87 (2017) 62–68.

L. De Bruin and D. Strijbos, 'Does Confabulation Pose a Threat to First-Person Authority? Mindshaping, Self-Regulation and the Importance of Self-Know-How', *Topoi*, 39 (2019) 151–161.

C. Duffield, ''Freedom Day' in pictures: England marks easing of lockdown restrictions on amid rising covid cases', i news, https://inews.co.uk/news/uk/freedom-day-pictures-england-lockdown-easing-19-july-rising-covid-cases-1110556. (2021) Accessed July 2021.

P. Foot, *Virtues and Vices*, (Oxford: Oxford University Press, 2002).

M. B. Ganapini, 'Confabulating reasons', *Topoi*, 39 (2020) 189-201.

J. Haidt, 'The Emotional Dog and Its Rational Tail: A Social Intuitionist Approach to Moral Judgement', *Psychological Review*, 108 (2001) 814–834.

L. Hall, P. Johansson, B. Tärning, S. Sikström, and T. Deutgen, 'Magic at the marketplace: Choice blindness for the taste of jam and the smell of tea', in *Cognition*, 117 (2010) 54–61.

W. Hirstein, *Brain fiction: Self-deception and the riddle of confabulation,* (MIT Press: USA, 2005).

M. Honeycombe-Foster, 'MPs in fresh demand for Big Ben chime to mark Brexit 'Freedom' day', Politics Home, https://www.politicshome.com/news/article/mps-in-fresh-demand-for-big-ben-chime-to-mark-brexit-freedom-day. (2019) Accessed July 2021.

Ipsos Mori, 'Perceptions are not reality: Things the world gets wrong', https://www.ipsos.com/ipsos-mori/en-uk/perceptions-are-not-reality-things-world-gets-wrong. (2014) Accessed July 2021.

A. Jefferson, 'Confabulation, rationalisation and morality', *Topoi*, 39 (2020) 219–227.

B. Johnson, PM speech in Greenwich: 3 February 2020, https://www.gov.uk/government/speeches/pm-speech-in-greenwich-3-february-2020. (2020) Accessed July 2021.

McGeer, 'Mind-making practices: the social infrastructure of self-knowing agency and responsibility', *Philosophical Explorations*, 18 (2015) 259–281.

R. E. Nisbett and T. D. Wilson, 'Telling More Than We Can Know: Verbal Reports on Mental Processes', in *Psychological Review*, 84 (1977) 231–259

L. Örulv, and L. C. Hydén, 'Confabulation: Sense-making, self-making and world-making in dementia', in *Discourse Studies*, 8 (2006) 647–673.

Rev Transcript, 'Donald Trump Tours the Ford Plant Without a Mask, Explains Why', Rev, https://www.rev.com/blog/transcripts/donald-trump-tours-the-ford-plant-without-a-mask-explains-why. (2020) Accessed July 2021.

R. Scaife, 'A problem for self-knowledge: the implications of taking confabulation seriously', in *Acta Analytica*, 29 (2014) 469–485

S. Stammers, 'Confabulation, explanation, and the pursuit of resonant meaning', in *Topoi*, 39 (2020) 177–187

J. Stanley, *How propaganda works*, (Princeton University Press, 2015).

D. Strijbos and L. de Bruin, 'Self-interpretation as first-person mindshaping: Implications for confabulation research', *Ethical Theory and Moral Practice*, 18 (2015) 297–307.

E. Sullivan-Bissett, 'Implicit bias, confabulation, and epistemic innocence', in *Consciousness and Cognition*, 33 (2015) 548–560.

J. D. Velleman, 'The Self as Narrator', in *Self to Self: Selected essays*, (USA, Cambridge University Press, 2006).

Yahoo News, 'Florida's Anti-Maskers Are Taking A Stand', *Yahoo News*, https://news.yahoo.com/floridas-anti-maskers-taking-stand-231500975.html. (2020) Accessed July 2021.

T. D Wilson, D. J. Lisle, J.W. Schooler, S.D. Hodges, K.J. Klaaren and S.J. LaFleur, 'Introspecting about reasons can reduce post-choice satisfaction', in *Personality and Social Psychology Bulletin*, 19 (1993) 331–39.

# Cultivating Curiosity in the Information Age

LANI WATSON

**Abstract**

In this paper, I explore the role that the intellectual virtue of curiosity can play in response to some of the most pressing challenges of the Information Age. I argue that virtuous curiosity represents a valuable characterological resource for the twenty-first century, in particular, a restricted form of curiosity, namely inquisitiveness. I argue that virtuous inquisitiveness should be trained and cultivated, via the skill of good questioning, and discuss the risks of failing to do so in relation to the design and use of novel technologies. If left unchecked, I argue, vicious forms of curiosity can emerge, with broad implications for society as a whole. Thus, we should seek to cultivate virtuous curiosity and teach the skill of good questioning to those of us (in principle, all of us) who use and rely on technology in our work and lives.

The nature and rate of change over the past century have brought about a number of distinct challenges that now face us on a global scale. These include rapid globalisation and increasing inequality associated with widespread societal and environmental damage, a new era of instant connectivity facilitating the spread of 'fake news' and conspiracy theorising, the effects of increased (actual or apparent) polarisation across the political spectrum, the rise of social media, and a complex range of associated harms brought about by a combination of online anonymity, novel technologies, and incentive structures driven by the attention economy. In order to meet these varied challenges, we must, it seems, continue to change – as individuals, as communities, and even as a species.

In this paper, I explore the role that curiosity has to play in this changing world. I treat curiosity as an intellectual virtue and argue that virtuous curiosity has important features that render it a valuable characterological resource in light of many of the complex and immediate concerns of the twenty-first century. I examine the role of a restricted form of curiosity, namely inquisitiveness, and argue that virtuous inquisitiveness should be trained and cultivated, via the skill of good questioning. Lastly, I discuss the risks of failing to cultivate virtuous curiosity (and good questioning), particularly in relation to the design and use of the novel technologies of the twenty-first century. If left

doi:10.1017/S1358246122000212

unchecked, I argue, vicious forms of curiosity can easily emerge, with broad implications for society as a whole. Thus, we should seek to cultivate virtuous curiosity and teach the skill of good questioning to those of us (in principle, all of us) who use and rely on technology in our work and lives. This is one valuable characterological strategy for tackling some of the most distinctive and pressing challenges we face.

## 1. Why curiosity

Why focus on the virtue of curiosity, in particular, as opposed to any one of the other intellectual, or indeed moral or civic virtues? Of course, my aim is not to suggest that cultivating curiosity is the only characterological strategy worth pursuing. Far from it. Nonetheless, curiosity has a distinctive role to play insofar as it features prominently in our intellectual lives from an early age and is, arguably, a (perhaps *the*) foundational intellectual virtue.

This view of curiosity as foundational is shared by a number of scholars. In *The Philosophy of Curiosity*, for example, Ilhan Inan (2012) writes: '[I]t is difficult even to imagine how our intellectual achievements would have been possible without the basic motivation of curiosity' (p. 1). Similarly, Nenad Miščević (2007) describes curiosity as the 'mainspring of motivation' and identifies it as 'the *core motivating* epistemic virtue' (p. 246, emphasis original). Jason Baehr (2011) places curiosity in the first of his categories in a taxonomy of the intellectual virtues, labelled 'initial motivation' (p. 21), and regards curiosity as a key intellectual virtue to educate for. I have argued elsewhere for the primacy of curiosity (more specifically, inquisitiveness) in educating for intellectual character, in part due to its status as a foundational intellectual virtue (Watson, 2016). Curiosity serves as a basic motivation for much of our intellectually virtuous activity and, as such, plays a significant role in initiating intellectually virtuous inquiry and shaping intellectual character.

The significance of curiosity is also highlighted by observing its shifting reputation throughout history (particularly in the West). In the twenty-first century, curiosity is typically represented in almost entirely positive terms but historically it has also accrued negative connotations. Throughout a significant period of Western intellectual history, curiosity was vilified as a vicious form of pride, particularly scorned in the early Christian context of Medieval Europe (Harrison, 2001). As a result, even today curiosity can be associated with prying and meddling in the affairs of others, or simply wanting to know more than is appropriate or proper. One can think of 'morbid curiosity', whereby a person seeks out particularly gruesome or unsavoury details, or of the well-known aphorism that curiosity 'killed the cat', warning of the dangers of an improper desire to know. The historical vilification of curiosity, and its subsequent mixed associations in common parlance, underline the complex and significant role that it plays in our intellectual and, indeed, moral and political lives.

A second reason for focusing on curiosity in the context of this volume derives directly from the nature of the change that we have seen in recent decades. That change has been largely brought about by significant technological and scientific progress. In its positive contemporary manifestation, curiosity is often associated with just such technological and scientific progress. It is NASA's Curiosity rover, for example, that was sent to explore the surface of Mars. Curiosity is, likewise, revered as an essential quality of many of the most famous scientists of the past century. The Nobel Prize committee asserts that it was 'Marie Curie's relentless resolve and insatiable curiosity [that] made her an icon in the world of modern science.'[1] Likewise, Einstein is well-known for extolling the value of curiosity and questioning:

> The important thing is not to stop questioning. Curiosity has its own reason for existing. One cannot help but be in awe when one contemplates the mysteries of eternity, of life, of the marvellous structure of reality. It is enough if one tries to comprehend only a little of this mystery every day. (*Life Magazine*, May 2, 1955).

These associations suggest an important role for curiosity, not only as a basic motivation for intellectually virtuous inquiry in general, but more specifically, as an essential ingredient of fruitful technological and scientific inquiry. It is precisely technological and scientific inquiry that have determined many of the recent rapid changes in our ways of living and communicating with each other, the results of which now dominate the daily work and lives of a large proportion of the global population (arguably everyone, whether in virtue of access or exclusion). Thus, as it has done throughout history, curiosity continues to feature centrally in our intellectual and moral lives. In particular, it has an important and distinctive role to play in setting and steering the course of technological and scientific progress and thus in tackling many of the challenges we now face as a result of rapid technological and scientific change. In short, it is worth

---

[1]    https://www.nobelprize.org/womenwhochangedscience/stories/marie-curie [Accessed: 11 Nov 2021]

paying special attention to the virtue (and associated vices) of curiosity in the contemporary world.

## 2. What is curiosity

Curiosity has attracted increasing attention from a variety of perspectives in recent years, including epistemology, psychology, linguistics, and political theory (see, for example, Inan, 2011; Inan, Watson, Whitcomb, Yigit (eds.), 2018; Zurn and Shankar (eds.), 2020; Zurn, 2021). Different authors treat curiosity variously as an emotion (Silvia, 2008; Brady, 2009), a mental state (Inan, 2011), or (more traditionally) a desire (Kvanvig, 2003; Whitcomb, 2010). Still others treat curiosity as a character strength (Peterson and Seligman, 2004) or as an intellectual or moral virtue (Baumgarten, 2001; Miščević, 2007; Baehr, 2011; Watson, 2018a; 2018b). It would, moreover, be misguided to assume that these characterisations are mutually exclusive. Rather, they represent different angles and perspectives taken by authors across disciplines and sub-disciplines, involved in a wide range of research concerning curiosity.

My own work has focused primarily on curiosity as an intellectual virtue. This treatment is particularly salient if one is concerned, not merely with an analysis of curiosity but with advancing an argument in favour of its cultivation. As opposed to emotions, desires, and mental states, virtues are more often the focus of training and education. The intellectual virtues are perhaps especially apt for this given the role of intellectual skill in the manifestation of intellectual virtue (which I will return to in due course). Aristotle himself saw intellectual virtues as a proper object of education, stating in the opening line of Book II of the *Nicomachean Ethics* that 'intellectual virtue owes both its inception and its growth chiefly to instruction' (*NE*, Book II, 1103a).

What then does it mean to be virtuously curious. According to my view, the virtuously curious person is *characteristically motivated to acquire worthwhile epistemic goods that she believes she lacks*.[2] This account of virtuous curiosity follows the model of defining intellectual (and moral) virtues in terms of a 'characteristic motivation', employed by authors such as Linda Zagzebski (1996) and Jason Baehr (2011). The motivation is characteristic in the sense that it constitutes a stable disposition in the curious person's character (as opposed to a

---

[2]    I have presented and defended this account of the intellectual virtue of curiosity in detail elsewhere (Watson, 2018a; 2018b).

fleeting whim). Moreover, this characteristic motivation, according to Zagzebski (1996), is action-guiding, providing us with 'a set of orientations toward the world' (p. 136), and it must be attached to some kind of reliable success or skill such that, '[A] person does not have a virtue unless she is reliable at bringing about the end that is the aim of the motivational component of the virtue' (p. 136).

In addition, my account of virtuous curiosity has three distinctive features that are worth highlighting. Firstly, virtuous curiosity concerns the *acquisition* of what I will collectively term 'epistemic goods'. These are goods such as information, knowledge, understanding, and truth – all of which pertain to the epistemic dimension of our lives. While all intellectual virtues aim, in some sense, at epistemic goods or, in Zagzebskian terms, at 'cognitive contact with reality' (Zagzebski, 1996), curiosity is defined in terms of the acquisition of these goods (for the purpose of cognitive contact with reality). Contrast this with other intellectual virtues, such as open-mindedness or intellectual humility, where the distinctive aims are not so much acquisition as perhaps evaluation or regulation. In the case of virtuous curiosity, acquisition itself is the defining aim. Notably, it is, I think, this distinctive feature of virtuous curiosity that suggests it as a plausible candidate for a (perhaps *the*) foundational intellectual virtue.

Secondly, virtuous curiosity is defined in terms of the acquisition of *worthwhile* epistemic goods. This feature of virtuous curiosity entails that the virtuously curious person is not simply motivated to acquire any and all epistemic goods. Rather, she is motivated to acquire those epistemic goods that are worthwhile, relevant, or important in some sense. Determining what precisely it means for epistemic goods to be worthwhile is a significant task concerning epistemic value. I will return to this in due course. For now, one need only agree that not all epistemic goods are equally worthwhile all of the time, in order to allow for this constraint on virtuous curiosity. The virtuously curious person does not seek out any and all epistemic goods (think again of 'morbid curiosity'). She seeks out those that are worth having from the point of view of intellectually virtuous inquiry.

Thirdly, the virtuously curious person is only motivated to acquire those worthwhile epistemic goods that she believes she *lacks*. I am not curious (virtuously or otherwise) if I seek out information that I already possess (although it might naturally be described as a curious thing to do, in an alternative sense of the word). Curiosity is fundamentally born out of a recognition of ignorance. This connection between curiosity and ignorance is examined in detail by Ilhan Inan (2012), who notes that when 'awareness of ignorance is coupled with an interest in the topic, it motivates curiosity' (p. 1). Much like the acquisitive nature of curiosity, this distinctive feature of the virtue speaks to its characterisation by various authors as an 'initial' or 'mainspring' motivation for intellectually virtuous inquiry (Miščević, 2007; Baehr, 2011). It is in virtue of recognising that one is ignorant, that one first begins to inquire. To reiterate, then, the virtuously curious person is *characteristically motivated to acquire worthwhile epistemic goods that she believes she lacks*. We can now consider the distinctive value of this virtue.

## 3. The value of virtuous curiosity

There is much to be said about the value of virtuous curiosity. I have already suggested that curiosity plays an important role in the initiation of intellectually virtuous inquiry and in the development of intellectually virtuous character. A stable, consistent form of curiosity has also been associated with increased wellbeing (Lydon-Staley, Zurn and Bassett, 2020) and has been advocated as a form of political resistance (Zurn, 2020; 2021). Let us focus, however, on the value of virtuous curiosity in light of recent and rapid technological and scientific change.

Arguably the most significant technological change that has occurred in the past century has been the invention of the Internet, making possible the almost instantaneous exchange of information across global distances, among large sections of the population (in principle, everyone). As such, we are now, more than ever, living in a deeply information-centric world: the so-called Information Age. This Age is characterized (according to one source that surely typifies it – Wikipedia) as 'a rapid epochal shift from the traditional industry established by the Industrial Revolution to an economy primarily based upon information technology.'[3] This shift to information technology, vastly expedited by the Internet, has resulted in the exponential growth of available information alongside a new immediacy with which it can be accessed and communicated. These are some of the hallmarks of our changing world.

Curiosity plays a valuable, indeed vital role in this world of information. It is, after all, curiosity that frequently guides the search for

[3]    https://en.wikipedia.org/wiki/Information_Age [Accessed: 12 Nov 2021].

information in the first place and steers our course as we hunt through the multitude of epistemic goods that are on offer. This role for curiosity is not new to the Information Age, *per se* – it is as old as information itself. But the affordances of the Internet – the sheer amount and breadth of information now at our fingertips – have placed new emphasis on our ability to search and find the information that we need in useful and efficient ways. Put simply, the Internet has made it ever more essential, epistemically and practically, that we use our curiosity well; that we are virtuously curious.

This is perhaps especially clear in the context of the purported 'post-truth' socio-political climate of recent years. Post-truth was famously defined (and crowned 'word of the year') in 2016 by *Oxford Dictionaries* as 'Relating to or denoting circumstances in which objective facts are less influential in shaping public opinion than appeals to emotion and personal belief.'[4] This post-truth condition suggests a deterioration of the defining features of curiosity among the general population. A dual failure whereby people are increasingly disinclined to acquire worthwhile epistemic goods (or indeed any epistemic goods) and, at the same time, increasingly disinclined to acknowledge their own ignorance or other intellectual shortcomings. The cultivation of virtuous curiosity is one characterological strategy that can and should be deployed to combat the emergence of these epistemic and characterological failings in the post-truth world.

In addition, as a foundational intellectual virtue, curiosity has a number of characterological effects that render it particularly valuable in the face of pressing contemporary challenges. By 'characterological effects', I mean effects that the exercise of virtuous curiosity has on the character of the virtuously curious person, beyond the manifestation of virtuous curiosity itself. One might also think of these as features or aspects of virtuous curiosity that have distinctive profiles as intellectual virtues in their own right. Thus, if I am praised for being virtuously curious, then I can also be praised for these other intellectual virtues, which are, in this case, brought about by my being virtuously curious. Much like a person who trains to be physically strong may be admired for her physical strength and, at the same time, for her core stability. Her strength and her stability are distinct physical attributes but they bear a close relation to each other; her strength has the physical effect of increasing her stability

---

[4]  https://languages.oup.com/word-of-the-year/2016/ [Accessed: 15 Nov 2021].

and, at the same time, her stability is an important aspect of her strength.

Likewise, virtuous curiosity has the characterological effect of increasing the exercise of certain other intellectual virtues and, at the same time, these are an important aspect of virtuous curiosity. A very strong version of the claim that curiosity is a foundational intellectual virtue might in fact suggest that *all* of the intellectual virtues are aspects of virtuous curiosity and can thereby be considered characterological effects of virtuous curiosity (a kind of unity of the intellectual virtues thesis, with curiosity at its heart). I will not defend that strong claim here, so for present purposes, I will focus on just two.

The first of these characterological effects derives from the first two distinctive features outlined in Section II: the virtuously curious person is characteristically motivated to *acquire worthwhile epistemic goods*. As such, the virtuously curious person exhibits a kind of intellectually virtuous *attentiveness*. Ironically, relatively little attention has been paid to virtuous attentiveness among virtue epistemologists to date. This virtue nonetheless appears on several standard lists of intellectual virtues, including Baehr's (2015) nine 'Master Virtues', deployed as a basis for much of his work in intellectual virtue education. In his discussion of attentiveness in the classroom, Baehr (2015) identifies three key features of the virtue: the attentive person is 'present' when learning, listens, and 'is quick to notice and is capable of giving sustained attention to *important details*' (p. 95, emphasis original). As such, virtuous attentiveness is not merely about 'paying attention' but is about actively engaging with and carefully attending to the 'important details' of one's environment or the subject matter under consideration.

On this plausible account of virtuous attentiveness, it shares something in common with virtuous curiosity. Namely, the motivation (and ability) to pick out and attend to the information, knowledge, understanding, and truth that is worth having in a given context. As such, intellectually virtuous attentiveness naturally features in the exercise of virtuous curiosity. If one succeeds in being virtuously curious, then one has also exhibited a degree of virtuous attentiveness in the acquisition of epistemic goods, attending to the worthwhile goods and ignoring the rest. Thus, virtuous attentiveness is a characterological effect of virtuous curiosity.

This close relationship between attentiveness and curiosity speaks to the value of curiosity, in and of itself. The virtuously curious person enjoys the benefits of not one but (at least) two intellectual virtues. In other words, virtuous curiosity offers good 'bang for one's intellectual buck'. In addition, it is not difficult to appreciate the particular significance of this characterological effect in the Information Age. In an increasingly fast-paced, information-centric world, the ability to pick out and attend to the information that is worth having and ignore the overwhelming flood of information that is not, is highly significant. Indeed, much like curiosity itself, this ability is arguably becoming ever more essential in light of the growing prevalence of online misinformation and 'fake news', as well as potential abuses of the attention economy (Marwick, 2015; Wu, 2017; Williams 2018). The fact that virtuous curiosity increases the exercise of something else that we value – virtuous attentiveness – provides further reason to value curiosity, over and above the value that has already been identified.

The second characterological effect of virtuous curiosity derives primarily from the third distinctive feature outlined in Section II: the virtuously curious person is characteristically motivated to acquire worthwhile epistemic goods *that she believes she lacks*. As such, the virtuously curious person exhibits a kind of intellectually virtuous *humility*. Unlike attentiveness, intellectual humility has received significant attention from virtue epistemologists in recent years (Roberts and Wood, 2007; Hazlett, 2012; Kidd, 2015; Whitcomb et al., 2017; Tanesini, 2021). Prominent accounts differ to some degree, particularly concerning the question of whether intellectual humility is best understood as an absence of the vices of pride (Roberts and Wood, 2007) or the presence of a particular ability, namely, the ability to recognize and 'own' one's intellectual limitations (Whitcomb et al., 2017). Most recently, intellectual humility has been characterised by Alessandra Tanesini (2021) as a kind of accurate assessment of one's intellectual strengths and weaknesses.

On any of these accounts of intellectual humility, there is a natural correlation with virtuous curiosity. The intellectually humble person must recognise and own her intellectual limitations, including acknowledging when she is ignorant. As we have seen, curiosity is born out of precisely this recognition of ignorance. In the case of virtuous curiosity, moreover, a person must have also discerned (consciously or not) that whatever knowledge or information she is missing, is worth having. In any number of situations where there exists a real or perceived expectation that one already knows this or that piece of worthwhile information, exposing the fact that one does not may require intellectual humility. Even without this expectation, the acknowledgement itself constitutes a (perhaps weaker) exercise of the virtue. As such, like virtuous attentiveness, intellectually virtuous humility naturally features in the exercise of virtuous curiosity. If one succeeds in being virtuously curious, then one has also exhibited a degree of intellectual humility by accurately assessing and 'owning' one's ignorance. Thus, intellectual humility is a characterological effect of virtuous curiosity.

Again, this close relationship between intellectual humility and curiosity speaks to the value of curiosity, in and of itself. The virtuously curious person enjoys the benefits of not one but now three intellectual virtues. Yet more 'bang for one's intellectual buck'. Moreover, as with attentiveness, it is not difficult to perceive the particular significance of this characterological effect in the contemporary world. The increased attention that has been paid to intellectual humility across several disciplines, including philosophy, psychology, theology, and political theory, is at least in part due to a perceived rise in the threats born of a notable absence of the virtue in both public and private life. The rise of extremism in various forms, increased political polarization, and post-truth conspiracy theorising are just three phenomena that appear to expose particular failures of intellectual humility in the contemporary epistemic and political landscape. The cultivation of intellectual humility is viewed by numerous commentators as a viable characterological strategy to address at least one underlying cause of these, and other issues (Baehr, 2011; Hazlett, 2012; Kidd, 2015; Lynch, 2017; Tanesini, 2018; 2021; Pritchard, 2021).

The existence and nature of these multiple threats to epistemic and political life, moreover, can be in part attributed to the novel technologies of the Information Age, including via mechanisms such as online 'echo chambers' and 'bubbles', which shield users from ideas and information that may challenge or undermine their own convictions. The interaction between novel technologies and novel expressions of vices such as arrogance and 'superbia' (Tanesini, 2021) is a rich topic for investigation. For our purposes here, it suffices to note that intellectual humility is an important virtue to cultivate in the social and political climate of the twenty-first century. Again, the fact that virtuous curiosity increases the exercise of intellectual humility provides further, independent reason to value curiosity in the contemporary world.


## 4. Cultivating (a restricted form of) curiosity

I have indicated that virtuous curiosity has an important role to play in the initiation of intellectually virtuous inquiry and, specifically, in the fruitful progress of technological and scientific inquiry. In addition, I have argued that virtuous curiosity is vital for navigating a deeply information-centric and problematically post-truth world, and that it has at least two significant characterological effects in the form of intellectually virtuous attentiveness and intellectually virtuous humility. These latter are both valuable virtues in and of themselves, with distinctive salience in the twenty-first century. Thus, virtuous curiosity is a valuable characterological resource that should be cultivated to help address a number of society's most complex and immediate concerns.

How then should we go about cultivating virtuous curiosity (in ourselves and others). I will indicate one key strategy that emerges from consideration of a restricted form of curiosity, namely inquisitiveness. I call inquisitiveness a restricted form of curiosity because, like the virtuously curious person, the inquisitive person is characteristically motivated to acquire worthwhile epistemic goods that she believes she lacks. However, she goes about this in a specific way, that is, by asking questions. In contrast, the curious person does not *necessarily* ask questions. She may, for example, acquire worthwhile epistemic goods by going for a walk or watching YouTube videos. The inquisitive person manifests her curiosity specifically by asking questions. Thus, inquisitiveness is a restricted form of curiosity, much like, for example, deadlifting is a restricted form of strength training. Put another way, inquisitiveness is one way of being virtuously curious. More fully, I characterise the virtuously inquisitive person as one who is *characteristically motivated and able to engage sincerely in good questioning* (Watson, 2015).

Virtuous inquisitiveness thus entails the intellectual skill of good questioning. It is this skill that suggests inquisitiveness as a particularly promising candidate for cultivating virtuous curiosity. To see this, it is worth taking a closer look at good questioning itself. The practice of questioning in general is, of course, both familiar and ubiquitous, but good questioning is a skill and, like all skills, some people are better at it than others. So, what exactly does it mean to be a good questioner. We can typically identify good questioning when we see it. Perhaps even more typically we know when we have seen or experienced bad questioning. Think of the standard questions in a customer satisfaction survey or an off-the-shelf employee progress review. Similarly, good and bad questioning occur in interpersonal interactions. Most of us know someone who has a knack for asking important or insightful questions and, alternatively, someone who manages to ask exactly the wrong questions every time.

Despite its intuitive familiarity, however, good questioning is a complex and dynamic skill. In order to offer an account of this skill, I begin by taking questioning in general to be a form of information-seeking.

When one engages in questioning (good or bad), one is typically in the business of 'finding things out'.[5] Transforming questioning into *good* questioning means engaging in this activity in a skilful manner. This elevates good questioning above mere information-seeking in two ways. When we engage in the skill of good questioning we do not simply seek information, rather we *competently* seek information that is *worth having*. I will elucidate each of these conditions.[6]

Firstly, good questioning requires seeking *worthwhile* information. This means attending to the 'what' of the question; what information is the questioner attempting to find out. I call this 'what' the content of a question. This content comprises the target information that the questioner is seeking when asking a question; it is 'what' they are trying to find out. This feature of good questioning entails that the good questioner is not simply trying to find out any and all information. Rather, she is seeking information that is worthwhile, relevant, or important in some sense. Recall that the same condition applies to virtuous curiosity. This makes sense because good questioning is a defining feature of virtuous inquisitiveness, which is a restricted form of curiosity. We can now look at this 'worthwhileness' condition in a little more detail.

There are two basic senses in which information can be considered worthwhile in the context of good questioning (and virtuous curiosity). In the first sense, good questioning excludes cases of trivial or disvaluable information-seeking. We might think, for example, that tracking down the precise alphanumeric URL of one's most recent internet search results constitutes trivial information-seeking, especially when the same or similar results can be found by simply re-typing the search terms into a search engine. Finding out that the URL ends with an '8' is unlikely to amount to important or valuable information, in most cases. Likewise, there is plenty of information and, especially, misinformation available online that is not merely trivial but actively disvaluable or harmful to seek. The search term

---

[5]   Of course, this is not the only reason we engage in questioning. We ask questions for many different reasons, such as engaging in polite conversation, impressing colleagues, and so on. Nonetheless, I take questioning to be fundamentally an epistemic practice, and a question to be definitively an information-seeking act. I have defended these claims in a number of places, including most extensively in Watson (2021).

[6]   I have presented and defended my account of good questioning in a number of places, including Watson (2018c) and Watson (2019).

'red pill', for example, returns among other things, large amounts of misogynistic misinformation concerning sex and gender, rooted in the men's rights movement. Falling down this kind of online misinformation rabbit hole may be both epistemically disvaluable and actively harmful to the information-seeker. The good questioner, online or otherwise, will avoid seeking out trivial, disvaluable, or harmful information (and misinformation).[7]

Worthwhile information-seeking, in the second sense, requires the good questioner not only to avoid seeking certain information but actively to seek out relevant, valuable, or significant information, when engaged in questioning. The good questioner will seek only the information that she needs or wants and, in doing so, will avoid the large amount of irrelevant, insignificant, or harmful information that is also available to her. If I am using the internet to understand how the Japanese parliamentary system operates, for example, I should use search terms like 'Japanese parliamentary system' and avoid search terms like 'red pill' or 'top ten cat videos'. Put like this, the point is a simple one but it is nonetheless significant in an age where endless distraction is at our fingertips and there is profit to be made from proactively directing our attention online. It is not hard to see that some instances of questioning falter precisely in virtue of the questioner's failure to seek out relevant, valuable, or significant information; in short, information that is worth having. Thus, the skill of good questioning requires the questioner to engage in worthwhile information-seeking, both through the avoidance of trivial, disvaluable, or harmful information and in the acquisition of information that is relevant, valuable, or significant.

Secondly, good questioning requires seeking (worthwhile) information *competently*. Competently seeking information requires attending to the 'who', 'when', 'where', and 'how' of the question; who is being asked, when and where are they being asked, and how are they being asked. I call these the contextual and communicative components of good questioning. In addition to targeting worthwhile content, these further components reveal the dynamic

---

[7]  Determining precisely why examples such as these constitute trivial, disvaluable, or harmful information-seeking is both complex and contentious. There is nonetheless broad consensus that some information is indeed trivial, disvaluable, or harmful to possess. As such, it is also broadly uncontentious to maintain that one can seek this information by means of questioning and that doing so is not something we typically consider to be worthwhile. Good questioning requires the questioner to avoid this.

complexity of good questioning as both an epistemic and practical skill. One's questions can misfire in numerous subtle and interconnected ways. One may go wrong by asking the wrong person or source, for example. Consider the difference between consulting a search engine and a loved one for advice on a major life decision. Likewise, a question may miss its target because it is badly timed or the situation in which it is asked is misjudged. Even more subtly, the tone or delivery of a question can affect its reception and effectiveness, even when the information sought is worthwhile. All of these factors can prevent a person from engaging in good questioning.

Notably, competent information-seeking does not permit information that is acquired by accident or luck. On the other hand, it does not always require that the information sought is in fact acquired. Rather, in certain circumstances one may competently seek information without actually acquiring it. One may, for example, competently search for a colleague's contact details online, but fail to acquire them because the colleague has not updated their contact information. Good questioning requires competent information-seeking but successfully acquiring information is neither necessary nor sufficient. Thus, questioning is good in virtue of competent and worthwhile information-seeking. A good questioner competently seeks worthwhile information.

Let us now return to inquisitiveness. Good questioning is the defining feature of virtuous inquisitiveness and, as noted, it is this skill component that allows us to effectively cultivate inquisitiveness, and thereby to cultivate virtuous curiosity. This is because, in contrast to virtues, skills are more commonly and explicitly trained and taught in schools and workplaces, using a range of tried and tested pedagogical techniques, according to the specific skill in question. We know how to teach young children to read, write, and multiply, how to teach a teenager to code, and how to train a new employee to use the in-house company software. Most of us will continue to learn new skills, formally or informally, throughout our lives. The development of skills, then, is a familiar process for both teachers and learners.

Like other skills, good questioning can be taught and doing so has many potential benefits including the cultivation of virtuous inquisitiveness (Watson 2016; 2018a; 2019). Teaching or training good questioning may involve focusing on one of its individual components – content, context, or communication – or on the practice as a whole. In the former case, for example, one may draw on resources designed to help students distinguish between reliable and unreliable online sources, and so direct the contextual 'who' of their questions.

Alternatively, one may focus on developing thought-provoking in-
structional materials on useful or important topics and so provide a
valuable baseline for the 'what', or content, of students' or employees'
questions. Many other similarly targeted strategies exist. Similarly,
strategies exist for teaching or training the skill of good questioning
directly, including techniques such as 'question-storming', ques-
tion-based assessment, and the *Right Question Institute's* Question
Formulation Technique.[8] However one approaches the task, given
its defining role in the exercise of virtuous inquisitiveness, teaching
or training the skill of good questioning is a promising means of cultivating virtuous curiosity.

That is not to say that one can guarantee curiosity in those who
learn how to question well. Good questioning does not necessarily
translate to intellectually virtuous inquiry because, as a skill, it may
remain dormant or underutilised. To achieve the cultivation of a
virtue such as curiosity, one must also foster the characteristic motivation common to all the intellectual virtues - the aim of cognitive
contact with reality. Doing so is a challenge in its own right. That
said, much like curiosity, good questioning is arguably foundational
to success in many aspects of our cognitive and intellectual lives. As
such, teaching or training in the skill of good questioning may well
have a wide-ranging and significant impact on intellectual conduct
and motivation more generally.[9]

Moreover, as with curiosity, the skill of good questioning has a distinctive role to play in the Information Age. In particular, as several
of the examples above indicate, the arrival of the search engine within
the infrastructure of the Internet has placed specific emphasis on the
ability to ask questions. We must be able to ask the right thing, of the
right sources, in the right way, in order to ensure that the results we
receive from search-based algorithms are those that we need and
want. A task that is made only more demanding by the existence of
paid advertising and search engine optimisation (SEO) strategies
that can and do fundamentally alter the information that we are
most likely to see when we search (whether we want that information
or not). It is not simply curiosity, then, but inquisitiveness that is required in order to effectively navigate the Internet through the use of
search engines. Good questioning in the form of virtuous inquisitiveness allows us to seek out the worthwhile information that we need or
want and avoid the potential information overload afforded by an

---

[8]    A list of these resources and others can be found on my website at
www.philosophyofquestions.com/resources
[9]    A rich topic for further theoretical and empirical work.

otherwise overwhelming and disordered repository of information, knowledge, opinion and, yes, cat videos. In order to cultivate virtuous curiosity in this information-centric world, we should teach and train the skill of good questioning.

## 5. Failing to cultivate virtuous curiosity

I have presented the case in support of cultivating virtuous curiosity primarily on the basis of the numerous benefits that I believe are afforded by doing so. In this final section, I outline some of the potential risks of failing to cultivate virtuous curiosity (and good questioning), particularly in relation to the design and use of the novel technologies of the twenty-first century. If left unchecked, vicious forms of technologically-induced and mediated curiosity can easily emerge, with broad implications for society as a whole.

We are all users of technology of one form or another, including many of the novel technologies of the twenty-first century. Many of us rely on these technologies for everything from buying food and navigating, to connecting with friends and following the news. The Internet, in particular, is increasingly omnipresent in our lives and, as already noted, search engines are the key to making it work in a structured way. I have suggested that reliance on search engines places an emphasis on our ability to ask good questions in order to get the information that we need and want. Simply put, the ability to competently seek out worthwhile information has a significant impact on what we see and what we do not see online. Ultimately, this determines much of what we come to know and believe on the basis of our online searching.

Arguably, however, rather than promoting the skill of good questioning, search engines are actually deskilling us in this regard. This is because they seek to predict, as far as possible, the information that a user wants from as little input as possible. The algorithms are, in essence, working to predict what we want to know before we have attempted to properly articulate it. Even the literal forming of our questions has become redundant online – how often do you type a full interrogative sentence into a search engine, as opposed to a string of syntactically disconnected search terms. We are thus not given opportunities to practice and refine the skill of good questioning online and are actively dis-incentivised from trying.

Yet, an *inability* to ask good questions can put one at a significant epistemic and practical disadvantage. It can both prevent a user from accessing the information they need and expose them to irrelevant or harmful information or misinformation. Consequences include everything from the user experiencing a slight inconvenience to the emergence of radical polarisation and extremism in society at large (depending, of course, on many additional factors). Whatever the particular effects, the general point is not hard to appreciate: the more extensively we (collectively) rely on information technologies, such as the Internet, the more widespread and intractable the consequences of an inability to navigate it will be. The deskilling of our ability to question online is thus a significant cause for concern in this regard.

Furthermore, even without this active deskilling, the profit-driven structure of large portions of the Internet poses a threat to the epistemic community at large. Online attention is a resource that advertisers and social media platforms, among others, must mine in order to survive. Search engine results are one of the most effective ways of doing this, directing the user's attention to this or that information in ever subtler and more sophisticated ways. There is, therefore, big business in modifying search engine results through SEO and paid advertising. Crucially, however, these approaches are not typically governed by exclusively (or remotely) epistemic ends. Rather, they are governed by profit. Thus, mere reliance on search engine algorithms cannot guarantee a valuable set of results.

Users who do not engage in good questioning when searching online are therefore liable to, at best, waste time and effort wading through unhelpful search results and, at worst, be once again exposed to false or misleading information. When the latter is sufficiently widespread, the consequences can be significant and harmful, as noted above. That is not to say that the good questioner can avoid the risks altogether, but without this skill, the user is more vulnerable.

Similarly, the user who cannot or does not exercise virtuous curiosity online risks falling foul of active efforts to direct their cognitive life in the form of, for example, recommendation algorithms like those of YouTube or Netflix. Such algorithms seek to guide the user's choices concerning what content to consume, often in the form of videos, images, and memes. Once again, the user's ability to make autonomous judgements about this content is diminished and actively dis-incentivised by such algorithms. But it is precisely this discernment of worthwhile epistemic goods that is required for virtuous curiosity. Without this, we are all at risk of failing to exercise due caution with respect to the content we are exposed to, resulting at best, in too many hours spent watching cat videos, and at worst, phenomena such as 'doom-scrolling', where users addictively consume a seemingly never-ending cycle of bad news stories online. Both good questioning and curiosity can provide an antidote to these distinctive concerns.

We live in a challenging world. I have argued in this paper that the intellectual virtue of curiosity, alongside virtuous inquisitiveness and the skill of good questioning, have a number of important features that render them valuable characterological resources in light of the complex and immediate concerns of the twenty-first century, many of which have been brought about by significant and rapid technological progress. Thus, we should seek to cultivate virtuous curiosity and teach the skill of good questioning to those of us (in principle, all of us) who use and rely on technology in our work and lives. This is one valuable characterological strategy for tackling some of the most distinctive and pressing challenges we face.[10]

*University of Oxford*
*lani.watson@theology.ox.ac.uk*

## References

Aristotle, *Nicomachean Ethics.* Translated by J. A. K. Thomson, (London: Penguin Classics, 2004).

Jason Baehr, *The Inquiring Mind,* (Oxford: Oxford University Press, 2011).

Jason Baehr, *Cultivating Good Minds: A Philosophical & Practical Guide to Educating for Intellectual Virtues* (2015) Accessed online via < http://intellectualvirtues.org/why-should-we-educate-for-intellectual-virtues2/>.

Peter Harrison, 'Curiosity, Forbidden Knowledge, and the Reformation of Natural Philosophy in Early Modern England', *Isis* 92 (2001), 265-290.

Allan Hazlett, 'Higher-order Epistemic Attitudes and Intellectual Humility', *Episteme* 9 (2012) 205-223.

Ilhan İnan, *The Philosophy of Curiosity,* (New York: Routledge, 2012).

[10] This work was supported by a John Templeton Foundation grant (no. 61413). The views expressed are those of the author and do not reflect the views of the John Templeton Foundation. Thanks to colleagues at the Oxford Character Project for a useful discussion of these ideas and to the participants of a work-in-progress seminar for contributors to this volume, especially Jonathan Webber for helpful written feedback.

Ian Kidd, 'Educating for Epistemic Humility'. In: (ed.) Baehr, Jason, *Intellectual Virtues and Education: Essays in Applied Virtue Epistemology* (New York: Routledge, 2015).

David M. Lydon-Staley, Perry Zurn, and Danielle S. Bassett, 'Within-person variability in curiosity during daily life and associations with well-being', *Journal of Personality* 88 (2020) 625–641.

Michael Lynch, 'Teaching Humility in an Age of Arrogance', *The Chronicle of Higher Education* (2017).

Alice E. Marwick, 'Instafame: Luxury selfies in the attention economy', *Public culture* 27 (2015), 137-160.

Nenad Miščević, 'Virtue-Based Epistemology and the Centrality of Truth (Towards a Strong Virtue Epistemology)', *Acta Analytica* 22 (2007) 239-266.

Duncan Pritchard, 'Intellectual humility and the epistemology of disagreement', *Synthese* 198 (2021) 1711-1723.

Robert Roberts and Jay Wood, *Intellectual Virtues: An Essay in Regulative Epistemology,* (Oxford: Oxford University Press, 2007).

Alessandra Tanesini, 'Intellectual Servility and Timidity', *Journal of Philosophical Research* (2018).

Alessandra Tanesini, *The Mismeasure of the Self: A Study in Vice Epistemology* (Oxford: Oxford University Press, 2021).

Lani Watson, 'What Is Inquisitiveness', *American Philosophical Quarterly* 52 (2015), 273-288.

Lani Watson, 'Why Should We Educate for Inquisitiveness'. In: (ed.) Baehr, Jason, *Intellectual Virtues and Education: Essays in Applied Virtue Epistemology,* (New York: Routledge, 2016), 38-53.

Lani Watson, 'Educating for Curiosity'. In: İnan, Ilhan, Watson, Lani, Whitcomb, Dennis, and Yigit, Safiye (eds.) *The Moral Psychology of Curiosity* (London: Rowman & Littlefield, 2018a) 293-310.

Lani Watson, 'Curiosity and Inquisitiveness'. In: (ed. Battaly, Heather) *Routledge Handbook of Virtue Epistemology,* (London: Routledge, 2018b).

Lani Watson, 'Educating for Good Questioning: A Tool for Intellectual Virtues Education', *Acta Analytica* 33 (2018c), 353-370.

Lani Watson, 'Educating for Good Questioning as a Democratic Skill'. In: *The Routledge Handbook of Social Epistemology* edited by Miranda Fricker, Peter J. Graham, David Henderson and Nikolaj J.L.L. Pedersen (New York: Routledge, 2019) 437-446.

L. Watson, 'What is a Question', *Philosophy, RIP Supplement* 89 (2021) 273-297.

Dennis Whitcomb, 'Curiosity was Framed', *Philosophy and Phenomenological Research* 81 (2010), 664-687.

Dennis Whitcomb, Heather Battaly, Jason Baehr, and Daniel Howard-Synder, 'Intellectual Humility: Owning Our Limitations', *Philosophy and Phenomenological Research* 94 (2017), 509-539.

James Williams, *Stand out of our light: freedom and resistance in the attention economy,* (Cambridge: Cambridge University Press, 2018).

Tim Wu, *The attention merchants: The epic scramble to get inside our heads,* (Atlantic Books, 2017).

Perry Zurn, 'Curiosity and Political Resistance'. In: Zurn, Perry and Shankar, Arjun (eds.), *Curiosity Studies: A New Ecology of Knowledge,* (Minnesota: University of Minnesota Press, 2020) 227-245.

Perry Zurn, *Curiosity and Power: The Politics of Inquiry,* (Minnesota: University of Minnesota Press, 2021).

Perry Zurn and Arjun Shankar, *Curiosity Studies: A New Ecology of Knowledge* (Minnesota: University of Minnesota Press, 2020).

# Practical Wisdom and the Value of Cognitive Diversity

ANNELI JEFFERSON AND KATRINA SIFFERD

**Abstract**

The challenges facing us today require practical wisdom to allow us to react appropriately. In this paper, we argue that at a group level, we will make better decisions if we respect and take into account the moral judgment of agents with diverse styles of cognition and moral reasoning. We show this by focusing on the example of autism, highlighting different strengths and weaknesses of moral reasoning found in autistic and non-autistic persons respectively.

Probably the best-known campaigner for climate action is a young woman called Greta Thunberg who is diagnosed as being on the autistic spectrum. The fact that Thunberg is autistic and that she is a dedicated and highly successful campaigner may of course be a coincidence. Just as we may have blond-haired or black-haired climate campaigners, we can, and do, have autistic and non-autistic ones. And yet, Thunberg ascribes a key role in her journey as climate activist to her condition. She says that the focus, even obsessiveness, that is one characteristic of autism spectrum conditions was one the reasons why it was impossible for her to forget about the danger of climate change once she had become aware of it. Being different is a gift, she says, because it allows her to be laser-focused on the moral imperative presented by our warming climate. 'I don't easily fall for lies; I can see through things. If I would've been like everyone else, I wouldn't have started this school strike for instance' (Thunberg, cited in Birrel, 2019).

Autism is a spectrum condition that encompasses a wide range of traits that can be more or less pronounced. Nevertheless, there are key characteristics associated with the condition: problems with social communication and interaction, and rigid and repetitive behaviours and interests (APA, 2013). These traits have been framed as deficits that compromise autistic persons' capacity for moral reasoning and action (Shoemaker, 2015; Schramme, 2018). Autistic traits also seem to pose problems for acquiring a trait that is particularly stressed in virtue ethics, practical wisdom, which includes the

doi:10.1017/S1358246122000182     © The Royal Institute of Philosophy and the contributors 2022

# Anneli Jefferson and Katrina Sifferd

ability to react flexibly to moral challenges. This need for sensitivity to context when making the correct moral judgments may make such judgments more difficult for autistic persons. To be generous, for example, one must give to another as is required by the situation: it may be appropriately generous to give a person who is suffering from hunger money; but sometimes giving money to others can foster dependence. When exactly this is the case is a tricky issue, and it takes considerable knowledge of the context to make a judgment call. Kristjánsson (2022) stresses the importance of context-sensitive practical wisdom in the 21st century, where complex problems such as the Covid-19 pandemic make it hard to assess what is the correct, virtuous thing to do. Does compassion require us to make sure people get back to school and the workplace to secure incomes and avoid mental health problems? Or does it require protecting the clinically vulnerable by locking down society?

In this paper, we disagree with the narrative that autistic persons are necessarily disadvantaged in practical wisdom when compared to non-autistic persons. We aim to show three things: first, that in non-autistic individuals, context-sensitivity can often have detrimental effects, as moral thinking becomes skewed by irrelevant features of the situation, motivational factors, and peer pressure. Thus, both autistic individuals and neurotypicals fall short of practical wisdom in different ways when it comes to moral decision making.[1] Second, autistic traits such as decreased context-sensitivity in making moral judgments can be a moral strength, because those traits are associated with decreased cognitive biases.[2] Finally, on a group level, these moral strengths and weaknesses can balance each other out, so that the moral community benefits when individuals succeed and fail in our moral thinking in different ways. Thus, while practical wisdom in moral judgment is hard to achieve for both autistic and neurotypical

[1] The term 'neurotypicals' is used to refer to individuals who have a 'style of neurocognitive functioning that falls within the dominant societal standards of 'normal.' (Walker, 2014). It is thus more narrow than 'non-autistic'. We will nevertheless be using the term 'neurotypical' here. This is because while we focus on autism, it is likely that other conditions such as ADHD also raise issues concerning ways in which virtuous agency and practical wisdom may be affected (for example in the realm of impulse control).

[2] We are aware that there are dangers of overgeneralization. Just as people without autism can be moral or immoral and have different character traits and psychological dispositions, autistic people vary greatly in their personality profiles. Nevertheless, links can (and have been) established between autistic traits and moral reasoning styles.

persons at the individual level, cognitive differences may enhance it at the group level, so long as we stay in a moral conversation.

## 1. How we go wrong in our moral judgments

In order to act well, we need to know what the appropriate response is within a given situation. Should we honestly tell someone that their painting isn't very good, or should we support their efforts by mentioning the positive aspects of their work and silently passing over the deficits? From Aristotle onwards, virtue ethical accounts have stressed the importance of this skill, termed practical wisdom or *phronesis,* to moral character and action. Character traits like honesty, kindness and courage are thought to be developed and become stable as a result of the process of habituation and learning (Aristotle, 1985). Persons must learn – typically, through the normal processes of moral development and via trial and error – how to discern which actions are morally appropriate or required in any given situation. As an end result of this learning process, a stable disposition to be, for example, honest may be built up as a result of making appropriately honest choices in different contexts over time, where practical reason guides our assessment of how much information we must divulge to be appropriately honest. A virtuous trait such as honesty becomes habituated when there is a stable disposition set – in this case, where the disposition to be honest is so well-established that effortful use of practical reason to determine the honest action becomes less necessary. Developing virtuous character traits can therefore be understood as similar to developing expertise in some area (e.g., when a long-term car mechanic can very quickly assess problems and solutions regarding car engines), and practical reason is crucial to honing this expertise (Annas, 2003).[3]

It is hardly surprising or controversial that moral character and action requires development, learning, and reasoning. Moral judgment and practical wisdom are complex abilities, and many different psychological features will be involved here. Practical reasoning would seem to include cognitive capacities such as top-down attentional focus, as we must be able to attend to the salient features of a

---

[3]   A car mechanic in training is likely to have to work hard to pay attention to the right features of a car engine and find the problems that need fixing. Over time, the process becomes much quicker and less conscious, and an expert mechanic may find diagnosing faults in an engine becomes almost second nature to him.

situation to notice a moral problem. For example, only once a lecturer notices that a student's joke is off-colour because it is sexist or racist can she indicate to the student that the joke is inappropriate. Practical reason also requires self-control, as we must set aside impulses to gratify ourselves and instead focus on the features of a moral problem. In addition, in order to make good moral decisions we need to be able to understand the possible outcomes of an action – to return to our example, whether a certain person will benefit from being told the truth and to what extent they may be harmed by having their feelings hurt. In their introduction to Virtue Ethics, Rosalind Hursthouse and Glen Pettigrove argue that in deciding whether to tell the truth, the virtuous agent needs practical wisdom to know when to speak and when to be silent. 'It is part of practical wisdom to know how to secure real benefits effectively; those who have practical wisdom will not make the mistake of concealing the hurtful truth from the person who really needs to know it in the belief that they are benefiting him.' (Hursthouse and Pettigrove, 2018, Section 1.2.)

The traits associated with a condition such as autism may impact a person's ability to be virtuous in at least two ways. First, they might affect the development and exercise of a particular character trait, like kindness. For example, problems in gauging others' thoughts and emotions may affect the development of the trait of kindness due to a difficulty in assessing a person's psychological needs. A well-meaning person who wants to be kind or compassionate needs the practical wisdom to gauge others' beliefs, feelings and emotions. In a discussion of autism and moral agency, Jeanette Kennett (2002) presents the case of 'an autistic teenager with a passion for the piano and perfect pitch [who] suggested a constitutional amendment "to require that every home have a piano with 88 keys, and to require that the piano be kept in tune"' (p. 351). As an act of kindness, this is well-meant but lacks practical wisdom in that it fails to detect what will actually benefit others. Consequently, some authors argue that problems autistic people have gauging other people's thoughts and emotions constitute a problem for their moral agency (Stout, 2016; Shoemaker, 2015). However, it should be pointed out that the problem with gauging other people's emotions is a mutual one. Neurotypical individuals often struggle to empathize with autistic individuals and to gauge or understand their emotional reactions. This has become known as the double empathy problem (Milton, 2012). Indeed, autistic scholar Robert Chapman (2020) notes that neurotypicals are often poorly equipped to empathize with autistics because in an ableist society they usually don't *have* to think about autistics' needs; whereas autistics work hard to empathize with neurotypicals due to the obvious benefits of doing so.

What the piano example shows is the necessity of taking into account the differences between individuals – in terms of their needs and preferences – in deciding what the morally best action is in a situation. While many responsibility theorists focus on how autistic persons might struggle with this due to difficulties in accessing others' mental states, a second problem may arise when autistic individuals employ moral rules in an overly rigid fashion. It is plausible that in some cases, difficulties with gauging what other people are thinking is what leads to rigidity and a strong reliance on explicit rules. However, this is unlikely to be the whole story, as rigidity and need for sameness in autistic persons also apply in the non-social domain. For our current purposes, we can think of moral reasoning in autistic individuals as more rule focused and less sensitive to context than that of neurotypicals. To illustrate, consider the case of a young autistic man confronted with the scenario where an unemployed woman with several young children steals a small amount of food in a store. He insists that what she is doing is illegal and that she should therefore be arrested (example from Keel, 1993 cited in McGeer, 2008, p. 240). This is a case where the context of the woman is not taken into account in coming to a moral judgment.

It thus seems that virtue ethicists' justified emphasis on cognitive flexibility and assessing situations case by case entails a moral weakness associated with autistic traits such as rigidity and need for sameness, as well as difficulty in reading social situations and predicting others' mental states. To be good moral actors, we do need the ability to pick out the morally salient aspects of new situations, weigh competing moral values against each other, choose amongst moral options, etc. Of course, neurotypicals also frequently fail to exercise practical reason in an appropriate way, so the difference is better conceptualized as one of degree. As Kenneth Richman argues, when neurotypicals are tired, stressed, or even lonely they may '…simply not register facts or fail to perceive options even when they are paying appropriate attention' (Richman, 2018, p. 29). That is, neurotypicals also fail to pay attention to a moral problem or to reason regarding others' emotional needs. In this way, Richman argues, '…autists are not different in kind from neurotypical people, just subject to more of the common sorts of moral frailties' (Richman, 2018, p. 29).[4]

---

[4]    One might worry whether the difference in picking out salient moral factors is one in kind, rather than degree. We address this concern in section 2.

It should again be emphasized that virtue ethics construes practical wisdom as a goal we strive for that many do not achieve, rather than as the default mode of moral decision-making. Most of us fail to exhibit practical wisdom much of the time; and almost none of us are moral experts across the realms of different moral problems. However, this focus on the importance of flexible moral reasoning fosters an overly narrow and deficit-oriented view of the way in which autism can impact moral reasoning. Rather than emphasising the weaknesses, we should note that autistic individuals' style of reasoning has costs *and* benefits in terms of moral decision-making and action.[5] The costs and benefits of moral reasoning and decision-making styles in autistics are different than those of neurotypicals – who also suffer from certain deficits in practical reasoning.

A narrow focus on scenarios where we need a good understanding of others' inner lives to make the right decision distracts from the fact that all of us face a whole host of different kinds of challenges to moral decision making. Many challenges we face in acting morally are not those where the main difficulty is taking notice of others mental states or figuring out the right thing to do. Rather, neurotypicals often face the moral challenge of keeping the right course of action in mind when there are powerful countervailing factors that make it hard to follow. For example, if we look at the problem of climate change, the moral (and prudential) imperative to prevent global temperatures exceeding 1.5 degrees of pre-industrial levels is clear. And yet people who want to stop climate change still fly, eat meat, and buy new boilers and gas-guzzling SUVs. With the exception of the SUVs, we authors would include ourselves in the list of environmental akratics. Of course, weakness of will is not the only possible explanation for acting inconsistently with our professed values. People may also not care as much as they claim to, or not fully grasp the gravity of the moral situation, for example because they are unrealistically optimistic about likely outcomes. We take these explanations for moral weakness to be compatible and mutually reinforcing.

The moral weaknesses that many neurotypicals display are arguably aided by sensitivity to context and by a strong attunement to one's social environment, the very capacities often posited as

[5] This thought is already foreshadowed in work by Victoria McGeer (2008), who claims that there are different kinds or moral agency, and that individuals with autism may be more strongly driven by a desire for cosmic order, whereas neurotypicals are more strongly motivated by empathic concern.

necessary to practical wisdom. Furthermore, motivational and contextual factors don't just deter us from doing the right thing, they also affect our perception of what the right thing to do is. How so? Aristotle and neo-Aristotelians stress the importance of habituation and learning from moral exemplars, people who we admire and respect as moral role models. This means that we can be influenced by moral slippage within our moral community, because we calibrate our moral compass against others in our community (Merritt, 2009). Furthermore, the human tendency to self-justify morally problematic behaviour has more scope for coming up with creative self-justifications when we don't rely on explicit moral rules and take the context of a specific moral decision as a reason to justify our behaviour. We may for example say that of course flying is wrong, but *in this particular situation*, when we are visiting relatives abroad after a long time, it is perfectly justified.

A lack of cognitive flexibility may serve to keep certain moral reasons, such as environmental dangers, in focus in a way that is uncomfortable in light of societal norms but more conducive to consistent action. An anecdotal example is that of an autistic boy who cares a lot about the environment and is seriously upset by the fact that his family will happily consume chocolate which contains palm oil, even though palm oil farming is a major contribution to deforestation. Unlike his family, the boy cannot put this concern to one side when it comes to enjoying the chocolate. This action provides an example of the consistency but also rigidity often associated with autism. One might argue that part of situational flexibility and good moral agency is to know when to make an exception. But, on the flip side, we know that many of us are far too easily swayed to make exceptions. The boy is exhibiting a consistency of reasoning which is just as important to good moral judgment and decision making as situational flexibility is.

With these insights in hand, we turn to the moral strengths associated with autistic traits and survey the growing body of evidence that shows that autistic traits are associated with enhanced rationality in the form of more consistent and less biased reasoning.

## 2. Cognitive biases and enhanced rationality in autism

Although autistic persons may be less flexible on average, there is a raft of evidence that they are also more rational and less prone to cognitive biases than neurotypicals. Jeanette Kennett argues that rationality is core to autistic moral agency (2002). Kennett's approach is

# Anneli Jefferson and Katrina Sifferd

explicitly Kantian and therefore focused on universalizable rules for moral action. But even if we believe practical wisdom and sensitivity to context is necessary to making the right judgment in a given situation, there is a role for autistic traits. This is because autistic traits make individuals less prone to being influenced by *irrelevant features* of the context that tend to distort moral judgment. In this section, we look at how this plays out at the individual level. In the next section, we turn to benefits at the group level that result from having different cognitive styles.

Humans are famously subject to a large number of cognitive biases. How information is framed influences the way we evaluate it: for example, hearing that a new treatment will prevent 60% of deaths makes people evaluate it more positively than hearing that it cannot prevent 40% of deaths (Kahneman, 2011). This phenomenon is called the framing effect. People are also unrealistically optimistic; they think that bad events are less likely to happen to them than to others or than is objectively likely (Shepperd et al., 2013; Jefferson, Bortolotti, and Kuzmanovic, 2017). These are just two examples; there are many more biases that human cognition is prone to. We cannot review all the forms of irrationality reflected in human psychology here. Let's instead propose a general characterization. Human beings have cognitive biases, which are patterns of thinking where information processing isn't ideally epistemically rational; they are often not sensitive to available information in a way that would lead to the most accurate beliefs and decisions. This can mean certain pieces of information are given too much (or too little) weight, or that motivational factors affect what information is taken into account. It can also mean that one and the same piece of information is processed differently depending on how it is presented, as in the framing case.

Over the last 15 years, researchers have conducted studies that showed enhanced rationality in people with autistic traits. A recent review paper by Rozencrantz and colleagues (2021) compiles the findings on the topic from several studies. According to these studies, individuals with autistic traits are less prone to framing effects, the optimism bias, and other common biases. Furthermore, people with autistic traits rely less heavily on intuition and are more consistent in their choices (i.e., their choices are less influenced by irrelevant contextual factors than those of neurotypicals tend to be (Farmer, Baron-Cohen, and Skylark, 2017)).

Here are two examples:

In a 2017 study, Farmer and colleagues tested the susceptibility of people with lower and higher levels of autistic traits to being

156

influenced by contextual information that normally (in the non-clinical population) biases choice in ways that are irrational. The choice situation in these kinds of experiments is as follows: Participants are asked to choose between two options, A and B. In these choice scenarios option A is better than option B in one respect, but option B better than option A in a different one. So, for example, part-time job A might pay $ 6.60 per hour, whereas job B pays $ 8.20 per hour. However, the commuting time for job A is only 20 minutes, whereas the commuting time for job B is 60 minutes. People will choose according to how they evaluate the trade-off.

So far, so good. But if a decoy option is introduced, which makes one option look more attractive by comparison to the decoy, then choice behaviour changes in irrational ways. So, if a third job, C is introduced, where the commuting time is 30 minutes and the salary is $ 6.20 per hour, this influences choices in such a way that option A is preferred over option B because option C makes A look more attractive. While A is clearly more attractive than C, the respective advantages of A and B *compared to each other* have not changed. Similarly, if a decoy job option is introduced where a job pays $ 7.80 per hour but has a commuting time of 70 minutes, this has the effect of making B more attractive to participants, and B is chosen over A more frequently, even though its respective advantages and disadvantages compared to A have not changed. So in these cases, information that is irrelevant to the choice at hand (that a third option is worse than one of the existing options) influences the perception of attractiveness and the subsequent choice.

These experiments show that context affects our choices in ways that are irrational, because we lose sight of the respective advantages and disadvantages of the two best options. Farmer and colleagues found that this effect is reduced in people with an autism diagnosis compared to those without, and it is also reduced in those who score high on autistic traits (even if they don't have a diagnosis) compared to those who score low.

Similarly, Kuzmanovic and colleagues (Kuzmanovic, Rigoux, and Vogeley, 2019) compared optimistically biased belief updating of people with and without an autism diagnosis. In line with other studies that have found unrealistically positive expectations for oneself, they found biased belief updating that supports positive expectations for the future in neurotypicals. People were asked to estimate the likelihood of a number of adverse life events (experiencing dementia, getting burgled etc.) and were then given (fictional) population base rates. If these were lower than expected, meaning the bad event was on average less likely than participants had assumed, they updated their predictions accordingly, assuming the adverse life event was less likely to happen to them. However, they updated their predictions far less when they found out that the adverse event was on average more likely to occur than they had assumed (unwelcome news). When making predictions for similar others, this asymmetry in belief updating was not observed. By comparison, people with an autism diagnosis were less likely to update their beliefs in a way that ignored unwelcome news, making their belief updating more rational.

How are these studies relevant to moral decisions by autistic persons? The enhanced rationality associated with autistic traits is not specifically related to moral thinking, and the biases investigated are often highly specific. However, the research on enhanced rationality matters because moral decision-making depends on good practical reasoning skills, as virtue ethicists stress. There is much talk about the importance to reason flexibly and context sensitively, but obviously, practical wisdom requires us to use the context *in the right way*. It requires the individual *not* to be swayed by contextual factors that are irrelevant to the morality of an action, and it also requires them to not be overly influenced by motivational aspects such as the desirability of certain beliefs, be they moral or non-moral.

So, for example, when considering the optimism bias, we can see how this might be particularly harmful in making assessments of what action is needed to avert climate change. Of course, it isn't really possible to think that climate change will only happen to others.[6] But it is perfectly possible to rationalise the belief that climate change is less likely to affect oneself and family – to whom one has a heavy moral obligation – and to downplay one's moral obligation to those who are more likely to be affected. It may also be easy to decide that, because the problem of climate change is so large and difficult, one's own ways to contribute to solving the problem are too insignificant to be worth doing; and to note that one's actions seem in line with or endorsed by the actions of others. Here we can see how enhanced consistency and accuracy in evaluating scenarios with moral implications, as well as a lower dependence on contextual cues, can be desirable features in moral thinking and decision making. They prevent people from being distracted by the context, using the context for self-justification, or making decisions based heavily on wishful thinking in the ways we have described.

---

[6] Though even now some seem to find it entirely possible to deny that it is happening at all.

# Practical Wisdom and the Value of Cognitive Diversity

At this stage, one might object that autistic traits predispose individuals to a moral rigidity that is incompatible with true practical wisdom. Being *too* situationally flexible is not a good thing, as it comes at the price of consistency, but practical wisdom requires the *right* amount of flexibility. While many neurotypicals are overly morally flexible or swayed by irrelevant features of the context, autistic individuals err on the side of rigidity. We agree that most individuals, be they autistic or neurotypical, fall short of having fully developed practical wisdom – they fail to become moral experts in at least some moral realms. The boy who gets distraught at the fact that his friends and family are eating chocolate which contains palm oil may well be lacking a sense of perspective. But, so are his friends and family who only attend to the wider implications of their food consumption when this does not interfere with their pleasure. Real agents fall short of practical wisdom in many ways. Again, practical wisdom is an ideal rather than the normal state of adult humans. Some of us with more autistic traits fall short by not readily perceiving reasonable exceptions to moral rules, whereas others are driven by sensitivity to context to make so many exceptions that it is hard to still see that there is a rule.

However, it may still seem that there is a qualitative difference between autistic individuals and neurotypicals, because in principle, neurotypicals could overcome their biases and weakness of will, whereas this is not possible in the same way for autistic people. We note that the extent to which flexibility can be learned by autistic individuals and biases can be overcome by neurotypical ones is in the end an empirical question, so we won't be able to give a definite answer to this question from the armchair. Also, the relevant traits are a matter of degree, so there is unlikely to be a one size fits all generalisation that can be made of autistic and neurotypical people, respectively.

However, there are reasons to doubt that it really is more possible for neurotypicals to avoid cognitive biases than it is for autistics to become sensitive to environmental cues. There is evidence that autistic people can get better at taking relevant factors about context and what matters to others into account when making moral decisions. For example, Shulman et al (2012, p. 1375) noted that autistic persons can benefit from being explicitly taught the principles upon which behavior-governing rules are based, and from practicing transferring these principles from one situation to another. Autistic individuals describe a process of coming to grips with the moral rules and sensitivities in their environment by way of an expanding list of considerations that are relevant to the moral evaluation of a situation

# Anneli Jefferson and Katrina Sifferd

(Grandin, 1995).[7] So it's plausible that for autistic persons acquiring context sensitive moral judgment is possible, but that it will happen in different ways than it does for neurotypicals – it may in some cases require more explicit instruction and practice.

## 3. The benefits of psychological diversity in moral reasoning

In a society where people often fail in moral judgment and action, it is helpful for us to fail in different ways. It is worse for society if we are *all* too optimistic about morally relevant outcomes; or *all* find it difficult to flexibly take contextual information into account. It is also helpful for us to morally succeed in different ways: for example, it is better if some of us are quite good at assessing other people's needs, and some of us can offer intense focus on a moral problem. Different societal roles require different moral strengths and can be more or less tolerant of certain moral weaknesses. For example, if a person finds it hard to anticipate and understand the emotions of the average child, they are probably not well suited to being a primary school teacher.

The benefits of diversity in moral reasoning can be seen from other perspectives than through the lens of practical wisdom. In her paper 'The Advantages of Moral Diversity,' Amelie Oksenberg Rorty uses the differences in styles of moral reasoning related to different types of ethical theory as an example. Ethical theories tend to give rise to different approaches to solving moral problems, even though they often agree on which moral problems need to be solved. For example, deontologists may focus on the duty to follow moral rules, whereas consequentialists focus on picking actions based upon the likelihood that they will achieve better moral outcomes. According to Rorty, a society containing some acting as deontologists and others as consequentialists is better off because 'it is safer and easier to be a full-blown consequentialist if you know that there are

---

[7]    One might further argue that in order for an action be morally wrong or right, there needs to be a reason for this to be the case. This reason should be available to anyone who can reason morally, even if it is more difficult to isolate the morally relevant features in a given context. However, there is room for disagreement here, as Aristotle claims that only the phronimos (moral sage) can be relied on to make the right moral judgment reliably across all contexts. At least one of the authors would argue that Aristotle is wrong about this. But in any case, it need not overly worry us lesser mortals, who do not achieve full practical wisdom anyway.

enough deontologists around to prevent you from doing something awful for the sake of a distant good' (2009, p. 53). Similarly, it is safer to act for the sake of pure duty if there are utilitarians around to argue for the distribution of basic human goods (2009, p. 53).[8] In other words, focus on moral rules alone can lead to problematic outcomes (e.g. being honest in cases where it doesn't have good effects); but focus on outcomes alone can lead to violation of important moral rules (such as killing one to save five).

It is especially valuable that diverse moral reasoners are often drawn toward different types of moral *projects and roles*. Society at large has benefited from Greta Thunberg's focus on climate change – she has increased awareness of the problem, motivated many young people to get involved in the cause, and made it clear what sorts of actions might help us address the problem if we act collectively. This point is also made by Robert Chapman, who argues that while her autistic traits 'are both beneficial and disabling for her as an individual, Thunberg's role as a climate activist is arguably a vital niche from the group perspective' (Chapman, 2021, p. 7). Chapman claims that at the level of the group or society, having cognitive diversity is beneficial for the system as a whole, even if the individual traits can at times make life more difficult for the individual and be disabling. He introduces the example of individuals with autistic traits being over-represented in engineering and points out that having a subset of people with a cognitive profile that lends itself to working in engineering and technology is beneficial to society. Chapman stresses that looking at the system level effects of different cognitive styles allows us to acknowledge the benefits of cognitive diversity in ways that are overlooked when focusing on perceived deficits at the level of the individual.

Applied more specifically to the realm of the moral and the idea of practical wisdom, this means that, given human limitations, practical wisdom (or some group analogue of it) may be best achieved if we have a variety of moral reasoning styles that complement each other, especially if persons occupy moral roles well-suited to their moral strengths. Persons with different strengths and weaknesses in practical reasoning may determine that different actions are necessary to address the problem of climate change; and these different decisions and actions may at times serve as a correction to others' errors in judgment. That is, a person who is sensitive to context may

---

[8]  True believers in a given moral theory might disagree. Rorty's approach already presupposes that different theories of normative ethics have strengths and weaknesses. We agree.

decide that given time and resources, it makes sense to fly to the UN climate change summit COP 26 to make the case for climate action; and a person skilled at focusing on the importance of consistent action on climate change may warn others that refusing to fly is an important – even necessary – way to address global warming. By having these different voices in the mix, we as a society are aided in giving due weight to morally relevant considerations at play in the context we find ourselves in.

From this perspective, rigidity of thought and an intense focus on an object of interest, both of which are features frequently found in autism, can be moral strengths. The world is full of complex moral challenges and keeping all of them in view can lead to distraction and possibly paralysis and a feeling of hopelessness. In many cases, a person will achieve more in addressing current moral challenges if they put a lot of energy into one specific problem and consider how to best approach that problem than if they spread efforts thin. This is particularly true if the moral problem one focuses on is something like climate change, which is complex and requires quite a lot of fact finding to evaluate in the first place.[9]

## 4. Conclusions

In negotiating the moral trials that face us today, we need to draw on moral strengths where we find them, rather than being blinded to moral strengths because they may be different from our own or because they are associated with corresponding weaknesses in the interpersonal realm. Having respect for others requires us to recognize the strengths associated with cognitive difference. Importantly, on a group level, these differences can result in a level of decision making that reflects practical wisdom which we would not otherwise have been able to achieve. As Berys Gaut (2022) points out, we can gain benefits in creativity and problem solving at the group level that wouldn't be available to individuals, and this

---

[9] We have focused on enhanced rationality and rigidity associated with autistic traits, but here is a further, different, example: Temple Grandin, Professor of Animal Sciences and autism campaigner credits her autism with helping her design more humane slaughter-houses. She says that her autism leads to an extremely visual way of thinking, which in turn helped her to see what 'cattle were seeing' and design slaughterhouses in ways that cause the animals less distress (Grandin, 2010).

partly stems from the fact that different individuals bring different skills and knowledge to the table.

Of course, seeing diversity as valuable assumes that there is a basic shared commitment to moral principles within a society, such as the need for honesty or a livable climate. Rorty thinks this is not too demanding. We agree. Often fairly different action-guiding principles can be seen as related to some greater value or principle at a high level of generality (Rorty, 2009, p. 5). Agreement that something is to be morally valued does not require that we have the same reasons for valuing it; or that we will exercise our valuing in the same way. Isabel may care about climate change due to concerns about the next generation's future or because she thinks biodiverse ecosystems have intrinsic moral value. Or she may recognize both as good reasons but find that concerns for the next generation's well-being, which includes her children, is what motivates her to act. Joan, on the other hand, might want to stop climate change because she is concerned about the effects on poor countries here and now.

Diversity in moral reasoning serves us, just as diversity benefits universities and companies. Inclusion is therefore not just a demand of fairness, but in a community's interest, be that a workplace or society more generally. However, the benefits of cognitive diversity extend beyond workplace efficiency or representation of minorities in decision making processes that affect them. Differences in reasoning styles can lead groups to better moral judgments and outcomes. In the workplace and other settings, some autistic persons may apply their focus and unflinching assessment of a moral problem to generate agendas and priorities that many of us greatly admire.

This requires workplaces but also society more generally to be educated about the benefits of cognitive diversity such that views or contributions are not dismissed on the basis that somebody is cognitively different. To achieve this, people need to be educated about the different strengths individuals with diverse cognitive profiles bring to the table. Just as we already know a project can benefit from including people with different areas of expertise, it should be explained that different thinking styles can help to get a more comprehensive understanding of the moral challenges we face and of possible solutions. To return to an earlier example: seeing an autistic boy's distress when we eat chocolate can remind his peers, teachers, and family of the values we are committed to as a society, and to think more carefully about making exceptions. But this effect requires taking different forms of moral cognition seriously as forms of moral cognition.

Further, when important governmental, regulatory, and corporate committees are convened to address pressing moral issues, we should aim to increase the cognitive diversity of the persons attending. Racial, socioeconomic, and gender diversity in decision-making groups can result in better moral outcomes; but cognitive diversity in moral reasoning may be just as important. Cognitively diverse committees can display better moral imagination – they are open to a larger variety of moral reasons and outcomes in pursuit of a common value.[10]

*Cardiff University*
*jeffersona1@cardiff.ac.uk*
*Elmhurst University*
*sifferdk@elmhurst.edu*

## References

APA, *Diagnostic and Statistical Manual of Mental Disorders, Fifth Edition*. (Arlington VA: American Psychiatric Association, 2013).

Aristotle, *The Nicomachean Ethics*. Translated by Terence Irwin. (Indianapolis: Hackett Publishing Co. 1985).

Ian Birrel, 'Greta Thunberg teaches us about autism as much as climate change', *The Guardian*, 23,04.2019. Accessed 19.08.2021. https://www.theguardian.com/commentisfree/2019/apr/23/greta-thunberg-autism.

Robert Chapman, 'Do Neurotypicals Have Moral Agency?' *Critical Neurodiversity.com* (2020). Accessed 06.12.2021. https://criticalneurodiversity.com/2020/03/31/do-neurotypicals-have-intact-moral-agency/?fbclid=IwAR1P6bXNfmhuHeC1lHjT73bmsNWb33lHE838fSqBQapY_fFWcCKuJC1-isg.

Robert Chapman, 'Neurodiversity and the Social Ecology of Mental Functions', *Perspectives on Psychological Science*: 16 (2021) 1360–1372

George Farmer, Simon Baron-Cohen, and William J. Skylark. 'People With Autism Spectrum Conditions Make More Consistent Decisions', *Psychological Science* 28 (2017) 1067–1076.

[10] We presented material for this chapter at the Workshop 'Virtues and Values in a Changing World' at Cardiff University and received useful feedback. We would like to thank Daniel Morgan, Jon Webber, Panos Paris, Robert Chapman and Zsuzsanna Chappell for very helpful comments on draft versions of this chapter.

# Practical Wisdom and the Value of Cognitive Diversity

Temple Grandin, *Thinking in Pictures: And other reports from my life with autism*. (New York: Doubleday, 1995).

Temple Grandin. 'The World needs all kinds of minds', *Ted Talk* (2010), https://www.ted.com/talks/temple_'grandin_the_world_needs_all_kinds_of_minds?language=en. Accessed: 6.12.2021

Berys Gaut, 'Group Creativity', *Royal Institute Philosophy Supplementary Volume*, 92 (2022) 5–26.

Rosalind Hursthouse, and Glen Pettigrove, 'Virtue Ethics'. In *Stanford Encyclopedia of Philosophy*, (Winter 2018 edition) edited by Edward Zalta. Accessed 6.12.2021 https://plato.stanford.edu/archives/win2018/entries/ethics-virtue/.

Anneli Jefferson, Lisa Bortolotti, and Bojana Kuzmanovic, 'What is unrealistic optimism?' *Consciousness and Cognition* 50 (2017), 3–11.

Daniel Kahneman, *Thinking, Fast and Slow*. (London: Penguin, 2011).

Jeanette Kennett,. 'Autism, Empathy and Moral Agency', *The Philosophical Quarterly* 52 (2002), 340–357.

Kristjan Kristjansson, 'The Need for Phronesis', *Royal Institute Philosophy Supplementary Volume*, 92 (2022) 167–84.

Bojana Kuzmanovic., Lionel Rigoux, and Kai Vogeley. 'Brief Report: Reduced Optimism Bias in Self-Referential Belief Updating in High-Functioning Autism', *Journal of Autism and Developmental Disorders* 49 (2019), 2990-2998.

Victoria McGeer, 'Varieties of moral agency: lessons from autism (and psychopathy'. In: Walter Sinnott-Armstrong (ed.) *Moral Psychology, The neuroscience of morality: Emotion, disease and development* (Cambridge Massachusetts and London, England: MIT Press 2008), 227–257

Maria Merritt, 'Aristotelean Virtue and the Interpersonal Aspect of Ethical Character', *Journal of Moral Philosophy* 6 (2009), 23–49.

Damian E. M. Milton, 'On the ontological status of autism: the 'double empathy problem'', *Disability & Society* 27 (2012), 883–887.

Kenneth A. Richman, 'Autism and Moral Responsibility: Executive Function, Reasons Responsiveness, and Reasons Blockage', *Neuroethics* 11 (2018), 23–33.

Liron Rozenkrantz, Anila M. D'Mello, and John D. E. Gabrieli, 'Enhanced rationality in autism spectrum disorder', *Trends in Cognitive Science* 25 (2021), 685–696.

Thomas Schramme, 'The Role of Empathy in an Agential Account of Morality: Lessons from Autism and Psychopathy'. In: Neil Roughley and Thomas Schramme (Eds.) *Forms of Fellow*

# Anneli Jefferson and Katrina Sifferd

*Feeling: Empathy, Sympathy, Concern and Moral Agency*, (Cambridge, UK: Cambridge University Press 2018), 307–326.

James A. Shepperd, William M. P. Klein, Erika A. Waters, and Neil D. Weinstein, 'Taking Stock of Unrealistic Optimism', *Perspectives on Psychological Science* 8 (2013), 395–411.

David Shoemaker, *Responsibility From the Margins*, (Oxford, UK: Oxford University Press 2015).

Nathan Stout, 'Conversation, responsibility, and autism spectrum disorder', *Philosophical Psychology* 29 (2016), 1015–1028.

Nick Walker, 'Neurodiversity: Some Basic Terms and Definitions', (2014). Accessed 01.10.2021. https://www.planetneurodivergent. com/neurodiversity-and-neurodivergent-basic-terminology/.

# The Need for *Phronesis*

KRISTJÁN KRISTJÁNSSON

**Abstract**

This chapter explores the state of public and academic discourse about socio-moral issues elicited by the Covid-19 pandemic, through two informal case studies of Facebook statuses and columns in two leading UK newspapers. The Facebook statuses tended to focus on performance virtues as remedies rather than moral virtues, whereas a survey among the general public highlighted the role of moral virtues. Divisions of opinion among columnists in the *Guardian* and *Daily Telegraph* turned out to be about different prioritisations of moral virtues rather than a trade-off between virtues and economic values. However, missing from all those discourses was attention to the meta-virtue of *phronesis*, or practical wisdom, as an adjudicator of virtue conflicts. Recent psychological work on wisdom does not fully ameliorate this lacuna; the paper argues that a retrieval of the Aristotelian concept of *phronesis* is needed to help us make balanced moral decisions.

## 1. Polarisation and Pandemic

It has become almost a platitude to say that the 21st century has witnessed increased political and ideological polarisation as well as a surge in populism from both the right and the left. Phrases such as 'post-truth', 'fake news' and 'alternative facts' have become household terms; and after the divisive Brexit campaign in the UK, parents react much more negatively than before if an offspring dares form amorous bonds with an individual from the 'other' side of the political spectrum (Guardian, 2016). Conspiracy theories have garnered increased popularity: some of them so bizarre, such as QAnon, that they make far-fetched figments of the medieval imagination seem positively reasonable by comparison.

There are conflicting views on whether recent technological advances, especially in the field of social media, have simply taken the lid off a discourse that hitherto had been confined to the locker room, the staff coffee corner and the dining table, or whether there has actually been a turn for the worse (or at least for the more radical, divisive and inflammatory) in the way people discuss hot topics of the day. In any case, the worldwide pandemic has helped crystallise many of these developments. As well as bringing existing

doi:10.1017/S1358246122000236

polarisations into sharper relief, it created new ones of its own, such as the one between public health and economic prosperity – dividing people both along and across traditional conflict lines. For example, the Tory ploy of paying 50% of people's restaurant bills during the month of August 2020 would probably have made the *laissez-faire* Margaret Thatcher turn in her grave: a vivid reminder of the fact that the left–right divide is becoming more multi-dimensional and less focused on the economy than it used to be.

The socio-moral, psycho-moral and economic reverberations of the pandemic led to a proliferation of debates in public media that closely connect – albeit in new and unforeseeable ways – to proverbial debates about values and virtues. As a scholar interested in the role of virtues and character strengths in the good life (Kristjánsson, 2015; 2020), I have found those new debates fascinating, infuriating and intimidating in equal measure. Fascinating because of the way they replicate old debates in new contexts; infuriating in the way they reproduce old fallacies that I thought academic discourse had laid to rest; intimidating because of the immediacy of the practical consequences that acting on some of the more radical normative positions would have for people's daily lives.

Rather than continuing to rant about my own abstract thoughts on social media, as I did quite a lot towards the beginning of the pandemic, I decided to conduct two minor 'case studies' of my own, the findings from which inform the remainder of this chapter. Let me first make it clear, however, that I do not claim any strict methodological credibility for those 'case studies', and there is good reason why I put them in scare quotes. I did not thematically analyse findings in a systematic manner along qualitative lines, nor did I count statistical beans as a quantitative researcher would. I simply did two things. In Case Study 1, I read carefully through Facebook statuses by my 'friends' for a few months insofar as they had to do with reactions to the pandemic and the lockdowns; or more specifically still, insofar as they suggested or recommended any particular states of character and virtue that would help us survive through the ordeal. In Case Study 2, I skimmed through posts written by some of the most outspoken columnists of the *Guardian*, on the one hand, and the *Daily Telegraph*, on the other – meant to represent opposing stances on the great political divide – trying to analyse their views in characterological terms. More specifically, I wanted to find out whether only one of the two 'camps' represented the stance of virtue, or whether both used virtues as grist for their argumentative mills – simply *different* virtues or the *same* virtue instantiated differently. I could obviously have done this in a more scientific way, but I never intended to publish my findings in an academic outlet, so I am happy to designate the 'results' reported on below simply as anecdotal evidence, potentially liable to a biased interpretation by myself.

Without wanting to anticipate the findings in too much detail, it will be instructive for readers to know at this juncture that what I found was an unexpectedly strong reliance on character-and-virtue language from all the relevant discursive camps. For someone eager to apply that particular theoretical lens, this must count as a positive finding. Less positive, however, was the general lack of attention paid to one of virtue theory's profoundest problems: how to intellectually and metacognitively navigate and arbitrate conflicts between different virtues. In a nutshell, the meta-virtue of *phronesis* or practical wisdom (Darnell et al., 2019; Kristjánsson et al., 2021) almost never came up in those discussions, nor was it applied implicitly. What I found, rather, were hordes of people who were 'excessively good' (with respect to the 'golden mean' of virtue) in a certain domain-specific Aristotelian sense. Before explaining what I mean by this and drawing some relevant conclusions, I need to inform readers briefly about my theoretical commitments and assumptions.

## 2. Neo-Aristotelian Character in Focus

I work in the Jubilee Centre for Character and Virtues: the world's largest research centre dedicated to the study of character and virtues, from an interdisciplinary perspective of philosophy, psychology and education. Our theoretical basis is neo-Aristotelian (Kristjánsson, 2015), non-politically partisan and non-religious. A lot of our work focuses on character education in schools and in professional ethics education; and philosophically educated readers will understand the advantages of grounding character education in the time-honoured Aristotelian paradigm of virtue ethics, whose resurgence in moral philosophy, post-Anscombe's (1958) article, has been phenomenal.

Complementing its philosophical merits are various methodological and practical advantages. A model of character education as the educational incarnation of virtue ethics is grounded in an objective conception of the good life as 'flourishing' (Kristjánsson, 2020); it tells a fairly plausible developmental story of how character can be taught, caught and sought (Jubilee Centre, 2017); it incorporates an acute sensitivity to social context and individual variance (Kristjánsson, 2020); and it focuses on gradually developing critical metacognitions as forming an agent's moral (characterological) identity (Darnell et al., 2019). Moreover, such a model lends itself open to constant updates and revisions because of its naturalist assumptions according to which all moral and educational theorising is answerable to empirical research on what makes people tick (Kristjánsson, 2015). The last-mentioned advantage makes neo-Aristotelian character education resonate particularly well with practitioners.

Neo-Aristotelian character education tends to apply a model of character that considers character virtues to fall into four main categories: moral, intellectual, civic and performative (Jubilee Centre, 2017). We can think of those as instrument groups in a large orchestra. However, contrary to various other paradigms of virtue and character education, the neo-Aristotelian model reserves a major role for the 'conductor' of the orchestra – in the form of the meta-virtue of *phronesis,* which makes sure that the orchestra plays in harmony and that no single orchestra group or player, however powerful and competent on its own, overwhelms and overpowers the others. This categorisation is based broadly on Aristotle's own distinction between the moral and intellectual virtues versus technical executive skills, although he did not distinguish as clearly between the moral and the civic virtues. It helps also that this categorisation is in good harmony with millions of contemporary people's self-reported character strengths and virtues which, when factor analysed, tend to fall into three overarching themes: interpersonal or other-directed issues, called Caring; intellectual explorations, called Inquisitiveness; and behavioural control, called Self-Control (McGrath, 2015).

Apart from the growth of interest within philosophy and education, we are also witnessing a retrieval of character and virtue research in psychology (McGrath, 2015; Fowers et al., 2021; Wright, Warren and Snow, 2021). This retrieval, often referred to as a new 'science of virtue' (Fowers et al., 2021), has been spurred on by the advent of so-called positive psychology in general and in particular its research into universal character strengths and virtues (Peterson and Seligman, 2004; McGrath, 2015). Defying historic anti-virtue catechisms in psychology (Allport, 1937; Kohlberg, 1981), positive psychologists have conducted extensive research into the role of good character in the flourishing life (Seligman, 2011) and found surprisingly uniform views, regardless of time and geography, on how living well includes a specific set of (acquired) universal human character qualities. Nevertheless, there are considerable differences in foci and emphasis – and sometimes more substantial differences – between the positive psychological and neo-Aristotelian take on character strengths and virtues, as I explain in the following section.

Recently, the sort of neo-Aristotelian, virtue-ethics-based character education promoted by the Jubilee Centre has come under a heavy attack from a number of UK academics who accuse it of being neoliberal and possibly religiously motivated – and indeed part of a grand, single-network conspiracy to personalise the political (Allen and Bull, 2018; Jerome and Kisby, 2019). This may seem fairly odd at first sight because Aristotelian philosophy is often seen as the direct anti-thesis of liberalism (at least the classical type, from Locke to Rawls) and appears to have even less in common with the recent neoliberal outgrowth. However, the polarisation tendency that I described at the outset is simply rearing its ugly head here once again. One of its syndromes is the obsession with the politicisation of all public or academic discourse: seeing any theoretical argument as masking a politically motivated move in a power game. I simply note this line of criticism here without aiming to respond to it directly (cf. Kristjánsson, 2021). Indirectly, however, what transpires from the following section and my first 'case study' is that there is no single network of character education operating within the UK at the moment. Rather, there are at least two contrasting approaches to how character virtues are to be valued, prioritised and educated in our quest for the good life.

## 3. Facebook versus the Queen

The two academic approaches to character virtues that I referred to as competing for allegiance in the UK are on the one hand a positive psychological model, loosely based on Peterson and Seligman (2004) but with a narrower remit, and on the other hand a neo-Aristotelian model (Jubilee Centre, 2017). To summarise and simplify the differences between these models, the first one – which tends to be promoted by organisations such as the CBI (Confederation of British Industry) and at least implicitly adhered to by the civil servants in Whitehall – understands character as encompassing the 'non-cognitive' side of personality skills (so-called soft skills), whereas the neo-Aristotelian model understands character in terms of the morally evaluable part of personality. The main substantive focus in the first model is on performance virtues such as grit, resilience and self-confidence and on how those broaden and build personal resources, whereas the second model prioritises moral virtues such as compassion, justice and honesty. Accordingly, the first model considers the main value of the virtues to lie in their instrumental benefits for better behaviour, higher grades and better workplace performance, while the second model highlights the intrinsic value of the virtues for the flourishing life of which they are constitutive (although grades and performance will also supposedly improve as a happy side-effect). Finally, the positive psychological model assumes that the more of each virtue, the better – and that a chain of virtues is as strong as its strongest link – with little or no attention paid to virtue conflicts, trade-offs and adjudications. In contrast, the neo-Aristotelian model assumes that too much of a virtue becomes a vice, just like too little, and that a chain is only as strong as its weakest link – with significant attention being paid to virtue conflicts and how the intellectual meta-virtue of *phronesis* is needed to critically assess and adjudicate those (Kristjánsson, 2013).

Now, I happen to have more than 2000 Facebook friends, and traumatised and homebound as I was in March-April 2020, at the beginning of the first UK lockdown, I spent an uncharacteristically long time reading through their posts. I guess I was looking for reassurance and advice from them about how to deal with those turbulent times. Eventually, I decided to jot down the character virtues they mentioned: an exercise that I referred to above, somewhat tongue-in-cheek, as my 'Case Study 1'. To my surprise – given that a disproportionate number of my friends are indeed academic philosophers, many of whom have Aristotelian sympathies – I realised that the virtues mentioned were almost invariably performative ones. The advice proffered was all about keeping one's head above the water; avoiding danger; hanging in there; mobilising one's resources; not feeling too downhearted. Insofar as specific virtue terms were used, they belonged to the familiar 'resilience', 'perseverance', 'grit', 'calmness' category, with the Buddhist concept of 'mindfulness' often added to the mix.

I felt somewhat disheartened by this, although I am obviously aware of the fact that the language of moral virtue does not come easily to everyone, and there are those who feel that it sounds too touchy-feely and mawkish for modern sentiments. The use of some common virtue terms has indeed declined substantially in ordinary language (Kesebir and Kesebir, 2012) since the days of Queen Victoria and Jane Austin who would have found it natural and unintimidating. Yet speaking of a queen, the present UK Head of State, HRH Queen Elizabeth, happened to give a televised speech on April 5th, 2020: a rare public address concerning the ongoing Covid-19 pandemic (The Queen, 2020). The address was watched live by an estimated 24 million viewers in the United Kingdom alone. Just like my Facebook friends, the Queen focused on the virtues that are needed to take us through the pandemic, and revealingly her short speech included no fewer than eight virtue terms. Interestingly, six of the eight terms referred to the realm of the moral/civic rather than the psychological/performative: namely selflessness, appreciation, duty, humour, helping others and compassion. Perhaps nobody minds an old lady using terms like this; after all, mawkishness is highly context-and-individuality-sensitive.

In any case, the Queen seemed to have captured the public consciousness better than my Facebook friends, because a poll that the Jubilee Centre conducted of 2,093 adults in the UK, at about the time of the Queen's address, found that people valued care and compassion in others most of all virtues during the crisis (68%), and 55% agreed that the health of today's older generations is more important than long-term economic prosperity of future generations, with only 8% disagreeing (Arthur, 2020). Notably, when repeated a few months later, these numbers had not changed substantially. I cannot offer anything but educated guesses as to why the general public were more willing than my Facebook friends – a 'sample' highly skewed towards academics – to mention moral qualities. Perhaps it is easier to tick a box for compassion in an anonymous survey than to mention the term explicitly in a Facebook status. Perhaps the latter is just too 'uncool'. Or perhaps what we are seeing here is the increasing rift between the chattering classes on the one hand and the general public on the other, about which much recent political discourse has proliferated. If that is the case, Queen Elizabeth seems, as already noted, to have captured the public mood better than my intellectually oriented friends.

I do harbour worries about the recent academic obsession with performative virtues, as encapsulated in the positive psychological model. For one thing, resilience is an amoral trait; it can be the resilience of the repeat offender. More generally, this model psychologises and individualises problems that are often social or collective (e.g. a global pandemic), and it under-estimates the nature of human beings as 'political animals', thus severing the link between character and citizenship. I could go on and on, by way of comparison, about the advantages of the neo-Aristotelian model. However, what I want to point out instead at the end of this section is a common lacuna in both the Facebook statuses that I canvassed and the Queen's address to the nation. There was no mention of *wisdom* anywhere, let alone *phronesis* or practical wisdom as a metacognitive capacity to make complex moral decisions.

I found this lacuna astounding, especially as the weeks passed during the first lockdown and more scepticism emerged about governmental policies. With the discourse focusing more and more on

# Kristján Kristjánsson

the trade-off between health (especially the health of the old and vulnerable) and economic prosperity (especially that of younger generations), one could have expected the virtue discourse to change from a focus on individual, domain-specific virtues to meta-level ones. However, I did not notice any such change – at least not among my Facebook friends. I decided, therefore, that I would need a larger lens and another 'case study' to cast further light on this issue.

## 4. Columnists at War – and Virtues 'Wandering Alone'

As the summer of 2020 turned into autumn and a new lockdown was instigated in the UK, political debates crystallised more clearly into opposing camps and became fiercer. The opposing stances of the 'typical' *Guardian* 'liberal' columnists, such as Owen Jones, Polly Toynbee and Jonathan Freedland, coming down on the side of public health, and the 'typical' *Daily Telegraph* 'conservative' columnists, such as Sherelle Jacobs, Michael Deacon and Allister Heath, representing the stance of industry and economic health, seemed to me to capture this divide well, and I decided to subject their columns to a more systematic scrutiny for a few weeks in the autumn of 2020 – constituting my 'Case Study 2'.

I am quite ready to admit that I approached this study with the prejudices inherent in my liberal orientation – albeit of the Millian 19th-century rather than the 21st-century kind – that I happen to share with the majority of academics. My initial working hypothesis was that the *Guardian* columnists would invoke virtues, whereas the *Daily Telegraph* ones would concentrate on hard economic values. That prejudiced assumption aside, I did decide to take what these columnists said at face value: namely, as presenting their authentic views, rather than imputing to them any ulterior motives.

My aim was not to evaluate the logical rigour and substantive worth of the views expressed in those columns, but rather to scan them for direct and indirect references to character virtues. And here my initial hypothesis was decisively disconfirmed. To be sure, the *Guardian* columns teemed with references to compassion and care towards the vulnerable and the need to protect those at all costs. However, the apparent 'hardness' of the opposing economic argument for the lifting of all lockdowns was mitigated by the frequent use of virtue language (such as 'compassion') and allusions to 'soft' emotional values (such as 'empathy'). In other words, the language of the typical *Daily Telegraph* column speaking against governmental policy was strewed with compassionate references to the loneliness of the locked-up old, the misery of the furloughed or unemployed middle-aged and the despair of the studies-deprived and desolate young. Much was made of the plight of the 30,000 people who supposedly would die prematurely of cancer because of NHS's exclusive focus on the coronavirus. All in all, the language of both the *Guardian* and *Daily Telegraph* columns was steeped in moral language in general and virtue language in particular. The so-called 'good people' were apparently not confined to one side of the lockdown debate.

Yet what struck me here, just like in Case Study 1, was the complete elision of any master- or meta-virtue meant to secure a balance between the competing first-level virtues. The only serious exception was in an article by Allister Heath (2020), but in that piece he, so to speak, reverted to type by couching the trade-off between health and wealth in the crude utilitarian terms of a cost-benefit analysis where a monetary value is ascribed to anything, from people's lives (as 'quality-adjusted-life-years') to missed birthday parties because of lockdown rules. However, nobody ever brought up wisdom, not to mention *phronesis*.

As I completed this informal case study, I was reminded of an old work by G. K. Chesterton. Although his text was written from a fairly orthodox Christian perspective, there is a lot to be learned from it in the current intellectual climate, irrespective of one's religious views. 'A man was meant to be doubtful about himself, but undoubting about the truth; this has been exactly reversed' (1908, chap. 3), Chesterton remarks in a way that seems to anticipate the current era of post-truth coupled with unbridled enhancements of subjective identities. What he says about virtues is no less timely and topical:

> The modern world is not evil; in some ways the modern world is far too good. It is full of wild and wasted virtues. When a [moral] scheme is shattered [...], it is not merely the vices that are let loose. The vices are, indeed, let loose, and they wander and do damage. But the virtues are let loose also; and the virtues wander more wildly, and the virtues do more terrible damage. The modern world is full of the old [...] virtues gone mad. The virtues have gone mad because they have been isolated from each other and are wandering alone (Chesterton, 1908, chap. 3).

Chesterton goes on to reminisce about a lost system that 'could to some extent make righteousness and peace kiss each other. Now they do not even bow.' This is precisely what I found in Case

# Kristján Kristjánsson

Study 2. The virtues upheld by the *Guardian* columnists on the one hand and the *Daily Telegraph* ones on the other did not even bow to one another, let alone kiss or aim for any affective union. The *Guardian* ones simply celebrated one kind of compassion and their counterparts another kind, along with virtues of righteous indignation and deservingness. These virtues 'wandered alone', however, like a group of novice scouts on an excursion without a guide to lead them. The diverse moral values touted seemed to represent a world that is 'far too good', to use Chesterton's words, in the sense of being out of balance.

Both my case studies, therefore, led to the same conclusion. There is no shortage in the public domain of arguments drawing on character virtues and the flourishing life. In that sense, MacIntyre's (1998) dictum about most of us being Aristotelians in the way we speak still holds good. However, one core teaching from Aristotle's moral writings seems to have got lost somewhere along the way: the need for *phronesis*.

## 5. Can Contemporary Psychology Help Us Out?

It is probably just a coincidence that the journal *Psychological Inquiry* dedicated its whole second issue of 2020 to the topic of wisdom; this must have been decided long before the pandemic. In any case, it was most opportune, given the lack of attention that both academics and pundits seem to have been giving to the function of wisdom in our stormy times. In this issue, Grossmann and his colleagues (2020a), who include many of psychology's most prominent wisdom researchers, produced a comprehensive new 'common' wisdom model (CWM) – followed by no less than nine critical commentaries and finally a response by some authors of the target article (Grossmann et al., 2020b). In their response, Grossmann and colleagues helpfully related their wisdom model to the ongoing health crisis, presenting it as a contribution from the social and behavioural sciences to addressing the dilemmas caused by the new world-wide challenge, such as health versus wealth.

From an historical and philosophical perspective, previous conceptual work in psychology has been hampered by attempts to reconcile (at best) or elide (at worst) a standard distinction between three discrete historical concepts of wisdom derived from Aristotle: *sophia* (theoretical wisdom), *phronesis* (practical wisdom), and *deinotes* (instrumental wisdom or 'cleverness'). The new CWM comes in many ways close to *phronesis*. Pitched as unifying perspectival metacognition and moral aspirations, the CWM seems to align with the *phronesis* construct that, since Aristotle, has been understood as a meta-virtue driven by moral motivations (Darnell et al., 2019). This potential rapprochement, however, opens up various thorny questions – theoretical as well as practical – about a potential competition, or at least division of labour, between wisdom, as understood in the CWM, and *phronesis*.

To cut a long story short, I do consider the CWM a game-changer in the field of wisdom research in psychology (see Kristjánsson et al., 2021). It is not only that, as a neo-Aristotelian, I am enamoured of the way in which the wisdom construct in psychology has now been realigned with practical wisdom in a broadly Aristotelian sense; what is more generally appealing about this development is how timely it is, given the current challenges the world faces, and how directly it addresses a serious lacuna in academic and public discourse. On top of this, the target article introducing the CWM (Grossmann et al., 2020a) happens to constitute a *tour de force* of psychological scholarship, characterised by a deft handling of voluminous bodies of literature and a no-nonsense conciliatory spirit that is rare in academia.

All that said, it is the philosopher's prerogative to be curmudgeonly, and I will exercise that prerogative here. As indicated above, the CWM has two main pillars, 'perspectival metacognition' and 'moral aspirations' (Grossmann et al., 2020a; 2020b). The CWM does not explain how perspectival metacognition (i.e. contextual higher-order thinking) guides wise action, arguably the central function of wisdom, at least on Aristotle's understanding of practical wisdom or *phronesis*. But is this lacuna then filled by the other pillar: moral aspirations? From a neo-Aristotelian perspective, the fact that the CWM posits 'moral aspirations' as one of the two main pillars of wisdom counts as an extremely positive development, especially given psychology's earlier-mentioned penchant for the performative and instrumental over the moral. It is reassuring, from a neo-Aristotelian perspective, to see the word 'moral' appear almost 100 times in the target article on the CWM (Grossmann et al., 2020a). However, the way the concept of 'moral aspirations' is unpacked in the article is not as reassuring – at least not from the standpoint of those concerned about finding an action-guiding decision procedure to resolve virtue conflicts and trade-offs, such as those generated by the pandemic.

At the beginning of their target article, Grossmann and colleagues specify moral aspirations in terms of aspirational goals that aim for a balance of self-and-other interests and an orientation toward a shared humanity (2020a, p. 103). The main difficulty here is that these are vague referents that cry out for elucidation. Instead of providing such an elucidation, the remainder of their (2020a) article and the (2020b) rejoinder simply refer back to this specification without deepening it. In one place (2020a, p. 107), the word 'prosociality' is added to the mix, but 'prosocial' is not the same as 'moral' or an elucidation of it. 'Prosocial' is a behavioural concept, and behaviour can be prosocial without being moral (e.g. uncritically and unreflectively following another person's lead to do a good thing) and moral without being prosocial (e.g. showing justified anger which happens to upset and alienate the persons who transgressed in a way that gave rise to the anger). 'Orientation toward a shared humanity' and a 'balance of self-and-other interests' can also mean a number of different things with radically different moral ramifications. For example, balancing interests could be pursued through a *phronesis*-guided virtue of justice, through an amoral group-centric ethos, through formal legal rights and duties or through brute social exchange practices. Each of those is different, however, in what one means by 'balance' and how one pursues it.

## 6. How *Phronesis* May Help

To take stock, I have argued by dint of two 'case studies' that the modern world is full of what Chesterton called virtues 'wandering alone', and that the lack of virtue integration has been demonstrated vividly via the various dilemmatic trade-offs elicited by the pandemic. I introduced a new psychological model of wisdom that goes some distance in addressing the integration issue, but I then took this model to task for being under-developed with regard to moral motivations and for lagging behind Aristotle's old construct of *phronesis*.

A sceptic could accuse me of having argued slightly disingenuously here by assuming, without argument, that the intellectual virtue of *phronesis* does hold the key to the satisfactory adjudication of conflicting virtue injunctions. As a matter of fact, Aristotle himself was not very articulate with regard to either how *phronesis* develops or how it operates. He tells us that it is learned via teaching and experience (as distinct from the moral virtues themselves that are learned by habituation and emulation). For the rest of the story, he suggests we defer to the 'natural scientists' (Aristotle, 1985, p. 181 [1147b5–9]), which is somewhat comical as he was himself the leading scientist of his time, so this is almost like deferring to himself with another hat on. Perhaps he wrote something more about *phronesis* in one of his treatises known to have been lost, such as the one about child-rearing, but in default of those lost works, an account of *phronesis* that explains the necessary operations of a bespoke integrative meta-virtue calls for substantial reconstructive work.

We in the Jubilee Centre for Character and Virtue have been busy with such reconstructive work in the last few years, drawing both on original Aristotelian sources and contemporary work in moral psychology. We have come up with an account of four components making up *phronesis* and a model of how *phronesis* negotiates moral decision-making (Kristjánsson et al., 2021). Here are the components, differentiated according to their functions:

*Constitutive Function. Phronesis* involves the cognitive ability to perceive the ethically salient aspects of a situation and to appreciate these as calling for specific kinds of responses. This ability can be cultivated and should develop into the sort of cognitive excellence that merits the label of 'practical wisdom'.

*Integrative Function. Phronesis* integrates different components of a good life, especially in circumstances where different ethically salient considerations, or different kinds of virtues or values, appear to be in conflict and agents need to negotiate dilemmatic space. To return to the case of the *Guardian* and *Daily Telegraph* columnists, they all used the virtue term 'compassion' a lot. However, compassion can give rise to various intra-virtue and inter-virtue conflicts. As to the former, each virtue contains various components (of perception/ recognition, emotion, desire, motivation, behaviour and comportment or style), and those can create internal tensions. Does compassion in *this particular case* require an emotional reaction only or does it call for direct political action? As to the latter, compassion frequently clashes with other virtues. The standard textbook example is compassion versus honesty. Should we, in *this particular case*, opt for honest compassion or compassionate honesty – or even relinquish honesty altogether and choose a white lie? Moreover, compassion can clash with other (non-virtue-based) values, like economic prosperity. The integrative function of *phronesis* is meant to adjudicate such conflicts.

*Blueprint Function.* The integrative work of *phronesis* operates in conjunction with the agent's overall sense of the kinds of things that matter for a flourishing life: the agent's own moral identity, her understanding of what it takes if she is to live and act well and her need to live up to the standards that shape and are shaped by her understanding and experience of what matters in life. This function relates to what is called the person's 'moral identity'.

*Emotional Regulative Function. Phronesis* both requires and contributes to persons' emotional wellbeing by helping to bring their

# Kristján Kristjánsson

emotional responses into line with their understandings of the ethic-ally salient aspects of their situation, their judgement and their sense of what is at stake in the moment. For example, *phronesis* might show that a person is having an excessive or deficient emotional response, given her construal of the situation at hand, and then help her adjust accordingly by, for instance, giving herself an inner 'talking to' or asking herself questions about why she is so upset (or is not upset enough).

So, to flesh this out a bit, the constitutive function helps us to iden-tify a clash within or between virtues. This function is often referred to simply as moral sensitivity. The integrative function orders the conflicting motivations under the guiding light of our conception of the good life – provided by the blueprint function – while the emo-tional regulative function makes sure that we are not led astray by irrationally powerful emotions, throwing a spanner into the works of intellectual decision-making.

Figure 1 illustrates our overall conceptualisation of *phronesis*. Notice that we try to couch the components there in a language that will be more familiar to psychologists and ordinary people (fully capitalised words) than the names of the four 'functions'. Notice also the central role accorded to the blueprint component. While the primary motivation driving *phronesis* comes externally from the respective moral virtues that feed into it (say, compassion and justice), the blueprint component furnishes it with an internal motivation of its own: the motivation to adhere to one's sense of

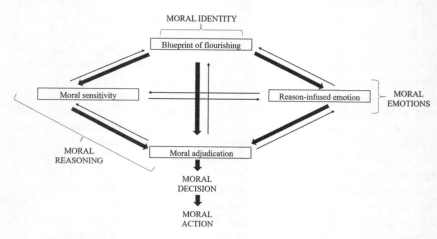

*Figure 1.* A Neo-Aristotelian Model of Wise (Phronetic) Moral Decision-Making

180

what flourishing it, or what contemporary psychologists would refer to as 'moral identity'. Without the central magnet of that blueprint component, all the other components would fall back into their respective heaps.

If we situate this in terms of how *phronesis* is meant to arbitrate in the case of a particular conflict, such as between the value of preserving the health of the old and vulnerable, on the one hand, and, on the other hand, the wellbeing of the young who need to study and work in the time of a pandemic, a well-developed capacity of *phronesis* helps us first to discern that there is a moral conflict at stake and identify precisely what that conflict is about. The blueprint function makes sure that we deliberate upon the conflict in light of our deepest held values about what we consider to be an overall flourishing life. The emotional regulation function secures the reason-embeddedness of the emotions that guide our motivation to engage with the problem (rather than trying to make our deliberation non-emotional and detached) and finally the integrative function weighs the pros and cons of each action option, through checks and balances, and comes up with a solution. Notice that this model is not a description of an *alternative route* to how people normally grapple with moral quandaries; rather it systematises what normally (or at least ideally) takes place in such processes and helps us improve the quality of our decision-making my making the steps we need to go through more specific and explicit. Moreover, it reminds us that simply following a single virtue, on a single generalised interpretation, is no royal road to getting things right.

I would not want to be seen to be arguing that the columnists explored in Case Study 2 should have taken us systematically through all the steps in an Aristotelian decision-making model. Obviously, they were bound by much stricter length restrictions than the normal philosophical essayist would be, and their remit is to write polemical and political pieces rather than philosophical reflections. However, I think the preceding paragraph indicates some of the considerations that I would ideally like to have seen grappled with even in a short column, for example in the many that one-sidedly advocated the immediate return of all children to school during the lockdown. Readers will also notice, more specifically, how I would have wanted to see the blueprint and emotional regulations functions dealt with in such an argument, and given my earlier critique of the CWM, why that model would not have been as useful in this regard as the *phronesis model*, because of its underspecified account of 'moral aspirations' and its avoidance of engagement with potentially aberrant (wisdom-undermining) emotions.

**Kristján Kristjánsson**

If a virtue-based approach to moral life ends up being hopelessly disintegrated without the unifying role of *phronesis* – as we have seen various examples of during the pandemic with people obsessively pushing specific virtue buttons without concerns for any holistic balance – why has *phronesis* faded from the public consciousness much more so than many other Aristotelian virtues? Answering that question satisfactorily would be a topic for another occasion. The reasons that come most readily to mind – and which are by no means original – will have to do, on the one hand, with the emergence of a law-like, codified model of morality, which reduces moral decision-making to mere compliance and, on the other hand, the prevalence of cost-benefit solutions to moral quandaries, which reduce moral values to monetary ones, couched in a single currency. The idea of virtue adjudications as critically guided and experientially grounded, but at the same time improvised and unforeseeably context-adjusted, has somehow gone missing in modernity. Our brush with the coronavirus has shown that it is high time to retrieve it: to rehabilitate *phronesis* and to make it the main pillar of moral education in the 21st century.

*University of Birmingham*
*k.kristjansson@bham.ac.uk*

## References

K. Allen and A. Bull, 'Following policy: a network ethnography of the UK character education policy community', *Sociological Research Online*, 23(2) (2018), 438–458.

G.W. Allport, *Personality: A Psychological Interpretation* (New York: Holt, 1937).

G.E.M. Anscombe, 'Modern moral philosophy', *Philosophy*, 33(1) (1958), 1–19.

Aristotle, *Nicomachean Ethics*, trans. T. Irwin (Indianapolis: Hackett Publishing, 1985).

J. Arthur, 'Coronavirus: Polling shows British public values compassion over economic stability', *The Conversation* (2020). Retrieved October 7, 2021, from https://theconversation.com/coronavirus-polling-shows-british-public-values-compassion-over-economic-stability-135962

G. K. Chesterton, *Orthodoxy* (1908) Retrieved October 7, 2021, from http://www.gkc.org.uk/gkc/books/orthodoxy/ch3.html

C. Darnell, L. Gulliford, K. Kristjánsson, and P. Paris, '*Phronesis* and the knowledge–action gap in moral psychology and moral education: A new synthesis?', *Human Development*, 62(3) (2019), 101–129.

B.J. Fowers, J.S. Carroll, N.D. Leonhardt, and B. Cokelet, 'The emerging science of virtue', *Perspectives on Psychological Science*, 16(1) (2021), 118–147.

I. Grossmann, N. M. Weststrate, M. Ardelt, J. P. Brienza, M. Dong, M. Ferrari, M. A. Fournier, C. S. Hu, H. C. Nusbaum and J. Vervaeke, 'The science of wisdom in a polarized world: Knowns and unknowns', *Psychological Inquiry*, 31(2) (2020a), 103–133.

I. Grossmann, N. M. Weststrate, M. Ferrari and J. P. Brienza, 'A common model is essential for a cumulative science of wisdom', *Psychological Inquiry*, 31(2) (2020b), 185–194.

Guardian, 'Parents disapprove of offspring marrying someone of different political persuasion' *Guardian*, Feb. 10 (2016). Retrieved October 7, 2021, from https://www.theguardian.com/politics/2016/feb/10/parents-disapprove-son-daughter-in-law-different-political-persuasion

A. Heath, 'The three taboos at the heart of Johnson's coronavirus fiasco', *Daily Telegraph,* September 24 (2020). Retrieved October 7, 2021, from https://www.telegraph.co.uk/news/2020/09/23/three-taboos-heart-ofjohnsons-coronavirus-fiasco/

L. Jerome and B. Kisby, *The Rise of Character Education in Britain: Heroes, Dragons and the Myths of Character* (London: Palgrave-Macmillan, 2019).

Jubilee Centre for Character and Virtues, 'A framework for character education in schools' (2017). Retrieved October 7, 2021, from http://www.jubileecentre.ac.uk/userfiles/jubileecentre/pdf/character-education/Framework%20for%20Character%20Education.pdf

P. Kesebir and S. Kesebir, 'The cultural salience of moral character and virtue declined in twentieth century America', *Journal of Positive Psychology*, 7(6) (2012), 471–480.

L. Kohlberg, *Essays on Moral Development,* vol. 1: *The Philosophy of Moral Development* (San Francisco: Harper & Row, 1981).

K. Kristjánsson, *Virtues and Vices in Positive Psychology: A Philosophical Critique* (Cambridge: Cambridge University Press, 2013).

K. Kristjánsson, *Aristotelian Character Education* (London: Routledge, 2015).

K. Kristjánsson, *Flourishing as the Aim of Education: A Neo-Aristotelian View* (London: Routledge, 2020).

# Kristján Kristjánsson

K. Kristjánsson, 'Recent attacks on character education in a UK context: A case of mistaken identities?', *Journal of Belief and Values*, 42(3) (2021), 363–377.

K. Kristjánsson, Fowers, B., Darnell, C. and Pollard, D., '*Phronesis* (practical wisdom) as a type of contextual integrative thinking', *Review of General Psychology*, 25(3) (2021), 239–257.

R. E. McGrath, 'Character strengths in 75 nations: An update', *Journal of Positive Psychology*, 10(1) (2015), 41–52.

A. MacIntyre, 'Plain persons and moral philosophers: Rules, virtues and goods', in K. Knight (Ed.), *The MacIntyre Reader* (pp. 136–152) (Notre Dame: University of Notre Dame Press, 1998).

C. Peterson and M. E. P. Seligman, *Character Strengths and Virtues: A Classification and Handbook* (Oxford: Oxford University Press, 2004).

M. E. P. Seligman, *Flourish: A Visionary New Understanding of Happiness and Well-Being* (New York: Free Press, 2011).

The Queen, 'The Queen's broadcast to the UK and Commonwealth', 5. April (2020). Retrieved October 7, 2021, from https://www.royal.uk/queens-broadcast-uk-and-commonwealth

J. Wright, M. Warren, and N. Snow, *Understanding Virtue: Theory and Measurement* (Oxford: Oxford University Press, 2021).

# Integrity as the Goal of Character Education

JONATHAN WEBBER

**Abstract**

Schools and universities should equip students with the ability to deal with an unpredictable environment in ways that promote worthwhile and fulfilling lives. The world is rapidly changing and the contours of our ethical values have been shaped by the world we have lived in. Education therefore needs to cultivate in students the propensity to develop and refine ethical values that preserve important insights accrued through experience while responding to novel challenges. Therefore, we should aim to foster the virtue of ethical integrity. This virtue is driven by a concern for ethical accuracy, which motivates and warrants respect for our existing ethical commitments as repositories of previous ethical reasoning, but equally requires recognition of our own fallibility and consideration of other people's reasoning. Ethical integrity thus comprises constancy, fidelity, humility, and receptivity, balanced and integrated by the aim of ethical accuracy. It is a kind of ethical seriousness, though it includes acceptance of some degree of ambivalence. It is an inherently developmental virtue distinct from the unachievable ethical perfection of practical wisdom. It is an Aristotelian virtue, even though Aristotle does not himself name it. The paper closes with an outline of what education for ethical integrity would look like.

Schools and universities should equip students with the ability to create new knowledge. This seems entirely uncontroversial. Not only is existing knowledge far from complete, but more importantly the world is always changing. If we treat education purely as a system for handing on information, then our collective knowledge will soon become outdated. We cannot prepare our students for the challenges they will face simply by telling them what we already know.

In this paper, I argue that the same is true of the ethical dimension of education. Schools and universities should equip students with the ability to deal ethically with the challenges ahead and cannot do this simply by imparting specific ethical values. For the world is rapidly changing, both socially and physically, as a result of technological change, and the contours of our existing ethical values have been shaped by the world we have lived in. Ethical education therefore needs to cultivate in students an ability to develop ethical values that preserve important ideas and insights accrued through our

doi:10.1017/S1358246122000273

# Jonathan Webber

collective experience yet respond to the novel challenges of a changing environment. I argue that this requires us to foster the ethical virtue of integrity.

The first two sections of this paper argue that responding to challenges in ways that promote worthwhile and fulfilling lives requires ethical virtues such as honesty, compassion, and justice, but also the virtue of reflecting critically on the contours of those virtues in relation to changing circumstances. The middle three sections then argue that the virtue of ethical integrity provides this critical reflective framework, emphasising that integrity involves being receptive to the ideas of others while being resistant to mere social pressure. Ethical integrity is driven by a concern to get things right, or ethical accuracy, but includes an acceptance of some degree of ambivalence about whether this is achieved. The final two sections distinguish ethical integrity from practical wisdom and roughly sketch a programme of education for ethical integrity.

## 1. The Need for Ethical Virtues

Ethics is the inquiry into how to live worthwhile and fulfilling lives. It is broader than the specifically moral question of what we should and should not do, what is right and what is wrong, though it does include that. Ethics is concerned with how we can flourish as human beings. Its aim is to identify the best ways to live and the conditions required for living in those ways. In responding to the difficult challenges of climate change, viral pandemics, widespread misinformation, and political polarisation, our aim as individuals or as a society should not be merely to survive, except when we know that is the most that can be achieved. Our aim should be to respond to these challenges in ways that promote the conditions for human flourishing as much as possible. For that, our responses need to be informed and guided by reflection on the ethical values of the goals we are pursuing, our methods of achieving them, and the outcomes we might produce.

Character education programmes often emphasise two closely related character traits that enable the discovery of new knowledge and its deployment in changing the world: grit or tenacity in maintaining the effort required to achieve a long-term goal, and resilience in learning from mistakes and adapting to changed circumstances. Some of the papers in this volume recommend further character traits of this kind, such as creativity as a collaborative virtue aimed at generating innovative solutions to problems, hope as the ability

186

to assess the importance and likelihood of achieving a goal in challenging circumstances, and epistemic forbearance as the ability to resist the temptation towards unjustified certainty about dangerous risks.[1]

Character traits of this kind are essential to responding effectively to the challenges of a rapidly changing world. However, they do not themselves promote human flourishing. They can be just as conducive to changing the world in ways that make no difference to our ability to live worthwhile and fulfilling lives, or indeed which make that more difficult. This is because they do not themselves embody any image of what would make a life worthwhile or fulfilling, never mind a picture of human flourishing that is at least roughly right. These character traits are valuable only because they enable us to prioritise between our existing ideas about what is important in life and to act in accordance with those ideas and priorities. This is why they are sometimes called 'structural virtues' or 'performance virtues'.[2]

If we are to respond to novel challenges in ways that promote human flourishing, we need firm commitments to the right substantive ethical values and the flexibility of mind to apply those values to the situations we face. We need an understanding of what matters in human life, what contributes to human flourishing, and how to secure those things. This will include commitments to such values as truth and fairness, for example, or the absence of pain and suffering. Firm commitments to these values for their own sake have traditionally been known as the virtues of honesty, justice, and compassion. Many other character traits have been promoted over the centuries as firm commitments to important values. Because this category of character traits is defined by their contribution to living a worthwhile and fulfilling life, we can label them 'ethical virtues'.[3]

[1]   Gaut (2022); Mason (2022); Shackel (2022).

[2]   For the concept of 'structural virtues', see Mason (2022), Adams (2006, pp. 33–34). For 'performance virtues', see: Kristjánsson (2022); Jubilee Centre (2017, pp. 1, 4, 5).

[3]   I intend this use of the term 'ethical virtues' to cover every character trait that includes a commitment to a substantive value that contributes to human flourishing. This is broader than the phrase 'moral virtues' used by Kristján Kristjánsson (2022), if 'moral' is understood in the narrower sense of relating specifically to right and wrong action, to what one ought or ought not to do. Valuing wit and good humour, for example, contributes to a worthwhile and fulfilling life without generating moral requirements. It is also broader than the phrase 'motivational virtues' used by Cathy Mason (2022), which she defines in terms of responses to perceived goods or evils in the world. Not all ethical virtues are reactive in this way. The ethical virtue

# Jonathan Webber

In order to equip students with the ability to respond well to the challenges of the future, where this means responding in ways that preserve and promote human flourishing, schools and universities need to foster in students the development of ethical virtues such as honesty, justice, and compassion, as well as structural or performance virtues such as creativity, hope, and epistemic forbearance. Doing so is really nothing more than taking explicit control of something educational institutions anyway cannot avoid doing. Educational theorists often emphasise that character traits are 'caught' from classroom practice, the school ethos, and the 'hidden curriculum' even when they are not explicitly taught in the formal curriculum.[4] Since educational institutions inevitably shape the characters and values of their students, they should design their environments, policies, and curricula to ensure that they do so in a way that contributes to those students and the people around them living worthwhile and fulfilling lives.

## 2. The Need for a Critical Reflective Ethical Virtue

Although every ethical virtue enshrines a commitment to some value that contributes to flourishing, ethical character education cannot simply aim to foster each of those values. The virtue of honesty, for example, involves a commitment to the value of truthfulness for its own sake. The honest person is averse to deception, whether that is through lying or other kinds of deceptive speech, through covertly violating agreements or cheating in other ways, or through theft or other varieties of falsely treating something as one's own. But this

---

of integrity, for example, is founded on a general commitment to ethical accuracy, as we will see. Finally, some ethical virtues in this broad sense can also be labelled 'epistemic virtues', where this phrase denotes character traits conducive to the development of knowledge or true belief. A good example is curiosity as described by Lani Watson (2022), which she defines as a motivation to acquire worthwhile epistemic goods (see also Watson, 2018, pp. 301–304). At least some epistemic goods – and maybe all of them – are worthwhile precisely because they contribute, directly or indirectly, to human flourishing. This concept of ethical virtues therefore encompasses the overlapping categories of moral virtues and motivational virtues, at least some of the category of epistemic virtues, and some virtues that do not fit any of those three categories.

[4]     For example: Ryle (1972, pp. 445–47); Warnock (1977, pp. 135-36); Lickona (1997); Noddings (1997, p. 10); Arthur (2003, pp. 117–21); Gross (2011); Jubilee Centre (2017, pp. 9–10).

does not mean that the honest person will never do any of these things. For example, there are clearly times when it is right to withhold secrets so that they cannot fall into enemy hands or, less dramatically, to boost someone's confidence by giving a more positive response to their work than you really think it merits. Aristotle famously argued that each ethical virtue is opposed not by one vice, but by two. Being insufficiently truthful is not the only way of failing to have the virtue of honesty. One can also be too truthful.

However, this 'doctrine of the mean', that every ethical virtue stands between a vice of deficiency and a vice of excess, is really only a very schematic approximation of Aristotle's view. No sooner has he said it than he clarifies that there are in fact a great many ways of going wrong, 'for single and straight is the road of the good; the bad go bad every which way' (Aristotle, 1106b35).[5] To possess a virtue is to feel and act on its characteristic motivation 'when one should, towards the things one should, in relation to the people one should, for the reasons one should, and in the way one should' (Aristotle, 1106b21-23). There are five different categories of potential failure listed in that phrase and within each of those categories there are many ways of failing. We might disagree with Aristotle over some of the details here, but his point does seem essentially right. Valuing truthfulness in itself is not enough for possessing the virtue of honesty. A sophisticated understanding of how and when to be truthful is also required.

It might be thought that the solution is to teach people a range of values including truthfulness, compassion, fairness, loyalty, and so on. The occasions when people should not be truthful are the ones when they should instead act on one or more of these other important values. However, this multiplies the problem rather than solving it. To have more than a vague and amorphous notion of the value of truthfulness, compassion, fairness, loyalty, or any other ethically important quality requires understanding its relation to the features of the situations one encounters. A nebulous understanding of truthfulness cannot be made more sophisticated by combining it with equally nebulous understandings of other values. What is required is regular experience of applying the value. One's decisions in each

---

[5]   This is the most lyrical translation of Aristotle's dictum 'ἐσθλοὶ μὲν γὰρ ἁπλῶς, παντοδαπῶς δὲ κακοί' that I have seen, but Harris Rackham's more telegraphic 'Goodness is simple, badness manifold' in the Loeb Classical Library edition seems the most literal.

situation will then define contours for that value and reflection on those decisions will refine those contours.[6]

It is a familiar point that virtues, like skills, are developed through practice. One aspect of this development is that it embeds the virtuous motivations into the individual's cognition so that they become habitual or automatic. Another is that in so doing these motivations become strong enough to take precedence over any desires or habits that favour less virtuous action.[7] But it is equally important that practice is what provides the detailed content of the virtue, the specific motivations built up in response to the situations that the individual encounters. The motivations that constitute a particular virtue, such as honesty for example, will therefore vary between people whose environments differ physically or socially in significant ways, even when those people are succeeding in only being truthful in the right ways and on the right occasions. Likewise, these contours of each virtue might vary between people in different positions within the same physical and social environment. And those contours are likely to vary across a person's lifetime as their environment and their social position change.

Schools and universities therefore cannot equip students with the ability to deal ethically with their situations just by imparting specific ethical values such as truthfulness and fairness. For these can only be vague and amorphous ideas until their content is defined through application in each individual's situation. To enable students to develop ethical virtues such as honesty and justice, character education needs to foster the attitudes and skills required for shaping the contours of those virtues in relation their own situations. To enable students to draw on these virtues to respond to novel challenges across their adult lives, character education needs to cultivate the traits required for continual reconsideration of the details of those

---

[6]  Aristotle claims that 'if those who have learned something for the first time can string the words together, they don't yet know what they have learned – because they have to assimilate it, and that requires time' (1147a21-2). Actually knowing something requires more than having been taught it, since it also requires integrating this information into one's general outlook through experience. His contrast between knowledge and merely stringing words together suggests that he considers this process of assimilation to be essential for understanding the detailed content of what has been taught, the real meaning of those words.

[7]  These two aspects are central to Aristotle's account. See, for example, 1103a15-b25, 1147a10-35, 1147b9-19, 1152a25-33. For a more recent version of these ideas grounded in experimental psychology, see Rees and Webber (2014).

virtues in relation to changing circumstances. In short, the funda-mental aim of ethical character education should be to produce a virtue of critical reflection on one's own ethical commitments.

## 3. Constancy, Fidelity, and Integrity

The virtue that is required is ethical integrity. However, this virtue is often misunderstood. It is often confused for a certain kind of inde-pendence of mind and resilience of commitment. The person of integ-rity will not be swayed by majority opinion, will not simply follow current trends, and will not succumb to peer pressure to behave in ways that are not in line with their own ethical judgment. From this ob-servation, it is sometimes concluded that the person of ethical integrity makes their own decisions based on their own ethical commitments ir-respective of the opinions of other people.[8] This confuses a regular manifestation of ethical integrity for the core nature of the virtue. Indeed, it is a mistake to think that someone impervious to the opi-nions of other people can be virtuous at all. Resistance to some kinds of social pressure needs to be combined with the recognition that other people may raise important points that need to be taken into con-sideration. Without that, it would merely be ethical arrogance.[9]

Similarly, the person of ethical integrity is often thought to be someone whose words and deeds are consistent over time, either because their motivations are well integrated into a coherent outlook on life or because their own sense of meaning and purpose is grounded in a set of fundamental commitments. It is sometimes concluded that ethical integrity is nothing more than consistency of one of these kinds.[10] This too is mistaken. Someone can display

---

[8]  Calhoun (1995). See also notes 13 and 15 below.

[9]  More precisely, this ethical arrogance can take either of two different forms. People who are ethically arrogant might consider themselves superior to other people in their ability to decide on the best course of action. This would be a form of what Alessandra Tanesini calls 'superbia' and can be manifested in treating other people as ethically inferior to oneself (2021, pp. 13–14, 98–100). A purer form of ethical arrogance is considering oneself to be entirely ethically self-reliant, so that one's own ethical judg-ments could never be improved by listening to other people's responses to one's ethical reasoning. On this form of arrogance, other people's reasoning is evaluated by the extent to which it concurs with one's own (Tanesini, 2021, pp. 14, 106–107).

[10]  For the view that integrity consists in having a coherent and inte-grated ethical outlook, see Taylor (1981). For the view that it consists in

Jonathan Webber

great integrity in changing their mind, especially where doing so requires them to admit that their previous judgments or actions had been wrong after all. Ethical integrity involves a kind of responsiveness to new considerations that may require revising deeply held commitments or disrupting a previously harmonious ethical outlook. In the absence of that responsiveness, a person with deep or well-integrated commitments is simply intransigent, stubborn, or pertinacious. Their consistency is a symptom of an ethical vice, rather than a manifestation of integrity.

Ethical integrity, therefore, does involve making up one's own mind about what one should do, but also requires giving due consideration to other people's ideas in doing so. Ethical integrity can be manifested in deep commitments or in a well-integrated outlook, but these must be susceptible to revision when there are sufficiently strong reasons to revise them. The characteristics of independent-mindedness and resilience of commitment form the trait of constancy, not the virtue of integrity. Constancy is the quality of being resolute in some commitments despite difficult circumstances that might undermine them. Similarly, acting on one's own deep or well-integrated motivations is the trait of fidelity to one's own commitments. Constancy and fidelity are aspects of the virtue of ethical integrity but are not themselves virtuous unless combined with a continuing responsiveness to reasons that might require revising one's commitments. The virtue of ethical integrity combines constancy and fidelity with this kind of respect for reasons.[11]

What is required to ground that respect for reasons is a concern for ethical accuracy. It is a concern for trying to act in ways that actually promote worthwhile and fulfilling lives, rather than simply acting in ways that might seem worthwhile or fulfilling at the time. Indeed, without this concern there is no justification for respecting one's own existing commitments. If those commitments have themselves been formulated and refined through trying to act in ways that promote human flourishing, then they are effectively repositories of reasoning about how best to behave. Rather than continually rehearsing the same sequences of reasoning, we should accept the conclusions of our prior reasoning, except where we seem to be presented with new reasons to take into consideration. Commitments that are

having a sense of meaning and purpose grounded in fundamental commitments, see Williams (1973) and Williams (1981).
[11] For a more detailed analysis of the nature of constancy and fidelity and their relation to integrity, see Rees and Webber (2013).

the repositories of ethical reasoning do indeed deserve our respect. By contrast, respecting one's own motivations where these are not the result of reasoning about how best to behave would be merely self-indulgent.[12]

A concern for ethical accuracy therefore grounds and delineates the virtuous forms of constancy and fidelity. This explains why ethical integrity is often manifested in independent-mindedness, resilience of commitment, depth of some core commitments, or the integration of commitments. It is ultimately the concern for ethical accuracy that produces each of these regular and salient features of ethical integrity. This same concern can lead to the disintegration of one's commitments or the abandonment of a deeply held commitment, either in response to reasons given by other people or through entirely independent reconsideration. The same concern that grounds the commonly observed features of ethical integrity, therefore, can also motivate thought and behaviour that seems on the surface to be contrary to those features. The deep structure of ethical integrity is not a kind of self-indulgence at all, but rather a kind of ethical seriousness.[13]

[12]   Bernard Williams argued that integrity would only be self-indulgent if it involved valuing one's own motivations purely because they are one's own. He proposed that integrity therefore consists solely in acting on one's deepest commitments without specifically valuing those commitments as one's own (1981, p. 49). However, it still seems self-indulgent to act on one's deepest commitments without regard for any good reasons to do otherwise. Cheshire Calhoun suggested that acting on one's own deepest commitments could itself be valuable either because it is integral to being an autonomous and responsible person or because it is essential to living a worthwhile and fulfilling life (1995, p. 255). However, unless those deepest commitments were themselves arrived at by reasoning and continue to be responsive to further reasoning, it is difficult to see why they should be integral to autonomy and responsibility or essential to a worthwhile and fulfilling life. Ultimately, it is because ethical integrity involves respecting and responding to reasons that it is not merely a self-indulgent concern for one's own preferences.

[13]   Calhoun points out that integrity involves not simply acting on one's own judgment, but acting on one's own *best* judgment (1995, p. 257). However, she does not explain what makes a judgment one's best. If we understand one's best judgment as that resulting from a genuine concern for ethical accuracy and we understand ethical integrity as driven by that same concern, then it is clear why ethical integrity involves acting on one's best judgment.

# Jonathan Webber

## 4. Accuracy, Humility, and Receptivity

At the heart of ethical integrity, then, is a concern for ethical accuracy that grounds a respect for one's own ethical commitments to the extent that they are products of reasoning about how to live worthwhile and fulfilling lives. This concern for accuracy produces the characteristic features of integrity that can be summarised as the traits of constancy and fidelity, but also produces thoughts and behaviours that run counter to those features. This is because a genuine concern for accuracy will not produce the arrogant attitude that one's own independent ethical reasoning is the best guide to behaving well. It will rather recognise one's own fallibility. The concern for ethical accuracy therefore produces a further feature of ethical integrity, which is ethical humility.

As a virtue, ethical humility is not merely the absence of the vice of arrogance. Rather, we can see it as lying in a mean between two vices. Ethical arrogance is the trait of being overly confident in one's own ethical reasoning and insufficiently aware of one's limitations in this regard. The opposite vice would be to underestimate the quality of one's own ethical reasoning and overestimate one's limitations in ethical reasoning. As with the Aristotelian doctrine of the mean generally, this is only a rough sketch of the true picture. Ethical humility is the virtue of correctly assessing the strengths and limitations of one's own ethical reasoning. Given the complexity of ethical reasoning about how best to behave in any given situation, there are many ways in which one's reasoning can go wrong, and therefore many ways in which one can fail to correctly assess the quality of one's ethical reasoning.[14]

[14] This analysis is modelled on Tanesini's description of intellectual humility as combining modesty about one's epistemic strengths with acceptance of one's epistemic limitations (2021, pp. 12–13, 74–84). Tanesini distinguishes four traits that I have here categorised together as arrogance, which she calls superbia, arrogance, narcissism, and vanity (2021, pp. 12–15). She also distinguishes four traits that I have categorised together as the opposing vice, which she calls servility, self-abasement, fatalism, and timidity (2021, pp. 12–15). I do not disagree with these distinctions. Indeed, they illustrate the point that the Aristotelian doctrine of the mean is only a rough sketch. Moreover, given that the first category can be described as excessive in self-confidence and deficient in appreciation of one's limitations while the second category can be described in the opposite terms, either category could be described as the 'vice of excess' or as the 'vice of deficiency'. The occasional cases where these traditional Aristotelian labels can be

# Integrity as the Goal of Character Education

Recognition of the limitations of one's own ethical reasoning entails some respect for other people's ideas. This is why ethical integrity does not require being impervious to persuasion. But a refusal to listen is not the only vice opposed to virtuous receptivity. For it is also possible to be too easily swayed by other people. Keep an open mind, as the old adage goes, but not so open that your brain falls out. Here too there are many ways in which one might fail to be properly receptive to the ideas of others, which are only very roughly clustered together as ways of being excessive or deficient in this regard. A more important way to cluster them is to distinguish between unreasoned social pressure and genuine ethical reasoning offered by other people. Ethical integrity does indeed require resistance to the former, but equally requires rational responsiveness to the latter, though even here the right response could be fairly swift if the reasoning only invokes considerations that one has already taken into account or that are not especially important.

Ethical integrity therefore has a social dimension. This explains a further feature of this virtue that is sometimes remarked upon: that it involves a willingness to articulate and defend one's own judgment of what should be done, or more broadly of what makes life worthwhile and fulfilling. Although there can be situations in which integrity requires keeping quiet about these matters, or at least not volunteering one's thoughts unsolicited, there are also situations in which keeping one's own ethical judgments to oneself would evidence a lack of integrity, especially when explicitly asked about them.[15] This openness about one's own ethical reasoning is essential to being receptive to other people's ethical reasoning. For it is only in response to the articulation of one's own perspective that other people

---

swapped around is another symptom of the doctrine of the mean being only a rough sketch.

[15] Calhoun describes this public articulation and defence of one's own ethical ideas as 'standing for something' and considers it 'central to the meaning of integrity' (1995, p. 253). However, she overlooks its reciprocity, describing other people only as obstacles to integrity and understanding ethical humility only as the recognition that other people should not be coerced (1995, pp. 258–60). This entails that integrity involves expecting that other people might learn from your ideas while denying that you yourself might learn from their ideas, which is a form of arrogance. More fundamentally, Calhoun does not consider *why* 'standing for something' is often characteristic of ethical integrity. The reason is that it evidences the same concern for ethical accuracy that ought also to motivate receptivity to other people's reasons.

# Jonathan Webber

can present a careful critique of that perspective. People who possess the virtue of ethical integrity explain their reasoning not simply to persuade others to agree with them, but to engage in the collaborative deliberation required by their ethical humility and their responsiveness to further reasons.

Conversely, the person of ethical integrity will actively seek out other people's reasoned ethical advice in some situations. This is partly because their own ethical reasoning is grounded in their own experience, which is limited and partial. Important insights into some difficult ethical problem might well only be available from somebody else's experience. It is also partly because ethical reasoning itself seems to be shaped by cognitive personalities, which differ from person to person. Listening to somebody else's perspective on a situation can help to counteract any biases or other cognitive structures shaping one's own reasoning.[16] In doing so, the person of ethical integrity is not merely seeking out the ethical judgments that other people make. What matters most is the reasoning in support of those judgments. In considering this reasoning, the person of ethical integrity not only works towards resolving their current ethical quandary. Equally importantly, they continue to shape the contours of their ethical outlook more generally.[17]

## 5. The Virtue of Ethical Integrity

The virtue of ethical integrity is therefore composed of constancy and fidelity in relation to one's own ethical commitments, driven by a concern for ethical accuracy that both justifies trusting in those commitments as products of prior ethical reasoning and requires reconsidering them when presented with reasons to do so. The virtuous forms of constancy and fidelity both display the classic Aristotelian structure: constancy lies between the vice of having no ethical

[16] For an important elaboration of this idea, see Jefferson and Sifferd (2022).
[17] Scherkoske argues that the value of integrity lies partly in the person of integrity being willing to offer reasons for their convictions and to be held accountable for them, which provides other people with the assurance that their judgments and reasons are credible grounds for belief and action (2013, pp. 34–35, 149–77). We should add that this credibility is partly demonstrated through taking other people's ideas seriously as potential reasons to revise one's own commitments, without which one's assurances would merely be arrogant condescension. Receptivity is therefore essential to this social value of ethical integrity.

196

commitments produced by prior reasoning and the vice of treating one's commitments as immune to further consideration; fidelity lies between the vice of failing to act on one's existing commitments and the vice of refusing to ever act against them. There are many ways of failing to exhibit these virtues. When one does possess them, it is because one's ethical reasoning is driven by a concern for accuracy. Constancy and fidelity, then, are only virtuous when subsumed into the virtue of integrity.

A genuine concern for ethical accuracy entails two further virtues, humility and receptivity. Humility lies in a mean between underestimating the quality of one's own ethical reasoning and overestimating it. Receptivity lies in a mean between considering oneself ethically self-sufficient and being too easily persuaded. In both cases, there are many ways of going wrong. The question of how best to succeed in humility and receptivity is itself one for the person of integrity to answer, motivated by their concern for ethical accuracy. This concern is therefore the core of ethical integrity. This is not to say that the person of ethical integrity is an obsessive ethical perfectionist. That would be a failure to live a worthwhile and fulfilling life, as anyone interested in ethical accuracy would soon realise. The concern for ethical accuracy must therefore also motivate and limit the extent to which the person of integrity allows that concern to rule their life.[18]

All of this shows that ethical integrity is a genuinely ethical virtue. It is founded upon a substantive value that contributes to human flourishing, the value of ethical accuracy.[19] The exact scope and

[18]    There are also restricted varieties of integrity, such as artistic integrity, personal integrity, and professional integrity. It is an important question how these are related to ethical integrity, but a full answer would take us far beyond the concerns of this paper. My view is that there is only one kind of integrity, which can be applied to different domains: ethical integrity encompasses every aspect of life; artistic, personal, and professional integrity are restricted to the aspects of life their names indicate. If this view is right, then educating for ethical integrity as described in this paper would also foster the restricted varieties of integrity.

[19]    Williams argues that integrity is not a virtue, since virtues are founded on characteristic motivations and integrity would be mere self-indulgence if it were founded on the motivation to preserve the projects and values one already has (1981, p. 49). Taylor concurs (1981, pp. 151–52). Scherkoske agrees with this as a claim about moral virtues but adds that epistemic virtues do not need characteristic motivations, since any stable cognitive trait that leaves its possessor in a good epistemic position is an epistemic virtue, and integrity fits that description (2013, esp. pp. 83–90). These arguments overlook that the constancy and fidelity involved in integrity are

limits of this value are in question for the person of ethical integrity, but the same is true of the substantive values at the heart of other ethical virtues. Indeed, ethical integrity is essential to developing the precise contours of those ethical virtues too. The honest person is committed to the substantive value of truthfulness, for example, which contributes to human flourishing, but the shape of this value depends on the changing demands of the situation. The commitment to ethical accuracy at the core of ethical integrity is essential to developing the contours of that commitment to truthfulness as one's situation changes. The same is true of the other ethical virtues, such as compassion and justice. Ultimately, this is why ethical integrity is essential to responding ethically to the unforeseen challenges of a rapidly changing world.

We can see clearly how ethical integrity operates if we consider one of the examples often discussed in philosophical literature on this topic. George has recently completed a PhD in chemistry, has a family to support, and has been offered a highly paid job developing biological and chemical weapons. George is opposed to this use of chemistry, but also knows that the job will otherwise go to someone who will be very diligent and successful. George has been finding it extremely difficult to get a job, due to an over-supply of people with PhDs in chemistry. George is here faced with reasons to revise one of his commitments, which his friends may well point out.[20] He would display ethical integrity by considering those

---

grounded in the concern for ethical accuracy that also drives humility and receptivity. This basic motivation makes ethical integrity a genuinely ethical virtue. However, this is perfectly compatible with it also being an epistemic virtue (see n. 3 above).

[20] Williams created this example in his critique of utilitarianism (1973, pp. 97–98). He argues that what matters most here is that George's opposition to this use of chemistry is one of his deepest commitments, one of the projects that his life is all about, which should not be subjugated to an overall calculation of what would be best given everyone else's projects (1973, pp. 116–17). Calhoun, by contrast, argues that what is at issue here is whose judgment should rule George's life: his own opposition to biological and chemical weapons, or other people's judgments that he should take the job (1995, p. 251). Taylor argues that whichever way George decides he will lose his integrity, by behaving inconsistently with either his commitment to his family or his opposition to using chemistry in this way, or by changing one of these for the sake of convenience (1981, p. 151). Williams and Calhoun are both mistaken to isolate George's integrity from the reasoning presented by other people. Taylor has overlooked

reasons, perhaps partly by actively seeking ethical advice on this difficult problem. It makes no difference whether doing so leads him to abandon his original commitment, revise it in some details, or reaffirm it entirely, so long as he has genuinely exercised the humility and receptivity required by a serious commitment to ethical accuracy.

Having made the decision, George may well find some ambivalence about the way his life then continues. The humility involved in ethical integrity can mean that one retains the concern that one's decision was indeed mistaken. However resolute one may be in acting on that decision, the thought that one is not infallible in one's judgments should indeed remain. It is not only in response to reasons provided by other people that ethical integrity can lead to ambivalence. For there are likely to be tensions within one's own set of ethical ideas and commitments. The concern for ethical accuracy does not entail the aim of removing all sources of ambivalence from one's own ethical outlook. A genuine concern with how to live worthwhile and fulfilling lives will soon uncover the quixotic nature of such perfectionism. Ethical integrity therefore does not rule out continuing to feel the force of reasons against decisions one has taken, reasons recognised in one's own set of motivations.[21]

## 6. Ethical Integrity and Practical Wisdom

Ethical integrity is a virtue founded on the substantive value of ethical accuracy. Where other ethical virtues are manifested in specific features of behaviour, so that honesty is manifested in acting and speaking truthfully, for example, or justice is manifested in promoting fairness, ethical integrity is manifested in the reasoning that leads to one's actions generally: the concern for ethical accuracy drives a respect for one's own prior ethical reasoning balanced with receptivity to other people's ethical reasoning and an awareness that both might be challenged by new situations. Through this distinctive approach to ethical reasoning, the virtue of ethical integrity defines its own contours and shapes the

---

that George might rationally revise his commitments in response to the reasons presented by this situation.

[21] Calhoun is right, therefore, to emphasise that ambivalence is compatible with integrity, because integrity involves some humility about one's own powers of judgment, which itself includes recognising the deliberative abilities of people who have come to different conclusions to one's own (1995, pp. 240–41). But we should also recognise that ambivalence rooted directly in one's own motivations is compatible with integrity.

individual's other ethical virtues, such as honesty, compassion, and justice. All of this might make ethical integrity sound rather similar to the Aristotelian virtue of practical wisdom, or phronesis (φρόνησις), which is often emphasised in discussions of ethical virtue.

However, ethical integrity does not fit Aristotle's description of practical wisdom. Aristotle understood practical wisdom not simply as an intellectual virtue that regulates other virtues. He saw it as the perfection of practical rationality, a single unified trait whose manifestations in relation to different aspects of life can be described in the language of specific virtues. The sophisticated understanding of how and when to be truthful can be described as the virtue of honesty, but can also be described as practical wisdom in the domain of truthfulness. Justice can equally be described as practical wisdom in relation to fairness. This is ultimately because Aristotle defines the correct understanding that constitutes each ethical virtue by reference to practical wisdom: any specific virtue requires consistently acting on the reasons that the person of practical wisdom would act on (1106b36–1107a2). Since situations are complicated, one cannot fully possess any one virtue without possessing them all; each virtue is essentially an aspect of the single quality of practical wisdom (1144b24–1145a1-2). Practical wisdom, as Aristotle understands it, entails complete possession of all the virtues, whereas ethical integrity aims to promote worthwhile and fulfilling lives by balancing one's existing ethical commitments with new reasons presented either by novel situations or through other people's perspectives.

Recent work on character education has used the terms 'phronesis' and 'practical wisdom' to describe the quality of drawing on an overall image of living well to discern the ethically relevant features of a situation, prioritise between them, and be motivated to act in line with this decision. Although this is derived from Aristotle's own concept of practical wisdom and inherits its name, this recent concept does not entail that the person who possesses this quality cannot be mistaken about ethical values, the relevant features of the situation, or their relative prioritisation. It is not the Aristotelian ideal. It is instead an eminently achievable quality that we could describe as 'ethical sensitivity' or 'good sense'. Rather than trying to develop such ethical virtues as honesty, compassion, or justice individually, according to this line of thought, programmes of character education should foster these virtues together through a continuous training of this intellectual quality that integrates and applies them.[22]

[22] Jubilee Centre (2017, pp. 4–5); Darnell et al. (2019, esp. pp. 118–20); Kristjánsson et al. (2021); Kristjánsson and Fowers (2022); Kristjánsson (2022); compare Masala (2016, pp. 244–45).

Despite the similarities between ethical integrity and this recent concept of practical wisdom, there remain two important differences. Fundamentally, ethical integrity is driven by a concern for ethical accuracy. The person of ethical integrity may well have a rough image of human flourishing, even if this is merely implied by their range of nuanced ethical commitments rather than something they have ever explicitly reflected on, but ethical integrity itself makes this image continually open to significant revision, even in profound and wide-ranging ways. Moreover, this concern for ethical accuracy entails humility about one's own ethical reasoning and receptivity to other people's reasons, which itself requires openness about one's own. Ethical integrity is an intrinsically social virtue. This essential dimension of good ethical reasoning is obscured by the recent concept of practical wisdom, which is focused entirely on the integration and application of the individual's own ethical outlook.

This is not to say that ethical integrity is opposed to the Aristotelian understanding of ethical virtue. Indeed, the structures of ethical integrity are all present in *Nicomachean Ethics*, even though Aristotle never draws them together as aspects of a single character trait. To develop ethical virtues, according to Aristotle, one must be responsive to reasoning about the nature of worthwhile and fulfilling lives (1095a6-11). This requires already being attracted by 'the fine' (τὸ καλὸν) and repulsed by 'the shameful' (τὸ αἰσχρόν), which entails being concerned with ethical accuracy (1179b29-31). With these conditions in place, one will be suitably receptive to other people's ethical reasoning (1095b4-13) and will develop through rational reflection the detailed contours of ethical virtues such as honesty, compassion, or justice (1105a28-b18, 1144b8-14).[23] This cluster of traits forms an inherently developmental virtue, which distinguishes it from Aristotle's perfectionist concept of practical wisdom, just as its fundamental concern with ethical accuracy distinguishes it from the recent concept of practical wisdom.

Ethical integrity is therefore a distinct Aristotelian virtue, even though Aristotle did not describe it in this way.[24] It does not fit

---

[23] Myles Burnyeat provides a careful analysis of these and other passages of *Nicomachean Ethics* to make clear the role of reasoning, its social dimension, and its relation to pleasure and emotion in the development of the virtues (1980, esp. pp. 75–79). But he stops short of identifying a single trait that integrates these features of reasoning.

[24] Kristjánsson argues that we can find a different concept of integrity within Aristotelian virtue ethics, since the trait possessed by self-controlled people, who bring themselves to do what they think is right despite strong

either of his two categories of 'natural' virtue, where one is committed to the right value but has only a nebulous understanding of it, and full virtue, where one has perfect practical wisdom (1144b2-17). If we want to promote worthwhile and fulfilling lives then we should aim for a mean between these two extremes: we should foster virtues that embody values with sophisticated and revisable contours, but should not allow ethical perfectionism to preclude our own flourishing.

## 7. Educating for Ethical Integrity

If we are to equip students with the ability to deal with a rapidly changing world in ways that promote worthwhile and fulfilling lives, then, we need to foster the trait of ethical integrity. We cannot predict the ethical challenges that will be posed by such interrelated and multidimensional challenges as climate change, viral pandemics, widespread misinformation, and political polarisation. This means not only that we should not simply impart our own ethical ideas, but also that we should cultivate in our students the tendency to continually develop their ethical outlooks in response to new reasons, rather than to apply their existing commitments to each new challenge or neglect the ethical dimension of the decisions they need to make. Educating for ethical integrity should encourage the virtue's core commitment to ethical accuracy, which is a kind of ethical curiosity.[25] In doing so, it should aim to develop the skills and motivations central to this virtue.

Ethical integrity requires a proper respect for one's existing commitments as repositories of prior ethical reasoning. Even commitments that have been inherited from the surrounding culture through upbringing, rather than arrived at independently, can be repositories of a communal tradition of ethical theorising. Education

---

desires to do otherwise, is a form of integrating their behaviour with their own best judgment (2019, p. 111). Given that integrity is not merely integration of motivations and behaviour, but is a respect for ethical reasoning driven by a concern for ethical accuracy, perhaps a better name for this trait of self-controlled people, which is also distinct from the 'self-regulation' described by Kathleen Murphy-Hollies (2022), would be 'self-control'.

[25] For some details on how to encourage curiosity in general, which can be applied to encouraging a commitment to ethical accuracy, see: Watson (2018, pp. 296–304).

for ethical integrity should therefore include a programme of what has become known as 'Social and Emotional Learning' (SEL), which teaches students not to act on their immediate emotional or intuitive responses, but rather to think more slowly and critically, drawing on a wider range of their existing beliefs and values. Studies have found these programmes to have lasting positive effects on both behaviour and academic achievement across the age range of compulsory education and across the range of student needs and backgrounds.[26] The same programmes also foster one central aspect of ethical integrity.

However, the concern with ethical accuracy requires balancing this respect for one's own commitments with humility about the quality of one's own ethical reasoning and receptivity to other people's ethical reasoning. These can be fostered through communities of ethical inquiry, where groups of students collaborate to address ethical questions together. These discussions should focus on distinguishing genuine ethical reasoning from three corruptions of ethical discourse that encourage and strengthen polarisation. One is mere peer pressure, especially allied with group identification. A second is the use of mere rhetoric, especially in the form of reasoning designed to support a conclusion already chosen in advance. A third is the widespread presence of misinformation within public ethical and political discourse, especially on social media.[27] Communities of ethical inquiry should aim to cultivate genuinely open-minded reasoning, which requires learning methods of identifying and resisting peer pressure, mere rhetoric, and misinformation.[28]

Through combining SEL with communities of ethical inquiry, we should aim to foster tolerance of some degree of ethical ambivalence. We need to resist the temptation of aiming for ethical certainty, not

---

[26]   Durlak et al. (2011); Belfield et al. (2015); Taylor et al. (2017).

[27]   For some thoughts on how to develop a sensitivity to misinformation, see Matthews (2022). For an argument that this approach is insufficient without regulating the design structures of social media, see Tanesini (2022).

[28]   This approach to ethical deliberation is the antithesis of the formal debate structure that has often been employed for discussing moral and political issues in educational settings. In a formal debate, students are assigned to one of two adversarial teams to develop and articulate arguments in favour of the conclusion assigned to their team. Usually, an audience vote at the end determines which team has been most successful. This crude gamification of ethical discourse positively incentivises peer pressure, mere rhetoric, and misinformation as techniques for 'winning' at the expense of genuine ethical inquiry.

# Jonathan Webber

only because an obsessive pursuit of ethical perfection is incompatible with living worthwhile and fulfilling lives, but also because the desire for certainty itself can corrupt ethical reasoning. We need to remain open-minded even after a decision has been made, though of course in aiming to make the best decision we can with the information and time available we are aiming to reduce our ambivalence.[29] In learning how and when to tolerate ethical ambivalence, students will also be learning to identify the times when it would be good to seek out ethical advice or collaborative deliberation and the times when it would not.

This is just a rough sketch for a programme of educating for ethical integrity.[30] The details of how best to combine SEL and collaborative ethical inquiry to foster this virtue will depend on the experiences and interests of each institution's students. It may also need to be tailored for different cognitive personalities. The pedagogical question of how to cultivate a commitment to ethical accuracy that grounds and integrates respect for one's own ethical commitments, appropriate receptivity to other people's ethical reasoning, and tolerance of some degree of ethical ambivalence, therefore, cannot be given a detailed general answer. Even so, the need for responses to the challenges of a rapidly changing environment to be shaped by the virtue of ethical integrity cannot be met unless cultivating such a commitment becomes the fundamental goal of ethical character education.[31]

*Cardiff University*
*webberj1@cardiff.ac.uk*

[29] The tolerance of ethical ambivalence required for ethical integrity seems to me a species of what Nicholas Shackel calls 'epistemic forbearance'. For the attractions and dangers of unwarranted certainty, and why epistemic forbearance is necessary, see Shackel (2022).

[30] For some further ideas about this kind of ethical education grounded in empirical psychology, see Athanassoulis (2016, esp. pp. 223–25), and Masala (2016, esp. pp. 229–43).

[31] I am very grateful to Anneli Jefferson, Orestis Palermos, and Panos Paris for their insightful comments on the first draft of this paper.

## References

Robert Merrihew Adams, *A Theory of Virtue: Excellence in Being for the Good* (Oxford: Oxford University Press, 2006).

Aristotle, *Nicomachean Ethics*, translation and historical introduction by Christopher Rowe, philosophical introduction by Sarah Broadie (Oxford: Oxford University Press, 2002).

James Arthur, *Education With Character: The Moral Economy of Schooling* (London: Routledge, 2003).

Nafsika Athanassoulis, 'The Psychology of Virtue Education', in *From Personality to Virtue: Essays in the Philosophy of Character*, edited by Alberto Masala and Jonathan Webber (Oxford: Oxford University Press, 2016).

Clive Belfield, A. Brooks Bowden, Alli Klapp, Henry Levin, Robert Shand and Sabine Zander, 'The Economic Value of Social and Emotional Learning', *Journal of Benefit-Cost Analysis*, 6 (2015), 508-544.

Myles Burnyeat, 'Aristotle on Learning to be Good', in *Essays on Aristotle's Ethics*, edited by Amélie Oksenberg Rorty (Berkeley: University of California Press, 1980).

Cheshire Calhoun, 'Standing for Something', *The Journal of Philosophy*, 92 (1995), 235–260.

Catherine Darnell, Liz Gulliford, Kristján Kristjánsson, and Panos Paris, 'Phronesis and the Knowledge-Action Gap in Moral Psychology and Moral Education: A New Synthesis?', *Human Development*, 62 (2019): 101-129.

Joseph A. Durlak, Roger P. Weissberg, Allison B. Dymnicki, Rebecca D. Taylor, Kriston B. Schellinger, 'The Impact of Enhancing Students' Social and Emotional Learning: A Meta-Analysis of School-Based Universal Interventions', *Child Development*, 82 (2011), 405–432.

Jubilee Centre for Character and Virtues, 'A Framework for Character Education in Schools' (2017). Available at: https://www.jubileecentre.ac.uk/1606/character-education/publications (accessed 30 May 2022).

Anneli Jefferson and Katrina Sifferd, 'Practical Wisdom and the Value of Cognitive Diversity', *Royal Institute Philosophy Supplementary Volume*, 92 (2022) 149–66.

Kristján Kristjánsson, 'Is the Virtue of Integrity Redundant in Aristotelian Virtue Ethics?', *Apeiron*, 52 (2019) 93–115.

Kristján Kristjánsson, 'The Need for Phronesis', *Royal Institute Philosophy Supplementary Volume*, 92 (2022) 167–84.

# Jonathan Webber

Kristján Kristjánsson, Blaine Fowers, Catherine Darnell, and David Pollard, 'Phronesis (Practical Wisdom) as a Type of Contextual Integrative Thinking', *Review of General Psychology*, 25 (2021), 239-257.

Kristján Kristjánsson and Blaine Fowers, 'Phronesis as Moral Decathlon: Contesting the Redundancy Thesis about Phronesis', *Philosophical Psychology*, online publication 2022. DOI: 10.1080/09515089.2022.2055537

Berys Gaut., 'Group Creativity', *Royal Institute Philosophy Supplementary Volume*, 92 (2022) 5–26.

Jean Gross, 'Should Character Be "Taught" Through The School's Curriculum Or "Caught" Through A School's Ethos?', in *The Character Inquiry*, edited by Jen Lexmond and Matt Grist (London: Demos, 2011), 90-96.

Thomas Lickona, 'Educating for Character: A Comprehensive Approach', in *The Construction of Children's Character*, edited by Alex Molnar (Chicago: University of Chicago Press, 1997), 45-62.

Alberto Masala, 'Mastering Virtue', in *From Personality to Virtue: Essays in the Philosophy of Character*, edited by Alberto Masala and Jonathan Webber (Oxford: Oxford University Press, 2016).

Cathy Mason, 'The Virtue of Hope in a Turbulent World', *Royal Institute Philosophy Supplementary Volume*, 92 (2022) 293–306.

Taylor Matthews, 'Deepfakes, Intellectual Cynics, and the Cultivation of Digital Sensibility', *Royal Institute Philosophy Supplementary Volume*, 92 (2022) 67–86.

Kathleen Murphy-Hollies, 'Self-Regulation and Political Confabulation', *Royal Institute Philosophy Supplementary Volume*, 92 (2022) 111–28.

Nel Noddings, 'Character Education and Community', in *The Construction of Children's Character*, edited by Alex Molnar (Chicago: University of Chicago Press, 1997), 1-16.

Clea Rees and Jonathan Webber, 'Constancy, Fidelity, and Integrity, in *The Handbook of Virtue Ethics*, edited by Stan van Hooft (Abingdon: Acumen, 2013), 399-408.

Clea Rees and Jonathan Webber, 'Automaticity in Virtuous Action', in *The Philosophy and Psychology of Character and Happiness*, edited by Nancy Snow and Franco Trivigno (Abingdon: Routledge, 2014), 75-90.

Gilbert Ryle, 'Can Virtue Be Taught?', in *Education and the Development of Reason*, edited by R. F. Dearden, P. H. Hirst, and R. S. Peters (London: Routledge and Kegan Paul, 1972), 434-447.

Greg Scherkoske, *Integrity and the Virtue of Reason: Leading a Convincing Life* (Cambridge: Cambridge University Press, 2013).

N. Shackel, 'Uncertainty Phobia and Epistemic Forbearance in a Pandemic', *Royal Institute Philosophy Supplementary Volume*, 92 (2022) 271–91.

Alessandra Tanesini, *The Mismeasure of the Self: A Study in Vice Epistemology* (Oxford: Oxford University Press, 2021).

Alessandra Tanesini, 'Affective Polarisation and Emotional Distortions on Social Media', *Royal Institute Philosophy Supplementary Volume*, 92 (2022) 87–110.

Gabriele Taylor, 'Integrity', *Aristotelian Society Supplementary Volume*, 55 (1981), 143-159.

Rebecca D. Taylor, Eva Oberle, Joseph A. Durlak, Roger P. Weissberg, 'Promoting Positive Youth Development Through School-Based Social and Emotional Learning Interventions: A Meta-Analysis of Follow-Up Effects', *Child Development*, 88 (2017), 1156-1181.

Mary Warnock, *Schools of Thought* (London: Faber and Faber, 1977).

Lani Watson, 'Cultivating Curiosity in the Information Age', *Royal Institute Philosophy Supplementary Volume*, 92 (2022) 129–48.

Lani Watson, 'Educating for Curiosity', in *The Moral Psychology of Curiosity*, edited by Ilhan Inan, Lani Watson, Dennis Whitcomb, and Safiye Yiğit (London: Rowman & Littlefield, 2018), 293-310.

Bernard Williams, 'A Critique of Utilitarianism', in *Utilitarianism: For and Against*, by J. J. C. Smart and Bernard Williams (Cambridge: Cambridge University Press, 1973), 77-150.

Bernard Williams, 'Utilitarianism and Moral Self-Indulgence', in *Moral Luck: Philosophical Papers 1973-1980*, by Bernard Williams (Cambridge: Cambridge University Press, 1981), 40-53.

# Empathy and Loving Attention

CARISSA PHILLIPS-GARRETT

**Abstract**

The failure to understand the needs, beliefs, and values of others is widely blamed on a lack of empathy, which has been touted in recent years as the necessary ingredient for bringing us together and ultimately for tackling issues of social justice and harmony. In this essay, I explore whether empathy really can serve the role it has been tasked with. To answer this question, I will first identify what empathy is and why its champions believe it plays such an essential role in social life. With this in mind, I contend that promoting empathy on its own may make solidarity among diverse populations more difficult to achieve and undermine social reconciliation. Instead, I argue for a different approach that begins with acknowledging our self-oriented perspective and how it shapes what we see, appreciate, and interpret, before turning to others with a kind of loving attention. Unlike empathy, loving attention allows us to see others as they really are, not as we imagine we would be in their shoes, and is that kind of perception that is necessary for bridging divides and building solidarity in our contemporary world.

The escalating social and political tensions of the last few years in many democracies force us to reckon with the fact that even in diverse nation-states, many live segregated lives, surrounded by those who think, believe, and look like them. Though democracies were designed to foster productive disagreement and to allow people of varied values, creeds, and identities to live together, they instead now encourage echo chambers that produce increased self-sorting, shutting down conversations and the possibility of tolerating disagreement. Bitter social and political divides forestall the possibility of productive communication about goals that should be shared, including rectifying the failures of political and social institutions to live up to the ideals of justice, while ensuring that all are able to secure their own flourishing.

Moreover, as climate change and the Covid-19 pandemic have most recently forced us to grapple with, the problems that we face now are also increasingly globalized; they cannot be solved by any one nation-state on their own, and what happens in one part of the globe inevitably affects everyone. Given the complexity of the problems and the diversity of those affected, this makes it even more challenging to solve problems exacerbated by deep differences in power, values, and interests.

doi:10.1017/S1358246122000200    © The Royal Institute of Philosophy and the contributors 2022

*Royal Institute of Philosophy Supplement* **92** 2022

**Carissa Phillips-Garrett**

Philosophers have long championed the power of reason and argument to test our own ideas and challenge those of others, allowing us to find the right practices and solutions to promote flourishing for all. This approach to promoting healthy civic life and global justice, however, has been increasingly criticized for failing to recognize the power of emotion in shaping our beliefs and allegiances. We do not make decisions based on reason alone, and research has shown that even when presented with evidence, our decision-making is based not on the evidence but on what reinforces our existing beliefs and identities or we wish were true (Kunda, 1990).

The failure to understand the needs, beliefs, and values of others is widely blamed on a lack of empathy, which has frequently been touted as the necessary ingredient for bringing us together and tackling issues of social justice and harmony. For example, U.S. President Joe Biden argued that 'empathy is the fuel of democracy': since empathy is what enables those with different perspectives to understand others, even when they disagree, the preservation of democracy itself requires empathy (Biden, 2021). We use our own feelings as a starting place to extend empathy to others; since we know what it feels like to suffer, experiencing the suffering of others moves us to act in response. Through empathizing with those very different than us, we can come to understand how to respond in ways that meet the needs of particular individuals and build solidarity to promote the common good.

In this essay, I explore whether empathy really can serve the role it has been tasked with. To answer this question, I will first identify what empathy is and why its champions believe it plays such an essential role in social life. With this in mind, I examine why it will be difficult for empathy to effectively bridge the epistemic divides we face and how empathy may make solidarity among diverse populations more difficult to achieve. Instead, I argue for a different approach that begins with acknowledging how our self-oriented perspective shapes what we see, appreciate, and interpret and then focuses on lovingly attending to others. Unlike empathy, loving attention allows us to see others as they really are, not as we imagine we would be in their shoes, and it is that kind of seeing that is necessary for building solidarity in our contemporary world.

## 1. What Empathy Is

Empathy, as commonly understood in the psychological and philosophical literature, includes both a cognitive and an affective response to the experience of others, so I experience what another feels when I engage empathetically – or at least what I imagine that the other feels (Slote, 2007, p. 14). The simplest form of empathy is a biologically-based response to the emotional state of others that involves deep feeling but is not intentional and does not involve effort, so the empathizing person may simply feel sad herself when she senses another's sadness (Hoffman, 2014, p. 73). However, empathy may also be developed actively through verbally-mediated association and perspective-taking practices that develop explicit connections between one's own empathetic feelings and the suffering of others, and it is the development of this capacity that empathy's proponents champion. In this more complex form of empathy, the empathizer connects her own experience of sadness with the target's, utilizing the power of imagination to take up the perspective of someone who suffers by projecting herself into the experience of the target (ibid, p. 74). For instance, in empathizing with a friend upon the death of his spouse, the empathizer uses her own experience of loss to imagine how the friend must feel before experiencing his feelings of loss in herself. In imagining how she would feel, were she in his position, she aims to feel as her friend does though they occupy different positions.

What is distinctive about empathetic feeling, in contrast to other feelings such as sympathy and compassion, is that the empathizer does not merely feel concern or sadness *for* her friend, but *as* him (Cuff et al., 2016, p. 145). If she feels sympathy for her friend, the object of feeling is the friend's state (e.g., the friend's sadness), while empathy responds to the same object of the friend's feeling (e.g., the death of the friend's spouse) (Stueber, 2019). Sympathy is felt as concern for the friend's well-being, but what is distinctive about empathy is that the sympathizer vicariously shares the other's feeling of loss and sadness as her own. She does not simply feel bad *for* him, but she is sad *with* him. This, however, is not merely a form of emotional contagion; she recognizes that though she is sad with him for the same reason that he is sad, her sadness is separate from his, and she is not simply 'catching' sadness.

These aspects of empathy are critical for the benefits that empathy's proponents claim for it. It is the ability to cognitively understand the experience of another and respond affectively to it that has led public figures as diverse as former U.S. First Lady Michelle Obama and conservative pundit Glenn Beck to champion empathy as the solution to political and social ills. Empathy leads to understanding, and understanding is ultimately the basis for reconciliation and reconstruction of social community. Both Obama and Beck emphasized trying to understand the experience of other people, and in particular, the necessity of empathy for truly reckoning with the reality of racial inequality (Beck, 2016; Obama, 2020). They are not alone; newspaper editorials, political speeches, and academic papers all frequently decry a lack of empathy as the cause of social and political discord, tracing the discontents that the U.S., the U.K., and many other democracies have faced in recent years to a lack of understanding and concern for the other that can be remedied through empathy.

## 2. Empathy's Value

A key feature that proponents of empathy point out in its favor is that empathy requires us to understand and take up the perspective of others, which involves knowledge of the target. This does not simply involve intellectual acknowledgement of how others think and feel, but feeling as the target does creates an emotional connection between different people. By facilitating understanding between those who are very different from one another, empathy promotes an openness to others that allows for productive, not defensive, interaction.

The ability to project is precisely what many champions of empathy have focused on as most useful since it is perspective-taking that is said to develop openness. As the philosopher Adam Smith wrote, when we imagine what it is like to be someone else, 'we conceive ourselves enduring all the same torments, we enter as it were into his body, and become in some measure the same person with him' (Smith, 2002, p. 12). It is by empathy that we can come to know what this is like, and it is when we imagine our own suffering that we can respond to the suffering of others appropriately.

Sentimentalist philosophers such as Smith, David Hume, and Michael Slote argue that when it comes to determining what we ought to do, relying on reason alone will not get us far, since reason cannot explain why we are morally obliged to act in one way rather than another, unless we care about the reason for action first (e.g., Hume, 2000, p. 301). For example, if I care about fighting climate change, I can determine via reason alone that donating a large portion of my income to combat climate change is good for me to do, since that is a way I can realize my goal. Reason alone will not tell me to combat climate change simply because it is the right thing to do, however, even if I do not care about it.[1] If I do not

---

[1]    Of course, we could appeal to the fact that climate change will likely undermine my long-term interests, and therefore, reason might suggest

have this goal, then reason may tell me to spend my money on things I care about more. So, if reason is what we must derive morality from, we are unable to explain why I ought to follow the demands of morality. Instead, since it is empathy that interests us in the common good of all, not just in our own good, morality is derived from our passions and thus empathy is the 'chief source of moral distinctions' (ibid, pp. 393-94).[2] On this view, moral approbation identifies what is morally right, so what we naturally empathize with reveals what we should or should not do (ibid, p. 321). Thus, empathy provides a normative foundation for right action.

Furthermore, empathy not only explains what we ought to do, but it also enables us to recognize how we ought to respond, so it is a helpful tool for training us to respond rightly. Through the cultivation of empathetic feeling, we shape our responses, and hence develop the capacity to appreciate how to respond to the needs of others. We may be able to ascertain that inequality is unjust through reason alone, but it is not reason that allows us to appreciate the injustice inherent in particular situations. As illustration of empathy's usefulness in this way, psychologist Martin Hoffman draws upon the case of Harriet Beecher Stowe, who wrote *Uncle Tom's Cabin*, the nineteenth-century novel that galvanized the slavery abolition movement in both the U.S. and the U.K. Stowe began to viscerally appreciate what it was like for enslaved Black mothers to lose their children when she grieved the loss of her own son, and Stowe's empathetic engagement motivated her to write the novel that, in turn, facilitated empathetic feeling for her many readers. Stowe's portrayal of what it was like to be a slave in the American South humanized the situation of enslaved Blacks for many whites and led many of them to see that the abolition of slavery was morally required (Hoffman, 2014, pp. 86-87).[3]

---

that I donate for those kinds of reasons. But that doesn't seem to explain why, morally speaking, I ought to donate money to combat climate change, and so once again, the judgment of reason is simply prudential.

[2] While Hume uses the term 'sympathy' here, his use of the term corresponds to the contemporary English understanding of empathy, not to the contemporary notion of sympathy.

[3] Hoffman also argues that empathy helped to motivate Lyndon B. Johnson's support for the civil rights movement a century later (2014, pp. 87-88). He is careful to qualify the role played by empathy, however, and though he argues it plays an important role, he does not claim that it was the only generating reason motivating white abolitionists and civil rights supporters (2014, p. 94).

Finally, beyond explaining what we ought to do and helping us to see what that is, sentimentalists argue that empathy is important for developing the capacity for sympathy and making altruism possible (Slote, 2007, pp. 23, 127-28). By causing us to imagine the suffering of others, our feelings of empathy lead us to take an interest in the good of others. Since we would fail to take such an altruistic interest in others without empathy, empathy is necessary for motivating us to respond to the needs of others (Hume, 2000, p. 394). Thus, empathy is not merely useful but is also essential for addressing the national and global issues we face that affect different populations in disparate ways.

## 3. Bridging the Epistemic Gap

Proponents of empathy tout its ability to bring people who are different from one another together by reminding them of their similarities and thereby motivating them to act for one another's good. I contend, however, that we should be cautious about the extent to which empathy can do this. First, since empathy relies on recognition of similarity, empathy is more easily given for people like the empathizer, suggesting that while empathy may help us feel what we already understand, it will not help to close the epistemic gap with those who are least like one another.[4] Though Hoffman draws on the case of Harriet Beecher Stowe to illustrate how empathy can be an effective motivator, Stowe's case also demonstrates the limits of empathy. Though Stowe's experience as a middle-class white woman differed in important ways from the enslaved Black women she empathized with, it was her experience of a specific kind of loss that caused her to appreciate a similarity that she shared with many enslaved Black women. However, without that similarity in the first place, she might have felt compassion or sympathy but not empathy. To feel empathy, Stowe had to experience a loss similar to that of those she was empathetic toward and then she had to recognize its salience. Without such a loss, however, she would not have been moved to support abolition due to empathy, showing that deep similarities between people are necessary for empathy's effectiveness.

---

[4]    Numerous studies support the empirical claim that a lack of similarity between the would-be empathizer and the target impedes feelings of empathy. See, for example, Nelson, Klein, & Irvin (2003); Tarrant, Dazeley, & Cottom (2009); Cikara, Bruneau, & Saxe (2011); Gutsell & Inzlicht (2012); and Stevens et al. (2021).

The deepest problems that plague our contemporary world, however, often involve clashes between people who have little in common and whose interests are often in opposition. The tensions between members of those groups is complex, but is driven, at least in part, by huge differences in ways of life, values, and interests. Take, for instance, the divisions between rural and urban residents amidst an increasingly globalized economy in industrialized countries like the U.S. and the U.K. that gained prominence during the 2016 U.S. presidential election and the Brexit referendum. While overall economic measures in many wealthy nations have increased due to globalization, focusing primarily on the size of GDP does not capture the significant economic losses experienced by workers in manufacturing and agricultural sectors, nor why the loss of a way of life is so destabilizing for some, who have found their expected way of life shifting beneath their feet. Politicians and other urban, white-collar professionals directly benefitted from free trade policies, but local farmers and manufacturers who had benefited from previous protectionist policies often did not. When the policies that have directly benefitted urban white-collar professionals have, at the same time, undermined the livelihoods of rural, blue-collar workers, this direct conflict of interests is unlikely to be solved by empathy without addressing the real material differences at issue.[5]

Another example of how empathy is an ineffective motivator when it requires those who have power and resources to give them up is the fight for Black liberation. One popular narrative is that empathy is what led many white people to fight for the abolition of slavery in both the U.S. and the U.K. However, in spite of the common belief that empathy played an important role in motivating support for the end of slavery and the promotion of civil rights, this interpretation has long been questioned by scholars such as critical legal scholar Derrick Bell. Bell argued that many white Americans were not moved to action until they recognized the costs to their own interests through the disruption of social life due to civil unrest and

[5]    I do not mean to imply that economic concerns are the only issues at stake, or the only reason why rural and urban voters diverged so strongly. Nor do I mean to imply that the issues in the U.K. Brexit referendum and U.S. presidential election were identical. Cultural loss (the feeling of many that their 'way of life' as a white-dominant majority) surely played a significant role, as well as resentment toward urban elites. Nevertheless, the failure to acknowledge the divergent impacts on the economic opportunities for different citizens surely played a substantial role in the increasingly hostile and polarized political climate.

continued protests, the reputation of American democracy, and their own self-image as 'good people'.[6] Recognizing these costs caused the self-interest of many white Americans to align with Black interests in the U.S., and it was when this changed that enough white Americans began to actively support Black civil rights, not because of altruistic empathy (Bell, 1976, p. 12).

Aside from direct conflicts of interests, however, deep disagreement about core values poses an even more difficult issue for empathy. A common strategy for developing empathy encourages the empathizer to imagine how she would feel in the other's shoes, so the empathizer brings her own values into her empathetic feeling. But if the values of the would-be empathizer and the target are deeply at odds, the same experiences will result in very different feelings for each. It is easy to see how similar experiences engender the same feelings when the loss is something we might expect everyone to suffer from (e.g., the death of a loved one), but when the very thing one person might mourn is what another would celebrate, empathy will struggle to bridge that gap. For example, consider a politically-charged Supreme Court decision that leaves one person stunned and angry at the injustice (as she sees it), while the other rejoices at (what he sees) as justice done. While the empathizer may be able to intellectually comprehend the target's feelings, unless the empathizer's deepest values change, they will be unable to feel as the target does in response to the same object. This kind of disagreement reveals a distinct limitation for empathy, since empathy uses shared values and similarities to build understanding. Deep conflicts over the best values, therefore, pose a challenge, since for the empathizer to take up the same feeling as the target toward the same experience, they must first share an understanding of which values are worth endorsing.[7]

As an example, consider that while some who voted for Brexit supported it on largely economic grounds, others did because they saw leaving the European Union as a way of preserving British identity,

---

[6] This dynamic also plays out in contemporary situations where 'good liberals' refuse to recognize their complicity in racial discrimination and structural injustice. Some of this is an unwillingness to give up material resources to support the costs of righting injustice, but some of the resistance surely also has to do with their image of themselves as non-racists and an unwillingness to accept that they, too, might be complicit.

[7] See also Nelson and Baumgarte (2004), which shows how cross-cultural value differences inhibit empathetic understanding.

autonomy, and sovereignty.[8] For someone with a cosmopolitan outlook who sees their identity as primarily European and prefers greater integration with the E.U., valuing British identity and control will seem insignificant, and it is hard to see how such a person could feel the same as a Brexiteer unless she was first convinced that British autonomy was worth valuing. Likewise, without first convincing the other party that their intellectual reasons for being saddened (or gladdened) are sound, someone who sees her British identity as being very important could not come to appreciate how it actually feels for the cosmopolitan, since the imaginative function of empathy connects the empathizer's own emotions to the target's feelings in response to the same object. Here, however, the same object (the results of the Brexit referendum) inspires very different responses.

This also applies to considerations of how we view our obligations beyond our nation as well. Someone who sees their identity first as a citizen of the world and secondly as a citizen of a particular nation-state might advocate for a drastic redistribution of resources from wealthy countries to poorer ones, arguing that need, not national identity, is what matters for moral obligations. However, to the person who deeply identifies as a member of her nation-state and sees the primary role of the government as promoting the good of that particular nation-state, this moral claim will seem deeply wrong, at least as long as some of their own fellow citizens are in need. At the deep level of values and identities, empathy will struggle to bridge the epistemic gap between people who are very different, so empathy can least do the work that is asked of it in the situations in which we need it most.

## 4. Addressing Inequality

A second concern with empathy is that it can dangerously entrench us in our preferences for some rather than others, undermining the pursuit of justice for all. Specifically, since empathy leads us to feel a greater connection with some over others, we will often be motivated by affective connection to promote the well-being of those we relate to over those we do not. For example, a study conducted on the impact of empathy on resource allocation found that when

---

[8]    Multiple surveys found that for those who voted to leave, maintaining independence over U.K. policies was the most important reason (Carl, 2018).

participants were asked to empathize with a specific person, this often motivated participants to allocate resources to benefit that particular person, even when they also believed this allocation was unfair and knew that other people in the distribution pool had greater needs than the person they had been asked to empathize with.[9] This suggests the following worrying implication: not only will empathy be ineffective in the cases where we need it the most (as I argued in the previous section), but, in fact, it will often lead us to act in favor of those like us, furthering the gap between people who are already different from one another. In other words, in an increasingly polarized world, empathy serves to supercharge existing divides, not to bridge them. Given that we live in a world where power and access to resources is unequal, this also has the effect of perpetuating existing injustices since empathy encourages us to respond to the needs and desires of those we understand and connect with, rather than responding on the basis of objectively identified need.[10]

Even proponents of empathy recognize the concerns that empathy can interfere with fair treatment of all. In response to this concern, Hoffman proposed that the worries about bias could be tempered through explicit reflection on who else might be affected by this decision, as a way of attempting to extend empathy more broadly (Hoffman, 2000, p. 296). However, in a study designed to test whether Hoffman's suggestion would actually be effective at moderating bias in empathy, reflecting on who else might be affected by the decision did not change participants' decisions to benefit the particular person they empathized with (Oceja, 2008, pp. 181-182). Asking participants to explicitly reflect on principles of justice and fairness prior to making their decision *did* have an effect, which suggests that the problems with empathy cannot simply be fixed by extending its range more broadly. The problem is not with empathy's range, but the fact that when empathy is prioritized in decision-making, it may overrule what is fair or what promotes the good for all.

[9] Batson et al. (1995, pp. 1051-1052).
[10] Of course, even the identification of what counts as a need will be shaped by existing power relations and value systems, so I don't mean to suggest that this is a matter of simply seeing objectively what is necessary. As will become clear in the next section, I am not endorsing a straightforwardly objective way of ascertaining need. Nevertheless, the kind of attention I will propose seeks to call into question those beliefs, values, and expectations as given, whereas empathy often encourages us to take them as natural and unquestioned.

It is not simply that we are more likely to empathize with those whose stories we appreciate vividly, however; it is also that even the capacity to develop empathy in the first place will be constrained by those we feel affinity for, and it is well-established in the psychological literature that we have greater affinity for those who are like us, including people of the same race and ethnicity, gender, team, political persuasion, and in-group.[11] This is not just a matter of who we tend to instinctively connect with or feel for, but also how seriously we take their suffering and what we will be willing to sacrifice to alleviate their suffering.[12] For example, as political science scholar Juliet Hooker has argued, white empathy evoked during the U.S. civil rights movement was a double-edged sword: while some white Americans clearly were empathetically moved to support civil rights, other white Americans were spurred by the possibility of equality to form angry and often violent mobs in opposition (Hooker, 2016). For those who fell into the latter category, they empathized with the experiences of other white Americans more than with the suffering of Black Americans, and this led not only to disproportionate empathy for those who were like them and indifference for those who were not, but to outright opposition and violence against Black Americans. The problem was not that these white Americans failed to empathize, but instead, that because the capacity for empathy itself is shaped, from the beginning, by prejudices, preferences, and affinities, their empathy was activated only for those like them.

Proponents of empathy are right to take the motivational question seriously. It is one thing to recognize that there is a difficult problem whose solution may require me to give something up and quite another to be willing to do so. But while empathy may well motivate me to sacrifice, it will not do so for those whose positions I do not understand or do not feel affinity for. Not only, then, might empathy not do anything to solve the motivational problem

[11] For research on affinity for those of the same race and ethnicity, see Xu et al. (2009); Avenanti, Sirigu, & Aglioti (2010); and Gutsell & Inzlicht (2010). For research on gender, see Feshbach & Roe (1968); for team, see Smith et al. (2009); for political persuasion, see Stevens et al. (2021); and for in-group, see Meindl & Lerner (1984); Gutsell & Inzlicht (2012); and Cikara et al. (2014).

[12] For particular studies that demonstrate how agents are less willing to benefit those unlike themselves and more willing to sacrifice themselves for those they have greater similarities with, see Batson et al. (1995); Batson et al. (1999); Stürmer, Snyder, & Omoto (2005); Tarrant, Dazeley, & Cottom (2009); and Cikara et al. (2010).

between very differently situated individuals, it may make it worse since I will be inclined to take the perspective of those who are like me more seriously, even when their suffering is less severe and doing so causes me to exacerbate the suffering of those with whom I do not readily empathize.

Together, these two problems highlight the danger of empathy's indifference to those we do not connect with emotionally, raising the question of whether emotion-based strategies really can play a transformative ethical role. Depending on the affective element to motivate us to promote justice encourages us to engage those we find easy to understand, but to bridge the gap, we must develop the capacity for both understanding and taking action even when we lack an emotional connection and do not recognize similarities.

## 5. Loving Attention

I have argued so far there are two significant problems with viewing empathy as the solution to the globalized problems we face. First, since empathy depends on us finding similarity with people like us, it will be difficult to achieve in the cases where we need it the most: in engaging with those who have very different interests, situations, and values than our own. Second, not only is empathy often ineffective at bridging these gaps, but it also activates our tendency to promote the interests of those who are like us, thus further exacerbating the divides that exist. Both concerns about empathy arise from the idea that developing understanding of one another should begin with our own experiences and feelings and use those as the basis for connection with others. In contrast, I suggest that a more effective strategy for promoting social solidarity through understanding starts with the cultivation of loving attention.[13] While both loving attention and empathy aim at the same end of building understanding between diverse populations, loving attention more successfully targets the barriers that keep us from doing so.

The way that we come to see when we attend to the other is similar to how we develop the capacity to appreciate a particular example of art. This task involves creativity and generosity as I seek to

---

[13] The sense of 'loving attention', as I develop here, draws on Iris Murdoch's development of the philosophical conception, particularly as she discusses it in her essay 'The Idea of Perfection' in Murdoch (2014). Murdoch's own work on this was most significantly influenced by Simone Weil's essays on attention (Weil, 2002).

understand and appreciate the work of art. I do not merely passively soak it in or reflect on how I feel in response to it; rather, I make a conscious effort to appreciate and interpret its meaning and beauty. When I first encounter an unfamiliar painting, I notice only the most obvious elements: the bright colors, the unknown faces depicted, the strangeness of the tableau. In the first few moments, nothing much may change, but if I stop and focus my attention, I will start to notice details that give me insight. I observe the way the eyes of the two central figures express longing, how they are physically separated, the disapproval that is manifest in the face of an onlooker to the side. These figures that, minutes ago, seemed so distant take on a new familiarity in this light, and I begin to appreciate the story that is unfolding before me. The painting itself has not altered; instead, my capacity to *see* the painting has changed.

This approach to ethical development is exemplified in Iris Murdoch's narrative of the relationship between a mother-in-law, M, and her daughter-in-law, D. In the beginning, M judges that D is 'a silly vulgar girl', but over time, M acknowledges the role that her own prejudices and motivations play in interpreting D, and she begins to engage in a process of paying careful attention to D (Murdoch, 2014, p. 17). In doing so, M seeks 'not just to see D accurately but to see her justly or lovingly' (ibid, p. 22). In seeking to see D lovingly, M engages in a process that first acknowledges how M's own self-focused desires shape how she sees D, and then aims to see D anew by attending to D in this light. M comes to recognize that her own perspective obscures and shapes her interpretation of D, and so M's effort is aimed at expanding her own capacity for moral imagination so that she might come to 'see D as she really is', not as M currently understands D (ibid, p. 36). In time, this reshapes M's perspective of D, though not because D has changed; what has transformed is not D's behavior, but M's interpretation of it.

While the process of lovingly attending to the other begins by acknowledging that the observer's perceptual capacity is shaped by self-interest and attempting to appreciate the other as she is, empathetic identification tries to connect the empathizer's own feelings, values, and ways of seeing the world to the other. Were M to attempt to empathize with D, she might use what they have in common to imagine how she would feel if she were in D's position. However, since M's own values, personality, and interests are quite different from D's, this may not help M receive any more insight into D. Empathy invites us to extend the scope of who we attempt to understand, but understanding is still limited by our own point of view. Conversely, loving attention challenges us to expand our moral imagination itself, not just the scope it applies to.

Since the starting point for empathy is the empathizer's own emotions, the beliefs and values about what is important that give rise to those emotions are often taken to be natural and unquestioned. In contrast, since loving attention starts with the other, our own beliefs and values are necessarily interrogated. This is an advantage in the case of divergent values, since knowing how I would feel, were I in the other's shoes, is no help if we value very different goods. In lovingly attending to the other, the attender questions his own biases to concentrate on sharpening what he is able to see, rather than relying on similarity and emotional connection to motivate his understanding. Of course, there will still be disagreement about what values he ought to prefer and how to best achieve shared ends, but these discussions can be more productive once he acknowledges the limits of his own perspective. Additionally, since loving attention is not based on understanding through emotional connection but on coming to understand others through engaging our attention, this approach explicitly combats the biases that lead us to favor those who are like us. By shifting the focus away from our feelings and emotive responses to the needs and desires of those we are engaging with, this will also make it less likely that we will react to the suffering of others by simply emoting or engaging in Facebook-solidarity.[14]

It might seem odd that Murdoch uses 'justly' and 'lovingly' interchangeably to describe the way in which M attempts to see D. We often speak of love's gaze as distorting reality, so to look at someone in the clear-eyed, objective way that we might think justice demands is quite different than seeing him through the subjective gaze of love. The loving attention here, however, is not the gaze of the lover who thinks that her beloved is the most perfect creature in existence; that is mere infatuation. Rather, the attention here is loving because love motivates us to know and appreciate the other as he truly is, not simply for who we wish him to be. Love orients us outward, away from the self and towards what is good. As we attend to the other on his own terms, we come to recognize that what we can see in the other is itself shaped and distorted by our

---

[14]  Take, for example, the many white liberals and progressives who consider themselves Black allies but responded to the death of George Floyd and others by mainly posting about their sadness and anger on social media without taking more substantive action.

own prejudices and preferences. This kind of attending to the other is thus, at its root, necessarily relational.

That loving attention is relational, however, does not mean that it is only appropriate for intimate relationships. Manifestations of love are in the concrete and the particular, but the love that motivates attention toward particular individuals may be broader, such as love for fellow compatriots or for humanity. While the urban cosmopolitan may not encounter any rural compatriots in her day-to-day life, she nevertheless assumes certain values and motivations on their part, and committing to engaging in loving attention requires that she recognize the ways in which her assumptions should be open to revision. Listening to people's stories – what they value, what they fear, what they hope for the future – is a way in, since it helps the attender to see others and their context better. She may not be able to feel what her rural compatriot does (connection to this particular area of land, fear of the collapse of economic livelihood, anxiety about changes in social status), but when she lovingly attends to him, she attempts to appreciate why her compatriot feels these things by seeing him in context. She does not merely engage him to convince him of what she takes the correct view to be or to make sense of beliefs that she finds baffling. In lovingly attending, her aim is to come to appreciate him, which involves not merely recognizing why he acts or believes as he does, but coming to see him in the light of love, as a whole person whose flaws and strengths are contextualized. As she attends to him, she hopes for his good and looks for what is best in him. She replaces easy caricatures with more complex pictures that acknowledge the ways in which the current economic system benefits her, along with the very real losses to community and economic livelihood that globalization brings. This recognition allows her to see her rural compatriot in a different light, and to understand the reasons why he values what he does, allowing her to engage meaningfully and imagine better solutions. Similarly, the white individual who commits to lovingly attending to his Black compatriot will begin to see the ways in which he has been unable (or unwilling) to see racial inequality. His recognition that his interpretation of Black experience is distorted by his own blind spots forces him to confront the distance between how things are and how they should be. Through acknowledging that his own self-interest might prevent him from appreciating the ways in which he has benefitted from injustice, he better develops the capacity to perceive the world and those around him as they are. The humility that this recognition produces then reorients his response to injustice to better reflect what those who experience injustice say they need, not what he assumes is best from the outside.

# Carissa Phillips-Garrett

When we come to see in this way, it is also not just a matter of opening our eyes or emptying ourselves; rather, to attend in this way is a creative act of moral imagination that does not occur purely through either rational argument or emotional connection. What we can see will be shaped by both, but loving attention differs by acknowledging that what is needed is not a purely objective position to neutrally evaluate arguments from nor a purely subjective emotional connection. Rather, in taking seriously that the capacity to see is misshapen by self-focus, this approach takes an intersubjective and relational perspective that facilitates appreciation of those we are engaging. None of us has full access to the world as it is, so we need an approach that expands what we can see to address conflicting interests and competing values. Since the aim is to see one another and the problems we face as they really are, an intersubjective approach is not only necessary for understanding those who are quite different from us but also for ultimately understanding which values we ought to hold. Through reorienting what we pay attention to, we expand what we can see and question how we interpret one another, and it is this reshaping of our moral imagination that is necessary to create the conditions for the flourishing of all in our diverse and changing world.

*Loyola Marymount University*
*carissa.phillips-garrett@lmu.edu*

## References

Alessio Avenanti, Angela Sirigu, and Salvatore M. Aglioti, 'Racial Bias Reduces Empathic Sensorimotor Resonance with Other-Race Pain', *Current Biology*, 20 (2010), 1018–1022.
C. Daniel Batson, Tricia R. Klein, Lori Highberger, and Laura L. Shaw, 'Immorality From Empathy Induced Altruism: When Compassion and Justice Conflict', *Journal of Personality and Social Psychology*, 68 (1995), 1042–1054.
C. Daniel Batson, Nadia Ahmad, Jodi Yin, Steven J. Bedell, Jennifer W. Johnson, Christie M. Templin, and Aaron Whiteside, 'Two Threats to the Common Good: Self-Interested Egoism and Empathy-Induced Altruism', *Personality and Social Psychology Bulletin*, 25 (1999), 3–16.
Glenn Beck, 'Empathy for Black Lives Matter', *New York Times*, September 7, 2016, https://www.nytimes.com/2016/09/07/

opinion/glenn-beck-empathy-for-black-lives-matter. html?searchResultPosition=1.

Derrick A. Bell, Jr., 'Racial Remediation: An Historical Perspective on Current Conditions', *Notre Dame Law Review*, 52 (1976), 5–29.

Joseph R. Biden, 'Remarks at the 153rd National Memorial Day Observance', May 31, 2021, https://www.whitehouse.gov/briefing-room/speeches-remarks/2021/05/31/remarks-by-president-biden-at-the-153rd-national-memorial-day-observance/.

Noah Carl, 'CSI Brexit 4: People's Stated Reasons for Voting Leave or Remain', *Centre for Social Investigation*, April 24, 2018.

Mina Cikara, Emile G. Bruneau, and Rebecca R. Saxe, 'Us and Them: Intergroup Failures of Empathy', *Current Directions in Psychological Science*, 20 (2011), 149–153.

Mina Cikara, Emile G. Bruneau, J. J. Van Bavel, and Rebecca R. Saxe, 'Their Pain Gives Us Pleasure: How Intergroup Dynamics Shape Empathic Failures and Counter-Empathic Responses', *Journal of Experimental Social Psychology*, 55 (2014), 110–125.

Mina Cikara, Rachel A. Farnsworth, Lasana T. Harris, and Susan T. Fiske, 'On the Wrong Side of the Trolley Track: Neural Correlates of Relative Social Valuation', *Social Cognitive and Affective Neuroscience*, 5 (2010), 404–413.

Benjamin M. P. Cuff, Sarah J. Brown, Laura Taylor, and Douglas J. Howat, 'Empathy: A Review of the Concept', *Emotion Review*, 8 (2016), 144–153.

Norma D. Feshbach and Kiki Roe, 'Empathy in Six- and Seven-Year-Olds', *Child Development*, 39 (1968), 133–145.

Jennifer N. Gutsell and Michael Inzlicht, 'Empathy Constrained: Prejudice Predicts Reduced Mental Simulation of Actions During Observation of Outgroups', *Journal of Experimental Social Psychology*, 46 (2010), 841–845.

Jennifer N. Gutsell and Michael Inzlicht, 'Intergroup Differences in the Sharing of Emotive States: Neural Evidence of an Empathy Gap', *Social Cognitive and Affective Neuroscience*, 7 (2012), 596–603.

Martin L. Hoffman, *Empathy and Moral Development: Implications for Caring and Justice* (New York: Cambridge University Press, 2000).

Martin L. Hoffman, 'Empathy, Justice, and Social Change', in *Empathy and Morality*. Ed. Heidi L. Maibom (Oxford: Oxford University Press, 2014), 71–96.

Juliet Hooker, 'A Black History of White Empathy', *Telesur*, February 12, 2016, https://www.telesurenglish.net/opinion/A-Black-History-of-White-Empathy-20160211-0011.html.

David Hume, *A Treatise of Human Nature*, ed. David Fate Norton and Mary J. Norton. (Oxford: Oxford University Press, 2000).

Ziva Kunda, 'The Case for Motivated Reasoning', *Psychological Bulletin*, 108 (1990), 480–498.

James R. Meindl and Melvin J. Lerner, 'Exacerbation of Extreme Responses to an Out-Group', *Journal of Personality and Social Psychology*, 47 (1984), 71–84.

Iris Murdoch, *The Sovereignty of Good*, 2nd edition (London: Routledge, 2014).

Donna Webster Nelson and Roger Baumgarte, 'Cross-Cultural Misunderstandings Reduce Empathic Responding', *Journal of Applied Social Psychology*, 34 (2004), 391–401.

Donna Webster Nelson, Cynthia T. F. Klein, and Jennifer E. Irvin, 'Motivational Antecedents of Empathy: Inhibiting Effects of Fatigue', *Basic and Applied Social Psychology*, 25 (2003), 37–50.

Michelle Obama, 'Address to the Democratic National Convention', *CNN*, August 17, 2020, https://www.cnn.com/2020/08/17/politics/michelle-obama-speech-transcript/index.html.

Luis Oceja, 'Overcoming Empathy-Induced Partiality: Two Rules of Thumb', *Basic and Applied Social Psychology*, 30 (2008), 176–182.

Michael Slote, *The Ethics of Care and Empathy* (New York: Routledge, 2007).

Adam Smith, *A Theory of Moral Sentiments*, ed. Knud Haakonssen (New York: Cambridge University Press, 2002).

Richard H. Smith, Caitlin A. J. Powell, David J. Y. Combs, and David Ryan Schurtz, 'Exploring the When and Why of *Schadenfreude*', *Social and Personality Psychology Compass*, 3/4 (2009), 530–546.

Samantha M. Stevens, Carl P. Jago, Katarzyna Jasko, and Gail D. Heyman, 'Trustworthiness and Ideological Similarity (But Not Ideology) Promote Empathy', *Personality and Social Psychology Bulletin*, 47 (2021), 1452–1465.

Karsten Stueber, 'Empathy', *Stanford Encyclopedia of Philosophy*, Fall 2019. Ed. Edward N. Zalta, https://plato.stanford.edu/entries/empathy/.

Stefan Stürmer, Mark Snyder, and Allen M. Omoto, 'Prosocial Emotions and Helping: The Moderating Role of Group Membership', *Journal of Personality and Social Psychology*, 88 (2005), 532–546.

Mark Tarrant, Sarah Dazeley, and Tom Cottom, 'Social Categorization and Empathy for Outgroup Members', *British Journal of Social Psychology*, 48 (2009), 427–446.

Simone Weil, 'Attention and Will', in *Gravity and Grace*, trans. Emma Crawford and Mario von Der Ruhr (London: Routledge, 2002), 116-122.

Xiaojing Xu, Xiangyu Zuo, Xiaoying Wang, and Shihui Han, 'Do You Feel My Pain? Racial Group Membership Modulates Empathic Neural Responses', *Journal of Neuroscience*, 29 (2009), 8525–8529.

# On the Importance of Beauty and Taste

PANOS PARIS

**Abstract**

We have all heard people say 'Beauty is only skin-deep', or 'Beauty is in the eye of the beholder': our culture promulgates a conception of beauty as subjective, superficial, and independent of other values like moral goodness or knowledge and understanding. Yet our taste in beauty affects many aspects of our lives, sometimes playing a decisive – and often detrimental – role in areas as wide-ranging as our identity and self-esteem, our morally salient decisions, and our relationship to the environment. This presents us with a choice: we can either ignore the facts – leaving our conception of beauty unchanged and allowing our taste to influence much in our lives while either not acknowledging such influence, or perhaps seeking to reprimand it; or we can take the power of beauty seriously and seek to harmonise our taste with our values. I argue for the latter option and propose a way of bringing beauty and taste in line with what matters to us using the notion of functional beauty. Adopting this strategy, I suggest, can have a powerful – and positive – impact on our self-esteem and wellbeing, our relationship to others, as well as our attitudes towards the environment.

We have all heard people say 'Beauty is only skin-deep', or 'Beauty is in the eye of the beholder': our culture promulgates a conception of beauty as subjective, superficial, and independent of other values like moral goodness or knowledge and understanding. At the same time, our taste in beauty affects many aspects of our lives, sometimes playing a decisive – often detrimental – role in areas as wide-ranging as our identity and self-esteem, our morally salient decisions, and our relationship to the environment. This presents us with a choice: we can either ignore the facts – leaving our conception of beauty unchanged and allowing our taste to influence much in our lives while either not acknowledging such influence, or perhaps seeking to reprimand it; or we can take the power of beauty and taste seriously and seek to harmonise it with our values. I argue for the latter option, proposing a way to bring beauty and taste in line with what matters to us. Doing so, I suggest, can have a powerful – and positive – impact on our self-esteem and wellbeing, our relationship to others, and our attitudes towards the environment.

doi:10.1017/S1358246122000285

**Panos Paris**

I begin in section 1 by offering an overview of evidence showing that our taste in beauty currently influences us in ways that are rarely acknowledged, adversely affecting our wellbeing, as well as our relationship to others, and to the natural world. In section 2, I argue that beauty's unsavoury effects are explained by certain peculiarities of our collective taste, which has left us with an unhelpful conception of beauty as wholly subjective, skin-deep, and independent of other values. In Section 3 I present a conception of functional beauty that is not wholly subjective, skin-deep, or independent of other values, and which comprises many different subspecies. In sections 4–6, I offer reasons to think that attuning our taste to functional beauty can positively contribute to our mental health and wellbeing, social justice, and our relationship to the environment. I conclude with some reflections on what it would take to thus attune our taste.[1]

## 1. The Power and Perils of Beauty and Taste

Whether we like it or not, many of our attitudes, decisions and behaviours – from the most mundane to the most consequential ones – are shaped by our taste for beauty and distaste for ugliness. Such influence extends to areas where we are currently facing considerable challenges, including mental health and wellbeing, social justice, and the environment. Let me briefly summarise some of the evidence.

First, presumably most of those reading this article will be aware that beauty standards are playing a key role in promoting negative body and self images, spearheading a mental health crisis, especially among young people. At the most basic level, feelings of guilt and shame are prevalent among those trying to live up to current beauty ideals and, inevitably, failing (Widdows, 2018, pp. 31–35). More alarmingly, we know that rates of eating disorders and body-image related disorders like body dysmorphia or bigorexia have been on the rise in the last decade (ibid., pp. 60–62; Grogan, 2021). We also know that such disorders, as well as concerns over body image more broadly, are strongly correlated with mental health problems like anxiety and depression. Finally, the evidence suggests

---

[1]    My arguments here thus complement other proposals for redressing the harms due to contemporary beauty or other aesthetic norms in various domains (Saito, 2007; Eaton, 2016; Lintott & Irvin, 2016; Irvin, 2017; Minerva, 2017).

that such beauty-related mental health problems are correlated with social media use, and in particular platforms that are predominantly visual and that are formative of our beauty norms and tastes (MacCallum & Widdows, 2018; Fardouly et al., 2015).

A second set of evidence points to a plethora of social injustices explicable by beauty standards and tastes.[2] These begin from birth, with evidence indicating that infants perceived as physically attractive receive greater affection and attention compared to those perceived as unattractive (Langlois et al., 1995), and are judged to be more intelligent, likeable, and well behaved than unattractive ones (Stephen & Langlois, 1984). Later on in life, teachers' evaluations of pupils favour attractive over unattractive ones (Adams & Cohen, 1974), as do, further down the line, hiring decisions (Hosoda, Stone-Romero & Coats, 2003) and pay gaps in employment (Hamermesh, 2003). Juries give harsher sentences to those perceived as unattractive, while those perceived as attractive receive more lenient sentences (Darby & Jeffers 1988; McKelvie & Coley, 1993). Strangers' willingness to help others depends on those others' perceived attractiveness (Athanasiou & Greene, 1973), and even the willingness of doctors and nurses to conduct physical examinations on patients varies with whether they are perceived as fat (Fontaine et al., 1998). And this is excluding all the evidence that points to intersections between judgements of attractiveness and race, gender, or ability. The collective effect of such phenomena is known as 'lookism' (Minerva, 2017), designating a form of discrimination based on perceived physical attractiveness. This form of discrimination may be partly explicable by another well-documented and widespread phenomenon known as the 'halo effect'. This involves making wider evaluations about people on the basis of their appearance, such that those found beautiful are also found to have positive qualities, like being more intelligent, popular, etc., whilst those found ugly are found to possess the contrary, negative qualities (Nisbett & Wilson, 1977).

A third set of evidence indicates that beauty informs our relationship to the environment and our decisions towards it.[3] These fall into three categories. Firstly, in the case of landscapes and habitats, we tend to single out areas of 'outstanding natural beauty' on the basis of their picturesque or scenic qualities, and are concerned about

---

[2] This paragraph draws on issues and examples discussed by Irvin (2017) and Minerva (2017).

[3] This paragraph draws on issues and examples discussed by Saito (2007).

their preservation, but neglect places like wetlands, indicating a 'perceived need for protecting scenic wonders, but not ecological integrity, from cultivation and development' (Saito 2007, p. 63). Secondly, in the case of living creatures, Stephen Jay Gould notes that 'environmentalists continually face the political reality that support and funding can be won for soft, cuddly, and 'attractive' animals, but not for slimy, grubby, and ugly creatures (of potentially greater evolutionary interest and practical significance) or for habitats' (1993, p. 312). Relatedly, philosopher Marcia Muelder Eaton has noted the emotional reactions people have to the sentimental portrayal of deer perpetuated by Disney, dubbing it the 'Bambi syndrome'. This made it difficult to cull deer in the US, threatening the ecological equilibrium (2001, p. 182). Thirdly, in the case of the built environment, we often pit the beautiful against the ecologically desirable, whether that concerns our lived environment, where there is 'still a strong resistance to green architecture not only because of the initial high cost but also due to the assumption that ecological value compromised the aesthetic value of such projects' (Saito, 2007, p. 66); or projects beneficial to the environment outside towns and cities, like the ongoing resistance to wind farms, which are often seen as soiling the landscape. All of this, evidently, often comes with adverse environmental consequences.

The evidence above shows two things. First, that what we find beautiful or ugly can have powerful effects on our attitudes, decisions, and behaviours in relation to ourselves, others, and the environment. Second, many of these effects are undesirable; they have negative impacts on our mental health, contribute to social injustice, and even adversely affect our relationship with the natural world.

## 2. Beauty, Taste, and Value

Confronted with such evidence, one might point out that it is, in a sense, unsurprising. Beauty is a powerful force, its experience characterised by rich feelings of pleasure and delight, so much so that beauty has been linked to love and happiness (Nehamas, 2007). No wonder it has a powerful motivational pull. But beauty is liable to lead us astray, and the evidence simply reflects this fact. We should thus do our best to resist beauty's influence on our judgements, by being more suspicious of it and exercising greater vigilance. In this way, we will slowly be able to weed beauty's influence out of the domains to which it does not belong.

But this, it seems to me, would be premature. The question we need to ask ourselves is whether the deleterious effects outlined above stem from the fact that when we find something beautiful, our experience of beauty spills over into domains that are properly not in the jurisdiction of aesthetics; or if these negative effects are instead a product of what we currently find beautiful.

It should be obvious that finding something beautiful is not in and of itself bound to bring about undesirable consequences. Indeed, in contrast to the evidence discussed earlier, there is a different set of evidence which suggests that appreciating beauty can contribute to, rather than detract from, wellbeing, and can have a positive influence in domains that many would consider paradigmatically non-aesthetic. For instance, just as there is evidence that finding someone physically attractive may lead to certain unwarranted judgements or behaviours, there is evidence that finding someone morally good leads to finding them more beautiful.[4] This is important because it implies that experiences of beauty can also have a positive effect and lead us to embrace what is genuinely valuable. Experiences of beauty are credited as conducive to success in other domains too, including in mathematics and physics. Many great mathematicians (e.g., Hardy, 2004), and prominent physicists (e.g., Wilczek, 2016), claim to be drawn to their subject for its beauty, and to be guided by beauty in all of their most important discoveries and decisions. In such cases, beauty's influence is conscious and, moreover, if we are to trust such expert testimonies, both welcome and rewarding.

So it seems plausible that the negative effects in section one cannot be explained solely by the hypothesis that beauty sometimes over-reaches, as when finding something beautiful affects many of our non-aesthetic attitudes, decisions, or behaviours. This is just as well, since the evidence above suggests that whether we like it or not, and whether or not our society chooses to ignore the link between experiences of beauty and other values, beauty, like an ivy, latches onto our most important values and concerns. This is probably because the link between beauty and other values is deeply rooted in human psychology. This does not, of course, show that the link is desirable or worth preserving. But it does raise a question as to whether it can or should be severed. For the influence of our experiences of beauty on other domains in many of the cases mentioned in section one probably operates well below the level of consciousness. Otherwise, presumably, we would have already addressed

---

4   See my (2018a) for discussion of this evidence.

these issues. Moreover, unlike certain kinds of unconscious bias, which are undesirable through and through, a love of the beautiful is plausibly both desirable and a much more fundamental and deeply entrenched part of our psychology (cf. Ravasio, 2022). So even if it were possible to eliminate beauty's influence altogether, it is not clear that this would be wise. For, as we've seen, experiences of beauty can also exercise valuable and desirable influence over our decisions and behaviour. If this is right, then trying to eliminate beauty's influence altogether, in the hopes that reason or something similar will replace it, seems like throwing out the baby with the bathwater. It is, after all, unlikely that there's anything else that can take beauty's place when it comes to its affective and motivational power, and the problem is not that beauty is powerful, but that its power can sometimes prove perilous.

So perhaps the negative effects in section one stem from our current collective taste in beauty, that is, from what we find beautiful, rather than beauty itself or the experience of beauty (cf. Higgins, 2000). But what might it be about our current taste in beauty that makes it liable to lead to such unpalatable consequences? It is difficult to give a full characterisation of our current taste in beauty, not least because there are bound to be individual variations. Be that as it may, our collective taste does appear to favour certain kinds of qualities over others (cf. Irvin, 2017; Eaton, 2016), and while it would be futile to try to offer an exhaustive list of such qualities across all domains, it is worth noting certain features. Our taste in human beauty, for instance, focuses exclusively on the face and body, and specifically, for women, on certain qualities like thinness, smoothness, firmness, and youthfulness (Widdows, 2018, pp. 21–26). For many of us, whether we find a person beautiful is independent of their character, and their character tells us nothing about whether they are beautiful. When it comes to the natural world, we seem to find beauty in picturesque landscapes, in neat, orderly scenes, and in medium to large mammals with bright colours and fairly smooth, regular features. Whether we find an animal beautiful has nothing to do with its design, nor does its design affect its beauty – just look at a worm: exquisitely designed to decompose organic matter, and essential to soil health, on which much of plant and animal life depends, but disgusting to look at. The common denominator here is that the qualities that we find beautiful in both human beings and animals are not just exclusively visual, but indeed, are whatever visually pleases us pre-reflectively, and independently of other considerations of value.

# On the Importance of Beauty and Taste

Our taste in beauty has been crystallised in what is plausibly our commonplace conception of beauty today. This sees beauty as fundamentally skin-deep – as strictly limited to, and predicable of, perceptible objects, and pertaining in virtue of objects' perceptual qualities; beauty is said to be a matter of how things look or sound, and independent of what they are, what they do, what they are for, or where they are placed (cf. Zangwill, 2001). Consequently, and crucially, on this conception, beauty is construed as superficial, in the sense that it is independent of other properties or values, like moral goodness or truth, and virtues like honesty, courage, justice, or wisdom. In addition to these features, beauty is also thought to be irreducibly subjective, in the sense that it is a matter of personal preferences. This immunises our taste in beauty from criticism.

All this may actually be unsurprising given the culture we inhabit. Since the advent of photography – to which the origins of our contemporary taste and concomitant conception of beauty are arguably traceable (Richards, 2017) – our cultural environment has been visual in ways unparalleled in human history, and is increasingly virtual in ways that we may not even be able to predict. Together with other technological advances in both the digital manipulation of images and their accessibility, our environment nourishes our appetite for beauty on an exclusively visual diet. And given that we are highly visual creatures, we happily indulge in that diet, whilst it, in turn, shapes our taste, radically narrowing the scope of what we commonly find beautiful, and even determines what we understand beauty to be.

Against this backdrop, it seems plausible that what explains the negative effects of our taste in beauty are two important features of our taste and concomitant conception of beauty. First, our taste in beauty is misaligned with, or developed in isolation from, other interests and values. No wonder it can clash with them, and come out on top, given its power. Second, due to its exclusive focus on perceptual qualities, our collective taste in beauty is impervious to certain kinds of beauty that may lead to positive effects, like mathematical beauty or beauty in physics, which hold heuristic value, or the beauty someone can have in virtue of their character, which can lead to greater moral appreciation. This makes our taste and corresponding conception of beauty too narrow and deprives us of a great many experiences of beauty that we could be enjoying. Of course, it's not possible for all of us to enjoy mathematical beauty, but its existence points to the possibility that many domains of everyday life offer untapped opportunities to enjoy beauty, which may be aligned to values we collectively endorse or should endorse.

Panos Paris

Jointly the foregoing considerations provide both pragmatic and theoretical reasons to suspect that our current taste in beauty is deformed in at least two ways: it is too shallow and too narrow. Consequently, it is very limited and limiting, and is not serving our collective, or indeed, individual interests. This critique crucially depends, of course, on there being viable conceptions of beauty that do not share these flaws. It also requires us to reject the idea that beauty is purely in the eye of individual beholders, subjective and therefore immune to criticism. In the remainder of this article, I argue that there is a conception of beauty that is suitably broad and substantive, allowing us to anchor its influence onto what we care about, and helping us develop better and healthier relationships with ourselves, others, and the natural world.

### 3. Functional Beauty and Good Taste

There is, in the philosophical tradition, a well-established notion of what's recently been called functional beauty. This is a species of beauty that depends on wellformedness for function.[5] That notion was displaced by our increasingly narrow commonplace conception and was given a bad name through its association with form-follows-function principles in twentieth-century architecture and design (which, admittedly, were behind some rather ugly products). Yet this conception of beauty offers a valuable alternative to our commonplace conception.

Indeed, if we reflect on our experiences, many of us will realise that we are actually quite familiar with functional beauty, even if the concept eludes us. Before testing this thought, let me briefly explain how I understand functional beauty. My account of functional beauty holds that (i) something's being well formed for its

[5]   The notion of functional beauty (unqualifiedly called 'beauty') arguably originated in antiquity and survived into modernity. It was reintroduced in contemporary philosophy, and labelled 'functional beauty', by Parsons and Carlson (2008). For a history of the concept, see (ibid., pp. 1–30). Note that my version of functional beauty (Paris, 2020), which I sketch in this paper, differs from that offered by Parsons and Carlson, which, in my view, inherits certain undesirable features of our commonplace conception of beauty, notably its link to strictly perceptual properties and independence from other, importantly moral, values. Saying that functional beauty is a species of beauty allows for the possibility of beauty that is not dependent on function and is predicable purely on the basis of perceptual or intelligible configurations.

function, and (ii) pleasing most competent judges of that kind of thing insofar as it is experienced (in perception or contemplation) as thus well formed, together suffice for something's being beautiful (Paris, 2020).

Notice that this account comprises two conditions, of which one is objective, namely that a functionally beautiful object should be well formed for its function. This is something that, in most cases, will depend on comparison with other things with a similar function and so judging it correctly will require a considerable measure of experience. Assuming adequate experience, however, wellformedness is fairly straightforward to judge, even if open to debate. The only thing to note about this condition is that being well formed is not a matter merely of appearing a certain way, but of having a structure or form – which may be perceptible or intelligible – that is conducive to realising whatever the object's function is. This feature, then, introduces a measure of objectivity, the possibility of innumerable kinds of beauty, given the breadth of wellformedness, and a way of coupling beauty to other values.

This last point is perhaps clearer if we look at the second condition, which is a little trickier, since it specifies a partly subjective requirement, namely that the object's wellformedness please most competent judges. This raises an important and difficult question, which I have not yet addressed in my published work, and that adequately treating would take me beyond the remit of this paper. The problem becomes clear when we notice that there are arguably certain things that do not please competent judges despite being well formed for their functions. Examples of such objects might be things like rubbish bins, condoms, plain metallic bookcases, and, perhaps most perspicuously, torture instruments. These range from, plausibly, leaving most of us indifferent, to displeasing us proportionately with their wellformedness. But, one might wonder, if functional beauty is ultimately a matter of wellformedness for function, why would this be?

There are two things to say by way of explaining why certain things plausibly won't please even competent judges. First, wellformedness is a matter of degree, so with greater expertise and experience the threshold for pleasure becomes harder to meet. But that cannot be the whole story, for some objects may be ingeniously formed for their function, but pleasing to contemplate they are not. The thumbscrew, for instance, is a very well-formed torture instrument, ergonomically designed to deliver maximal anguish with great economy of size and materials.[6] If so, then we might expect a competent judge to take pleasure in the thumbscrew and to find it beautiful after all. This depends on whom we take to be a competent judge. I take it that being a competent judge is largely a matter of possessing the sorts of qualities identified by Hume (1987, p. 150). These include possessing relevant knowledge to understand and being able to experience how the different components of an object contribute to its function(s); having an appropriate degree of experience of dealing with objects of this kind so as to be able to assess the degree of their wellformedness for function in general and in comparison to other objects with a similar function; and being unprejudiced. But, importantly, a competent judge of beauty, especially when it comes to the beauty of human artefacts and practices (perhaps unlike abstract objects like mathematical proofs) must, I think, also be cognitively and affectively normal, including having a sound moral outlook and possessing a considerable degree of moral and emotional sensitivity (ibid., pp. 152–153; cf. Paris, 2020, p. 521). This is because failure to possess such qualities is liable to lead to a misapprehension of certain objects and therefore also to a mistaken affective response to them. To wit, although the sadist may take great pleasure in the thumbscrew's design, this cannot be taken as criterial of the object's beauty since the sadist's judgement is marred by an abominable moral outlook.

Ultimately, then, the reason why certain well-formed objects might not please us, even if we can appreciate how well adapted their designs are to their ends, is that pleasure is contingent not only on wellformedness for function, but also on whether the functions of an object are themselves desirable. In Hume's words, when 'the end [is] totally indifferent to us, we ... feel the same indifference towards the means' (1975, p. 286; cf. Plato, 1983). And, in the case of torture instruments like thumbscrews, we may even be displeased since their function is inimical to our ends, viz., is undesirable. Under this construal, then, functional beauty is informed by certain norms and values from non-aesthetic domains, notably the moral realm. Thus, functional beauty is aligned with other values.

Note here that it is compatible with functional beauty that one may find a thumbscrew beautiful if one abstracts from its function and inspects it as a purely visual object. This is fine, provided that we note that the thumbscrew is not functionally beautiful and may even displease us when appreciated for what it truly is. This showcases another merit of appreciating functional beauty, which will become

---

[6] Thanks to Anneli Jefferson for the thumbscrew example.

relevant in subsequent sections, namely that a taste for functional beauty can serve to put into perspective other, less cognitively-laden species of beauty, and can dampen their effects.

Now that we have a better grasp of the concept of functional beauty, we can perhaps begin to see its plausibility. Although our commonplace conception of beauty may prevent us from identifying experiences of functional beauty as genuine cases of beauty, once our attention is drawn to functional beauty, many of us will recognise it in our everyday lives, and cherish its experience as most rewarding.[7] For instance, those who work in professions that they consider 'vocations', from professional sports and architecture, to computer science and politics, probably recognise functional beauty when they encounter well-formed solutions to important problems in their fields, or when confronted with excellent specimens of work that contribute to certain purposes or ends that they see as desirable in that field. Some may even explicitly use aesthetic language, on occasion, as in talk of a beautiful political gesture, move in chess, goal in football, proof in mathematics, or computer software. Others, however, may hardly register such beauty, partly because they lack the requisite conceptual resources, having instead interna-lised something like the current commonplace conception of beauty described earlier. Still, the notion of functional beauty allows us to capture all these ways of being beautiful and illuminates a realm of beauty hitherto obscured by our current collective taste.

Besides being reflected in ordinary experience, then, the notion of functional beauty elegantly accommodates, and draws our attention to, certain examples of beauty that the taste perpetuated by our highly visual culture makes us insensitive to, including beauty that does not depend on sensory perception. In doing so, the notion of functional beauty appears to satisfy both requirements of a valuable conception of beauty that our commonplace conception violates: it offers a measure of objectivity; aligns with other values, or at least provides us with a way of developing taste that does so align; and offers the possibility of discovering and appreciating beauty in virtually every domain of ordinary experience and through different modalities. Hence, a taste for functional beauty promises to help

---

[7]  Many might be reluctant to describe experiences of functional beauty as of beauty, or even as aesthetic. This is probably another case where our commonplace conception of beauty has influenced our language and con-ceptual categories. Still, insofar as we take pleasure in the wellformedness of things for their function, then we are, *ipso facto*, experiencing functional beauty.

redress some of the ills resulting from our current collective taste, which hypothesis I now turn to consider in relation to wellbeing, social justice, and the environment.

## 4. Taste, Functional Beauty, and Wellbeing

The thought that beauty is linked to wellbeing is ancient. Plato went so far as to maintain that 'in contemplating ... beauty, if anywhere, is human life worth living' (1903, translation mine). Research in positive psychology supports Plato's insight, with evidence suggesting that being appreciative of beauty can be an important contributor to wellbeing. It is difficult to believe that Plato and the positive psychologists are talking about the same beauty that is behind the current mental health crisis. As we saw earlier, however, whether beauty's influence is negative or positive depends on our taste. I suggested that developing a taste for functional beauty is a promising route towards countering the negative effects of current beauty standards. When it comes to enhancing wellbeing, I think that there are at least two ways in which functional beauty can help. First, a taste for functional beauty can help transform our conception of, and relationship to, human beauty itself. Second, it makes us sensitive to other forms of beauty that draw our attention away from narrow human beauty norms.

The first way in which a taste for functional beauty may contribute to wellbeing is by allowing us to appreciate human beauty differently in a number of ways, all of which transcend current norms of physical beauty such as thinness, firmness, smoothness and youth, for women, and muscularity, thinness, and the like, for men. Firstly, because of its focus on wellformedness for function, a taste for functional beauty does not rest content with the mere appearance of fitness, as exemplified by rock-hard abs or toned legs. Instead, its focus is both on appearance but also the underlying state of physical flourishing, aspects of which include health, vitality, etc. Because of this, such physical beauty is partly appreciable from the inside, in the mindful experience of a healthy, well-functioning body. And while it can also be appreciated from the outside, i.e., from a body's physical appearance, such appreciation is not a matter of unreflective perception, but of regular acquaintance with, and observation of the various activities, poses, and tropes of bodies experienced in ordinary life rather than pictures. Because of its link to genuinely desirable ends, appreciation of this kind of functional beauty is more likely to enhance wellbeing than our commonplace conception. Additionally, it may, in turn, lead one to become more suspicious of images of Instagram-type bodies, which, more often than not, are not only digitally manipulated but, when it comes to the bodies underneath the image, tend to be products of either unhealthy regimens or shortcuts to the appearance of fitness, including supplements and assorted potions, that may even compromise wellformedness.

This hypothesis receives some empirical support from a recent review of relevant literature by Alleva and Tylka, who conclude that 'body functionality [is] a valuable construct with respect to positive body image and well-being, particularly when individuals appreciate what their bodies can do and conceptualise their body functionality holistically' (2021, p. 149). The hypothesis also enjoys some indirect support from studies by social psychologist Viren Swami, which show that spending time in nature can be beneficial for mental health generally, but also specifically by improving negative body image. Part of the explanation Swami gives for this is that 'being in nature ... shifts attention away from what the body looks like to what the body can do' (2020, p. 5). In other words, as per our functional beauty hypothesis, essentially placing subjects in positions where the body's wellformedness for its function can be appreciated. Another explanation Swami offers also links to functional beauty. He says that exposure to nature may promote a feeling of connectedness to nature which may in turn help 'develop greater respect and appreciation for our bodies as part of a wider ecosystem requiring protection' (ibid., p. 6).

Secondly, functional beauty allows us to appreciate a kind of physical beauty that depends on the physical expression of a person's character or personality through their body. This is because the effective expression of such inner states draws our attention to something that human bodies are particularly well designed to do, namely embodying and communicating certain psychological states and traits. To the extent that these, in turn, are desirable (in which case they themselves can be beautiful, as we will see presently), this amounts to a pleasing wellformedness for function that goes beyond current beauty norms. This phenomenon partly explains why we love spending time with our friends, and why it is hard to find them ugly even if they would be classified as such by commonplace standards (Nehamas, 2007; Protasi, 2017).

Thirdly, a sensitivity to and taste for functional beauty opens us up to moral beauty and other forms of inner beauty. Moral beauty is a kind of beauty of character, specifically the beauty of character traits like honesty, fairness, and kindness, in short, the moral virtues (Gaut, 2007, pp. 114–132; Paris, 2017; 2018a; 2020; Doran 2021; 2022). To be morally beautiful is to have a good moral character and to have such character is to be beautiful in one way. Moral beauty is arguably a subset of functional beauty because virtues can be appreciated as well formed psychological – cognitive, affective, and behavioural – dispositions designed to realise certain functions or ends – namely, what we might call the humanly good, or human flourishing (Paris, 2020; cf. Paris, 2018a). Hence, a taste for functional beauty allows us to appreciate moral beauty. And while philosophers have been largely ignoring moral beauty, themselves prey to commonplace conceptions of beauty and taste, psychologists have argued, in line with my suggestions, that the appreciation of moral beauty leads to a 'decrease in anxiety and depression and improved interpersonal functioning' (Diessner 2019, p. 189; cf. Paris, 2021).

Jointly, the foregoing variants of functional beauty serve to complicate the picture of human beauty significantly, revealing further dimensions of both physical and non-physical beauty, based on the genuine possession and manifestation of desirable qualities and ends like health, vitality, etc.; a conception of physical beauty inflected by (knowledge and understanding of) an individual's inner traits; and a form of inner, intelligible beauty. Hence, a sensitivity to and taste for functional beauty opens one up to rich varieties of beauty, indicating that many more individuals should be appreciated, and appreciate themselves, for their beauty, and in many more ways. Crucially, the beauty it points to is both largely attainable, albeit to different degrees, and in line with efforts to better oneself in ways we should all think are important, and that we already know contribute to our wellbeing.

The second way in which a taste for functional beauty may enhance wellbeing, is by opening us up to a range of beauties that we can appreciate and that may be hard to notice under the current, commonplace conception of beauty. This is because functional beauty can be found in virtually anything that can be said to have a function, or be the product of design. So everyone, regardless of whether their interests are in the arts, running, playing video games, just hanging out, or other purposeful objects or activities, will find something to appreciate for its functional beauty, provided they are also adequately sensitive to values. This will result in a decreased focus on our own bodies and those of others, and a greater focus on other aspects of our surroundings.

Moreover, since functional beauty is not strictly visual, its appreciation will, in turn, attune us to engaging with more cognitively-laden forms of beauty across many domains. From works of art, architecture, and nature, to sports moves, works of design, and thoughts and ideas, a taste for functional beauty opens up multiple levels of appreciation, whilst being guided by objective qualities and genuine values. This, in turn, can make our appreciation of beauty at once more meaningful and more valuable, again, promising enhanced wellbeing.

Still, one might worry that the kinds of functional beauty discussed above are not beauties that we can appreciate in just anyone or anything and certainly not beauties that are appreciable purely in virtue of looking at photographs of people. However, as also indicated above, one potential consequence of appreciating functional beauty is increased suspicion of merely visual forms of physical beauty. Relatedly, a taste for functional beauty and the various ways in which it can manifest itself may complement, and thereby plausibly result in decreased appreciation of, forms of beauty that are dependent on current beauty norms, or even purely perceptual beauty in general. This is something that should be familiar to many of us from artistic appreciation. Although we always retain a visual interest in the beauty of art, suitably educated and experienced appreciators of visual art will find most beautiful art which is not just visually pleasing, or indeed that may not be visually pleasing at all on the surface, but which possesses beauty in virtue of its subject matter, the skill and sensitivities of the artist that are expressed in the handling of it, and so on (cf. Nehamas, 2007; Paris, 2019). This is why it is plausible to claim that Rembrandt's late self-portraits – which tend to be visually rough but whose every brushstroke is permeated by a profound self-understanding hewn out of a hard-won humility – are more beautiful than portraits by Ingres or Bougeureau, whose attractions are mainly visual.[8]

Once again, available evidence points to interactions between the effects of appreciating beauty in multiple domains and an increase in wellbeing (Martínzez-Martí et al., 2016). Evidence supports this at least with respect to appreciating natural beauty, but there is also some evidence that supports that the trait of appreciating beauty more generally, including physical beauty (though presumably not physical human beauty construed under current norms), moral beauty, as well as other forms of inner beauty is associated with greater wellbeing. For instance, a recent set of studies found that simple interventions designed to draw the attention of subjects – by asking them to think of beautiful things and consider why they

[8] Actually, Bougeureau's are more readily described as kitsch, but one may still recognise a visual seductiveness, or at least an attempt at such, which would also explain his contemporary popularity.

find them beautiful – to non-superficially beautiful things, like morally good behaviour or nature and the environment, have positive effects on wellbeing, by producing an increase in happiness and a decrease in depressive symptoms at least one month after the intervention (Proyer et al., 2016).[9]

## 5. Taste, Functional Beauty, and Social Justice

Although arguably beauty has always been a source of discrimination, current beauty norms, partly because of their narrow focus on physical appearance, and their even narrower focus on specific physical qualities, are a source of social injustice, making such discrimination more prevalent, whilst weighing disproportionately on those who are already oppressed, such as women (Widdows, 2018), people of colour (Taylor, 2016), or differently-abled individuals (Irvin, 2017).

At first glance it may be difficult to see how developing a taste for functional beauty could contribute to social justice. One might even worry that functional beauty risks promoting ableism. But this would be too quick. It is generally plausible that beauty, health, and physical excellence are linked and that this link has been forged deep within our evolutionary history, thus having a powerful hold over us. Functional beauty simply develops this aspect of our taste in line with genuine health and physical fitness, rather than its mere appearance. But it does not mean that ableism follows from this picture. There are two reasons for this. First, functional beauty allows us to appreciate disabled bodies too, and does so more than current beauty norms which are based on a specific blueprint. This is because most disabled bodies are able to function and are wonderfully adaptive to the challenges posed or options afforded by their particular disability (cf. Alleva & Tylka, 2021, p. 150). Importantly, they are often able to express their possessor's personality and to be used for communicative purposes. All of these are appreciable through a taste for functional beauty. Second, as mentioned in the previous section, functional beauty opens up a range of ways of being humanly beautiful that go beyond possessing health and being physically fit. It thus offers a much more comprehensive conception of

---

[9]    While such studies do not mention functional beauty, they couch their questionnaires and discussions in explicitly aesthetic terms, while talk of appreciating, for instance, 'non-moral excellence', strongly point to features inherent and experiences grounded in the appreciation of functional beauty.

human beauty that depends on one's full humanity rather than one's mere body.

This last remark points to a form of beauty that can plausibly be appreciated through the lens of functional beauty but that is often missed. This is the possibility of beauty in humanity itself, as it is expressed and can be appreciated in virtually every human being who is not a moral monster. Humanity is not a particular trait or excellence, but is, essentially, a fact about every one of us that comprises a physiology and psychology that hold a potentiality for good (though also for evil) and that we can recognise and appreciate in most of those around us. This is important to bear in mind because it can, to some extent, be recalled when meeting strangers, and dampen biases that someone falling short of other, particularly current commonplace physical beauty standards, may trigger. It is also important because it is one respect in which we are all beautiful in much the same way (cf. Protasi, 2017; Wolf, 1990). And it is this, I think, that lies behind calls by social justice groups to recognise various kinds of beauty, including most recently – in the context of the *Black Lives Matter* movement – black beauty, because to recognise the full humanity in someone is, if I'm right, to recognise a kind of beauty (cf. Okoro, 2019).

Besides the foregoing, I think that the elements of functional beauty making it conducive to wellbeing can also, *mutatis mutandis*, contribute to combatting social injustices perpetuated by current beauty norms and taste. Recognition of various forms of human beauty, including inner beauty, which depends on ends like the humanly good, partly consisting, as it does, in different individuals' wellformedness to realise such ends, brings beauty in line with other values and places all human beings on an equal, or at least unbiased, footing.

Here too, the evidence concurs, pointing to correlations between generally appreciating beauty and scoring more highly on morally relevant personality measures, like pro-sociality, agreeableness, and reduced neuroticism (Martínez-Martí et al., 2016). Moreover, albeit limited, relevant evidence suggests that a sensitivity to moral beauty in particular is linked to a number of morally desirable behaviours and attitudes, which, include 'increased cooperative behavior', 'reduction in prejudice against race or sexual orientation', 'increased belief in life as meaningful and in the benevolence of others', 'increase [in] positive affect and prosociality (affiliation and compassionate goals) and decrease [in] self-image goals' (Diessner, 2019, p. 189).

## 6. Taste, Functional Beauty, and the Environment

Finally, we turn to functional beauty's enhancement of our relationship to the natural world. What applies to human beauty will, to some extent, also apply to the beauty of the natural world. Being able to see more kinds of beauty and beauty in more kinds of natural objects will, presumably, reduce our tendencies to favour certain species or habitats over others irrespective of their ecological value, whilst putting a brake on the dominance and pervasiveness of a single dominant standard (or set thereof) (cf. Saito, 2007, pp. 69–96).

But arguably a taste for functional beauty in nature can also spur an ecological agenda. Consider some of the issues mentioned earlier. We have seen that beauty can be a powerful motivator due to its emotional hold over us, so that it leads to certain undesirable results, for instance, calls for the preservation and protection of certain species to the detriment of others, but also to decisions to do or not to do certain things, such as not going ahead with a windfarm because it is thought that it would ruin the landscape and constitute an 'eyesore' (Guardian, 2022).[10]

A recognition and appreciation of functional beauty could help alleviate some of these undesirable effects of beauty judgements based on narrow, visual norms.[11] Consider an example mentioned earlier, that of the earthworm. A slimy, wriggly, brown-red tubelike animal, it seems like a textbook argument for the existence of ugly nature. And yet, once we consider how well designed it is for its function, and how important its function is for a healthy natural world, then we might just begin to see it differently. All of its features that seem to make it visually ugly are evidence of how effectively this creature can discharge its functions, which in turn contribute to good soil structure and fertility, important for the life and health of a great variety of other plants and animals. Seeing it thus, one's experience may undergo a radical transformation, allowing them to appreciate a kind of beauty, previously unavailable to them.

[10] Debates over the aesthetics of wind farms and wind turbines have been going on for over a decade now (e.g., Guardian, 2012).

[11] I don't in fact think that all of our current aesthetic norms concerning the beauty of nature are narrowly visual. However, many are and these are unhelpfully placed at centre stage by our culture, with its general visual focus, which tends to single out striking animals or landscapes, rather than more subtly beautiful ones.

It is not a coincidence that functional beauty (and ugliness) are commonly appreciated by naturalists. David Attenborough, for instance, in the television programme *A Life on Our Planet* (2020), contrasts the seeming visual beauty of a bleached coral reef resulting from global warming, with its ugly reality, when he notes that the 'when you first see it you think that perhaps it is beautiful, and suddenly you realise it's tragic, because what you're looking at is skeletons, skeletons of dead creatures. ... the reef turns from wonderland to wasteland'. By contrast, as in the earthworm example given above, seemingly visually ugly creatures can be aesthetically appreciated once we understand how they are designed to discharge their function. Richard Dawkins concurs, remarking of bats that '[t]heir faces are often distorted into gargoyle shapes that appear hideous to us until we see them for what they are, exquisitely fashioned instruments for beaming ultrasound in desired directions' (2006, p. 24; Parsons & Carlson, 2008, pp. 123–124). Appreciating the functional beauty of seemingly ugly creatures, then, may counteract the preference for the cute and cuddly in efforts for preservation and protection, while greater sensitivity to the functional ugliness of nature's suffering through global warming may motivate greater concern and spur more to action.

As for the wind turbines and farms, similar considerations apply. Assuming that they are one of, if not our best bets for clean energy and for protecting the natural world,[12] we may begin to see them as well formed artefacts that do not mar the landscape but are welcomed by it, insofar as their function is, ultimately, the protection of natural landscapes, ecosystems, and the environment more generally, through countering our reliance on non-renewable energy and fossil fuels. Seen thus, they are efficient and intelligent designs for producing clean energy and ultimately – though no longer seen in terms of functional beauty – a symbol of a commitment and effort to prevent environmental disasters.

---

[12] This assumption is important. If it's mistaken, then perhaps these structures are eyesores, after all (cf. Paris, 2018b). But it's important to be clear about the level at which we disagree. If participants in relevant debates who think that wind turbines are eyesores agree that they are well formed for generating clean energy and prolonging the life of the planet, then they fail to appreciate their functional beauty. This can be either because they fail to appreciate their wellformedness, or because they do not genuinely take ecological interests to heart.

## 7. Concluding Thoughts: Taking Beauty and Taste Seriously

I have been arguing that while our current taste in, and conception of beauty leads to certain undesirable consequences, due to its narrowness, shallowness, and its being decoupled from other values, a taste for functional beauty may help alleviate some of the harms arising from our current taste in beauty, contributing to enhanced wellbeing, social justice, and a better relationship to the natural world. This is because it encourages the appreciation of beauty on multiple levels and across sensory modalities, whilst aligning it with other values.

Given that this article has advanced a hypothesis, informed by available evidence, but largely theoretical, it is essential that more research looks into the relationship between taste in beauty and our attitudes and behaviours in other domains. More specifically, we need more research on the relationship between appreciating functional beauty and its various subspecies, including moral beauty, environmental beauty, etc., and attitudes, behaviours, and decisions in domains like those discussed here, where we currently face challenges.

Now, suppose that my hypothesis does hold up to further scrutiny. What can we do to ensure that we live in a society with a healthy, positive outlook on beauty? First of all, we should acknowledge the existence of functional beauty, and of the possibility of distinctions in the quality of different tastes and conceptions of beauty. Second, we should encourage the development of a taste for functional beauty. To achieve anything like a widespread appreciation of functional beauty, we need to develop a social and cultural environment that encourages and supports the development of a taste in such beauty, partly by embodying it. This minimally requires that the notions of beauty and taste inform public policy, legislation, and education.

Relevant public policy that acknowledges the importance of functional beauty may include planning permission requirements for buildings, which specify that they need to be designed with a view to genuinely embodying respect for the environment, the inhabitants of the relevant spaces, and the communities affected.

Relevant legislation can continue to aim to minimise the influence of social media and the use of manipulated photos across media, which shape the taste of both children and adults, and it can place greater restrictions on the so-called beauty industry, which, in many ways, acts to legitimise and propagate our current taste in beauty, while, as technology advances, making it increasingly inhuman and inaccessible.

Finally, when it comes to education, greater attention should be paid to beauty, and relevant principles instilled, through frank discussions of beauty in arts and humanities subjects like literature and art as well as sex education and other relevant subjects. These should aim to introduce students to the varieties of beauty in art and human beings, from moral beauty, to the beauty of language, personality-inflected faces and bodies, and so on. But also through incorporating aesthetic terminology and ideas in subjects that superficially seem non-aesthetic, like mathematics, science, or even PE, thereby introducing students to ideas like mathematical beauty, or the beauty of bodily functionality.

Whatever the precise programme for developing a collective taste for functional beauty and its subspecies, it is of the essence that beauty and taste feature regularly and explicitly in our thinking in the areas of wellbeing, social justice, and the environment, as well as other domains, and that their nature and role is further explored, debated and elaborated.[13] This will only happen once we acknowledge the power and importance of beauty and taste and begin taking them seriously.

*Cardiff University*
*parisp@cardiff.ac.uk*

## References

G. R. Adams and A. S. Cohen, 'Children's Physical and Interpersonal Characteristics that Affect Student-Teacher Interaction', *Journal of* Experimental Education 43 (1974), 1–5.

Jessica M. Alleva and Tracy L. Tylka, 'Body Functionality: A Review of the Literature', *Body Image* 36 (2021), 149–171.

Robert Athanasiou and Paul Greene, 'Physical Attractiveness and Helping Behavior', *Proceedings of the 81st Annual Convention of the American Psychological Association* 8 (1973), 289–90.

Bruce W. Darby and Devon Jeffers, 'The Effects of Defendant and Juror Attractiveness on Simulated Courtroom Trial Decisions', *Social Behavior and Personality* 16 (1988), 39–50.

Richard Dawkins, *The Blind Watchmaker* (London: Penguin, 2006).

---

[13] I'm grateful to my coeditors, Anneli Jefferson, Orestis Palermos, and Jon Webber, who encouraged me to write this paper and provided invaluable feedback every step of the way.

Rhett Diessner, *Understanding the Beauty Appreciation Trait* (New York: Palgrave MacMillan, 2019).

Ryan P. Doran, 'Moral Beauty, Inside and Out', *Australasian Journal of Philosophy* 99 (2021), 396–414.

Ryan P. Doran, 'Thick and Perceptual Moral Beauty', *Australasian Journal of Philosophy* issue/number [online preprint] (2022), 1–18.

A.W. Eaton, 'Taste in Bodies and Fat Oppression', in Sherri Irvin (ed.), *Body Aesthetics* (New York: Oxford University Press, 2016), 37–59.

Marcia Muelder Eaton, *Merit: Aesthetic and Ethical* (New York: Oxford University Press, 2001).

Jasmine Fardouly, Phillippa C. Diedrichs, Lenny R. Vartanian, and Emma Halliwell, 'Social Comparisons on Social Media: The Impact of Facebook on Young Women's Body Image Concerns and Mood', *Body Image* 13 (2015), 38–45

Kevin R. Fontaine, Myles S. Faith, David B. Allison, and Lawrence J. Cheskin, 'Body Weight and Health Care Among Women in the General Population' *Archives of Family Medicine* 7 (1998), 381–4.

Berys Gaut, *Art, Emotion and Ethics* (Oxford: Oxford University Press, 2007).

Stephen J. Gould, 'The Golden Rule – A Proper Scale for Our Environmental Crisis', in *Environmental Ethics: Divergence and Convergence*, eds. Susan J. Armstrong and Richard G. Botzler (New York: McGraw Hill, 1993), 310–315.

Sarah Grogan, *Body Image* (London: Routledge, 2021).

The Guardian, 'Turbines an Eyesore? Sounds Like a Wind-Up' (2022), URL = <https://www.theguardian.com/environment/2022/apr/05/turbines-are-an-eyesore-sounds-like-a-wind-up>.

The Guardian, 'Wind Turbines: Are They An Eyesore? An Open Thread' (2012), URL = <https://www.theguardian.com/commentisfree/2012/mar/15/wind-turbines-lyveden-new-bield>.

Daniel S. Hamermesh, *Beauty Pays: Why Attractive People Are More Successful* (Princeton, NJ: Princeton University Press, 2003).

G.H. Hardy, *A Mathematicians Apology* (Cambridge: Cambridge University Press, 2004).

Kathleen Higgins, 'Beauty and Its Kitsch Competitors', in Peg Z. Brand (ed.), *Beauty Matters* (Bloomington and Indianapolis, IN: Indiana University Press, 2000), pp. 87–111.

Megumi Hosoda, Eugene F. Stone-Romero, and Gwen Coats, 'The Effects of Physical Attractiveness on Job-Related Outcomes: A Meta-Analysis of Experimental Studies', *Personnel Psychology* 56 (2003), 431–462.

David Hume, *Enquiries Concerning Human Understanding and Concerning the Principles of Morals* (Oxford: Oxford University Press, 1975).

David Hume, 'Of the Standard of Taste', in his *Essays Moral, Political, Literary* (Indianapolis, IN: Liberty Fund, 1987).

Sherri Irvin, 'Resisting Body Oppression: An Aesthetic Approach' *Feminist Philosophy Quarterly* 3 (2017), 1–26.

Judith H. Langlois, Jean M. Ritter, Rita J. Casey, and Douglas B. Sawin, 'Infant Attractiveness Predicts Maternal Behaviors and Attitudes' *Developmental Psychology* 31 (1995), 464–472.

Sheila Lintott and Sherri Irvin, 'Sex Objects and Sexy Subjects: A Feminist Reclamation of Sexiness', in Sherri Irvin (ed.), *Body Aesthetics* (New York: Oxford University Press, 2016), pp. 299–317.

Fiona MacCallum and Heather Widdows, 'Altered Images: Understanding the Effects of Unrealistic Images and Beauty Aspirations' *Health Care Analysis* 26 (2018), 235–245.

María Luisa Martínzez-Martí, María José Hernández-Lloreda, and María Dolores Avia, 'Appreciation of Beauty and Excellence: Relationship with Personality, Prosociality and Well-Being', *Journal of Happiness Studies* 17 (2016), 2613–2634.

Stuart J. McKelvie and James Coley, 'Effects of Crime Seriousness and Offender Facial Attractiveness on Recommended Treatment', *Social Behavior and Personality* 21 (1993), 265–77.

Francesca Minerva, 'The Invisible Discrimination Before Our Eyes: A Bioethical Analysis', *Bioethics* 31 (2017), 181–189.

Alexander Nehamas, *Only a Promise of Happiness: The Place of Beauty in a World of Art* (Princeton: Princeton University Press, 2007).

Richard Nisbett and Timothy D. Wilson, 'The Halo Effect: Evidence for Unconscious Alterations of Judgments', *Journal of Personality and Social Psychology* 35 1977: 250–6.

Enuma Okoro, 'Blackness and Beauty', *Aeon* (2019), URL = <https://aeon.co/essays/how-we-think-about-beauty-and-blackness-can-save-lives>.

Panos Paris, 'On Form, and the Possibility of Moral Beauty', *Metaphilosophy* 49 (2017), 711–729.

Panos Paris, 'The Empirical Case for Moral Beauty', *Australasian Journal of Philosophy* 96 (2018a), 642–656.

Panos Paris, 'The Deformity-Related Conception of Ugliness', *British Journal of Aesthetics* 57 (2018b), 139–160.

Panos Paris, 'Moral Beauty and Education', *Journal of Moral Education* 48 (2019), 395–411.

251

Panos Paris, 'Functional Beauty, Pleasure, and Experience', *Australasian Journal of Philosophy* 98 (2020), 516–530.

Panos Paris, 'Exemplarism, Beauty, and the Psychology of Morality', *The Journal of Value Inquiry* (pre-print) (2021), 1–25.

Glenn Parsons and Allen Carlson, *Functional Beauty* (Oxford: Oxford University Press, 2008).

Plato, *Two Comic Dialogues: Ion and Hippias Major*, trans. Paul Woodruff (Indianapolis, IN: Hackett, 1983).

Plato, *Symposium*, in John Burnet (ed.), *Platonis Opera*, (Oxford: Oxford University Press, 1903).

Sara Protasi, 'The Perfect Bikini Body: Can We All Really Have It? Loving Gaze as an Anti-Oppressive Beauty Ideal' *Thought* 6 (2017), 93–101.

Rene T. Proyer, Fabian Gander, Sara Wellenzohn, and Willibald Ruch, 'Nine Beautiful Things: A Self-Administered Online Positive Psychology Intervention on the Beauty in Nature, Arts, and Behaviors Increases Happiness and Ameliorates Depressive Symptoms', *Personality and Individual Differences* 94 (2016), 189–193.

Matteo Ravasio,'Engineering Human Beauty', *Australasian Journal of Philosophy* (pre-print) (2022), 1–15.

Eveleen Richards, *Darwin and the Making of Sexual Selection.* (Chicago, IL: Chicago University Press, 2017).

Yuriko Saito, *Everyday Aesthetics* (Oxford: Oxford University Press, 2007).

Cookie White Stephan and Judith H. Langlois, 'Baby Beautiful: Adult Attributions of Infant Competence as a Function of Infant Attractiveness' *Child Development* 55 (1984), 576–585.

Viren Swami, 'How Being in Nature Can Promote Healthier Body Image', *Relate Insights* (Technical Report) (2020), 1–10.

Paul C. Taylor, *Black is Beautiful: A Philosophy of Black Aesthetics* (New York: Wiley Blackwell, 2016).

Heather Widdows, *Perfect Me: Beauty as an Ethical Ideal* (Princeton, NJ: Princeton University Press, 2018).

Frank Wilczek, *A Beautiful Question: Finding Nature's Deep Design* (London: AllenLane, 2016)

Naomi Wolf, *The Beauty Myth* (London: Vintage, 1990).

Nick Zangwill, *The Metaphysics of Beauty* (Ithaca, NY: Cornell University Press, 2001).

# Relativism, Fallibilism, and the Need for Interpretive Charity

NADINE ELZEIN

**Abstract**

'Relativists' and 'absolutists' about truth often see their own camp as promoting virtues, such as open-mindedness and intellectual humility, and see the opposing camp as fostering vices, like closed-mindedness and arrogance. Relativism is accused of fostering these vices because it entails that each person's beliefs are automatically right for the person who holds them. How can we be humble or open-minded if we cannot concede that we might be wrong? Absolutism is accused of fostering these vices because the view is seen as entailing certainty. This also seems to preclude us from conceding that we could be wrong. However, no relativist defends the Protagorean version of relativism that entails infallibilism. And no absolutist posits infallible certainty. Fallibilism really is a precondition of various virtues, but both camps take themselves to be defending fallibilist positions against opponents who they take to be committed to infallibilism. Philosophers may inadvertently end up promoting precisely the sort of infallibilism they oppose by creating a false dichotomy and caricaturing the opposing camp. This underscores the importance of interpretive charity in both academic and public debate.

It is hard to avoid getting a depressing sense that standards of argument are declining in the present age. While the internet has brought with it the possibility of getting vast amounts of information with ease, it also seems to have ushered in an age of 'post-truth' politics, misinformation, 'alternative facts', and intense intractable social and political polarisation.

Among academics, debates about bad reasoning and the erosion of the concern for truth and accuracy sometimes focus on worries about whether people are increasingly viewing truth in relativistic terms. This is reflected in our experiences in the philosophy classroom.

I often teach introductory philosophy classes, both to undergraduates and to members of the public, many of whom are new to philosophy. I usually begin by covering Plato's *Theaetetus*. Among other things, in this text, Socrates tackles the doctrine associated with Protagoras, that 'man is the measure of all things: of those that are, that they are; of the things that are not, that they are not' (*Theaetetus*, 152a; trans. Waterfield, 1987, p. 30).

doi:10.1017/S1358246122000169

# Nadine Elzein

Plato understands the Protagorean doctrine to entail that each individual's opinion is necessarily and infallibly true *for that individual*, and that there can be no absolute truth, outside of what it true relative to each individual's perspective.

This is a simple form of relativism about truth (or 'alethic relativism'). Roughly, it is characterised by the following claims: that there is no objective fact of the matter about what is true; that what each individual believes to be true really is true for that individual, and that where individuals have conflicting opinions, each of those conflicting opinions is true for the individual who holds it. In present-day broadly analytic philosophy, these commitments are typically understood as capturing the central tenets of relativism about truth.

Plato raises some serious puzzles for the Protagorean view (*Theaetetus*, 160e2–187b1; trans. Waterfield, 1887, pp. 47–91). Is the Protagorean relativist thesis itself supposed to hold true absolutely, or merely for those who hold it? It seems it cannot be absolutely true on pain of contradiction. But if it is false for the rest of us, why should we be troubled by it? And since the view is false for those of us who think it is, isn't it also true for us that the view is mistaken even for its *own* proponents? Can those proponents concede this point? The view also struggles to make sense of cases in which we change our minds, or in which our future experiences do not bear out our earlier predictions, and it eliminates expertise in any field.

Many philosophers see this sort of relativist position as lazy and incoherent. It is accused of eroding our sense of truth and falsity and committing to a sort of irrationalism that precludes clear and careful thought. If each person's beliefs are automatically right for that person, how could we ever be motivated to subject our own opinions to critical scrutiny or to try to improve our perspectives in any way? Sometimes, philosophers worry that this relativistic view is rife among certain areas of academia and is bleeding into popular culture, having a damaging influence on public thought. But this story seems dubious in many ways.

It is unclear whether even Protagoras himself ever quite held the view that Plato attributed to him (Maguire, 1973). As someone who received most of my training within the analytic tradition of philosophy, I have often heard this position attributed to various philosophers working broadly outside of it, especially Friedrich Nietzsche, Michel Foucault, Jacques Derrida, and Richard Rorty.

Even a cursory reading of Nietzsche and Foucault renders this interpretation doubtful. Both of those theorists seek to examine a wide variety of historical perspectives precisely in order to create some critical distance with which to examine our own practices. This strategy seems to aim precisely at freeing us from our culturally ingrained biases so that we can assess our practices with a greater degree of objectivity.[1] And Rorty and Derrida both explicitly deny embracing Protagorean relativism, and express sympathy for Plato's critique of it.[2]

William Knorpp (1998) notes that many theorists who label themselves relativists actually seem to be defending distinct positions, such as pluralism, scepticism, fallibilism, or even merely an attitude of tolerance towards those with conflicting viewpoints. Perhaps Protagorean relativists are mythical creatures. But if this is so, it becomes difficult to account for one puzzling fact. Whenever I teach the Protagorean argument, many *students* proclaim to accept it, despite Plato's critique. Even if no professional philosopher subscribes to the view, many other people do, even in its simple 'Protagorean' form.

Upon questioning students as to why they are swayed by Protagorean relativism, I tend to find that their motives are largely practical and social. They tend to suppose that relativism fosters open-mindedness, tolerance, and intellectual humility, whereas objectivism fosters closed-mindedness, tyranny, and intellectual arrogance. They are more concerned with the consequences of relativism than with its coherence.

This supports Maria Baghramian's conjecture (2019, pp. 250-57) that relativism ought to be understood as a 'stance' rather than a

---

[1]   Nietzsche's critique of the 'will to truth' in the *Genealogy* (Part III, especially sections 24-6, trans. Clarke & Swensen, 1998, pp. 108–15) is sometimes read as supporting a sort of alethic relativism, but his attack is plainly on the idea of *valuing* truth as a moralised ideal, divorced from any concrete interests. The question of whether we should disinterestedly value the pursuit of truth is unrelated to the question of whether truth is relative. Perhaps Foucault's critique of the sharp distinctions between 'reason' and 'sanity' in *Madness & Civilization* (1967) is thought to entail relativism, though the relativistic reading seems similarly dubious here.

[2]   Rorty defines relativism as 'the view that every belief on a certain topic, or perhaps about any topic, is as good as every other' and denies that anyone holds this position (Rorty, 1982, p. 166). Similarly, Derrida claims that relativism is the doctrine that 'there are only points of view with no absolute necessity, or no references to absolutes.' He goes on to claim: 'That is the opposite to what I have to say. Relativism is, in classical philosophy, a way of referring to the absolute and denying it; it states that there are only cultures and that there is no pure science of truth. I have never said such a thing. Neither have I ever used the word relativism' Derrida (1999, p. 78).

# Nadine Elzein

'thesis'. The distinction comes from Bas van Fraassen (2002, p. 47), who notes that a stance is more like an attitude than a collection of beliefs. Stances tend to be embraced precisely for their results rather than for their plausibility as doctrines. Proponents of relativism embrace it not because there are strong reasons to think it's right, but because they suppose that it will foster various virtues and prevent various vices.

I will follow Baghramian (2019) in arguing that that there is something seriously mistaken in the idea that Protagorean relativism will help to foster the virtues allegedly associated with it. However, it seems that the Protagorean doctrine is rarely, if ever, defended by professional academics. Insofar as theorists are willing to label themselves 'relativists' it is typically because they take it to be *opposed* to another doctrine. Typically, the doctrine that they are opposed to is labelled 'objectivism' or 'absolutism'.

While plenty of philosophers embrace these labels in describing their own views, their positions seem to have little connection to those that self-styled relativists oppose; they do not usually oppose the idea that there exist facts independent of anyone's perspective, but the idea that anyone can claim to have absolutely certain and infallible *access* to these facts, and this is a doctrine that also seems to have few, if any, proponents.

I will argue that there is a position here which is distinct from relativism and absolutism and which we really *ought* to see as a precondition of various epistemic and social virtues. That position is *fallibilism*. It is the simple point that our own opinions are capable of *falsity*: the view that we could always be wrong.[3]

An agent who cannot acknowledge her own fallibility is certainly an agent who must lack intellectual humility, open-mindedness, and flexibility. The problem is that it turns out that both those who call themselves 'relativists' and those who call themselves 'objectivists' generally take themselves to be supporting a fallibilist position against opposing views that commit us to *infallibilism*. Hence both sides take themselves to be sole protectors and promoters of various epistemic and social virtues.

---

[3]    The position known as *epistemic fallibilism* holds that the fallibility of our beliefs is consistent with our having knowledge, whereas epistemic infallibilism holds that our actual fallibility rules out any claim to knowledge. That distinction can be put aside for the present discussion. We are not concerned with epistemic fallibilism and infallibilism. We are only concerned with the fact that our opinions could be false. We may think of this as a sort of *descriptive* fallibilism.

256

I will suggest that a failure of theorists on both sides to interpret opponents charitably is at the root of the problem, and that this helps to perpetuate a false dichotomy which, paradoxically, may end up inadvertently promoting precisely the sort of infallibilism that both sides seek to oppose.

We see a parallel pattern emerge with respect to many debates involving highly polarised discourse. Consider the controversies surrounding vaccines. In the UK, vaccines have generally been encouraged for voluntary take-up, and there has been no suggestion that the Covid-19 vaccine would be made mandatory (although it has been made a precondition for being permitted to engage in other activities). Nonetheless, prior to the vaccine rollout, social media sites were flooded with comments from people vehemently opposing the policy of *forcing* everyone to get vaccinated. This immediately produces doubt regarding what the differing sides of the debate are actually arguing about and can open up a gulf between the commitments people actually hold and the commitments that their opponents take them to hold. Are apparent opponents to the vaccine rollout trying to stop vaccines from being made available, or merely trying to stop people from being forced to take them? And do proponents endorse coercively forcing people to take vaccines, or do they merely wish to encourage voluntary uptake? Given a little ambiguity about whether it is availability or coercion that is at issue, we may see polarisation even among those whose perspectives do not actually significantly differ, at least to begin with.

The debate about relativism exhibits a parallel pattern of polarisation. But it is also, surprisingly, often invoked within these very social and political controversies themselves, with accusations of relativistic or absolutist thinking often being thrown in conflicting directions. Allan Bloom (1987) influentially argued that the views of liberals in the US, which he opposed, were driven by a commitment to relativism about moral truths. But it's just as common in more recent discourse for liberals to be accused of 'absolutism' about morality, especially when connected to 'cancel culture' or controversies about free speech.[4] And while the American right are often accused of 'absolutism' in their moral perspectives,[5] Kellyanne Conway's infamous comments about 'alternative facts' have also given rise to

---

[4] For example, a recent *Observer* headline runs: 'Cancelled culture is moral absolutism, and it's unsustainable' (Zhu, 2020). See also: Costello, *et al.* (2021) who associate left-wing authoritarian traits with a tendency towards moral absolutism, along with various other qualities.

[5] E.g., Marietta, *et al.* (2017).

# Nadine Elzein

accusations that the right are engaged in relativistic thinking (which is often put forward as a potential explanation for Trump's apparent lack of regard for truth-telling).[6]

While the dispute about relativism is primarily an academic endeavour, it is often reflected in social and political controversies outside of philosophy classrooms too. And examining this dispute may help us to appreciate the mechanics of polarisation more broadly. My claim will be that we need to exercise a greater degree of charity in interpreting views that diverge from our own, because a lack of interpretive charity tends to lie at the heart of most cycles of increasing polarisation. This is certainly evident in the case of relativism about truth.

## 1. Relativism and Intellectual Humility

A number of philosophers who take themselves to be defenders of 'relativism' have argued that their position is associated with epistemic or social virtues, such as humility, open-mindedness, and tolerance.

Lorraine Code, for example, sees relativism as a defence against a conception of knowledge that presupposes a restrictive sort of homogeneity, one that involves the 'often coercive view that we all see everything in the same way' (1995, p. 201). Code associates relativism with various emancipatory social and epistemic values.

David Bloor (2011) similarly argues that relativism entails the rejection of absolutism, and that this encourages curiosity and discourages dogmatism. Paul Feyerabend (1975) associates relativism with opposition to uniformity, and argues that the proliferation of theories is good for science, since uniformity endangers the free development of the individual.

The basic idea is that any form of 'objectivism' or 'absolutism' will foster intolerance, dogmatism, closed-mindedness and intellectual arrogance. In contrast, 'relativism' is thought to promote tolerance, flexibility, open-mindedness, and intellectual humility.

Baghramian (2019) puzzles over why we should suppose that relativism promotes these virtues or that absolutism promotes opposing vices. While relativism is epistemically egalitarian, it does not promote open-mindedness since it undermines our ability to transcend our own standpoint and to consider the merits of alternative ones. The relativist insists on the accuracy of her own point of view

---

[6] E.g., Kakutani (2018).

258

for herself, and on the points of views of others for them (2019, p. 264). If anything, this leaves us trapped within our own narrow perspectives, and undermines the possibility of communication across different standpoints.

Similarly, intellectual humility requires not only that we concede that other viewpoints might be right for other people. It also involves being able to concede that our own opinions might be wrong. But Protagorean relativism entails infallibilism: If each individual's opinion is right for *that individual*, then it is impossible for anyone, from their own perspective, to have a belief that is false. Far from fostering humility and curiosity then, it seems to undermine all possibility of expanding or improving upon our own opinions.[7]

And even the idea of promoting tolerance make very little sense if an individual with intolerant opinions is held to be automatically and infallibly *right* in those opinions, at least from their own perspective. At best, intolerant opinions will be wrong for those who don't hold them, but right for those who do.

It is also hard to see how we might reach any agreement on controversial issues if each person is right from their own perspective. This becomes especially problematic for policies that require us to arrive at a shared understanding. On the Protagorean view, those who believe that we need to take effective action to stop climate change, for instance, will be right, but only from their own perspectives. Similarly, those who believe that we can continue to pollute the environment with no repercussions at all will be right, but also only from their own restricted perspective. This leaves us with a serious practical difficulty. Whether it's climate change, covid restrictions, or effective procedures for counting votes, it is essential that we have some motivation to reach a shared understanding and to determine the truth in a way that enables us to transcend our own prior beliefs and get beyond our own individual perspectives.

The problem is that on the Protagorean view, since whatever one believes is automatically thereby true, we can never concede that we ourselves might be wrong about anything. This infallibilism essentially undermines many of the epistemic goals that relativists aim to promote, and hence the relativist stance appears to be completely misguided, even when it comes to promoting the virtues that relativists themselves proclaim to value.

---

[7]  See Lani Watson (2022) for a discussion of some of the real-world complexities surrounding curiosity as a virtue.

Nadine Elzein

## 2. Who Defends Relativism?

Why, then, do these theorists imagine that relativism might be important to promoting virtues like open-mindedness and intellectual humility, when these virtues seem to require precisely the sort of fallibilism that is ruled out by relativism?

The simple answer is that they do not. While some theorists certainly call themselves 'relativists', very few adopt Protagorean relativism so defined. Knorpp (1998) points out that there is, generally, a great deal of confusion about relativism. It is often directly confused with scepticism, nihilism, pluralism, fallibilism, or theoretical egalitarianism, or even simply confused directly with tolerance. Martin Kusch (2019) notes that theorists like Code, Bloor, and Feyerabend are not actually committed to the claim that all standpoints are equally valid and that there is no neutral way to adjudicate between them. Moreover, it is *this* that gives rise to the infallibilist commitments that Baghramian critiques.

Kusch notes that Bloor (2011) explicitly ridicules the idea that all theories have equal validity. And Bahgramian (2019, p. 259) herself acknowledges that Bloor prefers the characterisation of his position as the view that all theories should be treated merely with 'equal curiosity'.

Similarly, Kusch notes that Feyerabend explicitly rejects the view that that all theories 'are equally true or equally false' (1978, p. 84). Relativism would entail that all views are true, but only from particular standpoints. If there is, further, no neutral perspective from which to adjudicate, it then becomes hard to see how one can avoid a commitment to the thesis that all viewpoints are equally valid. But this is, as Kusch notes, a commitment that Feyerabend explicitly rejects. The view that all opinions are equally false is *nihilism*, not relativism, and Feyerabend rejects this too.

So why does Feyerabend sometimes endorse relativism? Knorpp argues that Feyerabend conflates relativism with *fallibilism*. Feyerabend explicitly associates relativism with the view 'that even our most basic assumptions, our most solid beliefs, and our most conclusive arguments can be changed, improved, or defused' (Feyerabend, 1987, p. 74). Knorpp takes this to be ironic in light of the fact that relativism would seem to entail precisely *infallibilism*. Once we see Feyerabend as defending fallibilism rather than Protagorean relativism, it becomes clear why he associates the view with such notions as curiosity and open-mindedness.

Code certainly describes herself as a 'relativist', but Kathrin Hönig (2005) notes that some of Code's claims seem to suggest she endorses, at most, a mitigated form of relativism. For example, Code says explicitly that if one culture supports the view that the Earth is flat while another supports the view that the Earth is round, it would be absurd to treat these views as equal (1995, p. 202).

In fact, Code seems particularly opposed to a narrow positivist perspective in epistemology, which assumes a 'view from nowhere', and holds that there are certain knowledge claims that are universally justifiable with no consideration of context. Again, however, the mere rejection of this view does not seem to commit us to Protagorean relativism.

Hönig suggests that Code may be better understood merely as an 'anti-anti-relativist'. The idea that endorsing an 'anti-anti' position is not the same thing as a double negation that entails supporting the position one is 'anti-anti' was first suggested by Clifford Geertz (1984). As a comparison, we may think of those who opposed McCarthy era anti-communist propaganda. Being anti-anti-communist, in this sense, did not entail endorsing communism. It merely involved rejecting alarmist propaganda that demonises communists and creates an exaggerated caricature of the communist threat. Being opposed to anti-relativist rhetoric, similarly, does not entail endorsing relativism. Moreover, given that none of the theorists so far discussed who regard themselves as relativists are committed to what *opponents* typically regard as the central tenets of relativism, it certainly seems likely that their views have been uncharitably mischaracterised.

Thus, there is a great deal of confusion about what ought to be regarded as a relativistic theory and what ought to be regarded as an absolutist or objectivist one. The confusion appears to be almost comically captured in the following quote from Melville Herskovits (1951, p. 24), cited by Knorpp (1998, p. 293):

> As a method, relativism encompasses the principle of our science that, in studying a culture, one seeks to attain as great a degree of objectivity as possible

This is, of course, precisely how most opponents of relativism would define objectivism, and objectivists would take this to be directly *ruled out* by the relativist framework.

Kusch (2019) suggests that the main problem is that the relativist view has been so frequently caricatured and mischaracterised. This accusation seems just. It certainly seems unfair for Baghramian to treat any of these theorists as supporting the Protagorean doctrine that we are each infallibly right, whatever we believe, when none of them actually embrace it. Nonetheless, at least part of the reason for the confusion may also be because those who typically call themselves relativists often define themselves in opposition to a view that that has been similarly caricatured and mischaracterised.

Theorists who call themselves relativists often take themselves to be opposed to 'objectivism' or 'absolutism' precisely because they see proponents of those views not merely as supposing that there *are* independently true or false answers, but as supposing, variously, some claim to infallible certainty about what those answers are, some claim to be uniquely placed to arbitrate objectively about all other viewpoints, or as supporting a coercive (or even totalitarian) agenda that denies validity to all perspectives other than one's own.

So perhaps we also ought to examine what exactly those who call themselves relativists tend to be opposed to and why.

### 3. What is Meant by 'Absolutism' or 'Objectivism'?

Relativism is typically opposed either to 'absolutism' or to 'objectivism', with most theorists using the terms interchangeably (although some theorists, such as Bloor, argue that we ought to distinguish them, contrasting relativism with absolutism and subjectivism with objectivism). Proponents of 'objectivism' or 'absolutism' typically argue that while our *beliefs* may be shaped by the available evidence, or by our prior attitudes, or by our differing perspectives, what is *true or false* is not dependent on our prior attitudes or evidence in the same way (with the obvious exception of beliefs specifically about our own attitudes).

Bloor and Feyerabend associate 'absolutism' or 'objectivism', respectively, with policies that involve enforcing a single perspective on others. Hans Kelsen (1948) goes further and defines absolutism as a sort of 'epistemological totalitarianism', even suggesting that it invariably entails support of authoritarian regimes and opposition to democracy.

Knorpp (2019) notes that 'objectivism' is often confused with *success theory:* The view not only that there *are* truths to be gotten at, but that one can be certain that one actually has *access* to those truths. But obviously, there is all the difference in the world between the claim that there are objective truths and the claim that anyone has unique access to those truths.

Feyerabend's optimism about relativism and pessimism about objectivism make sense once we see that further to identifying relativism with fallibilism, Feyerabend characterises objectivism as a stance that involves supposing one's own way of life is universally and unquestionably right. Again, the contrast he seems to have in mind is perhaps not best understood as contrast between 'objectivism' and 'relativism' so much as a contrast between fallibilism and the unquestioning assumption of infallibility that would have to accompany success theory. For instance, he says:

> The idea of objectivity ... is older than science and independent of it. It arose whenever a nation or a tribe or a civilization identified its ways of life with the laws of the (physical and moral) universe (1987, p. 5)

Here, not only is the idea of objectivity conflated with the claim that some group of people *is able to attain* a perfectly objective perspective, but also with the further claim that one's *own* way of life, specifically, is akin to an unbreakable law of nature.

Bloor similarly defines relativism in contrast to 'absolutism', and has sometimes given an unusual characterisation of absolutism. In an interview in 2007 with François Briatte, he describes his advocacy of relativism as follows:

> I would say the essential feature of every type of relativism must be a rejection of absolutism. To be a relativist acknowledges that the knowledge claims of science do not and cannot live up to the title of absolute knowledge. If knowledge is going to be absolute then it has to be true without any qualification, it has to be known with certainty, to be completely stable and eternal truth: those are the sorts of connotations that give meaning to the word 'absolute'. And it is precisely all of these connotations that the relativist rejects. (Briatte, 2007)

In this case, it seems that 'absolutism' is directly conflated with *infallibilism*. Not only is absolutism associated with the idea that truths are known with *certainty* but, even more surprisingly, with the further idea that they are 'true without qualification' and that they are 'stable and eternal'. The idea seems to be that there can be no ambiguity, no possibility of mistake, and even no possibility that facts could ever *change*. It is unclear who could be taken to hold an 'absolutist' view so defined.

Elsewhere, however, Bloor (2011) is less hyperbolic in his characterisation of absolutism. His project primarily involves examining the standards by which we *determine* truth in a scientific context. He takes the relevant contrast to relativism to be 'absolutism' as opposed to 'objectivism' (which would be contrasted with 'subjectivism' – a view that he explicitly rejects). Absolutism, as applied to scientific theories, for Bloor, entails that those theories may be

**Nadine Elzein**

directly descriptive of the facts, independent of any context-sensitive features of human language, standards, practices, etc., such that that it may one day be safe to assume that the truth has been arrived at, and hence that there is no possibility of further scientific progress.

This form of relativism seems to require *fallibilism* and some degree of scepticism with respect to how close empirical practices and scientific descriptions could ever get us to conveying the world as it really is. But it does not require Protagorean relativism.

Insofar as his opponent is painted as an infallibilist, he seems to be attacking a strawman. But if his opponent is merely optimistic about the prospects of scientific theory one day hooking up to the world accurately, then this looks like more of a feasible target. But we should be able to agree that there is a debate to be had about *this* which is entirely separate to the debate about Protagorean relativism. Neither side in *this* dispute must commit to infallibilism.

Code's rejection of objectivism (which she contrasts with relativism) also seems to involve associating it with a wide variety of views, including positivism, reductionism, imperialism, and scientism. It is not entirely clear how objectivism is supposed to be related to these positions. Code seems to suppose that 'mainstream epistemology' necessarily involves a commitment to the idea that there is a culturally divorced perspective from which to evaluate knowledge claims, and that epistemologists take themselves to occupy such a perspective.

This view certainly does seem apt to promote intellectual complacence, even if it does not directly conflate objectivism with infallibilism. But the analysis somewhat blurs the distinction between objectivism and success theory. The problem is not with whether there is an objective reality, but with whether we can claim to *access* that objective reality, free from all biases and contextual limitations. For instance, Code criticises the assumption that the detached methods of physics, with its relative freedom from cultural constraints, can be taken as an absolute paradigm for attaining knowledge in all fields, and especially in the comparatively messy social realm, and is sceptical about our ability to view things from a purely objective perspective, free from any taint of subjectivity (e.g. see Code, 2018, pp. 27–70).

Code's prime target, then, does not seem to be an objectivist perspective on truth or knowledge, but may perhaps be better captured by Rae Langton's (2000) related but distinct target: The *assumption* of objectivity. This involves assuming that observation of the ordinary course of things actually *occurs* from an objective and unbiased standpoint, as well assuming that there is no possibility that one's own expectations and practices sometimes shape social phenomena that one is observing.

But the assumption of objectivity is not the same thing as objectivism. In fact, one of the prime problems, as Langton notes, with the assumption of objectivity, is that it leads us to *false beliefs*. This can only *be* a problem to the extent that we suppose that we are aiming to form accurate beliefs about the way things actually are, independent of our particular and limited perspectives. It could not be a problem if we embraced Protagorean relativism.

It is easy to see why we might suppose relativism is on the side of various social and epistemic virtues when the relativist's opponents are characterised as being committed to the claim that they necessarily have something like a 'God's eye view' of the world, which affords them virtually infallible *access* to the truth, and some right to inflict their own way of life or worldview on anyone who might disagree with them.

It seems what both sides to this dispute object to, and what both sides take themselves to be opposed to is precisely *infallibilism*. Moreover, as Baghramian points out, fallibilism really is a plausible precondition of various virtues, including intellectual humility, open-mindedness, and flexibility of thought. One would hardly have a reason to be curious or open-minded about alternative viewpoints if one did not take there to be some serious possibility that one's own viewpoint was in error.

What we find is that objectivists frequently take relativists to be committed to infallibilism, since they take relativism to be precisely the rejection of 'objectivism' or 'absolutism', as they *themselves* understand it. Hence relativism is taken to involve a commitment to the claim that each person's belief is necessarily true from their own perspective, that conflicting beliefs held by others are equally true from the perspectives of those others, and that there is no sense in which we might be able to characterise one perspective as more or less valid than any other. This view certainly does involve a commitment to infallibilism, but it is not the view that any self-styled relativists actually seem to accept.

Similarly, relativists tend to assume that their opponents reject their *own* far more modest position, which usually amounts to the claim that each of our perspectives is fallible and limited by various contextual constraints, that none of us has a 'God's eye view', and that we ought to be open to other perspectives. Defined like this, the objectivist is taken to be a sort of arrogant authoritarian, convinced not only that there is such a thing as truth, but that they have unquestionable sole access to it, and that it is impossible that they could be wrong. Understood like this, objectivists are similarly

Nadine Elzein

characterised by their opponents as being committed to a sort of infallibilism. Once again, however, this is not a view that any self-styled objectivist actually seems to accept.

## 4. The Need for Interpretive Charity

What impression is this debate apt to give rise to in a casual observer? A quick glance at what each side takes themselves to be opposed to is liable to give the impression of a terrible (though obviously false) dichotomy. On the one hand, we can take the side of the fuzzy relativists, who suppose that 'anything goes' and that no opinion is better supported than any other, and who are happy to entirely collapse the distinction between belief and truth, leading to the collapse of all reasoned dispute and undermining any conceivable motivation to subject one's own opinions to rational scrutiny. On the other hand, we can take the side of the arrogant authoritarian absolutists, who take themselves to be the sole possessors of knowledge, and who will tyrannically crush the views of anyone who opposes them, devoid of any capacity to seriously consider any viewpoint other than their own, and oblivious to the fact that their oppressive policies might play any role in shaping the social world that they take themselves to be objectively observing.

No wonder, then, that even while neither position is defended by any academic philosophers, as far as I can tell, students who are new to the discussion may be tempted to embrace views that seem implausible or puzzling to us. No doubt, students are sympathetic, even to the sort of crude relativism we find in Plato's portrayal of Protagoras, in part, because they associate opposition to that view with intolerance or authoritarianism. While proponents of this authoritarian caricature thankfully tend to be rare in philosophy classrooms (though sadly not non-existent), views quite like it are certainly found lurking in various internet chat forums. No doubt, proponents may take themselves to be providing the only line of 'defence' against fuzzy relativistic thinking, further entrenching the idea that this arrogant authoritarian stance is somehow the natural alternative.

The problem, then, is that extreme views often give rise to extreme counterviews. The more absurd or threatening the perspective, the more likely people are to side with those they take to be natural enemies of it, especially when they take themselves to be defending the 'reasonable' stance against those who threaten to undermine it. People cannot be adopting these views on the basis that academics defend them and this bleeds into popular culture, since academics largely *don't* defend them. But they may well adopt them because they see them as the only viable alternatives to views frequently *attacked* in academic writing (views which are, in fact, defended by virtually no one).

Perhaps then, we ought to embrace both anti-anti-relativist sentiments *and* anti-anti-objectivist sentiments. While 'relativists' and 'objectivists' understand those terms, respectively, in ways that both sides should acknowledge to be largely innocuous, it seems both 'anti-relativist' and 'anti-objectivist' rhetoric are reactions to caricatures.

Freed from this rhetoric, we stop seeing a 'culture war' between opposing sides, and instead see both sides as largely agreeing on a view that may seem so obvious that it borders on the trite: that there is very little that can be known for certain, that we had better be willing to acknowledge the possibility that we might be in error, that we would be well advised to listen to other viewpoints with an open-mind, and that we should probably strive to view our own opinions with some critical distance, maintaining an awareness of the fact that none of us has access to a 'God's eye view' immune from all biases and perspectival limitations. The problem is that some seem to label this innocuous stance 'relativism' while others label it 'absolutism'.

This suggests that views that actually entail infallibilism only really become appealing when pitted against strawmen, caricatured so as to appear opposed to the reasonable stance of fallibilism. So insofar as we want to emphasise the sorts of virtue that seem to depend on fallibilism, virtues like open-mindedness and intellectual humility, it seems that we need to cultivate the additional virtue of *interpretive charity*.

Interpretive charity entails a commitment to trying to interpret one's opponents' views in the most sympathetic light. It stands opposed to the vice of interpreting one's opponents unsympathetically, as happens when we caricature those views or mischaracterise them to suit our critique. Interpretive charity can be a difficult virtue to cultivate. In present academia, pressure to publish combined with intense competition can make the vice of uncharitably interpreting one's opponents irresistible, especially where there is a great deal of pressure to make one's own arguments seem novel and disruptive. This adversarial approach has advantages, but it may also contribute to the illusion of extreme polarisation.[8]

[8] This may require us to cultivate the collective virtue of responsibility. See Mandi Astola (2022).

# Nadine Elzein

The debate between 'absolutists' and 'relativists' shows that this impression of polarisation can persist even when there is barely any separation between the views embraced by most proponents of the two camps.

When it comes to polarised debates outside of academia, the drivers are slightly different, but the mechanics appear to be similar. People may not be under pressure to publish seemingly controversial opinions on social media sites (the way that academics may feel pressured to produce novel viewpoints) but the algorithms used to promote content will make controversial claims more visible and will drive us towards extremes. The more we can ridicule or caricature our opponents, the more exposure our opinions are likely to get and the more heavily they will be promoted. The cycle is a vicious one. Again, this is a pressure that we must learn to resist. Some responsibility for this obviously lies with social media companies themselves and with policymakers. It would help if charitable content was promoted over divisive content, but while there is a commercial incentive to secure ever-greater levels of engagement, social media companies are likely to keep these policies going unless legal regulations are introduced to stop them. But this vicious cycle also relies crucially on users themselves repeatedly being willing to buy into depictions of their opponents that confirm or magnify their own biases against them.

The ability to interpret one's opponents charitably requires us to be able to step back and question an ungenerous caricature. It requires us to voluntarily resist the slide into tribalistic thinking and to try to recognise a mean-spirited dismissal of an opposing viewpoint and question it, even if we do not support the view under attack. Interpretive charity may therefore become one of the key virtues that we must cultivate in order to navigate the modern world and restore the possibility of constructive debate between camps that seem to disagree. Moreover, it may actually help us to recognise common ground where the dynamics of social media work to actively obscure it.

Virtues are, according to the traditional Aristotelian view, character traits that relate to fundamental human tendencies of the sort that we often struggle to get right. Learning to get them right requires a great deal of practice and self-control. In the case of interpretive charity, we are prone to getting it wrong because there are mechanisms in human society that consistently drive us in this direction. Almost every source of information we encounter is there because it is in somebody's interests to persuade us of something (whether it's voting for a particular party, spending more time scrolling, buying more papers, contributing to a cause, etc.) We are more likely to keep reading and more likely to adopt one side of an argument when the contrast between the two sides is exaggerated. This means that there is a constant incentive for some to caricature their opponents and a constant incentive for each of us to buy into those caricatures. Cultivating interpretive charity requires us to continuously question these. This is inherently difficult, but so is the development of any virtue worth cultivating.

*University of Warwick*
*Nadine.Elzein@warwick.ac.uk*

## References

Mandi Astola, 'Collective responsibility should be treated as a virtue', *Royal Institute Philosophy Supplementary Volume*, 92 (2022) 27–44.

Maria Baghramian, 'I. The Virtues of Relativism', *Aristotelian Society Supplementary Volume*, 93 (2019) 247–69.

Allan Bloom, *The Closing of the American Mind: How Higher Education Has Failed Democracy and Impoverished the Souls of Today's Students* (New York: Simon & Schuster, 1987).

David Bloor, 'Relativism and the Sociology of Scientific Knowledge', in *A Companion to Relativism*, edited by Stephen Hales (Oxford: Blackwell, 2011) 433–55.

François Briatte, 'Entretien avec David Bloor', *Tracés. Revue de Sciences humaines* [En ligne], 12 (2007). English translation (unpublished but corrected and approved by David Bloor) available from url: https://halshs.archives-ouvertes.fr/halshs-01511329/file/InterviewDB_FBriatte2007.pdf (accessed 3rd July 2021).

Lorraine Code, 'Must a Feminist Be a Relativist After All?' In her *Rhetorical Spaces* (London: Routledge, 1995), 189–207.

Lorraine Code, *What Can She Know?* (Ithaca, NY: Cornell University Press, 2018).

T. H. Costello, S. M. Bowes, S. T. Stevens, I. D. Waldman, A. Tasimi & S. O. Lilienfeld, 'Clarifying the structure and nature of left-wing authoritarianism', *Journal of Personality and Social Psychology*, Advance online publication (2021).

Jacques Derrida, 'Hospitality, justice and responsibility: a dialogue with Derrida'. In *Questioning Ethics: Contemporary Debates in*

**Nadine Elzein**

*Continental Philosophy*, edited by Mark Dooley & Richard Kearney, (London: Routledge, 1999) 65–83.

Paul Feyerabend, *Farewell to Reason* (New York: Verso, 1987).

Michel Foucault, *Madness and Civilization: History of Insanity in the Age of Reason*. Trans. Richard Howard, (London: Tavistock Publications, 1967).

Clifford Geertz, 'Distinguished Lecture: Anti Anti-Relativism'. *American Anthropologist*, 86, (1984), 263–78.

Melville J. Herskovits, 'Tender- and Tough-Minded Anthropology and the Study of Values in Culture', *Southwestern Journal of Anthropology*, 7 (1951) 22–31.

Kathrin Hönig, 'Relativism or Anti-Anti-Relativism? Epistemological and Rhetorical Moves in Feminist Epistemology and Philosophy of Science', *European Journal of Women's Studies*, 12 (2005) 407–419.

Hans Kelsen, 'Absolutism and Relativism in Philosophy and Politics'. *American Political Science Review*, 42 (1948) 906–914.

Michiko Kakutani, *The Death of Truth*, (Tim Duggan Books, 2019).

William Max Knorpp Jr, 'What Relativism Isn't', *Philosophy*, 73 (1988), 277–300.

Martin Kusch, 'Relativist Stances, Virtues and Vices'. *Aristotelian Society Supplementary Volume*, 93 (2019) 271–291

Rae Langton, 'Feminism in Epistemology: Exclusion and Objectification'. In *The Cambridge Companion to Feminism in Philosophy*, edited by M. Fricker & J. Hornsby, (Cambridge: Cambridge University Press, 2000) 127–45.

Joseph P. Maguire, 'Protagoras – or Plato?' *Phronesis*, 18, (1973) 115–38.

Morgan Marietta, Tyler Farley, Tyler Cote and Paul Murphy, 'The Rhetorical Psychology of Trumpism: Threat, Absolutism, and the Absolutist Threat' *The Forum*, 15 (2017) 313–32.

Richard Rorty, *Consequences of Pragmatism,* (Minneapolis: University of Minnesota, 1982).

Bas C. van Fraassen, *The Empirical Stance,* (New Haven: Yale University Press, 2002).

Lani Watson, 'Cultivating Curiosity in the Information Age', *Royal Institute Philosophy Supplementary Volume*, 92 (2022) 129–48.

Caroline Zhu, 'Cancel Culture is Moral Absolutism, and it's unsustainable', *The Observer*, January 17th 2020. https://observer.case.edu/zhu-cancelled-culture-is-moral-absolutism-and-its-unsustainable/. Accessed 26 November, 2021.

# Uncertainty Phobia and Epistemic Forbearance in a Pandemic

NICHOLAS SHACKEL

**Abstract**

In this chapter I show how challenges to our ability to tame the uncertainty of a pandemic leaves us vulnerable to uncertainty phobia. This is because, contrary to what we might hope, not all the uncertainty that matters can be tamed by our knowledge of the relevant probabilities. Unrelievable wild uncertainty is a hard burden to bear, especially so when we must act in the face of it. We are tempted to retreat into uncertainty phobia, leading to fixed definite opinions precisely when acting on sound judgement requires our opinions to be hedged and mobile. Coping with a pandemic requires us to bear the burden rather than give in to temptation: it requires us to practise the virtue of epistemic forbearance.

In this chapter I show how challenges to our ability to tame the uncertainty of a pandemic leaves us vulnerable to uncertainty phobia. This is because, contrary to what many believe, not all the uncertainty that matters can be tamed by our knowledge of the relevant probabilities. We are vulnerable because unrelievable wild uncertainty is a hard burden to bear, especially so when we must act in the face of it.

The source of unrelievable wild uncertainty is that the nature of probability distributions matters for whether knowledge of them tames uncertainty. It matters because a warrant for the taming is provided by two theorems, but this warrant applies only to some kinds of probability distribution. Essentially, this is because the theorems are about what happens at a mathematical limit but real life never reaches the limit. Consequently, the warrant depends on how quickly the random processes producing the uncertainty converge towards their limit. If they are governed by one class of probability distributions, they converge quickly enough to possess the warrant. If they are governed by another class of probability distributions, they converge towards their limit too slowly and so do not possess that warrant. The random processes of pandemics involve the slow kind.

Faced with such a burden, as we are in a pandemic, we are tempted to retreat into uncertainty phobia, leading to fixed definite opinions, precisely when the exercise of sound judgement to determine our responses requires our opinions to be hedged and mobile. Coping with

doi:10.1017/S1358246122000248

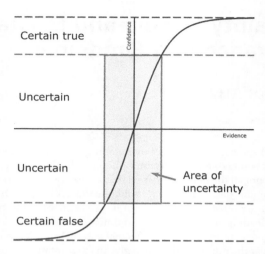

*Figure 1*. Mundane confidence; x-axis for the balance of the evidence for and against the proposition, i.e. balance positive is support for its truth, balance negative is support for its falsehood; y-axis for confidence: positive is confidence in truth, negative is confidence in falsehood.

a pandemic requires us to bear the burden of unrelievable wild uncertainty rather than give in to the temptation of uncertainty phobia. Pandemics require the virtue of epistemic forbearance.

## 1. Confidence: certainty, uncertainty, evidence and stakes

When we act on the basis of a belief what we do depends on our confidence in the proposition believed.[1] If we are certain, we usually act without hesitation: if we are not, we take precautions. Our confidence in a proposition should vary with the balance of evidence. Strong evidence in favour leads to certainty in its truth, strong evidence against leads to certainty in its falsehood. As evidence weakens, certainty weakens into uncertainty. Sketching this as a graph, this variation in our confidence would look something like figure 1.

Certainty has its own range, from fairly certain to absolutely certain, as does uncertainty. The boundaries are vague of course, and the box of uncertainty is just a rough indication of the extent

---

[1]    Here, a proposition is what is believed, or what is asserted by an assertion, rather than a proposal. For example, if I say or believe the bridge is safe, what I say or believe is the proposition that the bridge is safe.

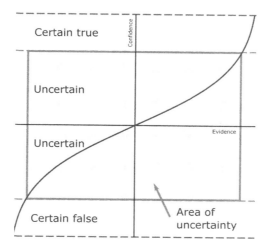

*Figure 2.* High stakes confidence.

of uncertainty's relation to evidence. But this is a useful model none-theless. (There are no units on the axes here because these graphs are intended only to illustrate the features of how confidence varies with evidence.)

Bearing in mind that the confidence I am speaking of is the confidence to act on a belief, it is clear that confidence does not depend only on the evidence. In mundane cases, where the practical consequences of our belief being mistaken are not severe, it makes sense for our confidence to increase quite quickly with the evidence. For example, if the badness of being late is mild then, being fairly certain from memory that the bus departs at 5.10pm and so we will get it if we leave now is reasonable (even if in fact it departs at 5.05pm and so we miss it). We will call such examples low stakes cases. For high stakes cases we need stronger evidence to be certain and the relation of our confidence to evidence looks more like figure 2.

Note how much greater the area of uncertainty is for high stakes cases. When our reliance on a belief has bad consequences if we are mistaken, then we should not be certain without stronger evidence. If missing the bus means missing the train which means missing the plane, for example, instead of relying on the evidence of my memory of the timetable, I should get stronger evidence by checking the various timetables.[2]

---

[2]    These kinds of rational influences of practical stakes are well known among philosophers from the contextualism versus invariantism for

Nicholas Shackel

## 2. Taming uncertainty

The main tool we have developed to tame uncertainty is the mathematical theory of probability. Our hunger for certainty about how things are can be satiated instead by certainty in the probabilities of how they might be. We bear the uncertainty by being able to plan on probabilities. Confidence in probability reassures us and thereby suffices for acting despite uncertainty whilst giving good guidance for how to act with the precaution required by uncertainty.

When it comes to sophisticated applications to complex problems, knowing the relevant probability need not be as simple as knowing a specific numerical value. Probability functions map entire sets of possibilities onto probabilities and knowing such a probability function – knowing the probability distribution over those possibilities – greatly increases our power to tame uncertainty. There are many classes of probability distribution and each member of a class is picked out by few parameters. For example, each Normal distribution is distinguished from all the others by its mean and variance.

It is often as important to know the class of probability distribution as to know specific numerical probabilities. Even when one does not know the parameters that are needed to derive the numerical probabilities, knowing the class of distribution allows knowing various qualitative features of the uncertainty faced, features which may be as important as knowing the exact probabilities in planning what to do and responding to a developing situation.

Furthermore, knowing the class of distribution allows us to know how good an estimate of the relevant parameters the available data give. So we can know how good our estimate of the probabilities is despite a paucity of available data. For example, if we know that the distribution of car crashes is a Poisson distribution (Nicholson and Wong, 1993), we may be able to get good estimates, and know just how good those estimates are, for a particular road with little traffic and little crash data.

Consequently, the power of probability to tame uncertainty goes well beyond numerical probabilities. Taming uncertainty is multifaceted, from knowing probabilities through knowing means and variances, knowing probability distributions, to knowing how well calibrated the predictions on which we base our actions are likely to be.

---

knowledge debate. They are used to motivate contextualism and challenge invariantism, although here I am not taking a side in that debate (but see Shackel, 2011; MS-a).

## 3. Tolerable and dangerous risks

In general, the uncertainties that most interest us are unknown facts and events which may bring benefits and may bring harms. A risk is a possibility of a harm and taking a risk is doing something that may bring a harm. A *tolerable risk* is one for which the possible harm is predictably endurable. A *dangerous risk* is one for which the possible harm is unpredictably unendurable. An *intolerable risk*, of predictably unendurable harm, is almost always stupid to take (the exceptions, if any there are, being where they are accompanied by the possibility of enormous benefits), so we won't bother thinking about those here. What is endurable, and therefore what is tolerable or dangerous, depends to some extent on context and feasibility, of course. What is tolerable or dangerous will also vary with who is doing the choosing. For example, what may be a dangerous risk for an individual may be a tolerable risk for a government, just because societies can endure despite the loss of some of their constituent individuals.

How, then, do we know which risks are tolerable and which dangerous? Much of life confronts us with this question, since much of life consists in taking opportunities for the sake of their possible benefit and doing so despite their risks. A pandemic confronts us with this question relentlessly.

The issue turns on predictability. Where we have certainty, predictability follows. Where we have uncertainty, there we have difficulty. There are usually many different uncertainties that we need to consider. The harm we risk for each opportunity need not be singular but may extend over a range of bad things. If we drive to the beach, the possible harms run from negligible to devastating damage to the car and ourselves, yet together these form a tolerable risk. So the phrase 'predictably endurable' does not mean no possibility of a harm great enough to be unendurable. It means the range of harms that we expect are endurable. Driving to the beach is a tolerable risk because devastating damage to the car and ourselves is sufficiently unlikely to be outwith the range we expect. In general, what we want to be able to do is predict that range.

Here is where the taming power of probability may enter. If we know the probability of harms, then we can predict that range. We can replace our uncertainty over the harm with certainty over probabilities of harms. We can then examine the tolerability of the risk in various ways: for example, we can consider the ratio of chances of the range of endurable harms versus unendurable harms; if the harms themselves are quantifiable we can calculate the mean (the

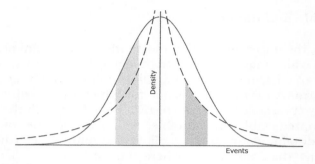

*Figure 3.* Probability density curves showing a thin and a fat-tailed distribution.

mathematical expectation), variance, skewness etc., and can give error bounds; and so on. In this way we can predict mathematically whether the harm is endurable or not.

Or at least, so it appears. The assumption lying behind this appearance is that good knowledge of probability tames uncertainty, by which I mean allows us to calculate probabilities that are close to true probabilities and to make reliable predictions. Unfortunately, whether this assumption is true varies with the class of probability distributions involved. Here is not the place to rehearse my formal arguments on this point.[3] Here is the place to simply report their results.

In short, uncertainty is born wild. Good knowledge of what I call tame probabilities suffices to tame uncertainty and good knowledge of what I call wild probabilities leaves uncertainty wild. Uncertainty involving wild probabilities can be entirely *untameable* or may instead take a very long time and a great deal of data to tame.

The borderline between tame and wild probabilities is usually the borderline between thin and fat-tailed probability distributions. What this means is illustrated in figure 3.

Here, the probability that an event is within a given range is the area under the curve (see shading for examples). The solid line distribution is called thin-tailed because its tails on either side get very close to zero quickly. The dashed line distribution is called fat-tailed because the tail takes a long time to get similarly close to zero. This means that extreme events are extremely unlikely for thin-tailed distributions but not for fat-tailed ones.

---

[3]    I provide these formal arguments in my forthcoming paper, 'Wild Uncertainty in a Pandemic' (Shackel, MS-b).

The distinguishing feature of a random process governed by a fat-tailed distribution is that events from that tail will dominate the cumulative result of repeated events from that random process, whereas for thin-tailed distributions it is events from the centre of the distribution that dominate. For example, if wealth has a fat-tailed distribution and we select at random a large enough sample of people, it is almost certain that nearly all of the total wealth is contributed by a single very wealthy person (e.g. a billionaire) than by a lot of wealthy people (e.g. millionaires). By contrast, height has a thin-tailed distribution and if we select at random a large sample of people, it is almost certain that nearly all of the total height is contributed by many people close to the mean rather than by a few extremely tall people.

If we have a process involving only thin-tailed probabilities, we can presume that good knowledge of the probability tames uncertainty. If the process involves fat-tailed probabilities, the uncertainty remains wild. These presumptions are not exceptionless, but an exception must be proved, not assumed. The reason for this is to do with the warrant from a pair of theorems, which is explained in section 5.

## 4. Taming Uncertainty in the Covid-19 Pandemic

We use epidemic models to attempt to tame the uncertainty of a pandemic. They have been widely used during the Covid-19 pandemic (e.g. Anastassopoulou *et al*, 2020; Calafiore *et al*, 2020; Cooper *et al*, 2020; Ferguson *et al*, 2020; Ferrari *et al*, 2021; Martínez, 2021; Shringi *et al*, 2021). In this section and the next I will give a very much simplified description of why, at the beginning of a pandemic and for some considerable time, epidemic models leave uncertainty untamed.[4]

The fundamental issue is that both in estimating the parameters of epidemic models and in then using those models to make predictions, we rely on two theorems, the central limit theorem and the law of large numbers. The power of these theorems is that they apply to any underlying probability distribution,[5] whether thin or fat-tailed, and they even apply when we don't know what those underlying probabilities distributions are. It is on this power that we rely for a warrant that the epidemic models tame the uncertainty.

---

[4]   For the explanations of what I here can only report, see Shackel (MS-b).
[5]   For the former theorem to apply, a probability distribution must have both mean and variance, for the latter it must have a mean.

# Nicholas Shackel

The central limit theorem assures us that the features of our observed samples are close to the features of the whole population, and thereby give us good inputs for our model. The law of large numbers tells us that the future observed outcomes will be close to our predictions. These theorems are therefore essential to justifying any claim that the probabilities of future eventualities determined by an epidemic model (such as the probabilities of numbers of hospitalizations next month) will be close to the truth. Without these theorems, we have no good reason to believe that these predictions will be reliable.

Consequently, these two theorems are needed for our epidemic models to tame uncertainty. Let us call their warrant to this effect *the warrant from theory*.[6]

Our attempts to tame the uncertainty of a pandemic involve complex concatenations of models. Estimates of pandemic parameters can themselves rely on models and the use of those models relies on those estimates, and this mutual feedback may involve a number of different epidemic models. There are also many other kinds of models involved in coping with a pandemic, which concern the effect on our myriad normal activities when large numbers of people are falling sick. For example, health services use models to plan priorities, beds, staffing and supplies. These other models take as inputs the outputs of the various epidemic models, thereby adding further concatenations into the mix. The extent of such concatenations of models makes it very hard to disentangle and trace the routes of reliance on our two theorems. We have no audits tracing where we rely on the warrant from theory and where we do not. In the absence of such audits, our use of epidemic models to attempt to tame the uncertainty of a pandemic depends quite generally on the warrant from theory.

## 5. Untameable uncertainty in the Covid-19 Pandemic

Unfortunately the warrant from theory, whilst satisfactory for thin-tailed random processes, can fail for fat-tailed ones. The source of

---

[6]    There are other warrants on which we rely as well, of course, such as the empirical science justifying the epidemic models. Their failure would pose a different problem from my concern here, since absent such warranted models, we would lack good knowledge of the probabilities and so we would know that we lack the basic tool to attempt to tame the uncertainty. So for our purposes we can assume all those warrants are in place.

the problem is that, technically, the two theorems are about what happens *at the limit*, i.e. as the number of observations tends to infinity. In real life, it can matter how quickly the accumulation of outcomes converges to the limit, i.e. how many observations you need to be within a specified distance of the limit. Thin-tailed random processes converge quickly, fat-tailed random processes converge slowly, sometimes very slowly indeed. This makes a huge difference to the sample size needed for an estimate of a parameter to be within a specified distance of its true value. For example, it can take only 30 observations of events governed by a Normal distribution (which is always thin-tailed) for our estimate to be highly likely to be that close. To get that close with a Pareto distribution[7] (which is always fat-tailed) it takes 100,000,000,000 (one hundred thousand million) observations (see Taleb, 2020, p. 40).

So where a random process involves fat-tailed probabilities, even if we know which class of fat-tailed probability distributions are involved, the warrant from theory fails because convergence is too slow. It can be so slow that we simply cannot get a large enough sample for the central limit theorem or the law of large numbers to apply. Even where over time we may accumulate large enough samples for them to apply, it may still take a very long time before we have achieved an accumulation sufficient for the warrant to be in place.

Here, then, is why the presumption must be that thin-tailed distributions are tame probabilities and fat-tailed distributions are wild probabilities. In general, and provably so, thin-tailed distributions converge quickly enough to have the warrant from theory whilst fat-tailed distributions do not converge quickly enough and do not have the warrant. To take an exception, therefore, requires fulfilling a burden of proof. For example, needing to rely on a specific fat-tailed distribution being an exception to this general rule requires being able to show that its convergence to the limit is sufficiently atypical for the class of distributions to which it belongs. Sufficiency here is determined by the purposes for which one needs to rely on it.[8]

---

[7]  This particular Pareto distribution generates outcomes fitting the Pareto 80/20 principle: see below.

[8]  For example, the class of log-normal distributions is at the borderline. Those with low variance can be thin-tailed but those with high variance are fat-tailed. We might be in the position to prove which we had, which might then allow us to treat it as an exception.

# Nicholas Shackel

Pandemic random processes involve a number of crucial fat-tailed distributions. The number of deaths caused by a pandemic is one good example. An analysis of 72 pandemics from the past 2500 years, with estimated deaths for each one scaled to the current world population, shows that the cumulative effect of these pandemics is dominated by a few extreme events: the Plague of Justinian (541–549 AD) and the Black Death (1346-1353 AD) each claimed the equivalent of more than two billion lives; the five next largest pandemics each claimed the equivalent of more than 100 million lives (Cirillo and Taleb, 2020, pp. 608-609). The characteristic of a fat-tailed distribution is precisely that the cumulative effect is dominated by a few extreme events from the distribution's fat tail. This analysis shows that deaths from pandemics form an extremely fat-tailed probability distribution (Cirillo and Taleb, 2020, p. 606).

Another good example is a critical input to epidemic models. The reproduction rate (also called the reproduction number) is the number of secondary infections per infected person, i.e. how many people an infectious person infects during the time they are ill. The reproduction rate is the mean of the random variable, $P$, which for each infected person takes the value of the number of people that that person infects.

Someone is called a 'superspreader' if their value for $P$ is high, although different authors give different thresholds. Recalling that fat-tails mean single events produce most of the cumulative effect, the existence of superspreaders is itself an indicator of a fat-tailed distribution. We have very good evidence that the transmission of Covid-19 has been heavily determined by superspreading. According to one study, 60–75% of cases infect nobody, while 10–20% of cases cause 80% of all secondary infections (Chen *et al*, 2021; see also Hasan *et al*, 2020; Lau *et al*, 2020; Sun *et al*, 2021).

This estimate fits the Pareto 80/20 principle, named after the economist who first drew it to our attention (Pareto, 1896). The class of fat-tailed probability distributions called Pareto are so-called precisely because random processes with such distributions exhibit this pattern. When we see a random process exhibiting such a pattern, the underlying random variables are probably fat-tailed. Hence, the underlying random variable $P$ for Covid-19 probably has a fat-tailed distribution. Recent research supports this conclusion. Wong and Collins have shown how where there is superspreading, the probability distribution of $P$ is fat-tailed, and conclude that

combine[d] empirical observations of SARS-CoV and SARS-CoV-2 transmission and extreme value statistics...show that the distribution of secondary cases is consistent with being fat-tailed, implying that large superspreading events are extremal, yet probable, occurrences. (2020, p. 29416)

Estimating the reproduction rate is, then, a matter of estimating the mean of a fat-tailed random variable. This is very hard to do well. We have already seen that it can require an enormous sample for our estimate to be as accurate as a sample size of 30 would give for the mean of a thin-tailed distribution. The second problem is that we will systematically underestimate the mean because the overwhelming majority of samples from systematic random sampling will not include those rare superspreaders at all.[9]

A third good example of a fat-tailed distribution involved in the spread of Covid-19 concerns the network of human acquaintances. The human world consists of many clusters of mutually acquainted people, some of whom are acquainted with people in other clusters. Pandemics can spread easily within a cluster, any member of which can then spread the infection to another cluster by infecting an acquaintance of theirs in that other cluster. Someone who is very well connected, which is to say, has many acquaintances, can therefore spread the infection to many clusters.

The number of acquaintances of a person is a random variable. If that random variable is fat-tailed the network will be what is called a small-world network, which in this case would mean that although most humans are not acquaintances, a path from one person to another consisting entirely of acquaintances has, on average, a fairly small number of people in it. A small enough mean path length implies that the random variable is fat-tailed.

We know that the network of human acquaintances is a small-world network (Milgram, 1967; Collins and Chow, 1998) with a remarkably short mean path length. Milgram's originating experiment (Milgram, 1967) found 5 or less steps of acquaintance sufficed within the US. and Watts and Strogatz estimated the global mean path length to be 6 (1998). Consequently this evidence shows human acquaintance is probably governed by a fat-tailed random variable.

The paths of pandemic transmission are significantly constituted by the network of human acquaintances. This is why the more complex stochastic epidemic models attempt to include the random processes of human acquaintance, movement and meetings that ground the causal transmission of a pandemic. The network is a

---

[9]  For the technical details of this, see Shackel (MS-b).

small world with a fat-tailed random variable governing the number of acquaintances. Watts and Strogatz have shown that

> infectious diseases are predicted to spread much more easily and quickly in a small world. (1998, p. 442)

Hence there are network features grounding the causal transmission of pandemics that have fat-tailed distributions and these are parameters for the more complex stochastic models.

Our epidemic models of Covid-19 thus depend on inputs and parameters that are derived from random processes governed by fat-tailed probability distributions. The probabilities are therefore presumptively wild. In the absence of proof that they are exceptions to the general rule of fat-tailed distributions, we would require huge samples to overcome their slow convergence to the limit before our estimates attained the needed accuracy for reliable model outputs. Since we do not have such enormous samples, the warrant from theory fails. The wild uncertainty of a pandemic remains.

Could we ever, given enough time, accumulate enough data to finally tame this uncertainty? The answer to this question is unclear. It may depend on the specific fat-tailed probabilities involved. Some fat-tailed distributions have no variance and even no mean and for them no warrant from theory is ever directly available.[10] Any uncertainty governed by such distributions may be completely untameable!

Our need for the warrant from theory is strongest at the beginning of a pandemic, because then our data is most limited. It continues strongly for some considerable time. First, and unavoidably, because of the slowness of convergence of any fat-tailed random processes involved and the consequent inaccuracy of estimation. Second, as the pathogen itself evolves, the parameters of the pandemic random process that we are trying to estimate may not be stationary phenomena. Similarly, our responses that attempt to constrain the pandemic change the environment within which it operates and this can produce a moving target for our estimates. All such non-stationarity weakens the extent to which the accumulation of data over time strengthens the quality of our estimates.

We need to be aware here of hindsight bias. Eventually, we will be able to fit our models to many years' worth of data and at that point our models will seem able to predict the course of that historical

---

[10] I say not directly because there are some technical things we can do when there is an upper bound on a random variable which may ameliorate (but cannot get around) this problem.

pandemic. But this does not mean that we could have built these models and tamed our uncertainty *when we needed to* during that pandemic.[11]

In conclusion, then, Covid-19, in common with pandemics in general, has exhibited fat-tailed random processes and we have no audit tracing the routes for the warrant from theory, so we have no audit of its failure. In the absence of that audit, the failure is quite general. So initially and for some considerable time, the Covid-19 pandemic faced us with untamed uncertainty.

## 6. Taming failures during the Covid-19 pandemic

At first slowly, and then quickly, we became aware of the dangerous risks of Covid-19. We saw repeated reversals in government policy as governments attempted to 'follow the science'. When we looked at the science, we saw persistent wide divergences in estimates and predictions coming from the models of different teams of experts and persistent failures of model predictions.

For example, in August 2020 Ioannidis et al pointed out that on 27 March 2020 'brilliant scientists expected 100,000,000 cases accruing within 4 weeks in the USA' (Ioannidis *et al*, 2020, p. 1). By contrast, the US Centre for Disease Control reports total cumulative positive specimens from 1st March to 25th April 2020 as 702,814 (United States Centre for Disease Control, 2020, p. 3). Of course, there were more infections than positive specimens, but this fact cannot account for such an enormous disparity.

Similarly, the team at Imperial College London predicted in March 2020 that there would be roughly 1,500,000 deaths across the UK and the USA by the middle of June 2020 (Ferguson *et al*, 2020).[12] In fact the number of deaths across the whole world by that date was less than one-third of that number ((Ioannidis et al

---

[11]    An illustration of the difficulty here is from the research on the stock market showing models well fitted to even many past years quickly fail to predict the future, and when a model is then built to countenance the new failures, it too fails for its future. (Fama, 1970; Summers, 1986; Bernstein, 1992; Mandelbrot and Hudson, 2004)

[12]    It is tricky to extract exactly the cumulative predicted figure from that Imperial College report (Ferguson *et al*, 2020), but mid-June is about the peak daily deaths in those predictions that were for total 500,000 UK deaths and 2,200,000 US deaths in that wave (assuming no mitigation). Since mid-June is halfway through that wave, this means predicted deaths of roughly 1,500,000 between the UK and the US by that point.

2020, p. 1). Ioannidis et al found instances of the same model going wrong in both directions: 'the model initially over predicted enormously, and then it under predicted' (2020, p. 4). Additionally,

> even for short-term forecasting when the epidemic wave waned, models presented confusingly diverse predictions with huge uncertainty. (2020, p. 3)

Ioannidis et al conclude that

> despite involving many excellent modellers, best intentions, and highly sophisticated tools, forecasting efforts have largely failed (Ioannidis *et al*, 2020, p. 1)

Subsequent research has confirmed this impression of unreliability. James et al note 'A proliferation of models, often diverging widely in their projections' (2021, p. 379). Poor calibration has been observed. Poor calibration means (in this case) that predictions diverge from actuality and do so with frequency lying outside predicted probabilistic error bounds. For example, predictions of 1000 deaths per day with a 95% confidence interval of 100 would be poorly calibrated if actual deaths were outside the range 900-1100 more than 5% of the time. Gnanvi et al (2021) report the poor calibration of the Covid-19 pandemic models they studied. 25% were outside their 95% confidence intervals for numbers of cases when only 5% should have been. Endo et al conclude that 'calibration of the [mortality risk] models were poor' (Endo *et al*, 2021, p. 1). See also Eker (2020); Holmdahl and Buckee (2020) and for a general overview see Cepelewicz (2021).

Evidently, such failures of prediction mean that calculations of probabilities and predictions using these models did not tame the uncertainty of Covid-19, at least initially and for some considerable time. The epidemic models used were well grounded in current methodologies and literature and, whilst no one would claim they are flawless, their warrant is commensurate with scientific warrants in medicine in general. The failure of those models therefore shows that the conclusion of section 5, that the Covid-19 pandemic faced us with untamed uncertainty, was manifest during the first six months of the Covid-19 pandemic.[13]

---

[13] For avoidance of doubt, I am not arguing that epidemic models have no use in managing a pandemic. Rather, when they leave uncertainty wild, we need to think harder about just what help they can yet provide. For more on this, see Shackel (MS).

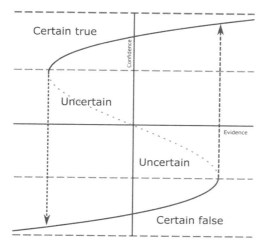

*Figure 4.* Uncertainty phobic confidence.

## 7. Uncertainty Phobia

Uncertainty is burdensome and it is especially burdensome in high stakes cases, when distinguishing tolerable and dangerous risks is very important. It is partly its burden that drives us to eliminate it by seeking better evidence. Yet sometimes no better evidence is available and still we must act. The burden of such unrelievable uncertainty can drive us instead to an irrationality I shall call *uncertainty phobia*. Instead of bearing the uncertainty we may end up responding as in figure 4.

The dotted diagonal of the S-shape may be steep or shallow. What is critical is that this fold in our response removes uncertainty by making the range of uncertain confidences unavailable. If the evidence changes against our belief, we may continue to be certain even when the evidence turns negative, until it reaches a point at which we suddenly switch from being certain true to certain false (and vice versa). Consequently, there is no area of uncertainty because our confidence can never take a place on the dotted diagonal.

If we fall into uncertainty phobia over a question, we will be certain even when we should not be. Which *way* we will be certain will be path dependent. Whichever side of a question we were on as the stakes rose, and however weakly we were on that side, we will end up certain on that side.

This also means that uncertainty phobia will amplify the effects of even very small irrationalities already in place. I doubt we have the ability to avoid small irrationalities, such as neglecting entirely some weak but uncongenial evidence. Were such an irrationality to place us very slightly on one side of a question when we should have been slightly on the other, that small irrationality determines where we end up fixed.

The upshot here is that anyone driven into uncertainty phobia on any questions will be stubbornly certain, unreasonably so, on those questions. How exactly we would sustain and rationalise our stubborn certainties is an open question. There are various well-known kinds of cognitive error that would suffice. One well known example is confirmation bias: our tendency to notice and remember evidence that seems to confirm the belief we already hold at the expense of evidence that counts against it. But really, the problem is far worse than that. In uncertainty phobia, even whilst we may be taking in the balance of the evidence accurately, we have almost entirely lost our graded sensitivity to it.

What has driven us here is that the height of the stakes makes distinguishing tolerable and dangerous risks very important and the unrelievable uncertainty has removed our ability to do that rationally. As a result, we have evaded the zone of uncertainty altogether. These practicalities are in the driving seat and cognition is, for the time being, their passenger.

There may be times when this is perfectly rational. For example, imagine that you must leap over a yawning chasm to save your life, and we know that you are more likely to succeed if you act with certainty that you will succeed. In such a case, it may be practically wise to become (however temporarily) uncertainty phobic so that you can acquire the certainty you need to succeed, despite this being theoretically irrational. That we have this ability may even be an evolved tendency.

That being said, a lot of the time uncertainty phobia is badly irrational. When we, both individually and together, are addressing sustained wavering evidence bearing on prolonged high stakes activities requiring good judgement to distinguish tolerable and dangerous risks, uncertainty phobia is going to be unwise just because it is theoretically irrational. In such cases, I think we can safely say that uncertainty phobia is an epistemic vice.


## 8. Polarisation in Response to Covid-19 Untameable Uncertainty

That our response to high-stakes unrelievable uncertainty can be uncertainty phobic makes an empirical prediction: when stakes are high and when the evidence is wavering around for a long time whilst action must be taken, we will see a polarisation of opinion on many of the relevant factual claims and consequent polarisation on what should be done. Such a polarisation is simply the upshot of widespread uncertainty phobia. Many people are stubbornly certain on all these questions and the polarisation between their individual certainties is the amplification of even the slightest original disagreement.

The conclusion of section 5, in short, is that pandemics in general and Covid-19 in particular face us with sustained, unrelievable, wild uncertainty. Of course, for any particular one of us, that the uncertainty is unrelieved need not depend on the fact that the uncertainty is wild. For example, in a case where tame probabilities tame the uncertainty, we may happen not to know of the taming. We may, however, learn of the taming and may see its manifestation in the management of a situation, and in that way have our uncertainty relieved. The problem in a pandemic is that (at least initially and for some considerable time) the uncertainty is not simply unrelieved but is unrelievable just because it is wild. In that case, any claim that the models are taming the pandemic uncertainty is not true. In fact, it is propaganda. The failure to tame will become evident soon enough and that failure itself may drive many people to uncertainty phobia when they realise they have been deceived.

So the prediction made by uncertainty phobia applies to the Covid-19 pandemic. It seems to me that the prediction is satisfied to a significant degree by what we have seen during the pandemic. We have lived through prolonged unrelievable uncertainty and on many questions of fact and policy opinions have become polarised. This suggests that a lot of us, perhaps all of us, have some tendency to uncertainty phobia. To what extent we might be uncertainty phobic is, of course, a question to be investigated by empirical scientists rather than by philosophers like myself.

## 9. The Virtue of Epistemic Forbearance

Thus, at least at the beginning and for some considerable time, a pandemic confronts us with wild uncertainty. We must therefore give up the belief that our models can generally tame the uncertainty. We must accept that pandemics face us with unpredictably unendurable harms. The risks we face are dangerous, not tolerable.

It may be that eventually we accumulate enough data and we know enough about the specific random processes of a pandemic that our models begin to give us sufficiently accurate outputs to tame the uncertainty. And that would be a good thing. But we must be careful not to jump the gun. We will be tempted to do exactly that.

The harms of a pandemic are very high stakes and their being unpredictably unendurable is very frightening. In such a situation uncertainty phobia is a standing temptation. Uncertainty phobia predicts widespread polarization of opinion and we have seen just such a polarization of opinion on almost all the questions of what we should be doing about Covid-19. Whether it is on masks, travel restrictions, border closings, or vaccinations, the prevailing opinions are fixed certainties on either side of each question. So we certainly can fall into this temptation.

Uncertainty phobia is not always a bad thing. But facing a pandemic is not like leaping over a yawning chasm. Similarly, polarization of opinion is not always a bad thing. There are moral questions on which there are quite rightly sharp disagreements (even though the fact of sharp disagreement should give us some pause). Yet this is not the situation with Covid-19. There are disagreements about the priorities of the various values bearing on what we should do, but not such as to justify the polarisation we have seen.

We are instead faced with needing individual and social responses, responses which must properly countenance the varying untamed uncertainties pandemics pose. Because the uncertainties cannot be tamed, these responses cannot be calculated. They must rely on sound, sober and considered judgement. Far from our opinions being fixed certainties, they should instead be mobile uncertainties.

So, the nature of the uncertainty of pandemics, being wild and unrelievable for a long time, threatens our ability to sustain what rationality requires, namely, uncertain belief. Initially, and for a considerable time, we must simply avoid the temptation of uncertainty phobia and bear the wild uncertainty that faces us. I am not saying that is easy to do. Nevertheless, it is what we must do.

This requires virtue. We need *honesty* with ourselves, to keep in mind the balance of evidence (as best as we can ascertain it). We need *discrimination*, to distinguish the temptation of uncertainty phobia from a justified choice. Our hunger for certainty is justified by the risk being dangerous, but we must distinguish that hunger from the proper motive for factual opinion and see that it is a temptation to certainty rather than a justification for certainty. We can identify that certainty would be a vice here by distinguishing the balance of evidence we have from the balance of evidence needed for certainty given the stakes we face. This in turn requires *epistemic sensitivity* to the degree of confidence warranted by the evidence given the stakes. Finally, so long as the wild uncertainty is unrelieved, so long must we sustain this honesty, discrimination and sensitivity. The virtue that avoids uncertainty phobia by combining and sustaining these virtues is a kind of patience and fortitude that we may call *epistemic forbearance.*[14]

*Cardiff University,*
*Oxford Uehiro Centre for Practical Ethics,*
*Oxford University*
*shackeln@cardiff.ac.uk*

# References

Cleo Anastassopoulou et al., 'Data-Based Analysis, Modelling and Forecasting of the Covid-19 Outbreak', *PLOS ONE*, 15 (2020), e0230405. https://doi.org/10.1371/journal.pone.0230405

Peter L. Bernstein, *Capital Ideas : The Improbable Origins of Modern Wall Street*, (New York: Free Press, Maxwell Macmillan Canada 1992).

Giuseppe C. Calafiore, et al., 'A Time-Varying Sird Model for the Covid-19 Contagion in Italy', *Annu Rev Control*, 50 (2020) 361–372. https://doi.org/10.1016/j.arcontrol.2020.10.005

Jordana Cepelewicz, 'The Hard Lessons of Modeling the Coronavirus Pandemic', *Quanta*, (2021).

Paul Z. Chen et al., 'Understanding Why Superspreading Drives the Covid-19 Pandemic but Not the H1n1 Pandemic', *The Lancet Infectious Diseases*, 21 (2021), 1203–1204. https://doi.org/10.1016/S1473-3099(21)00406-0

Pasquale Cirillo & Nassim Nicholas Taleb, 'Tail Risk of Contagious Diseases', *Nature Physics*, 16 (2020), 606–613. https://doi.org/10.1038/s41567-020-0921-x

James J. Collins & Carson C. Chow, 'It's a Small World', *Nature*, 393 (1998), 409–410. https://doi.org/10.1038/30835

Ian Cooper, et al. 'A Sir Model Assumption for the Spread of Covid-19 in Different Communities', *Chaos, solitons, and fractals*, 139 (2020) 110057 https://doi.org/10.1016/j.chaos.2020.110057

Sibel Eker,. 'Validity and Usefulness of Covid-19 Models', *Humanities and Social Sciences Communications*, 7 (2020), 54. https://doi.org/10.1057/s41599-020-00553-4

[14]   My thanks to Jon Webber for very helpful comments and suggestions. This paper was written during my tenure of the 2021-22 Mind Association Major Research Fellowship, for which award I am very grateful.

Hideki Endo, et al., 'Conventional Risk Prediction Models Fail to Accurately Predict Mortality Risk among Patients with Coronavirus Disease 2019 in Intensive Care Units: A Difficult Time to Assess Clinical Severity and Quality of Care', *Journal of Intensive Care*, 9 (2021), 42. https://doi.org/10.1186/s40560-021-00557-5

Eugene F. Fama, 'Efficient Capital Markets: A Review of Theory and Empirical Work', *The Journal of Finance*, 25 (1970), 383–417. https://doi.org/10.2307/2325486

Neil M Ferguson, et al. 'Impact of Non-Pharmaceutical Interventions to Reduce Covid19 Mortality and Healthcare Demand', 16 March 2020 *Imperial College London*, 1–20. doi. org/10.25561/77482

Luisa Ferrari, et al. 'Modelling Provincial Covid-19 Epidemic Data Using an Adjusted Time-Dependent Sird Model', *International Journal of Environmental Research and Public Health*, 18 (2021), 6563. https://www.mdpi.com/1660-4601/18/12/6563

Janyce Eunice Gnanvi, et al. 'On the Reliability of Predictions on Covid-19 Dynamics: A Systematic and Critical Review of Modelling Techniques', *Infectious Disease Modelling*, 6 (2021) 258–272. https://doi.org/https://doi.org/10.1016/j.idm.2020.12.008

Agus Hasan, et al., 'Superspreading in Early Transmissions of Covid-19 in Indonesia', *Scientific reports*, 10 (2020), 22386. https://doi.org/10.1038/s41598-020-79352-5

Inga Holmdahl & Caroline Buckee, 'Wrong but Useful – What Covid-19 Epidemiologic Models Can and Cannot Tell Us', *New England Journal of Medicine*, 383 (2020), 303–305. https://doi.org/10.1056/NEJMp2016822

John P. A. Ioannidis, et al., 'Forecasting for Covid-19 Has Failed', *Int J Forecast*, (2020) https://doi.org/10.1016/j.ijforecast.2020.08.004

Lyndon P. James et al., 'The Use and Misuse of Mathematical Modeling for Infectious Disease Policymaking: Lessons for the Covid-19 Pandemic', *Medical Decision Making*, 41 (2021), 379–385. https://doi.org/10.1177/0272989X21990391

Max S. Y. Lau et al., 'Characterizing Superspreading Events and Age-Specific Infectiousness of Sars-Cov-2 Transmission in Georgia, USA', *Proceedings of the National Academy of Sciences of the United States of America*, 117 (2020), 22430–22435. https://doi.org/10.1073/pnas.2011802117

Benoit B. Mandelbrot & Richard L. Hudson, *The Misbehaviour of Markets : A Fractal View of Risk, Ruin and Reward*, (London: Profile, 2004).

Vicente Martínez, 'A Modified Sird Model to Study the Evolution of the Covid-19 Pandemic in Spain', *Symmetry*, 13 (2021), 723. https://www.mdpi.com/2073-8994/13/4/723

Stanley Milgram, 'The Small World Problem', *Psychology Today*, 2 (1967) 60–67.

Alan Nicholson & Yiik-Diew Wong, 'Are Accidents Poisson Distributed? A Statistical Test', *Accident Analysis & Prevention*, 25 (1993), 91–97. https://doi.org/10.1016/0001-4575(93)90100-B

Vilfredo Pareto, *Cours D'economie Politique*, (Lausanne: Rouge, 1896).

Nicholas Shackel, 'Explaining Variation in Knowledge by Full Belief', *Proceedings of the 34th Ludwig Wittgenstein Symposium.* Eds Jaeger, C. and Loffler, W. Kirchberg am Wechsel, (Austria: Ontos Verlag, 2011) 95–102. http://dx.doi.org/10.1515/9783110329018.95

Nicholas Shackel, 'Stakes and Full Belief' (MS-a).

Nicholas Shackel, 'Wild Uncertainty and Pandemics' (MS-b).

Sakshi Shringi, et al. 'Modified Sird Model for Covid-19 Spread Prediction for Northern and Southern States of India', *Chaos, Solitons & Fractals*, 148 (2021), 111039. https://doi.org/10.1016/j.chaos.2021.111039

Lawrence H. Summers, 'Does the Stock Market Rationally Reflect Fundamental Values?' *The Journal of Finance*, 41 (1986), 591–601. https://doi.org/10.1111/j.1540-6261.1986.tb04519.x

Kaiyuan Sun, et al. 'Transmission Heterogeneities, Kinetics, and Controllability of Sars-Cov-2', *Science*, 371 (2021), https://doi.org/10.1126/science.abe2424

Nicholas Nassim Taleb, *Statistical Consequences of Fat Tails: Real World Preasymptotics, Epistemology, and Applications*, (Scribe Media, 2020).

United States Centre for Disease Control 'Covidview-05-01-2020' 2020. https://www.cdc.gov/coronavirus/2019-ncov/covid-data/pdf/covidview-05-01-2020.pdf

Duncan J. Watts & Steven H. Strogatz, 'Collective Dynamics of 'Small-World' Networks', *Nature*, 393 (1998), 440–42. https://doi.org/10.1038/30918

Felix Wong & James J. Collins, 'Evidence That Coronavirus Superspreading Is Fat-Tailed', *Proceedings of the National Academy of Sciences*, 117 (2020) 29416–29418. https://www.pnas.org/content/pnas/117/47/29416.full.pdf

# The Virtue of Hope in a Turbulent World

CATHY MASON

**Abstract**

I argue that hope is an ethical virtue. Hope, I suggest, is necessary for engaging in a broad kind of project which is essential for living a meaningful human life, and this gives us reason to think that it is non-instrumentally valuable in our lives. Specifically, I claim that hope is well understood as a 'structural virtue' without which we are prone to slip into despair, fantasy and cynicism. Moreover, I argue that this virtue will be particularly significant in turbulent times, when we may not be in a position to have outright (positive) expectations about the future.

> Hope is the story of uncertainty, of coming to terms with the risk involved in not knowing what comes next, which is more demanding than despair and, in a way, more frightening. And immeasurably more rewarding.
>
> … I believe in hope as an act of defiance, or rather as the foundation for an ongoing series of acts of defiance, those acts necessary to bring about some of what we hope for while we live by principle in the meantime. There is no alternative, except surrender. And surrender not only abandons the future,
>
> it abandons the soul. (Solnit, 2004, p. 7, 110)

In *Hope in the Dark* (2004), the writer and activist Rebecca Solnit calls on us to adopt and value hope as a personal and political ideal. Living with hope, she suggests, is difficult and perhaps frightening, but it brings with it the possibility of rewards worth this risk. Moreover, she suggests that there is no feasible alternative to living in hope, no other way of living that would not be an abandonment of our souls.

Is Solnit right to think that hope is indispensable for living well, and if so, what exactly is its role in a good life? On the one hand, hope can be a powerful force for personal and political good, and maintaining hope in unpromising circumstances can be praiseworthy. The hope that there would be a successful covid vaccine, for example, motivated many scientists to pursue research that has and will continue to save countless lives. Their hopeful actions will greatly benefit society at large. On the other hand, we can also hope for bad or evil things,

doi:10.1017/S1358246122000194

and hoping for such things seems to be part of what can make a person bad. These thoughts seem to pull us in opposite directions when we're considering hope's ethical standing. The former pulls us towards thinking that hope might be a virtue, a character trait that is a kind of excellence for a human being. The latter pulls us towards thinking that it's a state without any inherent ethical value.

There are some character traits whose role in a good life is fairly straightforward. Benevolence and justice, for example, seem to be valuable both in an individual life and for the good functioning of society as a whole. They are thus commonly thought of as inherently valuable traits and usually considered to be virtues. The place of other traits, however, is more ambiguous: cautiousness, for instance, is often a good policy, but a life without moments of uncalculated spontaneity would be lacking. As a result, cautiousness does not seem to be valuable in and of itself. It plausibly has only instrumental value and does not seem to be a good candidate to be a virtue. How should hope be situated in relation to traits like these? Should we understand hope as more like benevolence and justice or more like cautiousness?

In this chapter, I argue that (unlike cautiousness) hope itself makes a valuable contribution to our ethical lives, and that, like kindness and justice, it is a virtue. I argue that hope (or hopefulness, though I will treat these as interchangeable)[1] is necessary for engaging in a broad kind of project which is essential for living a meaningful human life (projects which I call 'vulnerable projects'), and that this gives us reason to think that it is non-instrumentally valuable in our lives. Without hopefulness, I suggest, we are prone to slip into despair, fantasy and cynicism. Specifically, I will suggest that hope is well understood as a 'structural virtue': an excellence regarding the organisation of one's life. As such, though it is a virtue, it is more like courage and fortitude than justice and kindness. Such a virtue will be particularly significant in turbulent times, when we may not be in a position to have outright (positive) expectations about the future, which can render it particularly difficult to avoid the above-mentioned vices. Hope is ethically valuable, then, but it will contribute to one's life going well as a whole only in the presence of knowledge (and motivation) about what is truly valuable. I will

[1] Talking about hope rather than hopefulness may initially sound odd, but compare this to other popular virtues: we talk about courage, not courageousness, love not lovingness and so on. Aaron Cobb (2015), Adam Kadlac (2015) and Nancy Snow (2018) all speak in terms of 'hope' rather than 'hopefulness'.

suggest, moreover, that this is well explained by understanding hope as a structural virtue.

To do so, I'll start in §1 by outlining one kind of virtue, which I'll call *motivational* virtue. I'll then explore why it does not seem plausible to think that hope is this kind of virtue. In §2, I'll outline a different kind of virtue, which I'll call *structural* virtue. In §3, I'll argue that hope is a structural virtue, and that it is necessary for engaging in a broad kind of project which is essential for living a meaningful human life (the above-mentioned 'vulnerable projects'). In §4, I will suggest that hope is particularly significant in turbulent times, since in those periods we may not be able to have confidence about the outcomes of our actions or the occurrence of good situations. Finally, having argued that hope is a virtue and explored its significance in turbulent times, in §5 I'll go on to contrast hope with corresponding temptations of despair, fantasy and cynicism.

## 1. Motivational Virtues

'Motivational' virtues are character traits that involve perceiving and responding correctly to particular goods (or evils) in the world.[2] The person who possesses such virtues will notice instances of these goods or evils, and will be motivated to promote or act in accordance with the goods – and vice versa for the evils. Justice and benevolence are paradigmatic examples of such virtues. Benevolence, for example, is a matter of responsiveness to other people's needs and well-being. The benevolent person will be sensitive to others' thoughts and feelings, for example, and will seek to avoid causing anyone suffering. They desire that others' lives go well, and are perceptive about when and how to bring that about. Similarly, the just person will be sensitive to matters of justice (or fairness), and motivated to correct injustices and bring about a fairer world. In each case, the thing responded to is worthy of a response and the particular response is merited by the situation. So, one cannot use these virtues for bad ends: they must be dispositions to respond in good ways to features of the world.

Could hope be understood as a motivational virtue in the above sense? Initially, we might think so. Hope plays an important role in lots of the activities we value, and hopefulness is a trait that we generally admire. The Black Lives Matter protests that took place in the summer of 2020, for example, did not only express people's disappointment and

---

[2] This distinction between motivational and structural virtues (as well as the names themselves) follows Robert Adams (2006).

outrage at racial injustices (though they certainly did do this). They also expressed, and depended on, the *hope* that things could be otherwise, that a more racially just world is possible and that it is within our power to bring it about. This hope was therefore a hope that something genuinely valuable would come about, and it was an appropriate response to the injustice in the world as it is. Similarly, the scientists working on covid vaccines presumably hoped to be able to save lives, and this is also a clearly valuable aim. Maintaining such hopes in the face of setbacks and difficulties can be a significant achievement, and we admire those who steadfastly persevere in such hopeful tasks.

Nonetheless, there are many ways in which hope can detract from our lives, have bad consequences for other people, or reflect badly on our characters. It seems possible to hope for bad things, and for this hope to sustain the hopeful person in pursuing bad ends. The terrorist involved in plots to kill large numbers of people, for example, might be just as hopeful that the plot will be successful as the scientist seeking a covid vaccine might be about finding life-saving technology. The terrorists' hope is likely to have bad consequences for other people, and perhaps for society as a whole. But it also seems to leave them worse off as an individual: their hope is part of what makes them a bad person. In this case, the hope is not a response to anything genuinely valuable; they do not hope for something that is worthy of hope.

Hope therefore doesn't seem to be a motivational virtue. It can motivate us to act, but it doesn't always motivate us to act in ways that are good. Hope can lead us to respond to situations in ways that are unmerited or inappropriate just as much as it can lead us to respond in good ways. Moreover, the fact that it isn't a motivational virtue can initially make it hard to see why we should think of it as a virtue at all. There are all sorts of different things that one can hope for, and not all of these are admirable. Hope doesn't seem to obviously track any morally significant feature of the world, since although some hopes are for good outcomes ('I hope that a covid vaccine can be found'), others are for morally irrelevant outcomes ('I hope that my favourite food is available at the restaurant today') or even morally bad outcomes ('I hope my rival publicly embarrasses themselves'). Hope therefore cannot be a motivational virtue, and if hope is inherently valuable, it must be valuable in some other way.

## 2. Structural Virtues

A glance at some other traits considered to be virtues, however, shows that motivational virtues are not the only kind. For example, think of courage. Courage is a fairly uncontroversial virtue, yet it can plausibly be aimed at bad ends: plausibly, the terrorist can be highly courageous despite using their courage for bad ends. They can confront and recognise danger and remain uncowed by it, and this makes them seem courageous despite their task being deeply morally misguided. Fortitude, too, appears to be demonstrated as much by persevering in worthless tasks when faced with setbacks as it does by persevering in morally valuable ones. At least some virtues, then, are not a matter of responsiveness to moral goods, since these virtues can all be exercised when seeking bad goals.[3]

What else might make these traits valuable? Why might they still count as virtues despite not being distinguished as good responses to particular goods or evils? A plausible answer is that they are valuable forms of self-government, or 'structural virtues'. Structural virtues are not a matter of being well-oriented with regard to particular goods. Instead, they concern the excellent governance one's own life in accordance with one's aims and values. That is, these virtues concern one's ability to 'structure' one's life in the right kind of way. The self-controlled person, for example, is not pulled from their chosen path by momentary annoyance or distraction, and the conscientious person attends diligently to the projects they have committed to. Doing so allows the conscientious or diligent person to structure their lives well in certain respects.

Why do we need structural virtues? On first glance, it may seem rather a low bar for being a virtue that a trait merely enables one to live up to one's own aims and values. Such aims can be too low or misplaced altogether. However, this kind of excellent self-governance is no easy task for human beings. Fear, for instance, is a powerful force, and it can be very difficult to resist the temptation to avoid danger, even when one judges the goal to be worthwhile. So, courage is a noteworthy human excellence. Similarly, it can be very difficult to display fortitude in an undertaking, and to keep persevering despite trials and setbacks. Mere belief that the undertaking is worth attempting is not always sufficient to guarantee perseverance in the task. There are always temptations to give up, to take an easier or more convenient path, and it can be hard to stick with a difficult task even if one judges it to be worthwhile. Structural virtues thus

---

[3]  Philippa Foot (2002, ch. 1) similarly suggests that temperance can be displayed in bad actions, and can be involved in over-willingness to refuse pleasure as much as in cases where one gets things right. Of course, some might doubt here that this over-willingness to avoid pleasure counts as temperance, and instead regard it as asceticism or similar.

seem like considerable achievements given the difficulty humans experience in structuring their lives well.

Structural virtues function as counters to our natural temptations. Courage, for example, counters temptations to cowardice and recklessness. On the one hand, we are often too responsive to fear: we feel so overwhelmed by it that we avoid taking worthwhile but risky actions. On the other hand, we can also be insufficiently responsive to fear: perhaps we fail to try to minimise the dangers involved in an undertaking, or we take dangerous actions even when they're not worth the risks. Aristotle thus suggests that virtues stand at the 'golden mean' between excess and deficiency, and are flanked by vices on either side (Aristotle, 2014, II.6 1106a26–b28). Courage, for example, plausibly stands at a mean between being cowardly and foolhardy or rash. Temperance plausibly sits between self-indulgence and insensibility. The self-indulgent person is too prone to indulge each passing desire, but the insensible person is too prone to ignore their wants and needs, too rigid in their self-governance. The virtuous person avoids both excess and deficiency. Whilst the structurally virtuous person might not act in ways that are good overall, they are admirable insofar as they structure their life in the right kind of way, avoiding various temptations that are natural to us.

## 3. Hope, Vulnerability and Structural Virtue

Why might we consider hope to be a structural virtue? To begin with, note that there are distinctive scenarios in which structural virtues seem to be especially called-for: facing dangerous situations requires courage, for example, and continuing with projects in the face of difficulties or setbacks requires fortitude. For hope to be a structural virtue, there needs to be a distinctive kind of situation in which it is apt or called-for. I wish to suggest that the situations in which hope is called for are those situations in which our goals or projects are *vulnerable*.

In acting, we pursue various goals and projects, and these are often within our control. On getting up this morning, I pursued the goal of eating toast for breakfast, and I took it to be something that I could easily bring about. I straightforwardly believed that since I intended it, I would succeed. I therefore *expected* to have toast for breakfast. However, many of the goals we pursue are things that may not be realised, things that might not come about no matter how we act. The Black Lives Matter protests, for example, by no means guaranteed that a more racially just society would come about. In fact, it would have been irrational for the protestors to have had outright *beliefs* or *expectations* that a more just society would come about. Similarly, the scientists researching covid vaccines could not (at least initially) have had outright beliefs or expectations that their vaccines would be successful, nor that they would be able to save lives with them. Ends that might not be realised in this sense are 'vulnerable'; their realisation is in part down to circumstantial luck. The people in question could do everything as they ought to, and the projects might still fail.

In one sense, of course, *both* eating breakfast and bringing about a more racially just world are vulnerable to luck. After all, one's house could have been burgled during the night and the food might have been stolen. Or one might trip up whilst walking down the stairs and end up in A & E with a broken leg before having had the chance to eat breakfast. But this kind of luck seems significantly different to the kind of luck to which bringing about a more racially just world is hostage, and there is a distinctive need for hope in the latter circumstances.

In normal circumstances one can reasonably *believe one will* or outright *expect to* eat toast for breakfast if one has decided to do so. Although it is possible that one would fail to eat toast for breakfast despite having decided to, one relies on the belief that one will do so in forming further beliefs and intentions (one might plan, for example, to leave the house half an hour after getting up, as eating toast for breakfast takes little time). We usually think that one can have *knowledge* about such future events. That is, in the case of eating breakfast the realisation of the aim is dependent on factors outside of one's control, but these factors are things one can reasonably take for granted, things that do not preclude knowledge. This is not the case with the protestors' ends. The realisation of their ends was dependent on factors outside their control, but which they could not have simply expected to obtain. We would therefore be reluctant to attribute knowledge about whether society would become more just to even the most optimistic of protestors. Similarly, the factors determining whether the covid vaccine was successful are not factors one could take for granted, or simply expect. 'Vulnerable ends', then, are ends that are vulnerable to factors outside the agent's control which the agent does not or should not take for granted. The kind of luck that precludes knowledge or reasonable belief makes an end count as vulnerable.

Situations that call for hope are those involving vulnerable ends. In these cases, one cannot simply act in the belief or the expectation that the end one desires will come about. Humans are limited creatures:

our capacities to act and influence the world are highly restricted. We have limited physical and cognitive powers to bring about those things that we aim for, and our attempts often end in failure. The projects that make up our lives are often extended over time, and thus require a stable and supportive environment in order to come to fruition. They frequently require the success of multiple sub-plans, each of which may itself be risky. And they can depend on others' cooperation, as well as on non-human factors. A vast number of our possible projects thus require acting for the sake of vulnerable goals. As such, many of the valuable projects that we have reason to pursue are vulnerable. Hope is valuable because it allows us to act despite the vulnerability of our ends.

There are some widely accepted cases of hope where we can do little or nothing to bring about the end in question. Adrienne Martin (2014) discusses hopes for good weather or recovery from severe illness, for example, which may involve no agential control over the outcome itself. Still, there remain some relevant vulnerable projects that we might yet engage in that nonetheless *involve* these outcomes: planning picnics in the event of good weather, for example, or making plans for the future in the case of illness. Hope is required to engage even in these projects.[4]

To live a good human life, it is necessary to engage in some vulnerable projects, or pursue some vulnerable goals. The only way to avoid such vulnerability would be to take on only very limited and minimal projects: those that are well within our capacity to secure, whose realisation is not therefore vulnerable to significant luck. But taking on only such limited and minimal projects would be incompatible with living a good life. The projects one engaged in would be far too narrow and unambitious for one to be living well. Any life containing projects that are sufficiently rich and ambitious to be valuable will involve some vulnerable projects – parenthood, fighting racial injustice, learning to quit smoking. A good life, then, will inevitably involve pursuing some goals whose realisation cannot be guaranteed, projects that are vulnerable to failure no matter how well and committedly one tries. Actions in response to such goals are essentially hopeful actions, and such projects are essentially hopeful projects.

---

[4] Some of the instances Martin (2014) identifies as hope lack even the indirect connection mentioned above; they are unconnected to vulnerable projects. For example, she argues that one might hope that a past event happened, even though one's life and projects are completely unaffected. In Mason (forthcoming) I argue that things that are totally agentially inert should count as wishes rather than hopes.

This observation seems to explain Solnit's claim that the alternative to hope – which she identifies as surrender – 'abandons the soul'. Without hope, we would seem to lose out on something important about being human, the ability to dream and aspire, to value and care about things beyond our known capacities to bring about, and to act accordingly. Giving up on these hopeful projects would leave us with a narrowly circumscribed existence barely worth living.

Hopeful actions are a necessary constituent of the good life, then, because living a good life is partly constituted by pursuing vulnerable goals. The person whose life contains vulnerable projects has ordered their life, in at least one respect, in the right kind of way: their life has the right kind of overarching structure to be living well. Hope is thus a structural virtue, a trait that enables one to structure one's life in an excellent way in situations of vulnerability.

## 4. The Virtue of Hope in a Turbulent World

Hope is thus inherently valuable and a structural virtue. In particular, it is a virtue which is of particular value for us in times of uncertainty and instability – a virtue much needed in changing times.

Human beings are always limited creatures, and the goals we value are often outside the scope of our control. Still, within limits, there are aims that within stable conditions we *can* expect to be able to realise. In stable conditions, we can take for granted that some aspects of the future will be fairly predictable, and that we can take them for granted. Most of the time, those of us living in Western democracies don't have to hope that political institutions will not collapse overnight, for example, because we can simply take this for granted. We can reasonably expect that political institutions will not simply disappear when the environment in which we live is reasonably stable. Similarly, we can usually simply expect that the shops we buy groceries at will have the items we need.

In times of instability, however, there are far fewer things that we can take for granted than under stable conditions. In unstable conditions we may no longer be able to simply *expect* good outcomes to come about. As such, hope becomes a particularly precious virtue, enabling us to continue to pursue valuable goals and engage in meaningful projects despite no longer being able to rely on good outcomes. For example, during the recent storming of the Capitol building in the US, Americans would not have been justified in taking for granted that political institutions would not simply collapse overnight. As such, continuing to engage in political action in this context – whether through activism, running for office, etc. – requires hope. Similarly, the covid pandemic has overturned many of the everyday expectations that we can ordinarily rely upon. In ordinary contexts, we might simply expect to be able to buy what we need at the shops, for example. But during the early stages of the pandemic, when many shop shelves were empty, many people were no longer in a position to rely upon this. As such, the instability of the pandemic meant that many ordinary actions required hope.

Conditions of turbulence, instability, or change can make it hard to know what to expect about the future. In such situations, our ordinary expectations regarding the future are overturned. This can be disconcerting or even bewildering, and it can be difficult to continue to pursue valuable projects when we lack reassurance about their results. In these circumstances our lack of confident expectations in the future makes us particularly prone to giving up. Hope sustains us in those most difficult of circumstances, and it is therefore here that the value of hope can be seen most starkly.

## 5. Hope, Fantasy, Despair and Cynicism

Finally, we can best understand the value of hope when we contrast it with other possible responses to the vulnerability of our goals. In particular, hope stands as a corrective to the temptations of despair, fantasy and cynicism. Each of these is a bad response to the vulnerability of our goals, and responding to vulnerability in this way is usually a kind of ethical failing. Each is a kind of refusal to recognise the vulnerability inherent to human existence.

Faced with a valuable outcome that is possible yet whose realisation is far from certain, one faces a practical question of how to respond, and there are a number of different practical attitudes which we might take. Hope is one such attitude. In hoping, one values the end in question and recognises its vulnerability but nonetheless invests oneself in the outcome. Such investment might be practical or emotional. In this sense, hoping is a risk-laden activity: to hope is to knowingly make oneself vulnerable to disappointment, disappointment that in serious cases can be crushing. What's more, in addition to the pain of disappointment, the practical investment that one makes may in the end come to nothing. For example, in the cases of political activism that Solnit discusses, hope involves a considerable investment of time and energy into activities like political organising and protesting to try to bring about valuable outcomes. These hopeful actions risk failure, in which case the practical investment of time and effort will go unrewarded. Hope is a response to the vulnerability of certain possibilities that acknowledges and embraces that vulnerability, and brings with it considerable risks.

Faced with an outcome that could warrant hope, many of us might be wary about hoping, reluctant to adopt an attitude that carries such risks. In this case, one option is simply to give up on the outcome: to despair of it happening and to refuse to be practically and emotionally invested in it. Although this response may be merited in some cases (particularly where the value of the end in question is not very high), despair as a trait denotes a more general avoidance of risk. As such, it involves reluctance to confront or accept our vulnerability as limited human beings, and the vulnerability of those things we care about. Despair, in this sense, requires ignoring important features of the world: it involves ignoring the fact that these possibilities remain open, that they might yet be realised, and that whether they are realised may be in part up to us. Despair can be tempting because it absolves us of responsibility for acting or even for accepting risks. The despairing person can feel that nothing is required of them because they refuse to recognise the possibilities for their own action and the positive possibilities that remain open. But the passivity thus gained looks like a form of paralysis rather than freedom, and it empties their life of opportunities for meaningful projects that could be rewarding. Foot thus identifies despair as the key temptation to which hope stands as a corrective: 'hope is a virtue because despair too is a temptation' (Foot, 2002, p. 9).

Despair is not, however, the only way to refuse the riskiness of hope. Another way of avoiding vulnerability is fantasy. Whereas the despairing person over-emphasises the badness of vulnerability and ignores the openness of the future to good outcomes, the fantasist overemphasises their control over a situation and ignores the possibility that the desired outcome might *not* be realised. The fantasist ignores their limitations and is blind to the evidence that good outcomes may not be within their power to realise or that the world may not be how they would wish it to be. Instead, they insist that things will work out for the best and close their eyes to any evidence to the contrary. This, too, is a temptation, because this is how we would like things to be, and the fantasist avoids the difficult task of grappling with inconvenient truths. Life would be pleasant were this to be the case and so the fantasist believes it to be so, ignoring any evidence to the contrary. This response is clearly also ill-advised. The fantasist likely has greater short-term peace of mind than the despairing person but it comes at an extremely high cost.

Moreover, the repeated disappointment the fantasist is likely to face as their projects are repeatedly and unexpectedly thwarted means that the fantasist is likely in quick succession to end up despairing. They thus avoid confronting risk, but only by making themself blind and unresponsive to reality.

Hope thus tips into fantasy at the point where one closes one's eyes on reality and indulges in positive illusions about the hoped-for outcome, regardless of the evidence. As I have understood it, such fantasy is *in general* a dangerous temptation. Martin (2014), however, points out that *some* instances of fantasy can be useful. Fantasising about an outcome that we truly value and can bring about may be irresponsible, but fantasising as a way of exploring a possible outcome, for example, could be helpful in deciding if it's something that truly appeals and one should pursue. Nonetheless, the irresponsible kind of fantasy remains a common and generally dangerous temptation.

Finally, one might avoid the riskiness of hope by refusing to value the vulnerable end: that is, one might adopt cynicism. Faced with the high costs and vulnerability of hoping for an outcome that might not be realised, the cynic prefers to withdraw from valuing it, telling themself that it cannot be so valuable after all. The person who responds in this way refuses vulnerability by refusing to appreciate the full value that certain outcomes have for them. Like the fantasist, the cynic closes their eyes to certain features of the situation, but in this case, they close their eyes to the fact that this is an outcome they care about, a goal they value. This response is another way to attempt to render oneself invulnerable, but once again it involves an important kind of failure. In this case, it is an appreciative failure (or perhaps a failure of self-knowledge), and the cost is a diminishment in the richness of their own life. This response to vulnerability is thus also undesirable.

We can see, then, that there are a number of possible responses to the vulnerability of an outcome. Despair, fantasy and cynicism can all superficially seem like attractive options, and we are often tempted to opt for these easy resolutions to the difficulties of living with our vulnerability. But it is clear that they are ethically unattractive options, and that they are not virtuous responses to our own fragility and the fragility of our goals. As Solnit puts it, these all represent forms of surrender: surrender of the possibility of the thing we value (despair), surrender of our value system (cynicism), or surrender of our grasp of reality altogether (fantasy). Rather than grappling with our vulnerable condition, these responses all represent an evasion of it, and the person who responds in these ways would fail to live in accordance with their aims and values. Hope functions as a counter to these temptations, enabling us to have a clear-eyed assessment of the value and likelihood of a goal or project whilst remaining invested in it. It thus allows us to recognise our own vulnerability whilst remaining committed to those vulnerable goals that we ought to care about.

This is not, of course, to say that every instance of hope involves a clear-eyed assessment of the evidence, or that every good possibility is worth hoping for. One can hope too much, as well as hoping too little, and it's possible to hope indiscriminately as well as wisely. The person who hopes desperately for trivial things but not for important ends, for example, is clearly not living well overall. Miriam McCormick (2017) thus suggests that there are various factors aside from likelihood of the outcome that determine the rationality of a hope. However, it is the *trait* of hope (or 'hopefulness'), or the disposition to hope, that is a virtue, not individual instances of it. The hopeful person is the person who is disposed to hope to the *right* degree, in accordance with those things that they value. Excessive embracing of vulnerable goals and projects will tend towards fantasy, and deficient embracing of such goals and projects will tend towards despair or cynicism. The hopeful person is disposed to respond in the right kind of way to vulnerable situations, and this can be virtuous even if some instances of hope are misplaced.

In particular, despite hope being a virtue there remains the danger mentioned earlier, namely that the hopeful person may be disposed to act hopefully regarding even those ends that we think ought not to be valued. The scientist involved in manufacturing weapons used for nefarious ends, for example, might be sustained in their task by the hope that they will create destructive weapons. However, structural virtues are not a panacea for all evils; they do not guarantee that the person possessing the virtue is getting things right overall. Instead, they depend upon motivational virtues – or the presence of knowledge about what's truly valuable – to be conducive to overall good. Hopefulness does not guarantee that one is living well, then, and nor does any other structural virtue. However, it is an essential component of living well, and as such it is of immense value to vulnerable beings like us.

*University of Cambridge*
*cm865@cam.ac.uk*

**Cathy Mason**

## References

Robert Merrihew Adams, *A Theory of Virtue* (Oxford: Oxford University Press, 2006).

Aristotle, *Nicomachean Ethics*, ed. Roger Crisp (Cambridge: Cambridge University Press, 2014).

Aaron Cobb 'Hope as an Intellectual Virtue?', *Southern Journal of Philosophy* 53 (2015) 269–285.

Philippa Foot, *Virtues and Vices* (Oxford: Oxford University Press, 2002).

Adam Kadlac, 'The Virtue of Hope', *Ethical Theory and Moral Practice* 18 (2015) 337–354.

Adrienne Martin, *How We Hope: A Moral Psychology* (Princeton: Princeton University Press, 2014).

Cathy Mason, 'Hoping and Intending', *Journal of the American Philosophical Association* (forthcoming).

Miriam McCormick, 'Rational Hope', *Philosophical Explorations* 20 (2017) 127–141.

Nancy Snow, 'Hope as a Democratic Civic Virtue', *Metaphilosophy* 49(2018) 407–427.

Rebecca Solnit, *Hope in the Dark* (New York: Nation Books, 2004).

# Index of Names